Topics in Information Systems

Cooperative Interfaces to Information Systems

Edited by

L. Bolc and M. Jarke

With 62 Figures

Springer-Verlag
Berlin Heidelberg New York
London Paris Tokyo

Series Editors

Michael L. Brodie
Computer Corporation of America, Four Cambridge Center
Cambridge, MA 02140/USA

John Mylopoulos
Department of Computer Science, University of Toronto
Toronto, Ontario M5S 1A4/Canada

Joachim W. Schmidt
Fachbereich Informatik, Johann Wolfgang Goethe-Universität
Dantestraße 9, D-6000 Frankfurt a. M. 11/FRG

Volume Editors

Leonard Bolc
Institute of Informatics, Warsaw University
PKiN, pok. 850, 00-901 Warsaw/Poland

Matthias Jarke
Fachbereich Informatik, Johann Wolfgang Goethe-Universität
Dantestraße 9, D-6000 Frankfurt a. M. 11/FRG

ISBN-13: 978-3-642-82817-1 e-ISBN-13: 978-3-642-82815-7
DOI: 10.1007/978-3-642-82815-7

Library of Congress Cataloging-in-Publication Data. Cooperative interfaces to information systems. (Topics in information systems). Bibliography: p. Includes index. 1. On-line data processing. 2. Programming languages (Electronic computers) 3. Information storage and retrieval systems. I. Bolc, Leonard, 1934- . II. Jarke, Matthias. III. Series. QA76.55.C66. 1986. 004'.33. 86-13965.
ISBN 0-387-16599-1 (U.S.)

Softcover reprint of the hardcover 1st edition 1986

Typsetting, printing and bookbinding: Appl, Wemding
2145/3140-543210

Topics in Information Systems

Series Description

Dramatic advances in hardware technology have opened the door to a new generation of computer systems. At the same time, the growing demand for information systems of ever-increasing complexity and precision has stimulated the need in every area of Computer Science for more powerful higher-level concepts, techniques, and tools.

Future information systems will be expected to acquire, maintain, retrieve, manipulate, and present many different kinds of information. These systems will require user-friendly interfaces; powerful reasoning capabilities, and shared access to large information bases. Whereas the needed hardware technology appears to be within reach, the corresponding software technology for building these systems is not. The required dramatic improvements in software productivity will come from advanced application development environments based on powerful new techniques and languages.

The **concepts**, **techniques**, and **tools** necessary for the design, implementation, and use in future information systems are expected to result from the integration of those being developed and used in currently disjoint areas of Computer Science. Several areas bring their unique viewpoints and technologies to existing information processing practice. One key area is **Artificial Intelligence** (AI) which provides knowledge bases grounded on semantic theories of information for correct interpretation. An equally important area is **Databases** which provides means for building and maintaining large, shared databases based on computational theories of information for efficient processing. A third important area is **Programming Languages** which provides a powerful tool kit for the construction of large programs based on linguistic and methodological theories to ensure program correctness. To meet evolving information systems requirements, additional research viewpoints and technologies are or will be required from such areas as **Software Engineering, Computer Networks, Machine Architectures**, and **Office Automation.**

Although some integration of research results has already been achieved, a quantum leap in technological integration is needed to meet the demand for future information systems. This integration is one of the major challenges to Computer Science in the 1980s.

Topics in Information Systems is a series intended to report significant contributions on the integration of concepts, techniques, and tools that advance new technologies for information system construction. The series logo symbolizes the scope of topics to be covered and the basic theme of integration.

The logo will appear on each book to indicate the topics addressed.

	Artificial Intelligence	Databases	Programming Languages
concepts			
techniques			
tools			

The first book of the series, "On Conceptual Modelling: Perspectives from Artificial Intelligence, Databases and Programming Languages", Michael L. Brodie, John Mylopoulos, and Joachim W. Schmidt (Eds.), February 1984, which deals with concepts in the three areas, has the logo:

	●	●	●

The book at hand, "Cooperative Interfaces to Information Systems", Leonard Bolc and Matthias Jarke (Eds.), September 1986, which deals with very high level communication with computerized information systems, has the logo:

	●	●	
	●		●
	●	●	

In addition, the series comprises the following volumes:

"Query Processing in Database Systems", Won Kim, David S. Reiner, and Donald S. Batory (Eds.), March 1985,

"Office Automation", Dionysios C. Tsichritzis (Ed.), March 1985.

"On knowledge Base Management System: Integrating Artificial Intelligence and Database Technologies", Michael L. Brodie and John Mylopoulos (Eds.), June 1986.

Future books in the series will provide timely accounts of ongoing research efforts to reshape technologies intended for information system development.

September, 1986

Michael L. Brodie
John Mylopoulos
Joachim W. Schmidt

Preface

Information systems are large repositories of factual and inferential knowledge intended to be queried and maintained by a wide variety of users with different backgrounds and work tasks. The community of potential information system users is growing rapidly with advances in hardware and software technology that permit computer/communications support for more and more application areas.

Unfortunately, it is often felt that progress in user interface technology has not quite matched that of other areas. Technical solutions such as computer graphics, natural language processing, or man-machine-man communications in office systems are not enough by themselves. They should be complemented by system features that ensure cooperative behavior of the interfaces, thus reducing the training and usage effort required for successful interaction.

In analogy to a human dialog partner, we call an interface *cooperative* if it does not just accept user requests passively or answer them literally, but actively attempts to understand the users' intentions and to help them solve their application problems. This leads to the central question addressed by this book:

> **What makes an information systems interface cooperative, and how do we provide capabilities leading to cooperative interfaces?**

Many answers are possible. A first aspect concerns the *formulation and acceptance* of user requests. Many researchers assume that such requests should be formulated in natural language. In this area, a central problem of cooperativity is the comprehension of fragmentary and seemingly ambiguous problem statements; if the system could understand incomplete requests, it would save the user a lot of repetitious work. Sometimes, general linguistic analysis leads to the completion of gaps in a query expression, e.g., caused by elliptical references. Often, however, a clear understanding of a request can only be accomplished by taking into account application-specific knowledge; knowledge not only about the domain of discourse, but also about the capabilities, tasks, and intentions of the user.

A second aspect concerns the *presentation* of the answer. A cooperative interface should adapt its output presentation to the cognitive limitations and objectives of the user. If the answer consists only of a few data, the user may desire a natural language sentence rather than an incomprehensible table as an answer. If the answer is uninformative, there may even be a need to over-answer the initial question. For example, few people would be happy with the answer "yes" to the question: "do you know what time it is?" Conversely, if the answer contains a lot of detailed information, the user may wish to process it further before looking at the result on-line. One effective means of condensing complex output data is their presentation in graphical form.

A third aspect of cooperativity is related to the system's *reaction to exceptional situations*. Trivial errors (e.g., spelling) should be detected and corrected largely automatically. If the system returns an unexpected answer (especially no answer where the user expected one), it should explain the problem and guide the user in its correction. Long delays of an answer should also be explained, in order to avoid misleading the user.

The third aspect could be considered a special case of a fourth one: the problem of supporting the user in *navigating through complex dialogs*. Dialogs may have a complex structure, consisting of different modes of interaction, cross-references, etc. A cooperative interface should maintain a trail of the dialog, sufficient to understand references to previous results and to explain the status of the dialog, for instance, when the user resumes the dialog after an interruption.

Finally, a fifth aspect is the *adaptability* of the interface to new applications, databases, or even different natural languages. Cooperative interfaces should reduce the need for calling expensive external specialists - and the delays caused by their involvement - by providing tools that allow end users to develop, or at least extend, tailored applications interfaces.

These five aspects, although by no means complete, should serve as an initial circumscription of the idea of cooperative interfaces. Recent developments in the field of Artificial Intelligence - in particular, in natural language processing - have begun to offer promising solutions to some of these questions. This book presents a selection of detailed descriptions and empirical evaluations of natural language systems that have made substantial contributions to the idea of cooperative interfaces to information systems.

The contributions in this book approach the problem of cooperativity from rather different perspectives: further developments in the formal aspects of natural language or graphics technology, functional and empirical evaluation of existing systems, and utilization of domain-specific knowledge about the information system and its users. All of these seem to be feasible strategies to promote our understanding of the requirements and solution strategies for designing cooperative interfaces.

The book is divided into three parts. **Part I** addresses general issues in natural language comprehension and (graphical) output presentation. It describes two important systems that attempt to provide application-independent services.

Jane R. Robinson (SRI International, USA) presents "DIAGRAM: A Grammar for Dialogues", a large and complex grammar to be used by AI systems for interpreting English language dialog. DIAGRAM is an augmented phrase-structure grammer with rule procedures that cause phrases to inherit attributes from their constituents, and from larger phrases in which they themselves are constituents. DIAGRAM does not only analyze the basic kinds of phrases but also complex ones; its application is not restricted to a particular domain.

Chapter 2, by Frank Zdybel, Jr. (Xerox Palo Alto Research Center, USA) describes „An Engine for Intelligent Graphics", an Advanced Information Presentation System (AIPS) that constructs graphic displays according to incomplete declarative specifications of their content, structure, and appearance. A knowledge-based approach using the knowledge representation language, KL-ONE, provides non-programmers with the capability of viewing complex collections of information in arbitrary ways. Similar to DIAGRAM which is intended as an application-independent *language understanding* tool, AIPS offers a centralized cooperative *graphics output* facility which can present information from a wide variety of sources.

The remainder of the book deals with systems that have the explicit goal of providing cooperative natural language access to different kinds of information systems: relational or other commercial databases, information retrieval systems, image processing systems, and expert systems.

Many early systems have tried to deal with this problem on the basis of purely linguistic analysis. The application semantics of such systems is ideally provided by the users themselves through the definition of an application-specific vocabulary and grammar subset. Some of these systems have now reached a fair degree of maturity which allows them to be subjected to stringent empirical evaluation, thus revealing very clearly the requirements of cooperative natural language query systems, but also the achievements and shortcomings of existing technology.

Part II describes three such systems that were or still are considered for commerciae product development. Each chapter stresses one important aspect: functional requirements (Chap. 3), general desirability and feasibility (Chap. 4), and application development (Chap. 5).

Marjorie Templeton and John Burger (System Development Corporation, USA) discuss in Chap. 5 the functional requirements of cooperative natural language interfaces to commercial databases. Their proposal results from their experience with EUFID, a transportable natural language interface which has been used with database management systems (DBMS) as diverse as the relational INGRES system and Honeywell's World-Wide Data Management System. The chapter "Considerations for the Development of Natural-Language Interfaces to Database Management Systems" elaborates cooperativity requirements for application development, language processing, and underlying DBMS, and concludes with a comprehensive checklist of necessary functional capabilities.

Matthias Jarke, Jürgen Krause und Yannis Vassiliou (New York University, USA and University of Regensburg, West Germany) emphasize the need for a formal empirical evaluation of information systems interfaces in Chap. 6. They develop a framework for the design of such studies and describe its application to a domain-independent natural language query system. The paper "Studies in the Evaluation of a Domain-Independent Natural Language Query System" presents the combined results of three stages of evaluation with the German and English versions of the system, using about 100 experimental subjects and more than 12000 queries. The results demonstrate that natural language interfaces allow more concise query formulation when compared to formal query languages, and require only vocabulary subsets of manageable size. But they fail to prove the superiority of natural language interfaces in terms of problem-solving quality and efficiency.

Fred Damerau (IBM Yorktown Heights, USA) addresses the important problem of user-developed natural language interfaces. In Chap. 5 he presents "An Interactive Customization Program for a Natural Language Database Query System" which is based on the TQA/REQUEST natural language interface to relational databases. The customization program is viewed as a replacement for a general domain-independent natural language database interface. It employs a system-driven dialog to help end users define their own vocabulary and grammatical rules. These users need not be linguists but should be familiar with the database to be accessed.

Part III of the book describes three major projects in knowledge-based natural language processing.

Stimulated by the success of expert systems, most natural language projects started in the last five years stress the role of domain knowledge in interpreting natural language requests cooperatively. By this approach, a natural language interface should be closely related to the semantic meta-information stored with many modern databases, especially with the so-called deductive databases. A number of different knowledge bases can be provided, for example, on the domain, on the technical information system structure, or on the information system's user. Of course, linguistic knowledge bases remain necessary in this approach as well.

Chapter 6, by Jürgen Janas (Hochschule der Bundeswehr, Munich, West Germany), is a theoretical analysis of "The Semantics-Based Natural Language Interface to Relational Databases" which may serve as a formal introduction to an approach that is less interested in the surface structure of natural language but relies on the structural semantics of the underlying relational database. In particular, the problems of ambiguity, conjunction, and ellipsis are elucidated from the semantics point of view. As a cautioning remark, the author emphasizes that this approach is only suitable for serious users who need data from a database they know fairly well.

Wolfgang Höppner, Katharina Morik and Heinz Marburger (University of Hamburg, West Germany) discuss in Chap. 7, "Talking it over: The Natural Language Dialog System HAM-ANS", the role of language-oriented research in the field of Artificial Intelligence. HAM-ANS attempts to provide cooperative natural language access to a wide variety of information systems: a database for fishery research, an image processing system for scene analysis, and an expert system for hotel reservations. Detailed examples of all three applications are given, and the overall organization of the system and its knowledge bases is described using the hotel reservation example. The authors emphasize the need for user modelling and present suggestions for the representation and application of user models.

The final Chap. 8, by Giorgio Brajnik, Giovanni Guida, and Carlo Tasso (Universita di Udine, Italy) describes an expert interface to yet another kind of information system: the information retrieval interface IR-NLI. In the chapter "An Expert Interface for Effective Man-Machine Interaction", the authors argue for the use of rule-based systems for interface support. They present a task concept for the respresentation and utilization of meta-knowledge, and discuss the use of learning techniques as a method to facilitate cooperative behavior.

In contrast to many short conference reports, the contributions in this book provide fairly detailed descriptions and results for selected systems and studies at the leading edge of cooperative natural language systems technology. The authors are well-known scientists from several of the major natural language research centers. This organization of the book is intended to offer the reader - student, practitioner, or researcher - a comprehensive view of the problems related not only to the design but also to the evaluation of cooperative interfaces to information systems. The book demonstrates that this area of research is still in its early phases, although some impressive results have been achieved. We look forward to future work on cooperative interfaces, hopefully some of it stimulated by the collection of papers in this book.

Warszawa and Frankfurt
November, 1985

Leonard Bolc
Matthias Jarke

Table of Contents

Part I

Tools for Cooperative Man-Machine Interaction

Chapter 1

DIAGRAM: A Grammar for Dialogues

Jane J. Robinson

Abstract[1]. This paper is an explanatory overview of a large and complex grammar, DIAGRAM, used in an AI system for interpreting English dialogue. DIAGRAM is an augmented phrase-structure grammar with rule procedures that allow phrases to inherit attributes from their constituents and to acquire attributes from the larger phrases in which they themselves are constituents. These attributes are used to set context-sensitive constraints on the acceptance of an analysis. Constraints can be imposed by conditions on dominance as well as by conditions on constituency. For every expression it analyzes, DIAGRAM provides an annotated description of the structure. The annotations supply important information for other parts of the system that interpret the expression in the context of a dialogue. Rule procedures can also assign scores to an analysis to rate it as probable or unlikely, so that semantic procedures can ignore possible but unlikely analyses when assigning interpretations to syntactically ambiguous utterances.

DIAGRAM analyzes not only all the basic kinds of phrases and sentences but many quite complex ones as well; it is not tied to a particular domain of application and can be extended with relative ease. Design decisions for DIAGRAM were guided by considerations of the communicative functions that phrases serve and by considerations of efficiency in relating syntactic analyses to propositional content. Major decisions are explained and illustrated.

1 Introduction

"All grammars leak." Edward Sapir, *Language,* 1921.

DIAGRAM is a grammar used in an AI system for interpreting dialogue. The system is a tool for ongoing research to find what structures and processes are necessary for dialogue interpretation. A basic premise of this research is that dialogue participants interpret each other's expressions by taking into account not

---

[1] This paper is an expansion of an article with the same title that appeared in the January 1982 issue of Communications of the ACM. The work reported here was supported by the National Science Foundation under Grant No. MCS76-22004, and the Defense Advanced Research Projects Agency under Contract N00039-79-C-0118 with the Naval Electronic Systems Command.

only the truth-conditional meanings of what is said, but also each other's intentions, goals, plans, beliefs, states of knowledge, and focus of attention as these can be inferred from text and context. DIAGRAM is a grammar of English - not of the whole of English, of course, but of a substantial subset of it. It analyzes not only all the basic kinds of phrases but also complex ones, and is extendible in a principled way independent of a particular domain of application. The list that follows is a sampling of the kinds of syntactical constructions that are successfully analyzed at present:

Her uncle gave the girl several books.
She was given more difficult books by her uncle.
Which ones did he give her?
I saw many more books than she did.
Two of them were by her uncle.
Do it quickly but be careful!
Be careful not to break the vase when you put it down.
Tell me what he told you.
Don't tell me any more about it!
There are some men here from the city.
The vase could easily break, if you aren't careful.
You could break this vase with that hammer.
They found her gone.
On arriving, we had something to eat.
Have there been many people who tried it?
Didn't those people want him to try to do it?
Is this any harder for him to do than that was?
Who wrote it?
By whom was it written?
Who was it written by?
What could he have been doing there?
Why did you want John to attach it?
Why do you think he wanted to go?
What did they tell you Mary said John tried to do?
How many more of them do you want him to have?

All grammars leak and no grammar for a reasonably extensive subset of English can claim to provide *all* and *only* the correct analyses for the sentences for which it is applicable. What is claimed is that every structurally distinct semantic interpretation of the sentences shown receives a corresponding, structurally distinct, syntactic analysis. A simple example may make the point. Consider the sentence:

She was given more difficult books by her uncle.

The sentence contains two syntactically ambiguous phrases: either the books were more difficult or there were more books, and either the books were "by" her uncle or the giving was "by" her uncle. These two ambiguities combine to produce four different analyses of the sentence. (There is an additional lexical semantic ambiguity, since "by" has both a locative and an agentive sense.)

DIAGRAM successfully provides the four appropriate syntactic analyses. Figure 1 shows three of the four analyses and their corresponding interpretations. The fourth, in which the books were more difficult and were given by her uncle, is left as an exercise for the reader.

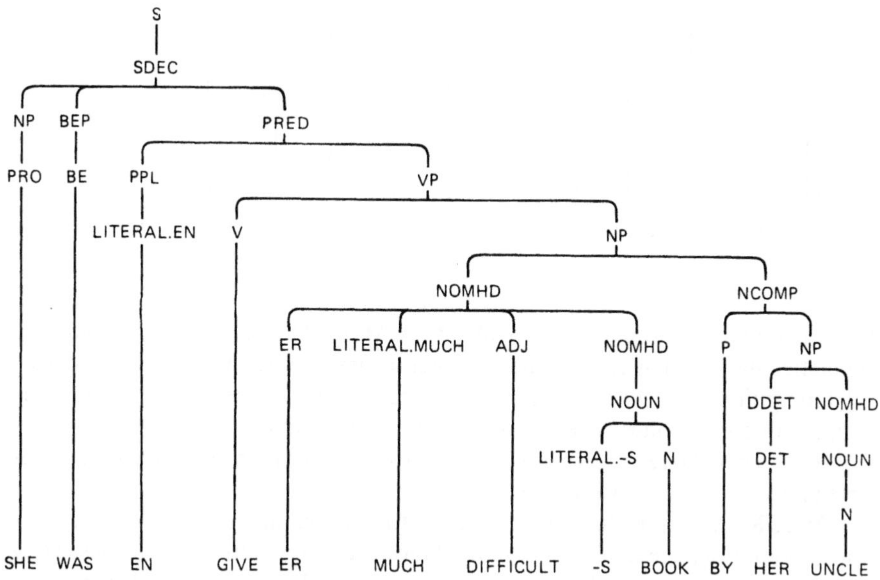

Fig. 1. a In this analysis, the books are more difficult (i. e., harder to read) and they are (written) by her uncle

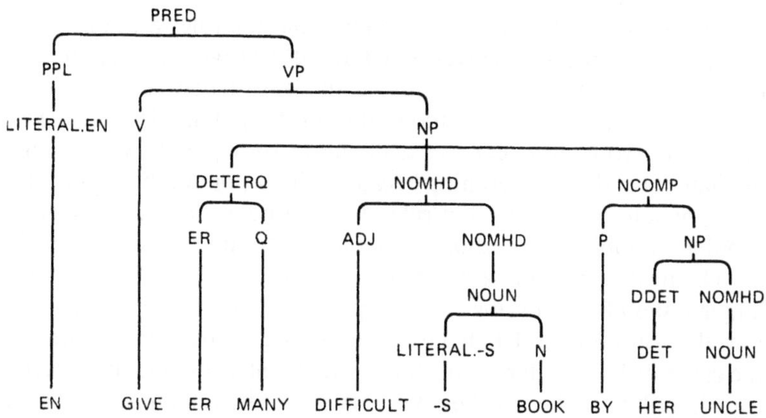

Fig. 1. b In this analysis, the difficult books were by her uncle and they were many

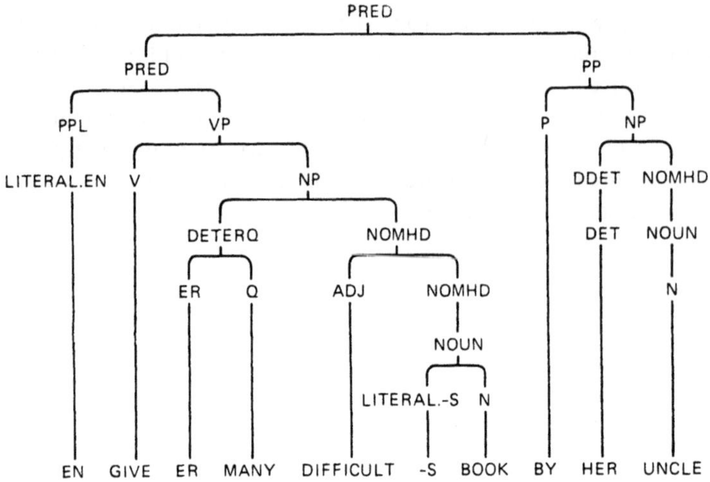

Fig. 1.c In this analysis, the giving was done by her uncle and the difficult books were many

For this sentence and many others like it, DIAGRAM provides all and only the syntactic analyses that correspond to semantic ambiguities not arising from lexical ambiguity. However, for some sentences there will be incorrect analyses along with correct ones. The reasons for this are relatively well understood and will be described later, together with methods for eliminating or controlling multiple analyses without losing correct ones.

DIAGRAM's rules have been written to capture the insightful generalizations about language that appear in the literature of theoretical linguistics. They have been written also with a constant awareness of the functional roles that syntactic phenomena play in communication. As a result, DIAGRAM contains some nonstandard definitions of syntactic categories and constituent boundaries along with much that is widely accepted. These definitions will be explained, but not always justified. "Justifying" implies that the rules are superior to any currently conceivable alternatives, but DIAGRAM will continue to be revised as better ways are found to accommodate the tension between the requirements for capturing linguistic generalizations and for designing rules suitable for processing and interpreting interactive dialogues. Consequently, we describe an intermediate stage that is interesting because it incorporates the results of experience with previous formulations of rules and procedures and because its unresolved problems establish a direction for significant future research and revision.

The next section presents an overview of DIAGRAM as a component in a larger system for analyzing and interpreting utterances in dialogues. This is followed in Sect. 3 by a detailed explication, beginning with a characterization of the category S (the category of independent sentences) and the subtypes of S, before describing, in Sect. 4, the categories of words and phrases that are the constituents of S. By starting top down in the order of description, a sense of the whole will be conveyed first so that light can be shed on how constituent parts function with respect to that whole. Indeed, the description will be as much in terms of functions as in terms of syntactic categories. Sect. 4 discusses the relationships of syntactic functions to syntactic categories. ("Function", here, is to be understood in two senses: the sense in which a phrase is capable of serving a purpose in discourse and the sense in which it serves one of the traditional syntactic functions such as subject, predicate, object, and modifier. Context should make clear which is meant.) Sect. 5 presents current plans for revisions and the motives for them.

2 What DIAGRAM Does and How It Does It

DIAGRAM is a phrase-structure grammar whose context-free rules are augmented by procedures that increase its descriptive power and give it limited context-sensitive capabilities. There has been a resurgence of interest in phrase-structure grammar with various augmentations as alternatives to transformational grammar. Generalized Phrase Structure Grammar (GPSG) [GAZD 81] and Lexical Functional Grammar (LFG) [BRES 82] are two notable examples. (See also [JOSH 80].) An extended comparison of the emerging grammatical formalisms with DIAGRAM's rules and procedures is perhaps premature and certainly beyond the scope of this paper, but some points of comparison are noted throughout, particularly in the final section.

For every expression it defines (or accepts) as syntactically wellformed, DIAGRAM provides an annotated description that makes explicit the structural relations holding among its words and phrases. It identifies the syntactic categories of each word and phrase and specifies properties that each contributes to the whole expression or that each acquires as a result of its relationship to the whole. For example, applied to the analysis of "The fish are in the river", DIAGRAM will not only label "the fish" as a noun phrase but also as definitely determined, plural, and the subject of the sentence. Note that the last two properties are not inherent to "the fish" in isolation, but are resultant properties of its use in the whole expression. (Compare "John caught the fish", where the syntactic number is indeterminate for "fish".)

All these properties provide important pieces of information for the other parts of the system that interpret the phrase when it is used in ongoing discourse. From the fact that the noun phrase is plural, it follows that more than one of a set of discrete entities are being referred to. From the fact that it is definitely determined, one can infer that the speaker assumes the entities to be already identified or readily identifiable by the hearer. From the fact that "the fish" is the subject, one can infer that the focus of attention of the speaker is on the fish rather than on the river or on other elements in the context of the discourse (Compare "The river contains many fish".)

2.1 Rules and Procedures

Appendix A contains a few of the rules and a sample lexicon. Here we are concerned with the formal properties of DIAGRAM rather than with details of its format.

The rules are augmented by procedures that constrain the application of a rule, add information to the structure created by the rule, and assign one or more interpretations to the resulting enriched structural analysis. These procedures apply at different points during processing. One, called a *constructor,* applies immediately as the constituents of a phrase are being assembled. After the entire utterance has been analyzed syntactically, a second procedure, called a *translator,* is applied. The following simplified example should clarify the interactions of the constituent-structure statements with the constructors and translators.

Rule SBE SDEC = NP BE ADJP;

Constructor: (1) If NP and BE disagree in syntactic number, then REJECT the analysis.

(2) If the syntactic number of NP is null (undefined), then set it equal to the syntactic number of BE.

Translator: (1) Apply the semantic translation of ADJP as predicate to the semantic translation of NP as argument.

(2) If BE contains "not", then prefix the negation operator to the translation.

The constituent structure portion states that a declarative sentence can be composed of a noun phrase followed by an auxiliary BE phrase followed by a predicate adjective phrase, as in "the fish are very big".

Within the constructor, the first (sub)procedure accepts or rejects a string of constituents according to the results of a number-agreement test. This prevents the rule from applying to "the girls was very tall" in the course of analyzing "the father of the girls was very tall". Notice that the second statement adds information about the number of the NP on the basis of its combinability with a BE phrase requiring plural number agreement. This addition of new properties to the description of a syntactic entity on the basis of its combinability with another is akin to the process of *unification,* a kind of pattern-matching technique first used in logic and theorem-proving and now provoking considerable interest among computational linguists. (See, for example, [KAY 83].) The successor to DIAGRAM, called PATR for PArse And TRanslate, uses unification as its basic operation in parsing [GROS 83b].

Constructors also have access to information about subconstituents of the constituents of the phrase. They can "look down" the parse tree, so to speak, in making decisions about acceptance. In addition, they can make semantic tests to decide whether constituents obey local selectional restrictions; that is, whether or not they are semantically as well as syntactically compatible. A translator has similar capabilities, and it is often not clear whether semantic tests are more efficiently made in the constructors, where the phrase may be eliminated from further consideration, or in the translator, where additional context is available for the decision.

The translator procedure for a rule derives one or more semantic interpretations of the phrase built by the rule. In doing so, the procedure can access all the attributes whose values have been set by translators of rules that have constructed the larger phrases in which the phrase to be interpreted forms a part. If the SDEC constructed by applying the rule in (1) is embedded in another SDEC, for instance, the translator for the embedding rule will add that information. This is necessary, since the independent sentence, "the fish are in the river", will be interpreted as an assertion about the world, but if it is embedded as part of a sentence beginning with "it is doubtful that..." or "I see that...", its interpretations will be very different.

A third procedure, called an *integrator,* which we will only mention here, is more domain dependent than the other procedures. (The separation of integrators from other procedures makes the grammar easier to adapt to new domains without extensive revision.) The integrator for a rule has access to facts in a knowledge base or in a data base, and can render decisions about the pragmatic well-formedness or appropriateness of a sematic interpretation. Quantifier scoping is handled in a special process intermediate between translators and integrators.

The capability to apply tests at any of three points during the analysis of a sentence - during application of the constructor, or the translator, or the integrator procedures - raises theoretical and practical questions concerning processing. The major question is: When should semantic and pragmatic criteria be invoked to avoid false parsing paths? The question involves matters of computational efficiency and also of psycholinguistic processing, on the assumption that people store a certain amount of incoming text before they process it for meaning. We speculate that experiments with computational efficiency, using DIAGRAM or some other sufficiently large grammar, may help us understand psycholinguistic phenomena and conversely.

In brief, the procedures of constructors and translators provide the overall system with the capability for context-sensitive intensional interpretations, and integrators provide the interface for extensional interpretations.

2.2 *Attributes and Factors*

Attributes that are set and tested by rule procedures are divided into two types: general and specific. Specific attributes are associated with specific categories of words and phrases and are often introduced in the lexical entries of words and inherited by the phrases in which the words are constituents.[2] Other attributes are introduced in the rule procedures themselves. One very important attribute, that of syntactic number, is introduced by both means. Syntactic number is primarily an attribute of the category NOUN and most NOUNs are formed by a rule that optionally combines a noun stem N with the plural suffix "-s". If the suffix is present, the value of the attribute is "plural" (PL); otherwise it is "singular" (SG). However, some words that do not combine with the suffix are inherently plural; e.g., "people". Such words are entered into the lexicon as members of the category NOUN with the value PL for the attribute @NBR. The ambiguous word "fish" is also a NOUN, but it has no attribute for syntactic number. The tests for number agreement accept null values (meaning that the attribute is undefined) as agreeing with any value, so that the NP "the fish", which has not inherited an attribute of number from its NOUN constituent, agrees with either a singular or plural auxiliary. As previously noted, this permits such NPs to combine with either singular or plural predicates, and to acquire the requisite value for the attribute of number in so doing.

Among the general attributes referenced and used in the procedures is one called @SPELLING. @SPELLING is an attribute of every word in the lexicon and its value is the literal form of the word. This attribute is referenced in rules that attach particles and inseparable prepositions (Ps) as constituents of the inner core of verb phrases. For example, the lexical entry for "give" will list the form UP as a possible value for the attribute @PARTICLE, and the rules (Rules VP1 and VP2) that analyze the phrases "give up the book" and "give it up" will test for agreement of the @SPELLING attribute of the preposition "up" with the forms listed as possible particles for the verb "give". The @SPELLING attribute is also used to check other "function" words and affixes.

Every phrase also has as attributes the categories of its immediate constituents, which can be referenced to any desired depth in the procedures that constrain the application of a rule. For example, noun phrases may contain modifying phrases that follow the central core (NOMHD) of the NP. Such modifying phrases belong to the category NCOMP, and NPs that contain them as immediate constituents will have an attribute @NCOMP with the value T, meaning that the constituent is present. The NCOMP itself may have a prepositional phrase constituent, in which case it has the attribute @PP.

DIAGRAM makes frequent use of such general attributes in the subprocedures called *factors* that are used to assign likelihood scores to syntactic or semantic analyses. Instead of simply accepting or rejecting an analysis, a rule can accept it with some assessment of the probability of its correctness. For example, the probability that a prepositional phrase is part of a nominal modifier

[2] Some of the syntactic categories assigned by DIAGRAM to words and phrases are listed in Appendix B. Appendix C lists some of the principal syntactic attributes associated with specific categories. The current version of DIAGRAM differs considerably from the version given in these appendices, especially in its use of *gap* attributes for associating WH constituents with argument positions.

NCOMP rather than a verbal modifier may depend on what the preposition is (i.e., how it is spelled), and on whether numerous other modifiers have already been added to NCOMP. Factors can specify the probabilities and attach scores to phrases that meet their specifications. Then when several possibilities for attaching the prepositional phrase result in multiple analyses of a sentence, the analyses can be ordered according to their likelihood by combining the judgments of the various factors for the various combinations. Less likely combinations can subsequently be ignored by semantic and pragmatic interpreters. Methods for combining scores derived from factors and ordering multiple analyses are described in [PAXT 77].

To give a simple example, consider the use of factors in assessing the probability that a prepositional phrase is part of an NCOMP. A factor in the appropriate NCOMP rule stipulates that the probability is low (UNLIKELY) if the NCOMP already has a relative clause constituent, SREL. The designation for the attribute is (@SREL NCOMP) and its value is T, meaning "true" or "present" for NCOMP modifiers like "that I saw" in:

the man that I saw.

In analyzing the larger phrase:

the man that I saw with the telescope

DIAGRAM currently assigns a higher score to the analysis in which "with the telescope" is part of the SREL "that I saw with the telescope", but will allow the alternate analysis in which "with the telescope" independently modifies "man".

It is worth noting that factors can be changed to adjust the analysis to particular styles and discourse domains without rewriting the grammar.

3 Sentence Categories and Structures

3.1 Major Sentence Types

We begin an account of the grammar itself with an explication of DIAGRAM's characterization of the category S, the category of independent sentences. Sentences, viewed functionally, perform many different tasks. Among other things, they encode propositional content that makes claims about the way the world is; they arrange that content so it meshes with what the speaker assumes the hearer knows and is currently attending to; and they express the speaker's attitudes toward the content and toward the hearer. The same propositional content may be encoded with different words in different syntactic structures. The differences reflect the influence of the other functions the sentence serves when it is used. Consequently, devising a grammar for recognizing and making explicit the significant variations in the syntactic structures of sentences and other phrases is a complicated affair. Decisions as to how some string of words should be structured and categorized in order to simplify the problem of interpreting them in a consistent and general way need to be guided by considerations of their communicative functions. These considerations should be kept in mind as part of the background in which various decisions about how to analyze English sentences were embodied in DIAGRAM.

Sentences are traditionally classified according to their modalities as imperative and indicative. Indicatives are subclassified as declarative and interrogative; interrogatives are further subclassified into two types according to whether the truth of a total proposition is being questioned or whether some argument of a proposition is marked as unknown. These two types of interrogatives are sometimes calles Yes/No (or polar) questions and WH-questions.

This hierarchical concept is not preserved overtly in DIAGRAM. All of the distinctions are treated as equally important and although the special relatedness of WH-questions to Yes/No questions is implicitly recognized in the constituent structure assigned to the WH-questions (see Sect. 3.1.1), DIAGRAM explicitly distinguishes four basic sentence types. These are given the mnemonic category names:

SIMP Imperative sentence
SDEC Declarative sentence
SQ Propositional interrogative
SWHQ Argument interrogative

The syntactic basis for this treatment is that each type has a distinctive initial category. SIMPs lack an initial NP; they typically begin with an uninflected auxiliary DO or BE or with an uninflected form of a verb. SDECs typically begin with a noun phrase that functions as the subject of the sentence. SQs begin with an auxiliary followed by an NP. SWHQs begin with a noun phrase marked by the presence of a WH-word (who, what, which, where, when, whose) in initial position or by an initial prepositional phrase with such a noun phrase as its object.[3] Examples are:

SIMP Put the apples in the basket.
Don't drop them.

SDEC He put the apples in the basket.
They are there now.
There are several of them.

SQ Did he put them in the basket?
Are they in the basket or in the sack?
Are there more than two there?

---

[3] WH-questions can also include sentences with noninitial WH-marked phrases, as in "He put them where?" DIAGRAM does not accept this kind of sentence, but extending it to do so should pose no major problems.

SWHQ How many apples did he put there?
Which basket did he put them in?
How many of them are there?

The differences in the types of messages each class of sentence is suited to convey are also equally important, conceptually. SIMP represents a directive speech act in which, to use Searle's terms, [SEAR 77], the direction of fit of the propositional content is from word to world; that is, the speaker asks the hearer to perform some action (putting apples in a basket) that will bring about a state of affairs in the world that realizes (makes true) the propositional content expressed in the words (the hearer has "put the apples in the basket"). For SDEC, the direction of fit is from world to word; that is, the speaker asserts that the propositional content expressed in the words is true ("they are there now"). SQ is a request for the hearer to judge whether the words fit the world and tell the speaker if the propositional content is true (if "he" did indeed put "them" in the basket). SWHQ presupposes the truth of some propositional content, but requests the hearer to supply a missing argument or quantifier. Extending Searle's terminology somewhat, we can say that WH-interrogatives (SWHQs) presuppose speaker and hearer agree that the words of the propositional content fit the world - the apples are in some basket - but that the speaker is missing a piece of the content that the hearer is requested to supply ("which basket").

Although the four sentence types are distinguished by their initial constituents, all are analyzable in terms of three basic functions: a subject, a predicate, and an indicator of mood. In most English sentences, these functions are served by overtly present constituents. For example:

Subject	*Mood*	*Predicate*
They	were	going there
That	is	a big bird
Your home	is	very beautiful
The cake	must be	in the oven

Under special circumstances, there may be no constituent to represent the mood; for example, in "they go here", where the sentence is affirmative, not interrogative, the predicate is a verb, the subject is plural, and there is no auxiliary to indicate perfective or progressive aspect. And, of course, imperatives lack subjects. Nevertheless, the association of constituent phrases with these functions is strong. In general, subjects are NPs, mood is indicated by various positions of auxiliary phrases, and predicates are phrases headed by one of the four major parts of speech - VPs, NPs, ADJPs or PPs.

Transformational grammars capture these generalizations by setting up canonical underlying forms of sentences in which each function is represented by an appropriate constituent category, arranged in declarative order. If we were writing such a grammar, we might represent the rules for S in a single schema like:

S = NP AUX [VP / NP / ADJP / PP]

and subsequently derive our four subtypes from the canonical forms by moving and deleting constituents to form interrogatives and imperatives. But although it employs some local string transformations on the sentences presented to it for parsing, DIAGRAM represents the various sentence types separately. Imperatives, for instance, are not derived from some appropriately restricted canonical form by deleting an initial NP realized as "you". They are analyzed directly by a rule (see Appendix B, Rule SIMP). Some relevant facts needed for interpreting imperatives are: that the subject is not overtly expressed but is understood to be the hearer; that the mood is indicated by the absence of subject, tense, and aspect; and that the predicating expression directs the hearer to perform some action to make the world fit the words. These facts are represented in the rule's translator, which assigns semantic interpretations to the syntactic analysis the rule provides for strings it accepts. This approach achieves the same effect as that achieved by formulating an imperative "transformation" that is constrained to operate on just those "underlying" canonical forms that obey the restrictions on realizing the subject as "you", omitting tense and aspect markers, and confining the predicates to certain semantic subclasses.

Nevertheless, we feel that there is some loss of generality in writing so many separate rules that have so many elements in common, and we are therefore exploring the possibility of using other metagrammatical devices to achieve generality while avoiding inefficiencies in the traditional transformational approach that requires first building and then transforming syntactic tree structures, some of which may have elaborate and redundant substructures that are not only moved around, but are subsequently deleted.

To sum up at this point, then, DIAGRAM does not derive sentences from underlying canonical syntactic forms, but directly defines four basic kinds of sentences. The syntactic bases for classification are the presence or absence of subjects, of tense and aspect auxiliaries, of a specially marked WH-phrase, and their structural arrangements with respect to each other when present. The classification is expressed in the first sentence rule, SO, which defines the root category of independent sentences as any of four types, with or without certain marks of punctuation. Square brackets enclose a list of alternatives, separated by "/". Parentheses enclose (a list of) optional elements.

Rule SO S = [SDEC / SIMP / SQ / SWHQ] (ENDPUNCT);

3.1.1 The Two Interrogatives

Mention has been made of an implicit recognition of the special relatedness of the two types of interrogatives, SQ and SWHQ. The recognition is implied by the analysis of SWHQs as containing SQ constituents in all cases except those in which the questioned argument is the subject of the sentence. The latter cases are handled by a distinct rule.

The rules defining SWHQs are:

SWH1 SWHQ = [WHNP / WHPP / WHADJP] SQ;
SWH2 SWHQ = WHNP (AUX) [VP / BE PRED];

Examples are:

(i)	WHNP[Which boat]	SQ[did you buy]	Rule SWH1
(ii)	WHPP[From whom]	SQ[did you buy it]	Rule SWH1
(iii)	WHADJP[How wide]	SQ[is it]	Rule SWH1
(iv)	WHNP[Who]	SQ[did you buy it from]	Rule SWH1
but (v)	Who bought it	(No embedded SQ)	Rule SWH2

When the SWHQ contains an embedded SQ, the initial WH-marked constituent is the filler for a "gap" (a missing constituent) in the SQ. In other words, an embedded SQ is always semantically incomplete or underspecified. When the missing constituent is an obligatory object of a verb or preposition, the SQ is syntactically incomplete too; that is, it is not a well-formed independent sentence. Such syntactically incomplete SQs are exemplified in the SWHQ examples above by "did you buy" and "did you buy it from". These incomplete SQs are currently marked with an attribute that is used to control their combination with an appropriate filler or to prevent them from being accepted as full sentences. This type of incompleteness is also present in relative clauses, and is handled by the same means. (See Sect. 3.4.)

3.1.2 Sentence Types and the Packaging of Information

Since the sentences analyzed by DIAGRAM are assumed to be utterances in a dialogue, it may be of interest to consider briefly how the information structures of sentences are related to their syntactic analysis. The preceding description of WH-interrogatives provides examples.

For SWHQs that embed SQs, the SQs contain the propositional material that is presupposed - the information that is ostensibly "given" or "already activated" [CHAF 76] and that is shared by both speaker and hearer. For the other SWHQs, the presupposed material is in the auxiliary and predicating constituents. Thus, "which boat did you buy" presupposes "you bought a boat", and "who bought it" presupposes "someone bought it". In both cases, the initial WH-marked constituent contains a pointer to the kind of information the speaker lacks and assumes that the hearer can supply. In declarative sentences, on the other hand, the initial constituent usually points to or contains the already activated, shared information, and the remainder adds the information the speaker assumes is not already activated and shared by the hearer. The most striking exception to this generalization occurs when the declarative is an answer to a WH-interrogative in which the subject is the WH-marked constituent. For example, in the first of the following exchanges, the declarative answer to the question packages the new information in the subject constituent, "John", which is likely to be stressed, and the already activated information is in the predicate that follows.

Who bought the boat?	
John bought it.	(The subject is "new" information.)
What did John buy?	
He bought a *boat.*	(The object is "new" information.)

This is just what we would expect from the way the preceding question serves to reverse the order in which given and new information is packaged. In the second example, the declarative answer contains a constituent in its predicate that is lacking in the predicate of embedded SQ of the SWHQ, a constituent that also contains the kind of information indicated by the WH-marked initial constituent of the interrogative. As we might expect, therefore, the predicate of the second declarative answer contains the new information, which is also likely to be stressed in speaking.

These considerations of how information is packaged become important in designing computer systems for interacting with human users. For instance, it is important that mistaken presuppositions be corrected and that new information be appropriately related to already activated information. Otherwise, there is risk of misunderstanding or incoherence. The risk cannot be avoided if only the propositional content of sentences is considered; the syntactic packaging must be related to the propositional content in analyzable ways. For a fuller discussion, see [HOBB 79].

3.2 Subtypes of the Basic Types of Sentences

3.2.1 The BE/DO Dichotomy

Each of the four basic sentence types is divided into two classes according to whether or not an auxiliary BE is required. Only sentences with verb phrase predicates can occur without any member of the BE paradigm. Such sentences require a form of DO if they are interrogatives or if they are negated or emphatic; otherwise, they may omit an auxiliary constituent entirely, except for the suffix "-s" marking present tense in sentences with third person singular subjects. Examples of the first class are "it *is* here" and "it could *be* a bear". Examples of the second class are "they go", "they *did*n't go", and "he goe*s*."

The rule schema for imperatives, shown below in simplified form, reveals the differences in the two subtypes. Rule SIMP1 allows an imperative with a VP predicate to occur without any auxiliary. When an auxiliary is present, it is the infinitive form of DO. An imperative with a non-VP predicate requires the infinitive form BE, but occurs with an infinitive DO in emphatic and negated forms.[4]

Rule SIMP1 SIMP=("DO" (NOT)) ["BE" PRED / VP]

Examples:	Don't be an idiot.	Don't try.
	Do be careful.	Do try.
	Be here by noon.	Try again.

Only a relatively small number of non-VP predicates are semantically appropriate as imperatives. Intuitively, the DO auxiliary and verbs are both associated semantically with actions, while BE is associated semantically with states, as are adjectives, nouns (static objects) and prepositions. Only those states that are conceived of as requiring an act of will to maintain can appropriately be expressed with non-VP predicates in imperatives.

Except for imperatives, sentences that *require* a BE form in the auxiliary cannot also occur with a form of DO in the auxiliary. For example, "He doesn't be an idiot" is not well-formed in modern English. DIAGRAM emphasizes the distinction by defining separate rules for the two subtypes of SDEC, although they could be represented in a single rule schema with some complication of the constructor and translator procedures. The two constituent structure statements are:

Rule SD1 SDEC=NP (AUX) VP
Rule SB1 SDEC=NP (AUX) BE PRED

3.2.2 Existential Sentences

Sentences requiring a form of BE in the auxiliary have a special subtype that is also distinguished in DIAGRAM. These are the existential sentences like "there is someone here", "are there any more oranges in that basket", and "how many are there". The rules defining existential declaratives and interrogatives form a separate set, in which "there" is explicitly quoted as a constituent, thus:

Rule STHERE1
SDEC="THERE"(AUX) BE (NP [ING (VP/"BE"PRED)/PRED]);

Examples: There could be two.
There is a man being held prisoner.
There is a man running away.
There are some oranges on the table.

[4] Quotation marks around an item mean that the item is interpreted literally; otherwise, it is interpreted as the name of a syntactic category. Some categories (e.g., NOT, OF) may contain only one or two members, however. DO and BE are categories of the auxiliary forms, including inflected forms such as "did" and "is". Instead of quoting "DO" and "BE", it would be possible to name the categories and then reject all inflected forms by performing a test in the translator for the rule, but this would clearly be inefficient.

Rule STHEREQ1
SQ = BE "THERE" (NP [ING (VP / "BE" PRED) / PRED]);

Examples: Are there?
Are there any going?
Are there any more here?
Are there some oranges left?

Separating the rules for existential sentences from the others allows much more economical treatment of certain special syntactic constraints. For example, unlike the other declaratives, number agreement in existential declaratives holds between the auxiliary and the NP that follows it, rather than one that precedes it. Compare: "this is a group" / "these are a group" / "there is a group". Also, the NP is typically indefinite rather than definite, and this fact can easily be stated in the constructors for the rules. Moreover, the NP is always a referring expression unless the sentence contains a negation, whereas in typical declaratives, the NP immediately following the auxiliary is a predicating expression. (Compare: "he is a man" versus "a man is here".)

These special syntactic and semantic facts stem from the special function that existential sentences perform in discourses. Some sentences in a discourse are analyzable as containing both 'old' (or 'given') information and 'new' information, but in existential sentences, all the information is presented to the hearer as 'new'. They are introductory sentences, quite literally, serving to introduce new objects into the domain of the discourse and focus the hearer's attention on them [GROS 80a, GROS 80b]. This is true even when the NP is definite. For example, "There's the book by Chomsky" (with the existential reading for "there") is appropriate only if there has been some previous denial or questioning of the existence of certain kinds of objects, as in "there aren't any good books on syntax". In this case, the previous speaker is *reminded* rather than *introduced* to the object (Chomsky's book), but in any case, that object is newly introduced into the *discourse*.

It is fairly common to overlook the special discourse functions of sentences when devising grammars, and appeals are frequently made to the principle that one should try to 'capture' generalizations when arguing for one syntactic analysis over another. On such grounds, many linguists have claimed that existential "there" is to be categorized as NP and existential sentences are to be defined by the same constituent structure rules that define the other sentence types. However, I know of only one property of the existential "there" that it shares with NPs, and that is its ability to function as the subject of a sentence.[5] But to say that "there" is the subject is to describe its syntactic function rather than its syntactic category. To claim that it is a NP is to ignore the fact that it cannot appear as a

[5] That it does have this property is shown by its behavior in tags, where "there are some men here, aren't there" is comparable to "John is here, isn't he". This syntactic behavior is plausibly described by saying that the subject of the sentence is reduplicated in the tag.

predicate nominal nor as the object of a preposition. If it is categorized as NP, this means that every occurrence of "there" in a nonsubject position will have to be checked for in the rules for phrases with NP constituents. Otherwise, semantic filters must reject inappropriate analyses that will be produced, for example, by parsing sentences like "John is there" with the same rules that parse "John is a linguist".

(In arguing against syntactic overgeneralization, I am not claiming that DIAGRAM's current rules for generating existential sentences are sufficiently general.)

3.3 Sentence Conjunction, Modification, and Embedding

Larger sentences can be created by conjoining sentences or by modifying or embedding them.

The rules for conjoining that are described in this section are no longer current. They were originally used as experimental placeholders, awaiting the time when linguistic theory yields more insight into the nature of conjunction and the constraints to be obeyed. They are currently being replaced by more general rules whose constructors and translators are being developed in greater detail. Their description here is only for purposes of illustrating some of the problems raised by conjunction.

Rules SX1 and SX2 define sentence conjunction and accept sentences like:

I went there but he wasn't there.	[Rule SX1]
He came, he saw, and he conquered.	[Rule SX1 followed by Rule SX2]

These rules do not cover sentences like "He came, he saw, he conquered". Also, DIAGRAM does not have rules capable of accepting sentences involving gaps of the kind found in

John gave but would have preferred to sell Mary a book,

where the sequence "Mary a book" is not a single constituent, but rather two constituents, serving as indirect and direct objects of both "gave" and "sell". The main problem with the conjoining rules, however, is not their failure to analyze some legitimate sentences. It is the problem that all syntax-based conjoining rules are prone to introduce; they assign too many structures. Attempts to constrain such rules syntactically will usually bar them from recognizing some legitimate structures.

The necessary constraints undoubtedly involve some notion of semantic parallelism. Meanwhile, DIAGRAM's conjoining rules for sentences are loosely constrained not to conjoin imperatives with nonimperatives. The constraint, which appears in the constructors, rejects the parsing of sentences like

I like to jog, swim and play tennis.

as the conjunction of a declarative "I like to jog" with an imperative interpretation of "swim and play tennis". However, it also rejects one possible correct parsing of the ambiguous sentence:

I like her but don't tell her that.

Sentence modification poses less severe problems. Rules SX3 and SX4 analyze sentences like

At midnight, satisfied, he left.
[Rule SX4 followed by Rule SX3]
After they arrived, he left.
[Rule SX3]

However, modifiers that follow the sentences they modify are attached as parts of the predicates of the four basic sentence types, rather than as modifiers of the S that dominates them. That is, in

He left after they arrived,

the phrase "after they arrived" is analyzed as part of the verb phrase. (See Rule VP9.) This attachment is theoretically justifiable, if one considers that Rules SX3 and SX4 define structures in which the modifiers have been fronted from a normally following position, analogously to the fronted object noun phrase "that man" in "that man I don't like". Even so, the rules for sentence modification will not at present allow a sentence modifier to modify jointly all sentence constituents of a conjoined sentence. For example, in parsing

He arrived and she left at two o'clock.

the modifier "at two o'clock" is attached only to the second SDEC of the conjoined pair. One remedy would be to add the rule

S = S (",") PP,

which is symmetrical to Rule SX3, but to do so would increase the already large number of parsings due to trailing prepositional phrases. For this reason, adding such a rule has been postponed, pending a more satisfactory solution to the general problems of conjunction.

In DIAGRAM, the root category of independent sentences, S, may be conjoined with other Ss or it may be modified. When it is conjoined or modified, it is embedded in a higher S, as in the structures S [PP S] and S [S CONJ S]. This self-embedding differs, however, from the embeddings in which sentences are constituents of phrases of a different, nonsentential category. In DIAGRAM, the root category, S, is embedded only as an immediate constituent of a higher S, and SQ, as we have seen, is an immediate constituent of some SWHQs. The only sentence type to be embedded as an immediate constituent of a nonsentential phrase category is the declarative type, SDEC. Languages achieve great complexity of expression in large part through providing for this latter kind of embedding of sentences inside nonsentential phrases.

Various rules define phrases in which SDEC is a constituent. It occurs as a complement of a verb phrase, as an object of a preposition, as a constituent in the complement of a comparative phrase and as a constituent of a relative clause modifier in a noun phrase, as in:

	[SDEC]	Embedding Rule
i)	I saw (that) SDEC [he had arrived].	Rule VP3
ii)	After SDEC [he had arrived], they left.	Rule PP1
iii)	It is wider than SDEC [it is high].	Rule THANCOMP
iv)	He is as tall as SDEC [she is].	Rule ASCOMP
v)	I saw the boat SDEC [you bought].	Rule SREL1

Recall that SWHQs cannot be embedded except as immediate constituents of the root category S. Therefore, the expression "who just came in", in "I recognize the person who just came in" is analyzed as a distinct relative clause type and not as an embedding of SWHQ, although it would be so analyzed in isolation. (Compare Rules SREL1 and SREL2 in Appendix B.) Like the sentence types SIMP and SQ, SWHQ is, in general, disqualified on both syntactic and semantic grounds from being a constituent of relative clauses. That is, *"the man go home" (with "go home" as SIMP), *"the man did you see him", *"the man to whom did you give it", and *"the man which man came" are all illformed. Only those SWHQs that have "who" or "which" as subjects have the right shape, so to speak, to be relative clauses, as in "who just came in" or "(the thing) which fell". But this seems as fortuitous as the fact that the string "open the door" could be analyzed as an imperative and then combined with the plural NP, "they", to form the declarative "they open the door". It seems more general therefore, to exclude all SWHQs from relative clause constituency and account for those SRELs in which the subject of the embedded clause is "who" or "which" by means of a separate rule, SREL2.

In addition to the SDEC sentence type that can occur as an embedded constituent of a matrix sentence, certain sentence-like phrases also occur as constituents of complex expressions. These include infinitive phrases and gerunds, like:

for John to have been going there yesterday and
John's having been going there yesterday,

which resemble embedded declaratives in having subjects, predicates and aspectual auxiliaries, but which do not contain any finite (tensed or modal) auxiliary or verb forms. They may also lack subjects, as in "to have gone there". One way of recognizing the similarities while acknowledging the differences is to say that infinitives and gerunds, like some embedded declaratives, may have the same propositional content as an independent sentence but that a propositional commitment is lacking. Compare, for example, the difference between the nonfinite phrases exemplified above with "John could have been going there yesterday", uttered as an independent sentence. Both the gerund and the infinitive can be embedded in contexts that relate them to reality in different ways, as in:

For John to have gone there was impossible.
John's going there was impossible.

For John to have gone there was regrettable.
John's going there was regrettable.

The possibility of John's going is denied in the first two examples; in the second two, its occurrence is presupposed. Embedded declaratives behave similarly, as shown by:

It is impossible that John could have gone there.
It is surprising that John could have gone there.

3.4 Relatives and WH-Questions

The SDECs embedded in relative clauses, like the SQs embedded in SWHQs contain gaps; that is, some normally present constituent is missing. In

I saw the boat you bought

the SDEC "you bought" is incomplete; the transitive verb "bought" lacks an object. The missing object is supplied by a constituent outside the SDEC; namely, by the nominal "the boat", which is a constituent of the NP in which the SDEC is embedded. Similarly, the SQ "did you buy it from" in "who did you buy it from", lacks the NP object of the preposition "from", which is supplied by the WHNP of the embedding matrix sentence. Gaps occur in other phrasal categories as well.

The problem of specifying where holes may occur and where the constituent can be found that provides the missing content is complicated because gaps can occur at arbitrary depths and distances from the constituents that fill the semantic gaps. In addition to the examples above, in which the gaps are in the next level of embedding, we also have

I saw the boat that Mary told me John claimed it was not likely that you were going to buy (___).
Who(m) did they think it was possible for you to manage to buy it from (___) if you needed it?

In other words, a phrase with a gap in it may depend on an arbitrarily distant constituent for its syntactic and semantic wellformedness.

The constituent-structure statements in DIAGRAM allow many constituents to be optional even in contexts where they may in fact be obligatory, but mark them with gap attributes that are propagated to the phrases that contain them. The semantic interpretation procedures in the constructors and translators share the task of constraining the choice of constituents that can fill the gaps in the interpretations of incomplete phrases or - in case of failure to find such constituents - to reject the analysis.

4 Constituents of Sentences

There are three important decisions that a grammarian has to make in proposing rules for analyzing sentences. They are:

1) what the ultimate unanalyzed constituents, the basic elements, are;
2) how the elements in the sentence are grouped into phrases (where the boundaries are); and
3) what the categories are.

The decisions are not independent of one another, and all are influenced by knowledge of the grammatical and communicative functions that are conceptually associated with a phrase of a given category. In this section, some of the problems and issues that arose in making these decisions in DIAGRAM are explored, focusing on the relationship of categories to the syntactic functions of predication and modification.

4.1 Words and Basic Elements

It is customary to think of sentences as ultimately decomposed into words and of phrases as sequences of words. It is also customary to think of words as appearing only in a lexicon where they are assigned to word-class categories, and of phrases as built out of word-class and phrase categories by rules that contain only categories and not actual word forms. These concepts are valid only as generalizations and none holds in a precise way in DIAGRAM.

Some categories (e.g., N, V, ADJ, P) appear in the lexicon, are never defined by rules, and consist mostly of single words (technically 'word stems'). These are sometimes referred to as 'lexical' or 'word' categories. But some words (e.g., "of") and parts of words (e.g., the plural suffix "-s") appear in rules. Word sequences like "out of" can appear in the lexicon and be assigned to the same lexical category as that of a single word like "from". A single word may be assigned by the lexicon to a category that is also defined by the rules. For example, "John" is assigned to the category of noun phrases (NP). In addition, an idiom like "kick the bucket" may appear as a multiword lexical entry, assigned to the category VP that is also defined by rule. However, any category in DIAGRAM that is designated as XP, where X ranges over various word categories, is a "phrasal" category, and there will be one or more rules defining it. Some reasons for these treatments of words, affixes, and phrases should become clear from the following description of the analysis of sentence constituents.

The sentences DIAGRAM analyzes have had suffixes stripped from inflected words like "bolts", "bolted", "running", and "taken". The suffixes are transposed to precede their stems, thus: "-s bolt", "-ed bolt", "-ing run", "-en take". (Reasons for preposing the suffixes will appear shortly.) The uninflected forms appear in the lexicon, where they are assigned to the appropriate categories. It is not necessary, however, to enter "bolts", "bolting", and "bolted", since these words are defined by rule. A single rule statement suffices to combine any member of the class N with a plural suffix, allowing the meaning of the combination to be computed as the meaning of the N plus the meaning of plurality by the semantic interpretation procedures. The lexicon also supplies regular forms for irregularly inflected words like "children", which is given as "child -s", and "took", which is given as "take -ed".

Affix stripping is a common practice in lexicography, and the economies it offers are obvious. DIAGRAM extends the practice to irregular forms. Only inflectional suffixes are stripped. Derivational suffixes, which may effect major changes in the category of the base to which they are attached, are untouched, so that "civil" (ADJ), "civilize" (V), and "civilization" (N), for example, will have individual entries. Derived words not only differ in category from their bases, the meaning of a word composed of a base combined with a derivational suffix cannot be regularly stated as a composite of the meanings of the base and the suffix, whereas the meaning of a base and an inflectional suffix can. A noun stem N plus the plural suffix regularly produces a NOUN meaning "more than one N", whereas the relationship of the meaning of "civilization" to the base "civil" is less straightforward.

The participle suffix PPL is a borderline case. It is regularly suffixed to verb stems preceded by the auxiliary HAVE, to mark the perfective aspect as in "they have brok*en* it". In this use, it is inflectional. Suffixed to transitive Vs, however, it can arguably be said to change the category of the stem from V to ADJ. Thus "broken", unlike "break", can modify a noun ("the broken vase", but not *"the break vase"), and can itself be modified by words like "very" and "completely" and the prefix "un-", which typically associate with adjectives. Compare: "completely broken" and "unbroken" with "completely happy" and "unhappy". Moreover, as a predicate, "broken" requires a form of BE in the auxiliary and does not occur with a form of "do". Compare: "It is broken" and "is it broken" with "they break it" and "do they break it", as well as with the intransitive sense of "break" in "it breaks" and "it did break".

Much of what has just been said of the suffix PPL applies also to the suffix ING, with added complications. Parallel to "the broken vase", there is "the breaking vase", though not *"the completely breaking vase". In addition, Vs suffixed with ING occupy syntactic positions and serve syntactic functions associated with NPs, as in "the singing was excellent but the dancing was poor". In spite of the shifts in syntactic function, and possibly in syntactic category, however, the meanings of the stem Vs appear to remain constant. It is this constancy of meaning that DIAGRAM seeks to preserve by stripping the two participial suffixes from verb stems.

4.2 Constituents

4.2.1 Suffixes and the Auxiliary Constituent

Decomposing words with inflectional suffixes has consequences for DIAGRAM's definitions of the immediate constituents of phrases. One reason for preposing inflectional suffixes is to regularize the form of the whole phrase in which the stem is an immediate constituent and which has a constant interpretation. Consider the sentences

			NP	AUX	VP
He	*gives*	her a book.	[He	-s	give her a book]
He is	*giving*	her a book.	[He	is -ing	give her a book]
He has	*given*	her a book.	[He	-s have -en	give her a book]
He	*gave*	her a book.	[He	-ed	give her a book]
He may	*give*	her a book.	[He	may	give her a book]

The VP "give her a book" remains constant in DIAGRAM's analyses of the three different sentences. The difference in meaning is ascribed to the differences in the auxiliary constituents.

Notice that in this analysis, the entire auxiliary, including tense and aspectual affixes, is an immediate constituent of the sentence rather than of the verb phrase. Functionally, the sentence is represented as composed of three constituents, with the subject NP and the predicate VP representing the timeless or neutral propositional content, while the auxiliary represents the speaker's attitude or perspective. It indicates whether the propositional content is considered to hold in the past or the present or in some possible world and whether it is considered to be ongoing or completed.

DIAGRAM's treatment of the form and meaning of auxiliaries and of their syntactic place in the sentence resembles that of [LANG 78], although independently conceived. Both treatments differ strongly from those in which suffixes are not stripped or preposed and in which modals, HAVE, and BE are categorized as verbs that accept VPs as complements. (Cf. [JACK 77, GAZD 81].) Whether or not DIAGRAM's current treatment of auxiliaries and its use of "affix hopping" can be claimed to represent some kind of psychological reality or to result in computational efficiencies in processing dialogue remains moot[6].

4.2.2 The Passive Constituent

DIAGRAM's analysis of suffixes and V stems also affects its analysis of the regularities in form and meaning that appear in active-passive sentences. DIAGRAM's input for two passive sentences with "give" as predicate are:

She is given a book.	[she	is	-en	give a book]
A book is given her.	[a book	is	-en	give her]

During analysis of these sentences, "give a book" and "give her" will be parsed as VPs by the same rule, Rule VP1, that applies to the active versions in the preceding examples. The constituent structures to which the rule applies include: a single V, a V followed by an object NP, and a V followed by two object NPs. Only those Vs whose attributes qualify them to take two object NPs will be recognized as predicates of well-formed active declaratives like "he gives her a book". As previously mentioned, DIAGRAM accepts such Vs as sole constituents of VPs when they occur without an obligatory object, to permit recognition of sentences like "what did he give" or "what did he give her". When a verb like "give" is parsed with its two object NPs to form a VP, the constructor procedure of Rule VP1 simply checks for the appropriate attributes, named DIROBJ and INDIROBJ, whose values are either T, for "present", or null. Here we are interested in the cases in which "give" occurs with only one or with none of its object NPs. In those cases, the procedure marks the resulting VP as lacking its full complement by setting the attribute DIROBJ of the V as an attribute of the VP. (In other words, the VP inherits the attribute of its 'head' V.) Subsequently, a rule PRED1 applies when such a VP is preceded by the participle PPL. The relevant parts of Rule PRED1 state the possible constituents of PRED and the conditions on wellformedness, thus:

PRED1 PRED=[ADJP / NP / PP / PPL VP]
Constructor: (Informally) If VP is a constituent of PRED, then VP must have the attribute DIROBJ and cannot have a prepositional phrase (PP) constituent.

In this manner, the passive construction joins the categories of NP, ADJP, and PP as a member of the inclusive category PRED, which is essentially "stative" in

[6] It should be noted also that the advantages of simplicity of statement afforded by this affix "hopping" are more easily achieved for some affixes than for others. Transposing the plural suffix to precede a noun does not prefix it to the entire phrase headed by the noun, and does not lead to the simplifying statements possible for the analysis of VP constituents. Although nouns and verbs are often homographic in English, it may still be practical to strip the homographic suffix "-s" from the category V and not from the category N.

contrast to the predicates formed with active verbs.[7] However, it is easy to distinguish subcategories of PREDs on the basis of the categories of its constituents because DIAGRAM's formalism assigns, to each phrase analyzed by a rule, a set of attributes whose names are the categories of its immediate constituents. A PRED formed with PPL and VP will have the attributes PPL and VP that can be tested for when their presence or absence is relevant.

4.3 The Major Categories

The phrases that are the major constituents of sentences are extensions of the four word categories, noun (N), verb (V), adjective (ADJ), and preposition (P). These categories contain the words in a dictionary. In particular, they include the so-called content words - words that, in some intuitive sense, denote entities, actions, processes, qualities, and spatial and temporal properties.

With the possible exception of the prepositions, these are large classes that can easily grow when the introduction of new objects and activities into a culture creates the need for new words for talking about them. They contrast with 'function' words, whose semantic content is very difficult to specify. The word "of" is an example. Although customarily classed as a preposition, "of" is strikingly different from words like "in", "over", "with", etc. In effect, it is treated as an inflectional prefix of the NP rather than as a preposition. The infinitival "to", as in "he wants to go" is another example. In contrast to the directional preposition "to" in "he came to the office", it carries no semantic information. "Of" and infinitival "to" are not assigned to categories in DIAGRAM; like some affixes, they are cited directly in the rules.

As their names indicate, the categories NP, VP, ADJP, and PP are regarded as phrasal extensions of the categories of the content words. Intuitively, each XP contains a word of category X that is the nucleus or *head* of the phrase.[8] In

those very young children requiring an escort,

the head is clearly the noun "children". Most other phrases within the NP are said to 'depend on' or 'modify' the head. These latter terms are not well defined and not matched in any simple way with syntactic categories. "Very young" (ADJP) and "requiring an escort" (ING VP) are modifiers, limiting the range of

[7] Another rule, Rule PRED2, analyzes prepositional phrase attachments to PREDs. The whole question of the treatment of the active-passive relationship raises many issues beyond the scope of this paper, issues that are also being vigorously raised in revisions of the theory of transformational grammar; e.g., by Bresnan [BRES 78] and Wasow [WASO 78]. We are examining them and exploring alternative ways of associating information about logical forms or predicate-argument structures with variations in syntactic arrangements of subjects, objects, and prepositional phrase complements.

[8] Cf. discussions of the X-Bar theory in the theory of transformational grammar in [ROBI 70] and [JACK 77], and references therein.

denotation of the head noun. In general, there is a tendency to call modifiers that follow a head 'complements'; however, the following modifiers or complements of VPs and PPs, which are typically NPs, are usually called 'objects'.

Function words are seldom classed with modifiers. They are variously called 'specifiers', 'determiners', or 'complementizers'. For example, "these" and "those" are not modifiers like "young", but belong to a small, closed class of function words labeled DDET in DIAGRAM. Elliptical headless NPs like "those requiring an escort" are possible when a function word specific to NPs is an initial constituent. Their full interpretation, of course, requires discourse context.

The foregoing description should provide a basis for understanding the interactions of the rules with the lexicon and with each other. Explication of a specific rule will further illustrate the principles involved.

The rule given below analyzes noun phrases like: water, boys, the boy, younger children than that, those very young children requiring an escort, those boys whom I had expected to see, every school boy on our block who has been driven to school by his parents. It will reject, as illformed: "many water", "much boy", "a boys", "two boys than that", and "those children who has been driven to school". It will mark as UNLIKELY an NP consisting solely of a singular count noun like: "boy", "bolt", etc., as in "I saw boy", but allow it, in case no better analysis can be found. The judgments of likelihood are partly, perhaps even largely, intuitive and subject to alteration in different discourse environments; for example, in an environment where the participants use a "telegraphic" style and omit function words like "the".

The first line specifies a possible constituent structure for a wellformed NP as consisting of a nucleus containing a head noun (NOMHD). The nucleus is optionally preceded by a determiner (D) consisting of the word "a" or a definite determiner (DDET) like "the" or "those" or a determiner of a different type (DETQ) like "much" or "many". It is optionally followed by a complement (NCOMP).

The constructor contains several statements, numbered here for ease of reference, including statements of conditions that must be met for wellformedness. The first two require that if there is a determiner, it must agree with the NOMHD constituent with respect to the property MASS. This condition rejects combinations of a determiner like "much" with a count noun like "child". Statements 3 and 5 require agreement in syntactic number (NBR) of all constituents and also assign the value of the property NBR to the NP on the basis of the values for the constituents. Statement 6 assigns the value of NBR from the NOMHD constituent when it is the sole constituent. Statement 4 rates as UNLIKELY the probability that an NP will lack a determiner if its head noun is a singular count noun like "child", a rating that will affect the score of any analysis containing such an NP. Statement 7 rejects as illformed such sequences as "two boys than that", although "taller boys than that" is acceptable. Statement 8 assigns to the analyzed NP the value COUNT or MASS for the attribute TYPE from the value assigned to the NOMHD constituent.

(NP1 NP= (D=[A / DDET / DETQ]) NOMHD (NCOMP);
(where D is a cover symbol for various determiners)

```
CONSTRUCTOR (PROGN (COND
                     ((@ D)
              1.       [COND
                         ((MASS? D)
                            (OR (MASS? NOMHD)
                                (F.REJECT (QUOTE F.MASS]
              2.       [COND
                         ((MASS? NOMHD)
                          (OR (NOT (@ A))
                              (F.REJECT (QUOTE F.MASS]
              3.       [COND
                        ((@ NCOMP)
                         (SET NBR (@ INTERSECT NBR D NOMHD NCOMP)))
                         (T (SET NBR (@ INTERSECT NBR D NOMHD]
              4.     ((AND (SG? NOMHD)
                           (NOT (MASS? NOMHD)))
                         (@ FACTOR (QUOTE F.NODET)
                                   UNLIKELY))
              5.     ((@ NCOMP)
                         (SET NBR (@ INTERSECT NBR NCOMP NOMHD)))
              6.       (T (@ FROM NOMHD NBR)))
              7.   [AND (@ THANCOMP NCOMP)
                        (OR (@ THANCOMP NOMHD)
                            (F.REJECT (QUOTE F.THANC]
              8.   (@ FROM NOMHD TYPE)))
```

Fig. 2. A rule for the analysis of NP

Other NP rules analyze elliptical NPs like “those requiring an escort”, comparative NPs like “more tall boys than that” and “as many more tall boys than that as there are girls”, and several other types.

4.4 Syntactic Functions

4.4.1 Predication and Modification

The NP rules analyze phrases that can function as subjects of sentences and objects in VPs and PPs. They can also function as predicates; i. e., as members of the category PRED. In

Children are sleeping

the NP "children" functions as sentential subject. In

Those boys are children

"children" functions as sentential predicate applied to the subject NP "those boys", in stating that they are members of the set of children. In

Those boys are the children of my friend

the NP "the children of my friend" is the predicate applied to "those boys" in stating that they are identical to the set of children of the speaker's friend.

We have already shown how DIAGRAM relates the major phrasal categories to the function of predication, making an important distinction between VP predication and predication by other categories. Because VPs can function as predicates without any accompanying auxiliary constituent, the term 'predicate' is sometimes taken to be commensurate with 'verb'. This usage mixes two levels of description of sentences, the categorical and the functional. Moreover, within the categorical level, it obscures the distinction between lexical heads of phrases (V) and phrases (VP). One consequence of such usage appears in the proposal that prepositions may be indistinguishable from verbs at some abstract level of description [BECK 69]. On similar grounds, Ross [ROSS 69] has argued that adjectives, verbs, and nouns have deep similarities that outweigh their superficial differences. The mixed properties of passive constructions heighten the confusion.

The same kind of confusion shows up with respect to 'modifier', which tends to be equated with 'adjective' and applied to any word that modifies a noun in prenominal position. However, three of the four major word categories appear in the function of prenominal modifier, as in:

a *stormy* sea	(ADJ)
a *storm* coat	(N)
a *threatening* sea	(ING V)

All major phrasal categories, including prepositional phrases, occur in postnominal modifiers or complements, as in:

a woman *of courage*	(OF NP)
a book *on the table*	(PP)
the cat *lying on the mat*	(VP)
diamonds *as big as your thumb*	(ADJP)

4.4.2 The Shifting of Categories

The pervasiveness of the association of particular categories with particular functions and notions ("a noun is the name of a person, place or thing"; "adjectives modify nouns"), is so notable that it cannot be ignored. Tesniere's notion of *translation* affords an interesting way of thinking about the interactions of syntactic categories with various functions of the kinds exemplified above.[9] Both function words and derivational affixes are considered to be *translatives* that serve to shift ("translate") a governor from one category to another, whenever it and the group of words it governs serve one of the functions of the category to which it is shifted. At first glance, these words and affixes would appear to be like the derivational suffixes that change the categories of word bases, previously exemplified in "civil", "civilize", and "civilization". The similarity is significant, but so are the differences. Translatives include words as well as affixes and they can shift the category of a phrase.[10] In constituent structure terminology, one would say that translatives are immediate constituents of *phrases,* even when they form parts of words.

There is a clear example of such a phenomenon in English. In NPs like "the mayor of Boston's hat", the constituent "the mayor of Boston's" is properly analyzed as having two subconstituents, "the mayor of Boston" and "-'s". In effect, the NP " the mayor of Boston" is now a determiner (DDET) of the larger NP of which it is a part. One could say that it had been "translated" from an NP to serve the function of a determiner by combining with the suffix. One of DIAGRAM's rules for analyzing determiner phrases could be so interpreted, namely Rule DDET2, whose constituent-structure statement is:

DDET2   DDET = NO "GEN"

where "GEN" is the lexical replacement for the genitive suffix.

It is customary to analyze preposed genitives in English in this fashion. DIAGRAM's extension of the concept to passive constructions in Rule PRED1 *(infra)* is not customary, but the extension seems quite natural.

5 Conclusion

DIAGRAM has been revised, extended, and adapted many times during its history and will undoubtedly have undergone many changes before this description is published. It is, after all, an experimental grammar. It has been a primary component in several systems developed in the Artificial Intelligence Center at SRI

---

[9] Tesniere's syntactic theories, first published posthumously in 1959 [TESN 76], center around the concept of the head of a phrase, which he calls a 'governor'. Governors are content words, categorized (roughly speaking) as nouns, verbs, adjectives, and adverbs. In analyzing a sentence, other words are attached to governors as 'dependents' (hence the name 'dependency theory'). Each category of governors has a typical set of syntactic functions. Verbs function as predicates, and they alone can occur as independent governors of an entire sentence. Nouns function as subjects and objects, adjectives as modifiers of nouns, and adverbs as modifiers of adjectives and verbs.

[10] Although he often speaks as if only the governor were involved, Tesniere is specific on this point: "C'est le mot ou le groupe de mots resultant de la translation". [TESN 76, p.367].

International. At present, it is a component in the TEAM system, a transportable domain-independent natural language interface to a data base [MART 83].

For an experimental grammar that is constantly being revised and extended, DIAGRAM is unusually large. As a consequence, introducing new rules almost inevitably has a perturbing effect as they interact with old rules in unforeseen ways. These perturbations are worth studying for the light they shed on the English language, or more precisely, on a grammarian's intuitions about the English language. However, the procedural nature of the statements of grammatical constraints in the rule constructors (they are essentially LISP procedures) makes it difficult to trace the consequences of revisions and extensions. This has led to new efforts directed towards development of a perspicuous declarative form for both attribution assignment and constraints on grammatical combinations.

References

[BECK 69], [BRES 78], [BRES 82], [CHAF 76], [GAZD 81], [GROS 80a], [GROS 80b], [GROS 83], [HOBB 79], [JACK 77], [JOSH 80], [KAY 83], [LANG 78], [MART 83], [PAXT 77], [ROBI 70], [ROSS 69], [SEAR 77], [TESN 76], [WASO 78]

Appendix A

Sample Lexicon and Rules

Sample Lexical Entries

(If a word W1 has the attribute LIKE with a word W2 as value, then word W1 has the same attributes as word W2 except for those specifically assigned to W1.)

Words for N

```
(APPRENTICE   (TYPE  COUNT)
              (GENDER M F))
(BOY          (TYPE  COUNT)
              (GENDER M))
(FISH         (TYPE  MASS))
(FOOT         (TYPE  COUNT))
(GIRL         (TYPE  COUNT)
              (GENDER F))
(MAN          (LIKE  BOY))
(THING        (TYPE  COUNT))
(WATER        (TYPE  MASS))
(WOMAN        (LIKE  GIRL))
```

Irregular Forms in N

```
(FEET         (FOOT -S))
(MEN          (MAN -S))
(WOMEN        (WOMAN -S))
```

Words in NOMHD

```
(FISH         (TYPE  COUNT)
(PEOPLE       (TYPE  COUNT)
              (NBR  PL))
(U.S.         (NBR  SG)
              (PROPN  T))
```

WORDS in NP

```
(JOHN         (NBR  SG)
              (DEF  T)
              (GENDER M)
              (PROPN  T))
(MARY         (LIKE  JOHN)
              (GENDER F))
((NEW YORK)   (NBR  SG)
              (TYPE  COUNT)
              (PROPN  T))
```

Words for V

```
(ASSEMBLE      (DIROBJ  T))
(BREAK         (DIROBJ  T)
               (PARTICLE UP OUT OFF)
               (PPL  EN))
(BUY           (DIROBJ  T)
               (INDIROBJ  T)
               (DIRECTION FOR FROM BY))
(FIND          (ADJOBJ  T)
               (DIROBJ  T)
               (INDIROBJ  T)
               (INFOBJ  T)
               (INGCOMP  T)
               (SOBJ  T)
               (DIRECTION FOR BY)
               (PARTICLE OUT))
(FINISH        (INGCOMP  T)
               (LIKE  ASSEMBLE))
(GO            (PPL  EN))
(GIVE          (LIKE  BUY)
               (DIRECTION TO BY)
               (PARTICLE UP)
               (PPL  EN))
(LOOK          (DIROBJ  T)
               (INSEPARABLE INTO)
               (ADJOBJ  T)
               (PARTICLE UP))
(TRY           (INFOBJ  T))
(WANT          (DIROBJ  T)
               (INFOBJ  T))
```

Irregular Forms in V

```
(BOUGHT        (BUY ED))
(BROKE         (BREAK ED))
(GAVE          (GIVE ED))
(GONE          (GO EN))
(WENT          (GO ED))
```

Words for Q

```
(FEW           (LIKE  MANY))
(LITTLE        (LIKE  MUCH))
(MANY          (TYPE  COUNT)
               (NBR  PL))
(MUCH          (TYPE  MASS)
               (NBR  SG))
```

Irregular Forms in Q

```
(MORE          (1 (MANY ER)))
(MORE          (2 (MUCH ER)))
```

Examples of Rules

```
(SD1    SDEC = NP (ADV) (AUXD) VP;
      CONSTRUCTOR [PROGN (COND
                             [@ AUXD)
                              (OR (AGREE NBR NP AUXD)
                                  (F.REJECT (QUOTE R.NBRSD1]
                             (T (OR (NEQ (@ NBR NP)
                                         (QUOTE SG))
                                    (F.REJECT (QUOTE F.NBR)))
                                (@ SET TENSE (QUOTE PRESENT]
      TRANSLATOR (PROGN (@ SET ROLE (QUOTE SUBJECT)
                             NP)
                        (@ SET SEMANTICS (COMBINE (@ SEMANTICS VP)
                                                  (@ SEMANTICS NP))

(VP1    VP=V (NP1 ([NP2 / P]));
      CONSTRUCTOR (PROG ((PARTICLE (@ DIAMOND.SPELLING P)))
                        (COND
                         [(@ NP1)
                          (OR (@ DIROBJ V)
                          (F.REJECT (QUOTE F.DIROBJ)))
                        (COND
                         [(@ NP2)
                          (OR (@ INDIROBJ V)
                              (F.REJECT (QUOTE F.INDIROBJ))))
                        ((@ P)
                          (OR (FMEMB PARTICLE (@ PARTICLE V))
                              (F.REJECT (QUOTE F.PARTICLE)))
                          (AND(@ PRO NP1)
                              (@ FACTOR (QUOTE F.PARTICLE)
                                        LIKELY))
                          (COND
                            ((@ NCOMP NP1)
                              (OR (@ NP NCOMP NP1)
                                  (@ FACTOR (QUOTE F.PARTICLE)
                                            UNLIKELY)
                              (AND (@ NCOMP NP NCOMP NP1)
                                   (@ FACTOR (QUOTE F.PARTICLE)
                                             UNLIKELY]
                        (T (@ SET BAREV T)
                           (@ FROM V DIRECTION DIROBJ))))
      TRANSLATOR (PROGN [COND
                          ((@ NP2)
                            (@ SET ROLE (QUOTE DIROBJ)
                                   NP2)
                            (@ SET ROLE (QUOTE INDIROBJ)
                                   NP1)
```

```
    (@ SET SEMANTICS (COMBINE
           (@ SEMANTICS V)
           (@ SEMANTICS NP2)
           (@ SEMANTICS NP1))))
  (T (AND (@ NP1)
          (OR (@ INDIROBJ V)
              (@ SET ROLE (QUOTE DIROBJ)
                     NP1)
  (@ SET SEMANTICS (COMBINE (@ SEMANTICS V)
                            (@ SEMANTICS NP1))))
```

Appendix B

Word and Phrase Categories and Constituent Structure Rules

Phrase categories are followed by the constituent structure rules that analyze them. Rule names are distinguished from category names by numerical identifiers.

ADJ	Adjective Stems big, difficult, allowable, frequent, careful, quick, great, tall, short, far, near, close, operational, necessary, possible. (Some, but not all, adjectives can be inflected with "-er" or combined with "as", "more", "too" in comparisons of degree.)
ADJCOMP	Adjective Complements for him, to go there (as in: difficult for him to go there; too heavy for me): that he went (as in: possible that he went).
ADJCOMP1	ADJCOMP = (ENOUGH) (FOR NP) (INFINITIVE)
ADJCOMP2	ADJCOMP = "THAT" SDEC
ADJP	Adjective Phrases too big, more difficult than that, allowable for him to go there, largest, as ready to go as he is, possible to do, necessary that it is done.
ADJP1	ADJP = ([(QPP) QDET / TDET]) ADJ (ADJCOMP)
ADJP2	ADJP = (DETQ) ("NO") ER ("MUCH") ADJP (THANCOMP (ADJCOMP))
ADJP4	ADJP = AS ADJP (ASCOMP)
ADJP6	ADJP = EST ("MUCH") ADJ (ADJCOMP)
ASCOMP	Adjective Complements for Equality Comparisons as that, as he appears to be.
ASCOMP1	ASCOMP = AS [NP / SDEC]

ADV	Adverbs frequently, soon, carefully, quickly, often, necessarily, possibly. (Words formed from adjectives by adding the suffix "-ly" or that occupy the same syntactic positions as words so formed.)
ADVP	Adverb Phrases as frequently as that, too often, more carefully than John did it, most rapidly, after he came, when he is here, if they come.
ADVP1	ADVP=((PQQ) QDET) ADV
ADVP2	ADVP=(DETQ) ER ("MUCH") ADV (THANCOMP)
ADVP7	ADVP=[P / "IF"] [SDEC / [PPL / ING] VP]
AUX	Auxiliary Phrases couldn't have been -ing, has, is, -ed, -s. (May consist of a single suffix.)
AUX1	AUX=(MODALP) (HAVEP PPL) (BEP ING)
AUXD	DO-Type Auxiliary Phrases could have -en, did, -ed. (See also DO and DOP.)
AUXD1	AUXD=C=[AUX / DOP]
DDET	Definite Determiner Phrases the, the many, all, all five, those, this, these two, the next man's.
DDET1	DDET=((NOT) "ALL") DET ([NUMBER / QPP])
DDET2	DDET=NP "GEN"
DETERQ	Compared Determiner Phrases more, that much more, too many more. (See also DETQ.)
DETERQ1	DETERQ=(DETQ) ER Q
DETQ	Determiner/Quantifier Phrases many, much, too many, any, any two, two, no two, some, most. (Indefinite determiners, including indefinite quantifiers. See also categories Q, QDET, QPP.)
DETQ1	DETQ=(C=[TDET / QDET / A]) Q (QPP)
INFINITIVE	Infinitive Phrases to have gone, to be informed, not to have realized, to have been very careful about that.
INFINITIVE1	INFINITIVE=(NOT) TO (HAVEP PPL) (BEP1 ING) [VP / BEP2 (PRED)]
INFINITREL	Nonfinite Relative Clauses to whom to give it, for you to do, being attached.

	(As in: the man to whom to give it; the thing for you to do; the part being attached.)
INFINREL1	INFINITREL=[([FOR NP / P RELPRO]) INFINITIVE / ING ("BE" PPL) VP]
MODALP	Modal Auxiliary Phrases
MODALP1	MODALP=MODAL (NOT) Z (ADV)
N	Noun Stems man, woman, box, foot, inch, water, length, U.S., United States, time, doctor.
NCOMP	Noun-Phrase Complements of tea, on the corner, for you to do, that I saw. (Modifying phrases that follow a head nominal or NOMHD).
NCOMP1	NCOMP=[OF / P] NP
NCOMP2	NCOMP=[INFINITREL / SREL / ADJP / THANCOMP]
NCOMP4	NCOMP=NCOMP PP
NHD	Pre-Noun Modifier Heads twenty-one gun, three mile, stone (As in: twenty-one gun salute, three mile swim; stone house. NHDs are constituents of compound nominals in which a noun stem (N) modifies a noun.)
NOMHD	Nominal Heads very big task, broken vases, running streams, more difficult task, fish, cats, people. (Constituents of NPs, containing the head noun and prenominal modifiers, but not determiners or quantifiers of the NP.)
NOMHD1	NOMHD=NOUN ([(",") "AND" / ","] NOMHD)
NOMHD2	NOMHD=[(QDET) ADJ / [ING / PPL] V] NOMHD
NOMHD3	NOMHD=(QPP) ER ("MUCH") ADJ NOMHD
NOUN	Nouns (N stems with or without a fronted plural affix; e.g., cat, -s cat, -s child (children), fish. May be pre-modified by NHD or NOMHD as in: cat foot containers. Unlike Ns, NOUNS have an attribute of syntactic number, SG or PL, unless they are ambiguous with respect to number.)
NOUN1	NOUN=("-S) N
NOUN2	NOUN=NHD NOUN
NP	Noun Phrases water, cats, very big cats that lie on mats, the length of that board, a length of two feet, as big a box as you could carry, two of them, more ships, a more difficult task than that, what he did, he, her, the best ones, the best I could find, his having

gone there yesterday, those, those few, some, all of them that are here, John, Mary, September.
(The most complicated category in the grammar.)

NP1 NP=(D=[A / DDET / DETQ]) NOMHD (NCOMP)
NP2 NP=D=[A / DDET / DETQ] (NCOMP)
NP3 NP=DETERQ (NOMHD) (NCOMP)
NP6 NP=DDET EST ("MUCH") ADJ (NOMHD) (NCOMP)
NP8 NP=AS QPP ([OF NP / NOMHD]) (ASCOMP)
NP9 NP=AS ((QPP) ER ("MUCH")) ADJ (OF) NP (THANCOMP) (ASCOMP)

P Prepositions, Particles, Subordinating Conjunctions
at, in, on, before, after, by, to, for, with.
(Does not include "of". Ps may occur as intransitives or particles, as in: break up the pavement; or as transitives with NP objects, as in: in the box. Combined with sentences and verb phrases, however, they become "translatives", and the resultant phrase is ADVP.

PP Prepositional Phrases
on it, after that, there (i.e., at that place).

PP1 PP=P (NP)

PRED Predicate Phrases (no VP)
(NPs as in: that is *a boy;* ADJPs as in: that could have been *very heavy;* PPs as in: that wasn't *in the box when I left;* Passives as in: that was *attached to it yesterday.*)

PRED1 PRED=[ADJP / NP / PP / PPL VP]
PRED10 PRED=PRED (",") [PP / ADVP]

Q Indefinite Quantifiers (nonstandard)
(A small set of words, including only: many, much, few, little. For other words usually called quantifiers, see DETQ and DDET. DETQs may have Q as sole constituents.)

QPP Q Phrases
much, too much, too many, too few, little.

QPP1 QPP=(QDET) Q (QPP)

S Sentences
(Independent sentences of various subtypes. Includes complex and compound sentences.)

SO S=C=[SIMP / SDEC / SQ / SWHQ] (ENDPUNCT)
SX1 S=CONJ S
SX2 S=S1 (MIDPUNCT) S2
SX3 S=[PP / ADVP] (",") S
SX4 S=[PPL / ING] VP "," S

SDEC	Declarative Sentences they went there; they might have been going there then; it could be difficult; he is here; that is the book; there are some apples in that basket.
SB1	SDEC = NP (AUX) (ADV1) BEP (ADV2) (PRED)
SD1	SDEC = NP (ADV) (AUXD) VP
STHERE1	SDEC = "THERE" (AUX) BEP NP ([ING [VP / "BE" PRED1] / PRED2 / SREL])
SIMP	Imperative Sentences Put them on the table; don't go; be careful; don't be difficult!
SIMP1	SIMP = ("DO" (NOT)) ["BE" PRED / VP A]
SQ	Yes/No Interrogatives Is he going; could he have been going; did he go; is it here now; are there any more; was it hard to do?
SBQ1	SQ = BEP NP ((ADV) (ING "BE") PRED)
SBQ2	SQ = MODALP NP (ADV) PPL "BE" ((ING "BE") PRED)
SBQ3	SQ = HAVEP NP (ADV) PPL "BE" ((ING "BE") PRED)
SDQ1	SQ = DOP NP (ADV) VP
SDQ2	SQ = MODALP NP (ADV) (HAVEP PPL) (BEP ING) VP
SDQ3	SQ = BEP NP (NOT) ING VP
STHEREQ1	SQ = BEP "THERE" (NP) ([ING ["BE" PRED1 / VP] / PRED2 / SREL])
STHEREQ2	SQ = MODALP "THERE" (NOT) (HAVEP PPL) BEP (NP) ([ING ["BE" PRED1 / VP] / PRED2 / SREL])
STHEREQ3	SQ = HAVEP "THERE" PPL "BE" (NP) ([ING ["BE" PRED1 / VP] / PRED2 / SREL])
SREL	Relative Clauses who went there yesterday; to whom he gave it; that was there; you saw yesterday; that you saw yesterday; that he attached it to; on which he placed it.
SREL1	SREL = RELPRO [(AUX) BEP PRED / (AUXD) VP]
SREL2	SREL = ((P) RELPRO) SDEC
SWHQ	WH-Questions who is it; who could it have been; what did he do; what could he have done; where did they go; on which table is it; which table is it on?
SWH1	SWHQ = [WHNP / WHPP / WHADJP] SQ
SWH2	SWHQ = WHNP (AUXD) VP
SWH3	SWH = WHNP (AUX) BEP (PRED)
V	Verb Stems go, move, do, have, give, arrive, attach, see, seem, break, take, tell, say, know, think, want, try, tend.

VP	Verb Phrases go there in September, move it from here to there, arrive, seem difficult, give her a book, give a book to her, tell him that it is here, want to go, tend to be careful, look at it, look up a book, look it up, look into it, saw him leave, saw him leaving. (Verb stems combined with following objects, particles, prepositions, and prepositional phrase modifiers.)
VP1	VP=V (NP1 ([NP2 / P]))
VP2	VP=V P (NP)
VP3	VP=V (NP) ("THAT") SDEC
VP4	VP=V (NP) INFINITIVE
VP5	VP=V (NP) [PPL VP / ADJP]
VP7	VP=V (NP) (ING) [VP / BE PRED]
VP8	VP=V (NP) [WHPP / WHNP / WHADJP] [SDEC / INFINITIVE]
VP9	VP=VP (",") [PP / INFINITIVE / ADVP]
WHADJP	Interrogative Adjective Phrases how big, how much bigger than that, how much more difficult to do.
WHADJP1	WHADJP=HOW ADJP
WHDET	Interrogative Determiners how much, how many more, whose, which man's.
WHDET1	WHDET=HOW Q1 (QPP) (ER Q2)
WHDET2	WHDET=WHNP "GEN"
WHNP	Interrogative NPs how many more women, how much water, whose book.
WHNP1	WHNP=WHDET (NUMBER) (NOMHD) (NCOMP)
WHPP	Interrogative PPs where, when, at what time, in which box, from where.
WHPP1	WHPP=[P WHNP / C=[TO / FROM] "WHERE"]

Appendix C

Attributes

The major specific attributes that currently affect DIAGRAM's syntactic analysis of a phrase are listed below, grouped with the relevant categories. The name of the attribute is followed by a list of the values it may assume. Where values are not listed, the attribute is binary; it is either present or absent, and if present, its value is T.

Attributes of S:

STYPE: (SIMP, SDEC, SQ, SWHQ). Sentence type; affects coordination.

CONJUNCT: Contains a conjunction; affects coordination.

Attributes of AUX, AUXD, BE, BEP, DO, DOP, HAVE, HAVEP:

TENSE: (PAST, PRESENT) Marked as finite; cannot combine with preceding auxiliaries.

NBR: (SG, PL) Number agreement feature.

INFINITIVE: May be nonfinite; compare: may have gone, they have gone.

Attributes of N, NOMHD, NP, PRO, WHNP:

TYPE: (COUNT, MASS)

NBR: (SG, PL) Syntactic number: singular or plural. Used heavily in number-agreement tests.

NOMCASE: Is marked as nominative pronoun; e.g., he (cf. him). Cannot be an object of V or P.

PROPN: Is a proper name; does not accept full range of determiners and complements of NPs; e.g., *every Mississippi.

Attributes of V and VP:

VPPL: (EN, ED). Form of participial ending; e.g., taken, waited.

DIROBJ: Accepts a direct object; e.g., assemble it.

INDIROBJ: Accepts an indirect object; e.g., give them something.

INFOBJ: Accepts an infinitive object; e.g., want John to go.

SOBJ: Accepts an S object; e.g., said that he would go.

INGCOMP: Accepts gerundive complement; e.g., saw her leaving.

PPLCOMP: Accepts a participial complement; e.g., found her gone.

PARTICLE: Accepts any member of a list of Ps as a particle; e.g., give up, give away, give it up, give up something.

INSEPARABLE: Accepts any member of a list of Ps as an inseparable preposition; e.g., look into.

BAREV: Is a VP with no objects or complements. Affects ability to modify nominals or functions as a passive predicate PRED.

Attributes of ADJ, ADJP:

SOBJ: Accepts an S complement; e.g., possible that he went.

ACOMP: Has a complement (of any type).

ERCOMP: Accepts a comparative complement, e.g., heavier than that.

Attributes of P, PP:

INGCOMP: Accepts a participial complement to form an ADVP; e.g., on going there.

SCOMP: Accepts S complement to form an adverbial ADVP; e.g., after he left.

BAREPREP: A PP consisting only of P. May be a stranded preposition or a particle. Cannot modify a nominal, e.g., gave the book up.

Attributes of Minor Categories:

The minor categories have some attributes of nominals and adjectivals, including TYPE, NBR, and THANCOMP.

Chapter 2

An Engine for Intelligent Graphics*

Frank Zdybel

Abstract. We describe a knowledge-based graphic display generation system called AIPS which accepts incomplete specifications and elaborates these into a display description structure specific enough to be drawn. A uniform knowledge representation, KL-ONE, is employed to capture both display content and display structure.

1 Introduction

Probably the single most important influence on man-machine communications during the last decade has been the development of bitmap graphics and inexpensive high resolution raster-scanned displays. This technology makes it possible to combine text and graphics freely in highly detailed information displays for a wide variety of computer applications. As a result, having the right information display has become more and more a matter of having the right display software.

In many cases this problem can be solved inexpensively by implementing a specialized and relatively simple user interface function as part of an application program. In other cases, such power and flexibility are demanded of the user interface that it is more effectively viewed as a companion system distinct from the application it serves. In this latter context, we sought to completely separate the two and develop a general interactive graphic interface capability that could be expanded to serve an open-ended group of applications.

We pursued this goal by applying Artificial Intelligence tools and techniques to the problem of automatically generating interactive graphic information displays. In this paper we describe a prototype display generation system called the Advanced Information Presentation System - AIPS. AIPS accepts incomplete specifications for a desired display and elaborates these into a display descrip-

* Funding was provided by the Information Processing Techniques Office of the Defense Advanced Research Projects Agency, whose support is gratefully acknowledged. The research group at BBN included Norton Greenfeld, Martin Yonke, Jeff Gibbons and Frank Zdybel. The work was carried out between January 1979 and March 1982.

tion structure specific enough to be drawn. The hallmarks of the AIPS approach are the explicit characterization of the semantic content of graphic displays and the use of a uniform knowledge representation formalism to capture both display content and display structure.

AIPS was developed at Bolt Beranek and Newman, Inc. of Cambridge, Massachusetts. One of our goals was to demonstrate the feasibility of a knowledge-based approach to information display. The applications context chosen for this demonstration was Military Command and Control. This influenced somewhat the generic kinds of displays we were most concerned with. More important, however, it forced us to face the issue of treating information from different sources and information from multiple sources. This in turn caused us to pay much attention to the issue of how to represent the information content of graphic displays.

At BBN, AIPS was developed alongside a large research effort in natural language understanding. We anticipated eventually combining the two research efforts in the demonstration of a generalized interface capability that would use both interactive graphics and natural language. This possibility, although it was a very long range one, had its effect on how we viewed the problem of representing knowledge about graphic displays.

In particular, we decided that both efforts would share a common knowledge representation apparatus: the KL-ONE knowledge representation language. Although much of the design of KL-ONE was dictated by its role in representing the semantics of natural language discourse, AIPS was the first demonstrated application of KL-ONE. Because KL-ONE was still evolving rapidly, AIPS used only a subset of the language. Even so, certain distinctive features of that subset proved to be very important to AIPS.

Finally, it was the BBN Jericho personal symbolic processor [YONK 78, GREE 81] - similar in function to the Xerox 1100 Scientific Information Processor - and the Interlisp-Jericho programming environment that made this work possible. Although we began our research using Interlisp-10 on a timeshared mainframe, we realized from the start that this would be inadequate. Even if it had been feasible to monopolize the entire processing capacity of a DEC PDP-10, the address space limitations of Interlisp-10 would have prevented this research. In addition to breaking these barriers, Jericho brought us an important resource in the form of flexibly configurable local bitmap display hardware.

In its approach to describing the structure of graphic displays, AIPS and most other work in this general area echoes a pioneer interactive graphic synthesis system called Sketchpad [SUTH 63]. This work is notable for its use of a uniform data structure for describing graphic displays, for its concern with the collection and interpretation of graphic input, and for its use of rudimentary constraints in characterizing graphic structures.

With regard to the use of structured graphics to display information, there is much other work contemporary with AIPS. In particular, the Model-View-Controller (MVC) paradigm for interactive graphics used by the Smalltalk programming environment [KAY 76, GOLD 76] is similar in spirit to AIPS because it makes an explicit connection between the display and an information model. A further similarity between this work and AIPS stems from the fact that both use a hierarchical structure that makes it possible to propagate very general display methods through inheritance and override them with specialized display methods where necessary.

Other parallel work on centralized information display includes the VIEW system [HERO 80] developed at the Computer Corporation of America. This effort demonstrated the feasibility of responding to database queries by automatically generating SDMS-like [DONE 78] displays. These displays consist of many individual graphic displays mapped into a single graphical space whose dimensions may correspond to distinctions or metrics in the data model.

Finally, with regard to the problem of automatically selecting appropriate display formats, our work with AIPS connects with Gnanamgari's work [GNAN 80] on characterizing the suitability of different graphic display formats for different kinds of information.

Our work differs from these efforts in two respects. First, we committed ourselves to generating (and interpreting user input over) a wide variety of graphic display formats, including not only tabular displays but also maps, graphs, and diagrams. Second, we viewed the problem of information presentation as fundamentally implying an extremely rich declarative characterization of the structure and semantic content of graphic displays, and we were technically prepared to pursue this implication.

We viewed the goals of our research in functional terms: in terms of new capabilities for interactive graphics. While we added and dropped peripheral goals over time, the essential targets remained the same from start to finish:

1) Afford non-programmers a larger measure of control over the selection and display of information;
2) Provide a knowledge architecture that could absorb a maximum of display generation knowledge with minimum need for restructuring;
3) Furnish an initial basis for formally characterizing the semantics of natural language dialogs about graphic displays.

Our most important goal was to provide an information display capability that could produce unanticipated displays without additional programming. This meant moving away from describing displays in terms of their realization process, toward specifying their content, structure and appearance declaratively.

This shift from the procedural to the declarative presents intriguing possibilities for almost every area of graphic interface design and engineering. To make the best use of our resources, we concentrated on what appeared to us to be the central issue: automatically generating graphic displays. If we were successful here, we could go on to experiment with techniques for expressing display specifications, for translating application-dependent information, for interpreting graphic input and for collecting knowledge about new graphic displays.

The remainder of this chapter divides into four parts. In the next section we discuss in general the problem of automatically generating graphic displays. In the section following that, we describe the KL-ONE knowledge representation language for the benefit of readers who aren't familiar with it. In the next section, we detail the internal construction of AIPS: the techniques used to describe display semantic content, to describe display internal structure, and to activate descriptions for purposes of display generation. In the final section of this paper, we will discuss the practical results of this work.

2 Foundations

The basic premise that underlies separating the information presentation function from the application system is that it is possible to make reasonable decisions about display appearance based on limited knowledge about display content. To the extent that this is not the case, the display generation function must remain application dependent.

Happily, it is usually only necessary to be able to make certain generalizations about domain entities in order to be able to depict them properly. For example, it is possible to draw a map of a college campus without knowing very much about what buildings are or what they are used for. One can get along with only the limited knowledge that buildings are discrete physical objects, occupy fixed regions in a two dimensional space, have names, etc. Moreover, the methods used to produce such a map would presumably suffice for any other set of discrete physical objects having these sorts of attributes. If this were not the case, a domain-independent display generation capability would be impossible.

Note that it is also possible to make discriminating choices among alternative display formats based on just such limited knowledge. A map is a good choice for showing the locations of physical objects; pie charts are good for depicting exhaustive partitions on enumerable sets, and so forth.

However, to apply this limited "common sense" knowledge to some particular application domain, there must be a mechanism for making generalizations. To continue the above example, there must be some way to bridge the gap between "building" and "physical object". Our approach assumes that the external knowledge base will provide this in the form of a generalization hierarchy which, at its least specific levels, matches or relates to the distinctions recognized by the display generation system. In other words, domain information must be expressed in terms of a hierarchical generalization structure, some portion of which is also recognized by the display generation system.

Fortunately, most current knowledge representation languages rely on this sort of hierarchy for organizing knowledge. AIPS requires that application dependent information be expressed in KL-ONE [BRAC 79a, BRAC 79b]. Of the current crop of knowledge representation languages, KL-ONE affords a particularly good basis for information presentation because it provides a richer-than-usual generalization structure: one that extends to the parts or attributes of descriptive entities as well as to the entities themselves. This extra structure enables more informed decisions about how to depict parts or attributes of a description. Without it, AIPS would be either dependent on attribute names for making these decisions, or would have to deal strictly in terms of whole entities, without regard to the functional roles they play as constituents of other entities.

This discussion has focused on what a domain-independent graphic presentation function requires in terms of the general structure of the subject knowledge base. If these requirements are satisfied, there remains the problem of how to make the display generator easily extensible to handle domain-specific display requirements. For example, the client who supports development of AIPS desires certain map and table formats that have an established currency in the domain of Naval Command and Control. Similarly, a knowledge-based system for assisting the design of LSI circuits may require special display formats which are roughly "maps", but which conform to the particular conventions and requirements of that domain.

Also, the end user may have his or her own unique requirements for the format of a display. Often, these can be expressed as slight variations on some display format already supported. For example, a naval tactician might want an otherwise standard format situation map in which ships with a certain capability are given a distinct depiction. In other cases, individuals may need to create their own formats starting more nearly "from scratch". For example, the implementor of a knowledge-based system may want a special display format that helps track down some specific class of bug.

In sum, the information presentation subsystem must comprise an open-ended and extensible model of the display generation process. Moreover, the structure of this model must be such that additions to it can make the maximum possible use of behavior that has already been captured. Accordingly, AIPS' most prominent architectural feature is a taxonomic hierarchy of display format descriptions. Inheritance of attributes and attached procedures down the structure of this hierarchy allows new display formats to be described to the greatest possible extent in terms of those already represented.

It is possible to pursue this kind of approach using a LISP enhanced with an object class hierarchy package, such as Flavors [WEIN 81], or an object-oriented language such as the Smalltalk-80 programming language. However, that would not address a remaining important issue affecting extensibility and flexibility: the extent to which the presentation system's behavior is expressed as an interpretive process written in some programming language. Particularly for non-programming users, control and modification of the presentation function ultimately depend on the degree to which display generation behavior can be declaratively described. Unless the interpretive component is very general, changes or additions to the graphics model will often require programming changes or additions to the interpreter.

In accordance with the above considerations, we implemented AIPS as a

KL-ONE taxonomic hierarchy of display structure descriptions. The interpreter for this knowledge base is written in LISP, and the bulk of it is distributed over the KL-ONE hierarchy in the form of inheritable attached procedures. AIPS treatment of procedural knowledge was less than ideal, but sufficed for an initial exploration of the functionality of domain independent information presentation.

3 The Knowledge Representation Language

AIPS uses KL-ONE to express both the structure and content of graphic displays. We chose KL-ONE for these functions because we hoped that its taxonomic character would facilitate adding knowledge about new kinds of displays, and because we hoped its epistemological orientation would make it general enough to serve as a kind of *lingua franca* for connecting up to diverse application domains. Because KL-ONE plays such an important role in AIPS, we will describe it here briefly before discussing AIPS' internal construction. This description is not complete by any means. It only introduces those aspects of KL-ONE which are of some importance to AIPS.

KL-ONE's designers were concerned with making a clean distinction between terminology and assertion. Accordingly they divided their language into terminological and assertional components, each of which defines certain distinct types of network nodes and relations. The terminological part of KL-ONE is concerned purely with descriptions and the internal structures of descriptions. It is the older and more stable of the two parts of the KL-ONE. For our work, we chose to limit our use of KL-ONE to this terminological portion of the language, and we will describe only that part of KL-ONE here.

KL-ONE has just two terminological node types, called "Concepts" and "Rolesets". Concepts describe entities or collections of entities in some world of interest. Rolesets in turn form the constituent parts or aspects of Concepts.

Concepts are related by subsumption: more general descriptions subsume more specific ones. Concepts can inherit structure from the descriptions they are subsumed by. This has important practical consequences, especially when adding new descriptions to an existing network. Nevertheless it is subsumption, and not inheritance, that shapes the KL-ONE network. Inheritance is merely a notational convenience feature.

KL-ONE's terminological component is "epistemologically principled": it gives no allegiance to any built-in set of descriptions, except for the distinguished Concept called THING. THING is the most general possible description and inhabits the topmost position of every KL-ONE network. Semantically speaking, it is a null description; a place holder. At the other end of the spectrum, at the lowest and most specific layers of the description hierarchy, are those descriptions (called "Individual Concepts") that intrinsically describe at

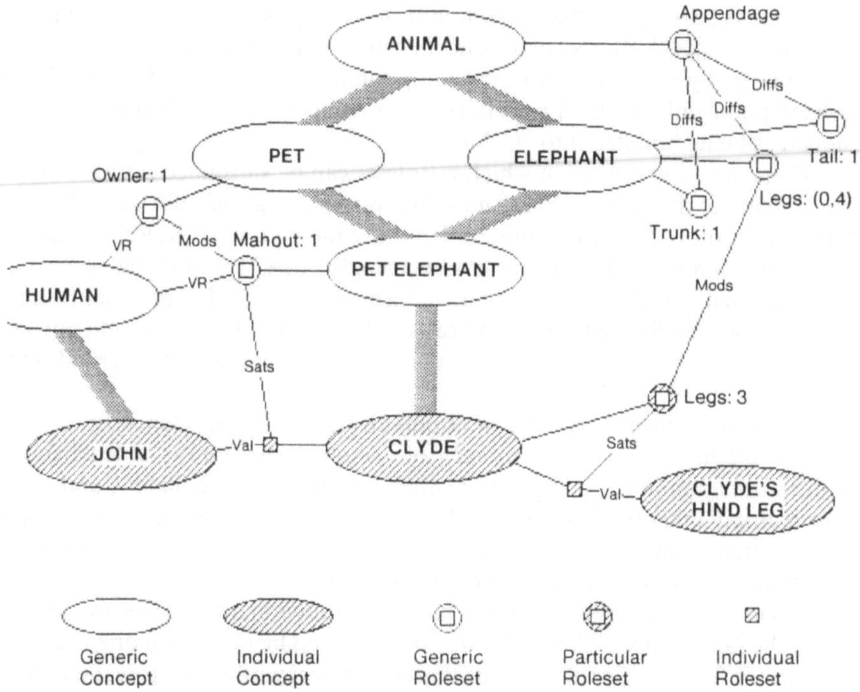

Fig. 1. An example portion of a KL-ONE network

most one entity. In between, the lattice is filled with descriptions that may apply to more than one entity. These potentially pluralistic descriptions are called "Generic Concepts."

One of the things distinguishing KL-ONE from most of the associative network formalisms which preceded it is that a Concept (a network node) has an internal structure of its own. It is, in effect, a small chunk of network in its own right. Concepts are made up of Rolesets. A Roleset describes a conceptually identifiable constituent of a Concept. The Roleset's structure includes a name (ideally a documentation feature used to suggest the function played in the conceptual complex), a description (called the "Value Restriction" or "VR") of the set of legal potential fillers for that Roleset in any Individual Concept subsumed by the generic description, and an optional "Number Facet": a restriction on the number of descriptive entities implied by the Role.

The term "filler" refers to an Individual Concept that satisfies a Roleset in the structure of some other Individual Concept. Figure 1 shows an example of Role structure at a Generic Concept and how a Roleset is satisfied at a subsumed Individual Concept. The Roleset node is drawn as a circle with a square inscribed. The connector to the filler (called an Individual Roleset) is drawn as a shaded square.

Rolesets participate in a subsumption hierarchy distinct from but similar to that of Concepts. A Roleset of a Concept can be linked to a Roleset of a subsuming Concept by means of a Role subsumption relationship called a "Wire". The subsumption links pertaining between two concepts and their parts are envisioned as being bundled into "Cables".

There are several ways in which a Roleset can be subsumed (as an unmodified version of the subsumer, as a modified version, or as one of a set of differentiated sub-Roles). Because of this, and because the number of Rolesets at a Concept is not constrained, there cannot be a single "ISA"-type link (as in "A Dog ISA Mammal") to carry the inheritance. Instead, the Cable has at least one internal wire for each Roleset. In the interests of brevity, KL-ONE notation and language implementations usually omit the Wires for unmodified inherited Rolesets.

KL-ONE Concepts can have multiple subsumers ("Super Concepts"). A separate Cable links the concept to each of its subsumers. Each Cable carries its own information about a particular super-concept and its Rolesets, and therefore multiply inherited Rolesets can be explicitly treated. This structured attribute inheritance mechanism avoids the problem of "slot" naming confusions common to most other network formalisms.

It is important to emphasize that KL-ONE Individual Concepts are descriptions: the same entity in the world may be described by more than one Individual Concept. The notational elements that denote real world objects (called "Nexuses") and the links (called "Description Wires") that tie them to the description hierarchy are, properly speaking, part of KL-ONE's assertional apparatus. However, a Nexus can be used to denote another KL-ONE description rather than some external object. Metadescription of this sort is facilitated in KL-ONE with a special notational abbreviation, the "Metadescription Link" that can be attached to any Concept, Roleset, Wire or Cable.

This ability to express "knowledge about knowledge" permits descriptions that are awkward or impossible in the base language alone. For example, metadescriptions can be attached to the Cables descending from a Generic Concept to indicate that the corresponding sub-categories comprised an exhaustive partition. As explained below, metadescription is used by AIPS in indicating the information contained in a Display.

Finally, in addition to KL-ONE metadescriptions, arbitrary LISP objects can be attached to the network as uninterpreted tags. Two types of tags are provided for: those that are inheritable at inferior points in the taxonomic lattice and those that are not. The principal importance of this feature to AIPS is that it allows LISP procedures to be attached to KL-ONE descriptions in support of an object-oriented scheme for manufacturing new Individual Concepts.

The foregoing discussion hews to the officially recognized dogma for the formal semantics of KL-ONE notation. In using KL-ONE to describe the structure of graphic displays, we violated this dogma in an important regard: we omitted the use of Nexuses to denote displays and parts of displays. The required additional structure would have been quite expensive in terms of memory, and we

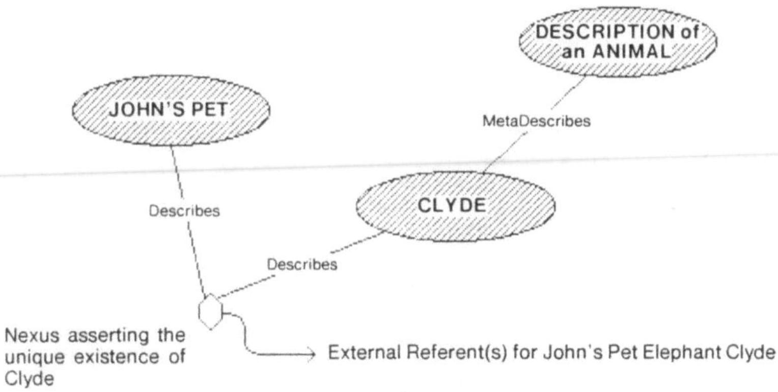

Fig. 2. Description, metadescription, and assertion

did not foresee any immediate need to deal with existential assertions about displays. Instead, the procedural parts of AIPS recognized certain Individual Concepts as implicitly denoting external objects such as displays.

4 The Presentation System

AIPS generates a graphic display by refining a KL-ONE description of the display to the point where the display itself can actually be drawn. The display description that begins this process may be limited to an account of the information content of the desired display, or it may include a partial description of the display's structure and appearance. To paraphrase in English, an initial description might be as vague as: "the locations of the Campus and Jane's house", or it might include rather more detail, such as: "A map 200 pixels by 200 pixels with circles showing the locations of the Campus and Jane's house."

The ensuing process of refinement is directed by a collection of KL-ONE Generic Concepts which describe a small but extensible variety of graphic display formats. One of these descriptions relates not only the internal structure of a format, but also the general type of information for which that format is suited. Procedural attachments to these format descriptions perform the functions of identifying and locating the constituent parts and pieces of a specific display.

The graphic elements of a generic format description are represented in turn by generic descriptions of more primitive graphic entities. These in turn are described in KL-ONE and so on, down to the level of atomic graphic elements such as points and lines. At this lowest level of structural decomposition, procedural attachments to the generic descriptions perform the function of drawing the display.

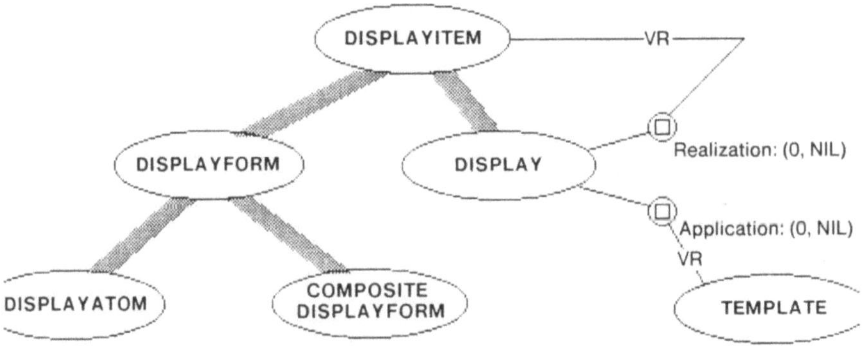

Fig. 3. Cardinal descriptions of the graphics taxonomy

To summarize, AIPS can be viewed as three separate groupings of generic descriptions and three separate groupings of procedural attachments:

- Descriptions of graphic devices capable of conveying information;
- Descriptions of graphic structures that don't bind information;
- Descriptions of very general categories of real world objects;
- Attachments for expanding the descriptions of individual displays;
- Attachments for locating the constituents of individual displays;
- Attachments for drawing the leaf descriptions of individual displays.

These six categories of information are used to expand and refine KL-ONE individual descriptions of specific displays, and then interpret these descriptions in order to produce the actual displays.

The remainder of this section details the internal architecture of AIPS. The system's taxonomy of display formats and display objects, its characterization of the information content of a display, and its use of procedural knowledge are all described.

For the sake of clarity, we will fully capitalize the names of KL-ONE Generic Concepts. The names of Individual Concepts and Rolesets will be shown in mixed case. Thus, DISPLAY refers to the description of a category, Display refers to a description of an individual of that category, and display refers to something seen on the screen of a graphics terminal.

4.1 Display Description Structure

DISPLAYITEM is the top-most description of the information presentation model. This description applies to anything that can be drawn. As already indicated, there is a distinction between those descendants of DISPLAYITEM that bind or present specific information and those that do not. The former are described by DISPLAY, a specialization of DISPLAYITEM. DISPLAY and its

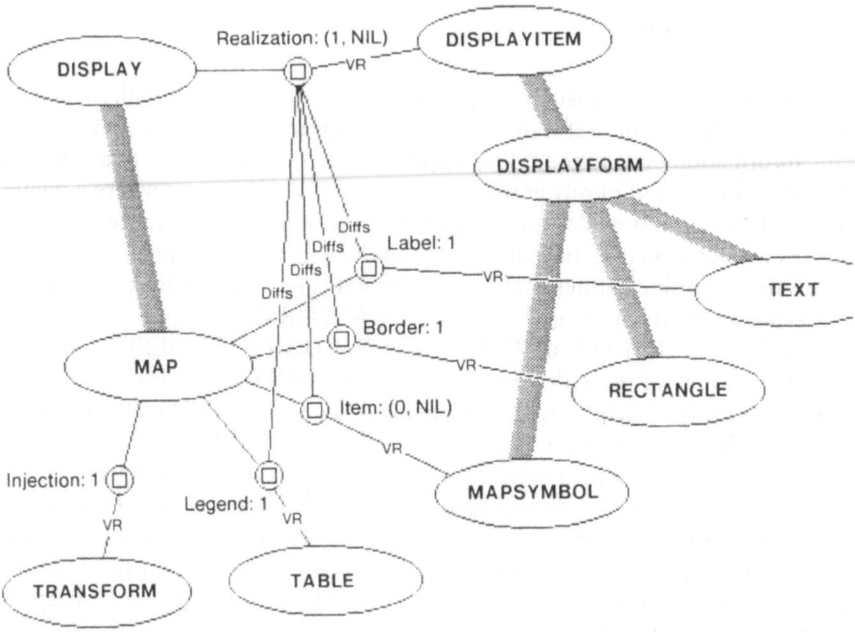

Fig. 4. Some of the structure of MAP

generic specializations roughly amount to descriptions of different kinds of graphic information display formats. For example, DISPLAY's descendants include TABLE and MAP.

DISPLAY has two parts: a Realization Roleset that describes the visible components of a display format, and an Application Roleset that is used by individual Displays to describe their information content. The Realization Roleset is differentiated and modified at the various descendants of DISPLAY. For example, MAP's visible parts and pieces are all represented as differentiating descendants of DISPLAY's Realization Roleset (see Fig. 4).

The Value Restriction of the Realization Roleset is the concept DISPLAYITEM. Because DISPLAYITEM subsumes DISPLAY, this means that the components of a generic format description may or may not be described as DISPLAYs, that is, they may or may not reflect specific information drawn from the client system's application domain. Also, DISPLAY and its specializations inherit DISPLAYITEM's Rolesets, which relate such things as the location, orientation, scale, width and height of a display element. The ability to treat structural components of a Display as Displays (thus making an explicit treatment of their semantic content) contributes to the structural uniformity of the presentation system and helps to provide a basis for interpreting graphic input.

Descendants of DISPLAY may also include Rolesets that are descendants of neither Realization nor Application. For example, MAP includes a Roleset named Injection, which characterizes a map's scaling transformation.

4.2 Display Primitives

The descriptive decomposition of generic display formats eventually reaches a level at which it is not useful to characterize graphic elements as conveying specific information of any kind. This happens where the appearance of a symbol is described in terms of purely graphical elements. It also happens where a display format description provides for components that enhance appearance but do not convey information (e.g. lines that separate the columns of a table.)

Generic graphic entities that are not formats are captured by a second specialization of DISPLAYITEM called DISPLAYFORM. Descriptions subsumed by DISPLAYFORM include POINT, LINE, CIRCLE, EDGESET, CURVE, and ARC. Some of these descendants, such as POINT and LINE, are atomic; others are further decomposed in terms of other varieties of DISPLAYITEM. For example, RECTANGLE is described in terms of LINE.

Descriptions of some of these composite display forms include prototype individual descriptions. These exemplify how the components are arranged and oriented to form the composite. For example, OCTAGON can be accompanied by an individual description descended from itself and built out of individual Lines whose location information can be scaled up or down for octagonal shapes of different sizes.

4.3 Characterizing Information Content

The information content of a particular display is described by its Application Roleset, which is filled with one or more individuals of the concept TEMPLATE. A Template is simply a means of indicating the cross product of some set of descriptions in the subject knowledge base with some subset of their Rolesets. Hence, TEMPLATE has two roles: ConceptGroup and RoleGroup. In an individual Template, the fillers of the ConceptGroup Roleset indicate the domain model objects of concern; the fillers of the RoleGroup Roleset indicate which attributes of those objects are involved. If the semantic content of a display does not factor into a single such cross product, several Templates may be used to capture the disjuncts.

A Template gets its necessary descriptive "grip" on Concepts and Rolesets in the domain knowledge base through use of KL-ONE's metadescription feature. The Rolesets to be included in the RoleGroup of a Template are described as individuals of ROLE. Similarly, Concepts are meta-indicated via individuals of CONCEPT. See Fig. 5 for an example of a Template used to meta-indicate some information about some ships.

Templates are also useful as meta-descriptions of display formats. For example, a Template can be used to indicate the kind of information that is well depicted in a particular format. In this case, the fillers of the ConceptGroup Roleset of the Template meta-indicate generic descriptions rather than individual descriptions.

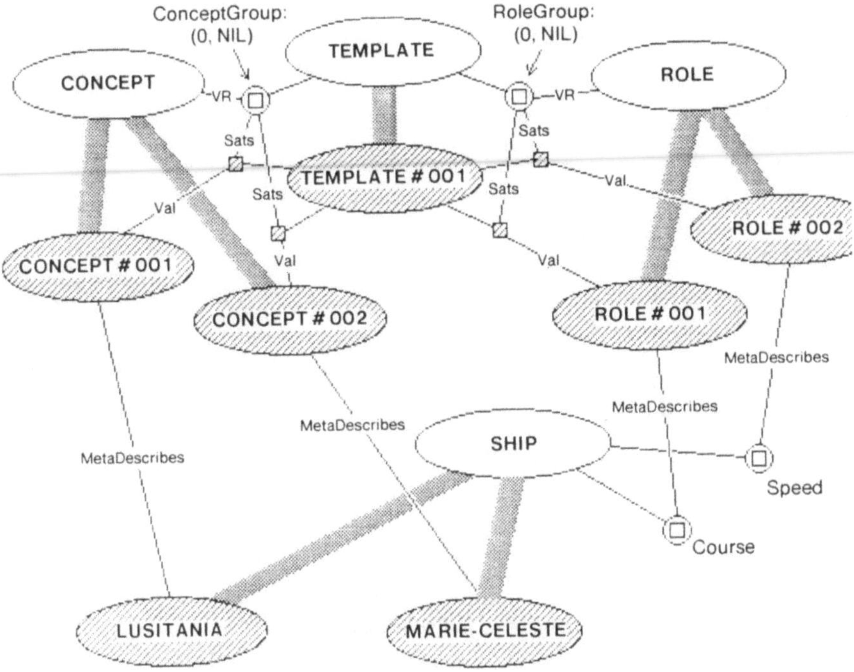

Fig. 5. Describing the course and speed of two ships

4.4 *Procedural Knowledge in the Presentation System*

The process of creating a display begins by creating a new individual of some sub-category of DISPLAY and filling its Application Roleset with Templates to indicate the information content of the desired display. At this point, only the Application Roleset is filled. If desired, the user can simply create an individual sub-concept of DISPLAY itself, and let AIPS choose a format. In this case, AIPS compares the Template with metadescriptions on the display formats it knows about in order to make an appropriate selection. From this starting point, display construction proceeds in three phases:

1) Derivation of descriptions of the new Display's components;
2) Location of these components in the coordinate system of the Display, and
3) Drawing of the graphic display itself.

Each phase is supported by its own set of procedural attachments to the knowledge base.

During the derivation phase, the description of the goal display is expanded at least to the extent that all descendant Rolesets of DISPLAY's Realization Roleset are filled with some DisplayItem; each of these descriptions is then recursively expanded in the same manner. For example, for the case shown in Fig. 6,

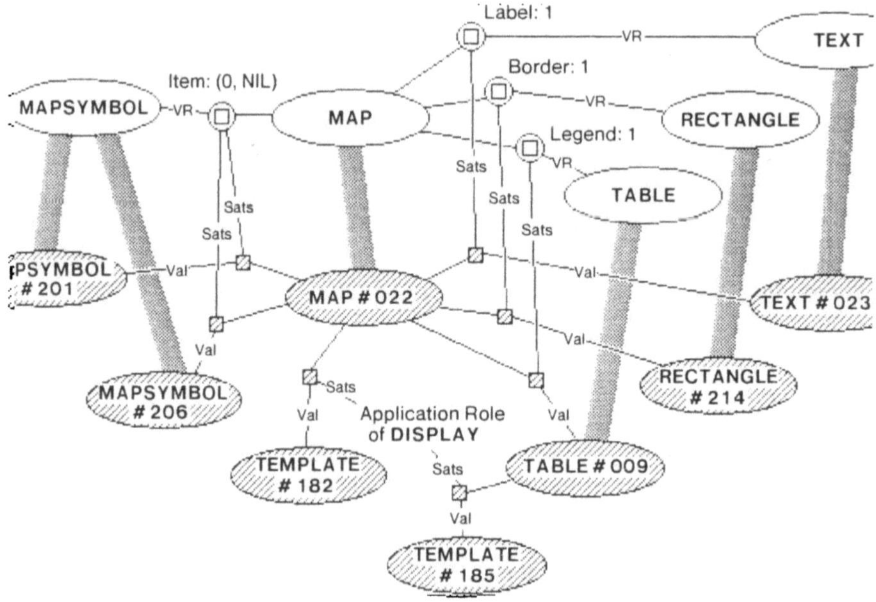

Fig. 6. Generating the description of an individual map

the Legend Roleset of the Map being constructed is filled with an individual of TABLE whose Application Roleset indicates the set of symbols used in the map. The derivation process then recurses on this Table to fill out its internal structure.

The derivation phase procedures are attached as tags to the Rolesets for which they produce fillers. These tags specify what information must already be known in order to run a procedure, so that a demand to fill a Roleset may first result in the filling of other Rolesets on which its derivation depends. Also, the body of an attached derivation procedure can dynamically call for the derivation of some other Roleset and suspend processing until the information is provided. Derivation procedures are inherited and more than one derivation procedure may be attached. At filler derivation time, all of the available procedures are tested for applicability and executed in order from the more specific to the more general until one succeeds.

When derivation phase recursion terminates, the second phase of locating the newly identified display components begins. This phase is driven by means of messages passed among the constituent descriptions of the Display. DisplayItems receive messages which tell them where they are located relative to the coordinate system of the display. If the recipient contains separately described components, the locating procedure computes the locations of these constituents and then recurses by dispatching this information to them as messages.

By the end of the locating phase, each description of a visible display component includes where it is located and how it is oriented in the coordinate system of its containing DisplayItem. At this point, the KL-ONE description of the goal display has been completely expanded and it remains only to do the actual drawing. This final operation is handled much like the location phase. DisplayItems receive messages that cause them to execute attached drawing procedures. Except for the lowest atomic level of DISPLAYFORM's, a single drawing procedure is inherited that re-broadcasts the drawing request to sub-components. For descendants of DISPLAYFORM that can be directly drawn, specialized drawing procedures call the routines of a graphics package to finally realize the requested display.

4.5 Interpreting Graphic Input

The display description built up in generating a display also serves as a framework for interpreting graphic input relative to the display. As a byproduct of the generation process, this framework includes an explicit description of the information content of each part and piece of the display. For example, in a map whose markers denote the locations of certain cities and aircraft, the description of each marker includes which city or aircraft it depicts. This allows us to compute, for some intensionally described set of domain model entities, the corresponding set of display objects in a given display. For example, we can compute the set of map markers that correspond to aircraft of a certain type. Once the set of display objects of interest has been determined, the location information included in their descriptions can be used to generate a list of envelope regions on the display. This, in turn, can be used for interpreting graphic input selection.

5 What Resulted

The prototype system that we built successfully demonstrated a minimal order of automatic display generation. To support this demonstration we built a testbed knowledge base of information to be displayed. It described a modest set of generic vehicle types and included information about some simulated situations involving specific vehicles. We then built a simple menu-driven interface for constructing Templates over this knowledge base. This allowed us to drive AIPS interactively from the Interlisp programming environment.

Unsurprisingly, we found that we had built a rather slow display generator. A moderately complicated map including half a dozen locator symbols, a bitmap backdrop with continental outlines, and a legend would take between two and three minutes of real time to produce. Although we demonstrated AIPS on the BBN Jericho Symbolic Processor, its performance would have been approximately the same on the Xerox 1100 Scientific Information Processor. Roughly five percent of the total time was spent in the LISP-coded portions of the procedural attachments; most of the rest was tied up in accessing and manipulating KL-ONE network structures. The only real conclusion to be drawn from AIPS' performance was that our implementation of KL-ONE was too slow.

The resulting performance is less discouraging than it seems: more recent implementations of KL-ONE have made two orders of magnitude worth of performance improvements [BOBR 84]. There were also at that time many performance shortfalls in the underlying Interlisp-Jericho programming environment. For example, the demonstration system was run on a version of Interlisp-Jericho that did not have garbage collection. As the virtual memory image of the system became more and more fragmented, performance degraded markedly.

At the time of the system's completion in 1981 we were discouraged by AIPS' performance. Looking back over three years worth of engineering progress in symbolic processing hardware, programming environments and knowledge representation languages, the approach that we took now seems eminently feasible, if only in a context of powerful personal symbolic processors.

5.1 Functional Contributions of KL-ONE

The significant questions to be asked about an experiment of this kind concern the benefits of using a knowledge representation language instead of some simpler or more efficient data representation. Practically speaking, there are two areas in which to look for these benefits: the ease with which the system is extended to describe various types of graphic displays, and the ease with which the system is connected to application domains. Unfortunately, due to time limitations, we got only limited experience in either area on which to base our evaluations.

With regard to the extensibility of graphics generation knowledge expressed in KL-ONE, the case is inconclusive because of AIPS' heavy reliance on procedural attachments. Certainly it was very easy to expand AIPS' collection of declarative display descriptions. The rub was that these additions tended to require adding fairly redundant procedural attachments. The fault for this lies not with KL-ONE, but with AIPS: we didn't understand how to atomize and distribute the procedural knowledge involved in display generation.

In building graphics knowledge into AIPS, we found the KL-ONE declarative notation to be remarkably accommodating for three reasons:

1) The KL-ONE implementors, recognizing that both the notation and its implementation in Interlisp were incomplete, included powerful escape mechanisms to bridge the gap between what could and could not be expressed in KL-ONE;
2) KL-ONE embeds fairly powerful notions of subsumption and inheritance: both generic and individual descriptions may be multiply subsumed;
3) Subsumption is described in KL-ONE in terms of the component parts of descriptions rather than merely in terms of complete descriptions.

KL-ONE's escape mechanisms include the feature that allowed us to tag Concepts and Rolesets with LISP expressions and procedures, and also a provision for recognizing certain Interlisp data types in terms of KL-ONE descriptions. These kinds of facilities are essential for engineering one's way around various limitations, particularly limits on available memory. They also facilitate building hybrid systems that use more than one representational formalism.

Multiple subsumption and inheritance allow great flexibility for adding to a taxonomy of descriptions so as to extract the maximum benefit from descriptions already encoded. However, this advantage has to be backed up with some means of disambiguating how attributes and other attachments are inherited when multiple sources are involved. KL-ONE's explicit Roleset taxonomy deals with this problem exhaustively by disambiguating on a case by case basis. This sometimes seemed verbose, but clarity benefitted because the taxonomic placement of descriptions didn't have to be compromised in order to suit some more general scheme for resolving inheritance conflicts.

While KL-ONE's notions of subsumption helped in describing the structure of graphic displays, they played a much more crucial role in connecting AIPS with the simulated client application. Here, the explicit Roleset hierarchy directly linked the Rolesets declared in the application domain model with Rolesets from AIPS' simplified domain model. This eliminated the need to use Roleset names for doing this kind of attribute matching. For example, Wires connected the Position Roleset of VEHICLE with the Location Roleset of PHYSICAL-OBJECT.

The problem of merging disparate knowledge bases did not really arise in our limited experience, but multiple subsumption of descriptions gives a means for working around any differences between the presentation system's domain model and the upper levels of the application system's domain model taxonomy. For example, if the former embeds a description named CREATURE while the latter declares only that ANIMAL subsumes ELEPHANT, multiple subsumption lets us merge the two by adding a link between CREATURE and ELEPHANT. Similar shotgun marriages can be performed between Roleset hierarchies.

Finally, KL-ONE's Roleset differentiation mechanism let us state how a group of Rolesets generalized to some single Roleset on a subsuming description. For example, the Displacement Roleset of VESSEL differentiated into the Submerged-Displacement and Surfaced-Displacement Rolesets of SUBMARINE. This made it easy to arrange for a table of displacements to include just one datum for a ship but two separate data for a submersible.

5.2 Extending Display Knowledge in AIPS

One of our goals was to be able to generate novel kinds of displays purely by describing them declaratively in KL-ONE. We did find that we could get certain kinds of structural recombinations purely by adding new descriptions. For example, it was easy to embed one kind of presentation in another, e.g. to embed tables inside of a map, or graphical symbols inside of a table. We also found we could vary the appearance of displays to a considerable extent, e.g. adjust their proportions, add or remove structural elements, or change texture or shading. Unfortunately, adding any really new display format, e.g. a new kind of graph, tended to require writing LISP code for procedural attachments.

We used two different mechanisms for activating procedural attachments in AIPS: directed interpretation for description derivation, and message passing for locating and drawing display elements. The most successful of these applications were the drawing procedures. Writing new drawing procedures was only necessary where a display element could not be described in terms of other, more atomic display elements. Otherwise, the new description simply inherited DISPLAYITEM's procedure for recursing on components. Altogether there were only about a dozen different atomic display elements.

The procedural attachments used for locating display elements, on the other hand, were the biggest barrier to extending AIPS to new display formats. New formats usually required their own locating procedures because locating strategy tended to depend on format structure. If we had treated the structural relationships between display components declaratively, we might have limited the procedural vector to a general, widely heritable strategy of constraint interpretation and a limited set of atomic constraints. Instead, we were forced for practical reasons to make a procedural treatment of these relationships.

In the case of simple composite display forms we got a somewhat more declarative treatment by using prototype descriptions to capture the fixed relative locations of their components. This simple means of expressing location information at least allowed us to add new display forms - e.g. map symbols - without adding new procedural attachments. Of course, this approach can't work for presentation formats because their structure is variable depending on information content.

For the process of deriving the components of an individual Display, we used a system of tags to advise the invocation of attached procedures. These tags captured some of the structural and computational dependencies. Otherwise, the situation was similar to that for the locating procedures: most Rolesets required their own tags and at least one associated derivation procedure. This was somewhat ameliorated because filler derivation procedures tended to apply correctly - even though inherited from several removes up the taxonomy.

To summarize, AIPS' commitment to procedural attachments tended to hamper the addition of new display knowledge, mainly because limitations on KL-ONE network size forced us to treat certain relationships procedurally. In the case of the locating process these were relationships between structural components; in the case of the derivation process these were relationships between structure and content. Despite this it was still possible to make considerable variations in the structure and appearance of display formats, purely by adding new KL-ONE descriptions to AIPS.

6 Conclusion

AIPS is an initial and tentative illustration of the issues and avantages in taking a knowledge-based approach to interactive graphics. Further progress will require a thorough treatment of the structural relationships involved in the display of information, and a yet more heavily declarative approach to characterizing graphic displays. These in turn will open up fascinating new possibilities for acquiring display knowledge, for interpreting graphic input, for dynamically modifying displays, and for interpreting the editing of graphic displays in terms of their underlying models.

References

[BOBR 84], [BRAC 79a], [BRAC 79b], [DONE 78], [GNAN 80], [GOLD 83], [GREE 81], [HERO 80], [KAYG 76], [SUTH 63], [WEIN 81], [YONK 78]

6 Conclusions

Part II

Evaluation of Domain-Independent Database Access Systems

Chapter 3

Considerations for the Development of Natural-Language Interfaces to Database Management Systems*

Marjorie Templeton and John Burger

Abstract. This chapter illustrates the difficulties of product development in the natural language interface area by describing experience with the End-User Friendly Interface to Data Management (EUFID). EUFID was designed to be both application and DBMS independent. Although most design goals were met, several limitations in application development facilities, cooperative language processing, and DBMS capabilities prevented successful product development. A set of functional requirements for marketable natural language query systems is derived and a checklist for evaluating the potential of a given systems is presented.

1 Introduction

Over the past two decades a considerable amount of work has gone into the development of natural-language systems. The field has moved forward, but there are still many remaining problems. Some of the problems specific to natural language access to database management systems (DMBSs) will be discussed in this chapter.

Early natural language research was in the areas of text processing, syntactic parsing techniques, machine translation, and early attempts at English-language question answering systems. Several early question-answering experiments are reviewed by R. F. Simmons in [SIMM65]. Waltz has edited a collection of short papers on topics related to natural-language and artificial intelligence in a survey of natural language interface (NLI) research [WALT77]. A survey of NLIs and evaluation of several systems with respect to their applicability to command and control environments can be found in [OSI79].

Today, new high-technology companies are being formed to create spinoff products that apply artificial intelligence technology to practical problems. [Tek-

* A previous version of this paper appears in the Proceedings of the Conference on Applied Natural-Language Processing, Santa Monica, California, February 1-3, 1983. The conference was sponsored jointly by the Association for Computational Linguistics and the Naval Research Laboratory.

nowledge; Symantec; Artificial Intelligence, Inc.; Machine Intelligence, Inc.; to mention a few]. Natural-language processing has been as responsible as any of the sub-branches of artificial intelligence in the generation of spinoffs. Unfortunately, only a very few of the many NLI attempts have actually resulted in a commercial product that can be deemed ready for the marketplace. Those that have are very limited with respect to the services, facilities, and capabilities that are provided.

In this chapter we will be using the EUFID system as an example of a research project that attempted to develop a product with a wide range of capabilities, but which never became a product because solutions could not be found for several severe problems that forced reductions in those capabilities. We hope that future developers and users of similar systems can benefit from our experience and this description of those problems.

1.1 EUFID

From 1976 to 1981 the System Development Corporation (SDC) in Santa Monica, California was involved in the development of the End-User Friendly Interface to Data management (EUFID) system, a natural-language interface that was designed to be independent of both the application and the underlying database management system (DBMS) [TEMP79, TEMP80, BURG80, BURG82]. The EUFID system permits users to communicate with database management systems in natural English rather than the formal query language of the DBMS. It is assumed that the application domain is well defined and bounded, that users share a common language to address the application, and that users may have little experience with computers or DBMSs but are competent in the application area.

As an overall system, EUFID was quite ambitious and, as a result, ran into an impressive set of problems. We feel that it is important and useful to describe and categorize these problems insofar as they pertain to NLIs in general. At least three broad categories of issues had to be addressed during EUFID development, and it is apparent that they are common to any general natural-language interface to database management systems.

The first category involves the application: how to characterize the requirements of the human-machine dialogue and interaction, capture that information efficiently, formalize the information and incorporate that knowledge into a framework that can be used by the systems. The major problems in this area are knowledge acquisition and representation. For many NLI systems, bringing up a new application requires extensive effort by system designers with cooperation from a representative set of end users. Tools that could assist in automating this process are badly needed.

The second set of issues involves language processing techniques: how to assign constituent structure and interpretation to queries using robust and general methods that allow ill-formed and unanticipated input, extension to additional lexical items, sentence types and semantic relationships. Some NLI systems distinguish the assignment of syntactic structure, or parsing, from the interpretation. Other systems, including EUFID, combine information about constituent and semantic structure into an integrated semantic grammar.

The third class involves database issues: how to actually perform the intent of the natural-language question by formulating the correct structured query and efficiently navigating through the database to retrieve the right answer. This requires a thorough understanding of the DBMS process, the structure underlying the application, the operations and functions that the query language supports, and the nature and volatility of the database.

Obviously issues in these three areas are related, and the knowledge needed to deal with them may be distributed throughout a natural-language interface system. The purpose of this chapter is to show how such issues might be addressed in NLI development, with illustrations from EUFID.

The next section of this chapter includes a brief review of related work and an overview of the EUFID system. The third section describes the goals that EUFID achieved, and section four discusses in detail some of the major application, language, and database problems that arose. Section five suggests guidelines for determining whether an application is an appropriate target for a natural-language interface.

2 Background

2.1 Related Work

While few NLIs have reached the commercial marketplace, many systems have contributed to advancing the state of the art. Several representative systems and the problems they addressed are described in this section.

The general trend in systems has been (1) to move from an integrated database and knowledge base using special storage structures to a separation of the database and knowledge base using general purpose database management systems; (2) to provide more tools so that end users can build and modify the knowledge base instead of requiring hand crafting by NLI experts; and (3) to include more knowledge about the semantics of the database in the parsing algorithms.

1. ASK [THOM83] is one of the newer generation of NLIs which emphasize ease of development of the knowledge base. It is aimed at the end user who wishes to create and query his own small, personal "knowledge base". The line between the database and the knowledge base is blurred. An existing database may be loaded into the ASK "context", and the new tuples as well

as new ways of talking about the database can be added by the user using the same type of dialogue.

2. CONVERSE [KELL71] used formal syntactic analysis to generate surface- and deep-structure parsings together with formal semantic transformation rules to produce queries for a built-in relational DBMS. It was written in SDC LISP and ran on IBM 370 computers. Started in 1968, it was one of the first natural-language processors to be built for the purpose of querying a formal data management system.
3. LADDER [HEND77a] was designed to access large distributed databases. It is implemented in INTERLISP, runs on a PDP-10, and can interface to different DBMSs with proper configuration. It uses a semantic grammar and, like EUFID and most NLIs, a different grammar must be defined for each application.
4. The Lunar Rocks system [WOOD72] was the first to use the Augmented Transition Network (ATN) grammar. Written in LISP, it transformed formally parsed questions into representations of the first-order predicate calculus for deductive processing against a built-in DBMS.
5. PHLIQA1 [SCHA77] uses a syntactic parser which runs as a separate pass from the semantic understanding passes. This system is mainly involved with problems of semantics and has three separate layers of semantic understanding. The layers are called "English Formal Language", "World Model Language", and "Data Base Language", and appear to correspond roughly to the "external", "conceptual", and "internal" views of data as described by C.J. Data [DATE77]. PHLIQA1 can interface to a variety of database structures and DBMSs.
6. The Programmed LANguage-based Enquiry System (PLANES) [WALT78] uses an ATN based parser and a semantic case frame analysis to understand questions. Case frames are used to handle pronominal and elliptical reference and to generate responses to clarify partially interpreted questions.
7. REL [THOM69], initially written entirely in assembler code for an IBM 360, has been in continuous development since 1967. REL allows a user to make interactive extensions to the grammar and semantics of the system. It uses a formal grammar expressed as a set of general re-write rules with semantic transformations attached to each rule. Answers are obtained from a built-in database.
8. RENDEZVOUS [CODD74] addresses the problem of certainty regarding the machine's understanding of the user's question. It engages the user in dialogue to specify and disambiguate the questions and will not route the formal query to the relational DBMS until the user is satisfied with the machine's interpretation.
9. ROBOT [HARR78] is one of the few NLI systems currently available on the commercial market. It is the basis for Cullinane's OnLine English [CULL80], Artificial Intelligence Corporation's Intellect (EDP82] and has recently been picked up by IBM for their Structured Query Language/Data System

[SYST83]. It uses an extracted version of the database for lexical data to assist the ATN parser.

10. TEAM [MART83, GROS83a] is another recent system which emphasizes the ease of development of a new application. The aim is to allow a domain expert rather than a linguist or artificial intelligence expert to develop a TEAM interface to an existing database. The system has well defined distinctions between the domain independent components and the domain dependent components. The parser considers English syntactic rules as well as semantic interpretations in database terms.
11. TORUS [MYLO76], like RENDEZVOUS, engages the user in a dialogue to specify and disambiguate the user's question. It is a research oriented system looking at the problems of knowledge representation, and some effort has been spent on the understanding of text as well as questions.
12. TQA [DAME81] (see also Chap. 5 in this volume) originally named REQUEST, is a system developed by IBM Yorktown. It uses a series of grammatical transformations to transform the user's question into a database query. It was used quite successfully by real users to access a real database, although the structure of the database was very simple.

2.2 The End-User Friendly Interface to Data Management (EUFID)

EUFID is a general purpose natural-language front-end for database management systems. The original design goals set out for EUFID when the project was begun were:

- to be *application independent*. This means that the program must be table driven. The tables contain the dictionary and semantic information and are loaded with application-specific data. It was desired that the tables could be constructed by someone other than the EUFID staff, so that users could build new applications on their own.
- to be *database independent*. This means that the organization of the data in the database must be representable in tables that drive the query generator.[1] A database reorganization that does not change the semantics of the application should be transparent to the user.
- to be *DBMS independent*. This means that EUFID must be able to generate requests to different DBMSs in each DBMS's own query language and that the interface of EUFID to a different DBMS should not require changes to the basic EUFID modules. All DBMs specific code is contained in a *translator* module which must be written for each different DBMS query language.

[1] We make a technical distinction between the words "question" and "query". A *question* is any string entered by the user to the EUFID analyser. A query is a formal representation of a question in either the EUFID intermediate language IL, or in the formal query language of a DBMS.

Transferring the same database with the same semantic content to another DBMS should be transparent to the natural-language users.

- to run on a mini-computer that might be different from the computer running the DBMS.
- to have a fast response time, even when the question cannot be interpreted. This means it must be able quickly to recognize unanalyzable constructs.
- to handle unanticipated, nonstandard or poorly-formed (but, nevertheless, meaningful) questions.
- to be *portable* to various machines. This means that the system had to be written in a high level language; initially a customer required code to be written in FORTRAN, and later the "C" programming language was used.
- to support different views of the data for security purposes.

The design which met these requirements is a modular system which uses an Intermediate Language (IL) as the output of the natural-language analysis system [BURG 82]. This language represents, in many ways, the union of the capabilities of many "target" DBMS query languages.

The EUFID system consists of three major modules, not counting the DBMS (see Fig. 1). The analyzer (parser) module is table driven. It is necessary only to properly build and load the tables to interface EUFID to a new application. Mapping a question from its user representation in the EUFID dictionary to DBMS representation is handled by mapping functions contained in a table and applied by a separate module, the "mapper". Each content (application dependent) word in the dictionary has one or more mapping functions defined for it. A final stage of the mapper is a query-language generator which transforms the query to IL. This stage writes a query in IL using the group/field names found by the mapper to represent the user's concepts and the structural relationships between them. This design satisfies the requirement of application independence.

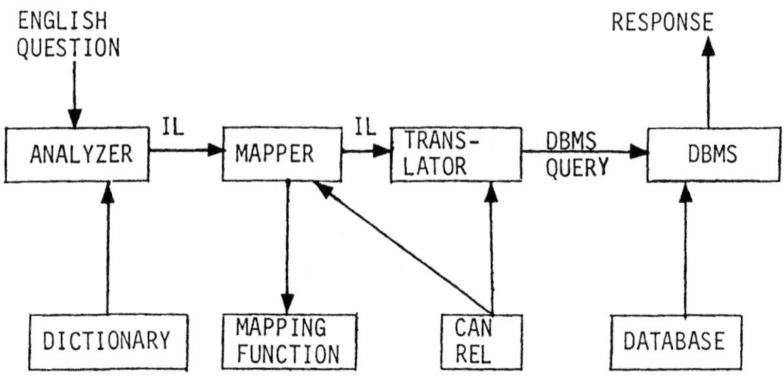

Fig. 1. EUFID block diagram

For each different DBMS used by a EUFID application, a "translator" module needs to be written to convert a query in IL to the equivalent in the DBMS query language. This design satisfies the requirement of DBMS independence.

Other modules peripheral to the three main runtime modules are the system controller, a "help" module, and a "synonym editor". An "Application Definition Module" is used off-line to assist in the creation of the run-time application description tables.

The following subsections describe each of the modules of the EUFID system, and give some of the motivation for design.

2.2.1 Application Definitions

A large conceptual gap exists between the way data are seen by the programmers and database administrators who organize and maintain the database and by the end users of the data (the researchers, administrators, or clerks for whom the data are collected). The former group tends to see data in terms of groups, records, fields, and aggregates. These terms reflect the structured organization given to the data in order to maximize efficency of storage, access time, update processing, and other procedural requirements. These requirements cause the data to be thought about and described in data management system software terms. The end users, on the other hand, think of the data in terms of persons, objects, events, and other entities, together with the attributes (or properties) of these entities, and the relationships they perceive between them.

These two perceptions of the data differ in many ways, and this difference must be recognized and dealt with by any system (computer or human) that communicates with a DBMS at the level of the end user. It is this difference that is involved in the conversion of an end-user's question ("When does flight 317 depart for Chicago?") into a DBMS's query which might look like ("RETURN DEPTIM WHERE FLGT# =317 AND DEST='CHICAGO'").

In support of the design goals of EUFID, it was felt that there should be a high degree of independence between the internal structures containing these two representations of the database content. Such independence allows user views to change without requiring that the database be restructured. No less significantly, it allows the database administrator to restructure the database without interfering with the concepts the end users have about the nature of the data.

The user's view in EUFID is embodied in the definitions of the English words recognizable for a particular application. These definitions are contained in an on-line dictionary. There are two primary catagories of definition in this dictionary: that of *content words* and *function words*.

One of the principle features of a definition of a content word is a list of all other word definitions in the dictionary to which the word being defined may be connected in order to form a phrase that has meaning in the context of the application. Such a connection would exist, for instance, between the word definitions for "employee" and "salary" if the concept of employee-salary has meaning in the application.

The EUFID language analyzer relies on these connection indicators to structure a sequence of words (the user's question) into a tree of connected meaning components. Thus, the driving element of the analyzer is the semantics of the application.

The meanings in DBMS terminology of the words themselves, and by extension, the meanings of connected phrases, are incorporated in *mapping functions* pointed to by individual word definitions. Mapping functions are interpreted by a separate EUFID module, the *mapper,* and are able to transform the definitions of words and connected phrases into the structure and terminology of the application's database.

Bringing up a new application in EUFID is a long and complex process. The database definition must be formalized and made machine-readable. A large corpus of "typical" user questions must be collected from a representative set of users and analyzed by the EUFID staff. The dictionary and mapping tables are designed from the results of this analysis.

A *semantic graph* is defined for the application. This is a graph of the meaningful relationships between word definitions that are recognized in the semantics of the database. The graph is implicitly realized for the run-time system in the dictionary where the nodes of the graph are the definitions of English content words and the connectivity of the graph is implied by connection pointers between the nodes. The pointers are implemented as case-structure relationships on the word definitions.

All dictionary and mapping-function data are then entered into computer files which are processed by the *Application Definition Module* (ADM) to produce the run-time tables. These final tables are complex structures of pointers, character strings, and index tables, designed to decrease access time to the information required by the analyzer and mapper modules. The ADM, typically, needs to be run several times to "debug" the tables.

EUFID tables were built for three applications. Building tables for a new application still requires several staff-months.

2.2.1.1 User-View Representation

All information on the user's view of the database is kept in the dictionary. The dictionary consists of two kinds of words and definitions. *Function words,* such as prepositions and conjunctions, are pre-stored in each application's dictionary and are used by the analyzer for direction on how to connect the semantic-graph nodes during analysis. *Content words* are application dependent. The definitions of content words are semantic-graph nodes. The connectivity of the graph is indicated by semantic case slots and pointers contained in the nodes. A form of semantic-case is used to indicate the attributes of an entity (e.g., adjectives, prepositional phrases, and other modifiers of a noun). This same formalism is applied to verbs to indicate subject, object, and many of the more common cases.

2.2.1.2 Mapping Functions

The set of mapping functions is derived by hand from observations of the dictionary. Every possible connection of every node has to be considered. Frequently, design decisions in the mapping-function list necessitate going back and modifying the content of the dictionary. This is an example of the overlap of the linguistic and database in assigning an interpretation to a question.

2.2.1.3 Database Representation

The structure of the data in the user's database is represented in two tables, called the CAN (for canonical) and REL (for relationships) tables. EUFID lists each database group (either a record or a repeating group within a record) as if it were a relation even if the DBMS is not "relational". Group-to-group linkage (represented in the REL table) is dealt with as if a join[2] were necessary to implement the link. For hierarchical and network DBMSs the join will not be needed: the link is "wired in" to the database structure. EUFID nevertheless assumes a join in order to facilitate the writing of group-to-group links in IL, which is a relational language. The CAN table includes database-specific information for each field (attribute) of each group (relation), such as field name, containing group, name of domain from which an attribute gets its values, and a pointer to a set of conversion functions for numeric values which can be used to convert from one unit of measure to another (e.g., feet to meters).

These data are used by the run-time modules which map and translate the tree-structured output of the analyzer to IL using the actual group/field names of the database, and then to the language of the DBMS. These modules are discussed in the next sections.

2.2.2 The EUFID Analyzer

Various versions of algorithms were used during the EUFID development years for reducing a string of English words into a structured tree of word-definitions. Principal among these are the *slope analysis* technique [BURG75], and the *Cocke-Kasami-Younger* (CKY) algorithm. The first two applications use a variation of the slope technique, while the third application is built on a variant of the CKY.

CKY is a classical nonpredictive bottom-up algorithm that has been used in a family of "chart parsers" developed by Kay, Earley, and others [AHOU72]. The main features of these parsers are:

1) They use arbitrary context-free grammars. There are no restrictions on rules which have left-recursion or other characteristics which sometimes cause difficulty.

2) They produce all possible parses of a given input string. The grammars they use may be ambiguous at either the nonterminal- or terminal-symbol levels.

---

[2] The term "join" refers to a composite operation between two relations in a relational DBMS.

In natural-language processing, this allows for a precise representation of both the syntactic and lexical ambiguities which may be present in an input sentence.

3) They provide partial parses of the input. Each non-terminal symbol derives some input substring. Even if no such substring spans the entire sentence, i.e., no complete parse is achieved, analyses of various regions of the sentence are available.

4) They are conceptually straightforward and easy to implement. The speed and storage considerations which have kept such parsers from being widely used in compilers are less relevant in the analysis of short strings such as queries to a DBMS.

The grammar used by the EUFID parser is essentially semantic. The symbols of the grammar represent the concepts underlying lexical items, and the rules specify the ways in which these concepts can be combined. More specifically, the concepts are organized into a case system. Each rule states that a given pair of constituents can be linked if the conceptual head of one constituent fills a case on the conceptual head of the other. A degree of context sensitivity is achieved by attaching predicates to the rules. These predicates block application of the rules unless certain (usually syntactic) conditions hold true. The parser uses syntactic information only "on demand", that is, only when such information is necessary to resolve semantic ambiguities. This adds to its coverage and robustness, and makes it relatively insensitive to the phrasing variations which must be explicitly accounted for in many other systems.

2.2.3 Mapping

The mapper module converts the output of the analyzer to input for the translator module. Analyzer output is a tree structure where the nodes are semantic-graph nodes corresponding to the content words in the user's question and obtained from the dictionary.

Input to the translator module is a string in the syntax of IL which contains the names of actual groups and fields in the database. The mapping algorithm, thus, has to make several levels of conversion simultaneously:

- it must convert a tree structure into a linear string of tokens,
- it must convert semantic-graph nodes into database group- and field-names, and
- it must convert the connectivity of the tree (representing concept-to-concept linkage in English) into the (frequently very different) group-to-field and group-to-group connections of the database.

The mapper makes use of a table of mapping functions. The table contains at least one mapping function for every content word in the dictionary. The analyzer's tree is traversed bottom up, applying mapping functions to each node on the way. A mapping function is context sensitive with respect to those nodes below its current argument in the tree: nodes that have already been mapped. A new tree is gradually formed and connected this way. Mapping functions may indicate that the map of a semantic graph node is a database node (that is, a group or field name), or a pre-connected sub-tree of database nodes. The mapping function may also indicate removal of a database node from the tree or modification to the existing structure of the tree being constructed.

The new tree is created in terms of the database groups and fields and its structure reflects the connectivity of the database. A final stage of the mapper traverses this new tree and generates the IL statement of the query using the database names from the tree and a table of the syntax and keywords of IL.

An alternative method of mapping that was investigated involves breaking the process into two basic parts. The first step would be to map the tree output of the analyzer to an IL query on what C.J. Date calls the "conceptual schema" of the database [DATE77]. A second step would take this IL input and re-arrange the schema connectivity (and names of groups and fields) from that of the conceptual schema to that of the actual target database, generating another IL query as input to the current translators. This appears to be a better approach but has never been implemented in EUFID.

2.2.4 Translating

The final run-time module in EUFID is a translator that converts the syntax and functional keywords of IL to those of the actual DBMS query language. Database group- and field-names as well as semantic relatedness is maintained. If necessary, the translator can also add access-path information related to database search. Two translators have been written. One converts IL to QUEL, a relatively simple conversion into the language of the relational database management system INGRES [STON76]. The other translator converts IL into the query language of the World-Wide Data Management System (WWDMS) [HONE76] used by the Department of Defense, and also handles additional access path information. This translator was quite difficult to design and build because of the highly procedural nature of the WWDMS query language.

The output of a translator is sent to the appropriate DBMS. In the EUFID system running at SDC, a QUEL query is submitted directly to INGRES running on the same PDP-11/70 as EUFID. For testing purposes, queries generated by the WWDMS translator were transmitted from a PDP-11/70 to a Honeywell H6000 with a WWDMS database.

2.2.5 Application Description

EUFID runs on three different application databases. The METRO application involves monitoring of shipping transactions between companies in a city called "Metropolis". There are ten companies located in any one of three neighborhoods. Each company rents warehouse space for shipping/receiving transactions and has local offices which receive goods. The database is organized relationally using the INGRES database management system. That means that there are no navigational links stored in the records (called "relations") and there is no predefined "root" to the database structure. Access may be made from any relation to any other relation as long as there is a field in each of the two relations which has the same "domain" (set of values).

AIREP (ADP Incident REPorting) is a network database, implemented in WWDMS. It contains reports about hardware and software failures and resolution of the problems in a large computer system. Active problems are maintained in an active file and old, solved problems are moved to an historical file. If a problem is reported more than once, an abbreviated record is made for the additional report, called the "duplicate incident" record. This means that there are four basic type of report: active incidents, duplicate incidents, historical incidents, and historical duplicate incidents. In addition, there are records about sites, problems, and solutions.

The APPLICANT database is a relational database implemented in INGRES that contains information about job applicants and their backgrounds. The central entity is the "applicant", while other relations describe the applicant's specialties, education, previous employment, computer experience, and interviews.

Each database has different features that may present problems for a natural-language interface but which are typical of 'real-world' applications. METRO has relatively few entities but has complex relationships among them. APPLICANT has many updates and many different values, some coming from open-ended domains. AIREP has a network database structure and contains the same data structure in four different files.

3 Level of Success

Most of the EUFID design goals were actually met. EUFID runs on a mini-computer, a DEC PDP 11/70. It is application, database, and DBMS independent. A typical question is analyzed, mapped and translated in five to fifteen seconds even with grammatically incorrect input.

The analyzer contains a good spelling corrector and a good morphology algorithm that strips inflectional endings so that all inflected forms of words need not be stored explicitly. Spelling correction can be done on any English word stored in the dictionary. The spelling corrector compares the unknown word to all words in the dictionary and assigns a score. If a single word scores above a threshold value it replaces the unknown word and the user is informed. If more than one word scores over the threshold, the user is asked to select the correct word or enter another.

A "synonym editor" permits the user to replace any word or string of words in the dictionary with another word or string to accommodate personal jargon and expressability and to allow personal abbreviations. Each user may have his own synonyms, or groups of users may share synonyms.

A "Concept Graph Editor" allows a database administrator to modify tables and define user profiles so that different users may have limited views of the data for security purposes. Access may be denied at the field or relation level.

The analysis strategy, based on semantic connectivity, permits easy and natural paraphrase recognition. Users may mix tenses, leave out determiners, and order phrases in any way. There are linguistic contructs it cannot handle which will be discussed below.

An English word may have more than one definition without complicating the analysis strategy. For example, "ship" as a vessel and as a verb meaning "to send" can be defined in the same dictionary. Words used as database values, such as names, may also have multiple definitions, e. g., "New York" used as the name of both a city and a state.

The mapper, despite many limitations, can correctly map almost all trees output by the analyzer. It is able to handle English conjunctions, mapping them appropriately to logical ANDs or ORs, and recognizes that some "ands" may need to be interpreted as OR and vice-versa under certain circumstances. It is able to generate calls on DBMS calculations (e. g., average) and user-defined functions (e. g., marine great-circle distance) if the user function exists and is supported by the DBMS.

Questions involving time are interpreted in a reasonable way. Functions are defined for "between" and "during" in the METRO application. The AIREP application allows time comparisons such as "What system was running when incident J123 occurred" which require a test to see if a point in time is within an interval.

The mapper can translate "user values" (e. g., English words like "Russian") to database values (e. g., "USSR"), and convert one unit of measure (e. g., feet) to another (e. g., meters). The value conversion is done by table lookup, and the numeric conversions are done by calling functions.

EUFID can interface to very complex relational and CODASYL-type databases having difficult navigation and parallel structures. In the AIREP application a consistent WWDMS navigational methodology is used to access non-key records. The system can also map to the parallel, but not identical, structures for duplicate and historical incidents.

In the INGRES applications, EUFID is able to use and correctly map to "relationship" relations which relate two or more other relations. For example, the METRO relation "cw" contains a company name, a warehouse name, and a date. This represents the initial business contact between a company and a warehouse. Company and warehouse records are each held in "entity" relations of their own. A user might ask, "When did Colonial [a company] start to do business with VAI [a warehouse]?" or "When did business begin between Colonial and VAI?", either of which refers to the "cw" relation. Companies and warehouses are also related through the "cwt" relation which is a transaction relation. "List transactions between Colonial and VAI." refers to the "cwt" relation. The mapper can map a concept such as "company" to any one of nine fields in any one of seven relations which contain company names.

The system control module keeps a journal of all user-system interactions together with internal module-to-module data communication such as the IL for the user's question and the generated DBMS query. This was intended to assist a security officer who might be monitoring the use of the system and checking for security violations, but it is an invaluable tool for debugging.

The system also employs a very effective HELP module which, under certain circumstances, is context sensitive to the problem affecting the user. Help messages are organized in a network of menus referencing numbered messages. The user can ask for general help and can browse through the menus and messages. Specific help is also available. Each time an error condition occurs in a EUFID module, a message number is stored in a global variable. This message number is used to retrieve both the error message itself and the help message related to the error message. If a user asks for help after an error has occurred, he jumps directly to the help message(s) related to the error message.

4 Problems

This section describes problems associated with EUFID development that appear to be common to natural-language interfaces to database management systems. They are loosely classified into the major areas of application, language and database management issues, although there is much overlap. Criteria for evaluating whether an application is appropriate for a natural-language front-end are also described.

4.1 Application Definition Problems

The primary issue in this area is concerned with problems of defining, creating, and bringing up the necessary knowledge base for a new application. The discussion points out the difficulties associated with systematic knowledge acquisition.

4.1.1 User Model

A single database may be used by different groups of users for different purposes. For example, some users of the APPLICANT database may wish to fill a specific job opening while others may collect statistics on types of applicants. The languages used for these two functions can be quite different, and it is necessary to have extensive interaction with cooperative users in order to characterize the kinds of dialogues they will have with the system.

Not only must representative language protocols be collected, but desired responses must be understood. For example, to answer a question such as "How many outstanding offers do we have?" the system must know whether 'we' refers to the company as a whole, the personnel department at one location, the specific recruiter asking the query, or some other unit. There may be different meanings for different groups of users.

The importance of this understanding between potential users and system developers should not be underestimated, as it is the basis for defining much of the knowledge base needed by the system, and may also be the basis for eventual user acceptance or rejection of the NLI system.

4.1.2 Value Recognition

A "value" is a specific datum stored in the database, and is the smallest piece of data obtainable as the result of a database query. For example, in response to the question "What companies in North Hills shipped light freight to Superior?" the METRO DBMS returns two values: "Colonial" and "Ajax". Values can also be used in a query to qualify or select certain records for output, e.g., in the above question "North Hills" and "Superior" are values that must be represented in the query to the DBMS. As long as the alphanumeric values used in a particular database field are the same as those of words in the English questions, there are no difficult problems involved in recognizing values as selectors in a query.

There are three basic ways to recognize these value words in a question. They can be explicitly listed in the dictionary, recognized by a pattern or context, or found in the database itself.

If the value words are stored in the dictionary, they can be subject to spelling correction because the spelling corrector uses the dictionary to locate words which are a close match to unrecognized words in a question. This means, though, that all possible values and variant legitimate spellings of values for a concept must be put either into the dictionary or into the synonym list. This is reasonable for concepts which have a small and controlled set of values[3] such as the names of the companies in METRO, but may become unwieldy for large sets of values.

If a value can be recognized by a pattern, it is not necessary to itemize all instances in the dictionary. For example, a date may be entered as "yy/mm/dd" so that any input matching the pattern "nn/nn/nn" is recognized as a date. This is the approach used for dates and for names of applicants in the APPLICANT database, where names of people match the pattern "I. I. Lastname".

In another approach, OnLine English [CULL80] and Intellect [HARR78, EDP82] (two variations of ROBOT) use the database to recognize values. This is a satisfactory solution if the database is small or if the small number of different values is stored in an index accessible to the NLI, and if the values in the database are suitable for use in English questions.

---

[3] A set of values is called a "domain".

Each of these solutions has disadvantages. If values are stored in the dictionary and there are many different ways to spell each particular value, maintainance of the dictionary is difficult. For example, the company name for "System Development Corporation" may also be given as "S. D. C.", "S D C", or "System Development Corp". While each different spelling could be entered as a synonym for the "correct" spelling in the database, this would result in an enormous proliferation of the dictionary entries and problems with concurrency control between the updates directed to the data management system and the updates to the dictionary. A creative solution might be to define rules for synonym generation and apply them to database updates.

A somewhat different example is from the APPLICANT application which has many open ended domains, such as names of applicants and previous employers. In this case, the application designer may have to treat certain fields as "retrieve-only", meaning that the data can be asked for but not used as a selection criterion. A database with a large number of retrieve-only fields may be a poor candidate for an NLI.

Patterns can be used only if they can be enforced, and probably few values really fit the patterns nicely. Proper names are a poor choice for patterns because of variations such as middle initial or title such as "Dr." or "Jr.". Also spelling correction cannot be performed unless the value is stored in the dictionary.

Finally, the solution of using the database itself to recognize values is unsatisfactory to a general NLI for anything other than trivial databases, unless an inverted index of values is easily accessible. There are the problems of spelling correction and synonyms for database values, the inefficiency involved in accessing the DBMS for every unrecognized word, the difficulty of knowing which fields in the database to search, and the fact that values stored in the database may be coded differently from the way that they are displayed.

4.1.3 Semantic Variation by Value

Databases are generally designed with a minimum number of different record types. When there are entities which are similar, but possibly have a small number of attributes which are not shared, the entities will be stored in the same record type with null values for the attributes that do not apply. The user, in his questions, may view these similar entities as very different entities and talk about them differently.

We did not encounter this problem in METRO or AIREP. For example, in METRO, the user asks the same type of questions about the company named "Colonial" as about the company named "Supreme". In APPLICANT, however, each applicant has a set of "specialties" such as "computer programmer", "accounting clerk", or "gardener". These are all stored as values of the specialty field in the database. Unfortunately, in this case different specialties evoke completely different concepts to the end user. The user may ask questions such as, "What programmers know COBOL?", "Who can program in COBOL?", and "How many applicants with a specialty in computer programming applied in

1982?". Notice the new nouns and verbs that are introduced by this specialty name.

A value domain such as specialties should be handled with an ISA hierarchy. Each different type of specialty such as gardener or programmer could have a different concept that is a subset of the concept "specialty". Some questions could be asked about all specialties and others could be directed only to certain subconcepts. However, there is no ISA hierarchy in EUFID, and it would have been inefficient to treat each specialty and subspecialty as a separate concept since there are 30 specialties and 196 subspecialties. Therefore, we required the users to know the exact values, to know which values are for specialties and which are for subspecialties, and to ask questions using the values only as nouns. This is not "user friendly".

Even if it were possible to build a different concept for each different skill, there is an update problem. When a new value is added to a domain with uniform semantics (as in adding a new company name in METRO), the new value is simply attached to the existing concept. When the new value has different semantics, the newly associated concepts, nouns, and verbs cannot be added automatically. If the NLI supports an ISA hierarchy, someone will need to categorize the new value and add a new node to the hierarchy or specify a position in the hierarchy.

4.1.4 Automation of Definition

A natural-language interface system will not be practical until a new application can be installed easily. "Easily" means that the end-user organization must be able to create and modify the driving tables for the application relatively quickly without the help of the NLI developer and must be able to use the NLI without restructuring the database.

Each EUFID application required "handcrafted" tables that were built by the development staff. Each new application was done in less time than the previous one, but each still required several staff-months to bring up. Clearly, the goal of facilitating the building of the tables by end users was not met. Computer-assisted tools for defining new applications are a prerequisite for practical NLIs.

4.1.5 Security View

Selective database security can be handled in an NLI like EUFID by giving each user his own set of NLI tables. A user with access to the entire database, then, would have a complete set of tables. Users with restricted access may have specialized tables built for them in which all references to restricted fields or relations have been removed.

In many applications (e.g., military applications) it is not enough, though, simply to withhold the answer to the user's question. In such applications it is desired to make the NLI respond to a question about a restricted field in exactly the same way that it would if the field did not exist in the actual database. In these applications then, removal of a field from the user's tables necessitates also the removal of any mapping functions that point to (create) the field in the IL, removal of any concepts (word definitions) that point to the removed mapping functions, and finally, removal of any English words that point to concepts that have been removed. If the user's environment (that is, his operating system) can enforce access to the database only via the NLI and the user's own specific tables, then selective access to the data can be achieved.

Removal of a database field or relation from the user's tables and the subsequent backchaining to remove the mapping functions, definitions, and words is a tedious process. EUFID makes a good attempt at implementation of this kind of security in a module called the *Concept Graph Editor.* However, due to the complexity of some of the internal structures of the FORTRAN-coded tables, it was decided not to remove everything described above when a database field is restricted to a user. EUFID operates with a single dictionary for all users and only the mapping functions and database description tables are user specific. EUFID can thus deny access to any field, but cannot restrict knowledge of the existance of the field from the astute user. If the field contains values that are themselves words in the dictionary, the user can, with persistence, discover these words.

Security is not an insurmountable problem, but it cannot be "tacked on" to an NLI design as a retrofit. The tables must be designed so that it is possible to remove all traces to a removed field. Of course, any word which references both restricted and unrestricted fields must remain after the removal of the restricted field, but the appropriate links through the concept graph and mapping functions must be removed.

4.2 Language Problems

The basic approach to language analysis in EUFID involves a bottom up parser using a semantic grammar. The symbols of the grammar are concepts underlying lexical items, and the rules of the grammar are based on a case framework. Essentially syntactic information is used only when needed to resolve ambiguity. The language features that this technique has to handle are common to any NLI, and some of the problem areas are described in the following sections.

4.2.1 Anaphora and Ellipsis

To support natural interaction it is desirable to allow the use of anaphoric reference and elliptical constructions across sentence sequences, such as "What applicants know Fortran and C?", "Which of them live in California?", "In Nevada?", "How many know Pascal?". One of the biggest problems is to define the scope of the reference in such cases. In the example, it is not clear whether the user wishes to retrieve the set of all applicants who know Pascal or only the subset who live in Nevada.

One solution is to provide commands that allow users to define subsets of the database and then address questions to the subset. This removes the ambiguity and speeds up retrieval time on a large database. However, it moves the NLI interaction toward that of a structured query language, and forces the user to be aware of the level of subset being accessed. It is also difficult to implement because a subset may involve projections and joins to build a new relation containing the subset. The NLI must be able dynamically and temporarily to change in the mapping tables to map to this new relation.

4.2.2 Intelligent Interaction

One of the EUFID design goals was to respond promptly either with an answer or with a message that the question could not be interpreted. The system handles spelling or typographical errors by interacting with the user to select the correct word. However, when all of the words are recognized but do not connect semantically, it is difficult to identify a single point in analysis which caused the failure.

It is in this area that the absence of a syntactic mechanism for determining well-formedness was most noticeable. There are times when a question has a proper syntactic structure, but contains semantic relationships unrecognizable to the application as in "What is the location of North Hills?". The intent of the user's question should be apparant to the system via the syntactic structure of the question and a response of "Location is not defined for North Hills in this application" or "North Hills is a location and does not have a location" should be derivable from the recognizable semantic failure. Similarly, it would be useful to have a framework for interpreting partial trees, as in the question "What companies ship to Mohawk?" where Mohawk is not a recognized word within the application. An appropriate response might be "Companies ship to receiving offices and companies; Mohawk is neither a receiving office nor a company. The names of offices and companies are ...".

Interpretation of partial analyses is not possible within the EUFID system; it either succeeds or fails completely. When the analysis forms a fully connected tree, it succeeds. When the tree is not fully connected there is a failure, but it is not obvious to EUFID where the failure occurred. One concept may be unconnected not because it is in error but because another concept connected in an erroneous way.

4.2.3 Yes/No Questions

In normal NLI interaction users may wish to ask "yes/no" questions, yet no DBMS has the ability to answer "yes" or "no" explicitly. The EUFID mapper maps a yes/no question into a query which will retrieve some data, such as an "output identifier" or default name for a concept, if the answer is "yes" and no data if the answer if "no". However, the answer may be "no" for several reasons. For example, a "no" response to the question "Has John Smith been interviewed?" may mean that the database has knowledge about John Smith and about interviews and Smith is not listed as having had an interview, or the database knows about John Smith and no data about interviews is available[4]. A third possibility could be that the database has information about John Smith and his employment situation (already hired), and the response might include that information, as in "No, but he has already been hired".

The NLI ought to have a post processor that looks at the data being returned. If there is data, a "yes" answer should be given along with some of the response. When there are many pages of output, the user probably does not want to see all of it. If there is no data, a "no" answer should be given. Determining why the answer is "no" might then require several separate queries to the database which could be done automatically if the user asks "Why?", or "Why not?".

4.2.4 Conjunctions

The scope of conjunctions is a difficult problem for any parsing or analyzing algorithm. The natural-language use of "and" and "or" does not necessarily correspond to the logical meaning, as in the question "List the applicants who live in California and Arizona.". The EUFID mapper will change English "and" to logical "or" when the two phrases within the scope of the conjunction are values for the same field. In this example, an applicant has only one state of residence.

Multiple conjunctions in a single question can be ambiguous as in "Which minority and female applicants know Fortran and Cobol?". This could be interpreted with logical "and" or with logical "or" as in "Which applicants who are minority or female know either Fortran or Cobol?". EUFID allows only a single conjunction or a single conjoined list as in "Who knows Fortran or Cobol or Pascal or C?". This is not sufficient. An NLI must have a method to recognize ambiguity and interact with the user to resolve it.

4.2.5 Negation

Negative requests may contain explicit negative words such as "not" and "never" or may contain implicit negatives such as "only", "except" and "other than" [OLNE78]. The interpretation of negatives can be very difficult. For example, "Which companies did not ship any perishable freight in 1976" could mean

[4] There is the important distinction between a "closed world" database in which the assumption is that the database covers the whole world (of the application) and an "open world" database in which it is understood that the database does not represent all there is to the real world of the application. In the open world database, which we encounter most of the time, a response of "not that this database knows of" might be more appropriate than "no".

either "Which (of all the companies) shipped no perishable freight in 1976?" or "Which (of the companies that ship perishable freight) shipped none in 1976?". Moreover, if some companies were only receivers and never shippers it is uncertain whether they should be considered as part of the answer.

An English expression of the form "X other than Y" such as "cities in the United States other than those with a population under 10,000" refers logically to what is called a *relative complement* (of Y with respect to X). It can be very difficult to compute the relative complement of a set of data using the many data management systems that do not support set operators between relations.

Questions which require a "yes" or "no" response are difficult to answer because often a "no" answer is due to a presupposition which is invalid. This is especially true with negation. For example, if the user asks, "Does every company in North Hills except Supreme use NH2?", the answer may be "no" because Supreme is not in North Hills.

The current implementation of EUFID does not allow explicit negation, although some negative concepts are handled such as "What companies ship to companies other than Colonial?". "Other than" is interpreted as the"!="operator in exactly the same way that "greater than" is interpreted as " > ".

4.3 Interpretation and Database Issues

Many questions make perfect sense to a user but are difficult to present to the DBMS because of the database structure. The problems become worse when access is through an NLI because of increased expectations on the part of the user and because it may be difficult for a help system adequately to describe the problem to the user who is unaware of the database structure.

4.3.1 IL Limitations

The design of the IL is critical. It must be rich enough to support retrieval from all the underlying DBMSs. However, if it contains capabilities that do not exist in a specific DBMS, it is difficult to describe this deficiency to the user.

In APPLICANT, the user cannot get both the major and minor fields of study (two different attributes both relating the applicant relation to a "fields of education" relation) by asking "List applicants and field of study", because a limitation in the EUFID IL prevents making two different joins between education and subject records. This problem was corrected in a subsequent version of IL with the addition of a "range" statement similar to that used by QUEL [STON76].

The current IL does not contain an "EXISTS" or "FAILS" operator which can test for the existence of a record. Such an operator is frequently used to test an interrecord link in a network or hierarchical DBMS. It is needed to express

"What problems are unsolved?" to the AIREP application, which requires a test for a database link between a problem set and a solution set.

The definition of a completely general IL is possible, but the mapping from that IL into the query language of a weak DBMS might not be possible. If some DBMS is extremely weak, it is a poor candidate to have an NLI front end. When a generally complete DBMS lacks some specific features, a good translator may be able to overcome the deficiency by building temporary relations, by calling user defined functions, or by producing a procedural query. When some function simply can not be performed, a good help message is important.

4.3.2 Mixed Upper/Lower Case in Values

EUFID allows a value in the database to be upper or lower case and will convert a value in the question either to all upper or all lower case or leave it as input by the user.

If the database values are mixed case, it is not possible to convert the user's input to a single case. If the user does not enter each letter in the proper case, the value will not match. There is no simple, application-independent solution to this problem. The field perhaps should be declared a "retrieve only" field, or another mode such as a "list selection" mode should be entered. In "list selection" mode, all values in the domain are retrieved and displayed to the user who checks off the value or values desired. This method can be used only if there is a small set of values or if a subset of values can be recognized.

Differences in letter case can be handled for small databases in a process like EUFID's value conversion routine, but overuse of such a method would be prohibitive. It is also possible to match values entered by the user with values in the database by converting all characters to a common case during comparison. This will work if the comparison can be done in the DBMS. The NLI cannot make the comparison because to do so would require retrieving all entries in the field to make the case change and match. It will not work in an application where a change in the capitalization of a letter reflects a change in words meaning, such as the difference between "Polish" and "polish".

4.3.3 Granularity Differences

The NLI user is not expected to understand exactly how data is stored, and yet must understand something about the granularity of the data. Time fields often cause problems because time may be given by year or by fractions of a second. Users may make time comparisons that require more granularity than is stored in the database. For example, suppose the user asked "What incidents were reported at SITE1 while system release 3.4 was installed?". If incidents were reported by day but system release dates were given by month, the system might return incidents which occurred in the days of the month before the system release was installed.

This problem exists whether or not access is through the NLI. If there is control over the development of the database application, an effort may be made to use a common granularity for all fields that share a domain. This can only be done if the data can actually be collected with all comparable fields at the same granularity level. When it can not, it may be reasonable to have the user's conceptual view use the lowest common granularity, but then the user who accesses the database through the NLI is blocked from getting complete information from the database.

4.3.4 Nested Queries

A very simple question in English can turn into a very complicated request in the query language if it involves retrieval of data which must be used for qualification in another part of the same query. In IL these are called "nested queries". Most often some qualification needs to be done both "inside" and "outside" the clause of the query that does the internal retrieve. For example, the question "What incident at SITE1 had the longest downtime?" from our AIREP application is expressed in IL as

```
retrieve [AIR.ID]
where (AIR.SITENAME = "SITE1")
and (AIR.DNTM =
  {retrieve [max (AIR.DNTM)]
    where (AIR.SITENAME = "SITE1")})
```

The nested part of the query is enclosed in braces. "AIR" is the database name of the Active Incident Records. Notice that removing the "AIR.SITENAME = SITE1'" clause from either the inner or outer query would result in an incorrect formulation of the question.

A similar example from the METRO application is the question, "In 1980, what company shipped more than the 1979 average amount of light freight?" which will generate the IL query

```
retrieve [cct.scname]
where (cct.date = 1980)
and (cct.lf > =
  {retrieve [avg (cct.lf)]
    where (cct.date = 1979)})
```

Here, "cct" is the name of the company-to-company transaction relation. "scname" is the name of a shipping company in this relation. Note that we are using a different qualification on the cct relation in the inner and outer queries.

In the query language for INGRES such a request is expressed in a manner very similiar to the IL expressions. For WWDMS a very complex procedure is generated. In all cases, the DBMS needs to answer the inner request and save the result for use in qualifying the outer request. There are many database management systems that cannot handle such questions and these IL statements cannot be translated into the system's query language.

4.3.5 Inconsistency in Retrieval

The NLI presents a uniform view of all databases and DBMSs, but it is difficult to truly mask all differences in the behavior of the DBMSs because they do not all process the equivalent query in the same way. For example, when data are retrieved from two relations in a relational database, the two relations must be joined on a common attribute. The join forms a new relation which may be displayed to the user or stored. Since the join clause acts as qualification, a record (tuple) in either relation which has no corresponding tuple in the other relation does not participate in the result. This is a different concept from the hierarchical and network models where the system retrieves all records from a master record and then retrieves corresponding records from a subfile. This difference can cause anomalies with retrieval. For example, in a pure relational system "List applicants and their interviews" would be treated as "List applicants who have had interviews together with their interview information." A hierarchical or network DBMS would treat it as "List all applicants (whether or not they have been interviewed) plus any interview information that exists.". This second interpretation is more likely to be the one expected by the NLI user.

The developer of the NLI translator must have a detailed understanding of the operation of the DBMS, and the NLI must clearly explain the interpretation of the query to the user through feedback. The query might be rephrased in English or in a structured language.

4.4 Overall NLI Design

There are several problems that affect the selection of applications for the NLI. Some databases and data management systems may not be appropriate targets for natural-language interfaces. Some DBMS functions may be difficult to support. It is important to have a clear understanding of these problems so that the NLI can mediate between the user view, as represented by the natural-language questions, and the underlying database structure.

4.4.1 A Design Consideration

For any database there are natural-language questions that cannot be interpreted because the concepts involved lie outside the world of the database. Questions can also involve structural complexity that is not representable in the DBMS query language. A particularly difficult decision in the overall design of an NLI is the issue of where to trap these questions and stop processing in the chain of events of processing a user's question into a DBMS query.

One approach is to decide that if a question is not meaningful to the world of the database it should not be meaningful to the NLI and, therefore, not analyzable on semantic grounds. Another assumes that if the NLI can analyze a question that cannot be asked of the database, it has a much better chance of telling the user what is wrong with the question and how it might be rephrased to get the desired information.

Codd made good use of the dialogue procedures of the RENDEZVOUS system [CODD74] to avoid questions that the DBMS could not handle, as well as avoiding generation of DBMS queries that did not represent the user's intent. Such a system, however, requires a very large semantic base (much larger than that of the database) in order to make meaningful communication with the user during the dialogue.

In EUFID, an attempt was made in the analyzer to anticipate questions that cannot be mapped into the DBMS query language, but this forces the dictionary to contain some idiosyncratic rules. We believe that a better approach is to allow the question to flow through the system to the level at which the problem actually occurs. That is, the parser may find spelling errors, unrecognized words, and unconnected concepts; the mapper may find errors in mapping the concepts to database concepts; and the translator may find errors in expressing a particular query in the DBMS query language. The problem then becomes one of giving a reasonable error message to the user after many transformations of the query have occurred.

4.4.2 Class of Database to Support

Some databases are simply not good candidates for an NLI because of characteristics mentioned in previous sections such as many retrieve-only fields or domains that have a high update rate but cannot be recognized by a pattern.

There are also some structural problems that must be recognized. If the database contains "flat" files about one basic entity, it is reasonably easy to map queries and to explain problems to the user when the mapping cannot be made. However, there can be "reasonable" queries that cannot be answered directly because of the database structure. Hierarchical DBMSs present the most problems with navigation because access must start from the root. For example, if the APPLICANT database were under a hierarchical DBMS, the question "List the specialties for each applicant" could be answered directly but not "What are the specialties?" as there would be no way to get to the specialty records except via particular applicant records.

The concept of an array is difficult to handle in natural language, because it requires that the user have some understanding of the underlying data structure. An array allows more than one instance of a field or set of fields in a single record. There may be arrays of values or even arrays of sets of values in nonrelational databases. When the user retrieves a field that is an array the DBMS requires a subscript into the array. Either the user must specify this subscript or the

NLI must map to all members of the array with a test for missing data. This is not reasonable for large arrays.

Some repeating groups (arrays of sets of values) may be handled as logically independent relations in the user view. However, the relational view does not support an order on the repeating groups which may be significant. For example, in some applications, a repeating group is implicitly time ordered. In order to correctly handle this, the database may need to be restructured to add a time field to impose an order.

4.4.3 Class of DBMS to Support

For systems such as EUFID, the database must be organized within a data management system so that the data is structured and individual fields are named. If the data is plain text, the EUFID approach cannot be used. Text does not have individual fields labelled in any way, and a general scan through records for a match of values will locate many records that should not be returned to the user.

Current NLI systems are designed to be used interactively by a user, which means that the DBMS should also have an interactive query language. However, not all data management systems are interactive. WWDMS [HONE76] has a user query language, but queries are entered into a batch job queue and answers may not return for many minutes. If an NLI front end is to be added to such a DBMS, it must have the capability to generate query programs without any access to the database for parsing or for processing the returned answer.

The query language should support operations equivalent to the relational operations of select, project and join. Also, the query language should support some arithmetic capability. Most have aggregate functions such as SUM and COUNT. WWDMS does not have an easy-to-use average operation, but it does have a procedural language with arithmetic operators so that EUFID can produce a query that procedurally calculates an average.

Basic calculations should be supported such as "age = today - birthdate". It is also desirable to be able to call special functions to do complex calculations such as navigational calculations required in a naval database.

Several developers of natural language systems have built their own DBMS and integrated this with the NLI in order to get the exact functionality that they need. This can work for small databases, but it is very unlikely that these systems will operate efficiently on large databases. The development of a complete DBMS is a substantial effort that requires tens of man years. The DBMS must support recovery, protection, and database development, as well as a query language with a good optimizer. We believe, therefore, that the practical NLI-builder of today is well-advised to optimize his natural-language processing system and to interface to one or more existing DBMSs unless he has considerable experience in database management design and is willing to invest the time and effort needed to achieve a good DBMS.

4.4.4 Support for Metadata

Metadata is data about the data in the database. For EUFID's METRO application, for example, it would include a description of the information the database has for warehouses, companies, and other entities in the application. Such metadata might be extensions of active integrated data dictionaries now available in some DBMSs.

Ideally, the user should be able to query the metadata to learn about the *structure* of the database in the same mode that he uses to learn about the *content* of the database. A different mode, such as the menus used by the EUFID help system, can also be used to access metadata.

4.4.5 Updates

Some potential users would like a natural-language interface to include the capability to update the database. Currently, updating through any high level view of the database should be avoided, especially when the view contains joins or derived data, because of the risk of inadvertently entering incorrectly-interpreted data. If updates are allowed, the scope of the updates must be well defined, must be nonambiguous, and must be limited to changes in specific attribute values. For example, "Colonial shipped 500 units of light freight in 1976" is possible to handle through an NLI since it is a direct update to an attribute of a named entity, but "Colonial opened an office in North Hills" may create many new relationships that may need values for attributes.

5 Functional Comparisons of Natural-Language Systems

A reader of the problems that were encountered with EUFID may conclude either that NLIs are impossible or that commercial systems such as Intellect are magic. The truth lies somewhere in between. When the EUFID project began in 1976, the extent of the problem was not fully understood and therefore expectations were high. Today's commercial systems do not try to provide full functionality and this is perfectly adequate for many applications. In order to evaluate an NLI and determine whether it does or does not satisfy the requirements for an application, a functional evaluation must be done - both of the application and of the candidate NLIs.

In this section we present an outline that may be used for such a functional evaluation. The needs of the application should be ranked using categories such as these. Candidate NLIs, either commercial systems or one to be developed, should be rated using the same categories. The result will indicate whether a specific NLI can be expected to satisfy the users and what further development work needs to be done.

1 Language Coverage

1.1 *Extent of Verb Understanding*

Is the system limited to "What is ...", "Who has ..."?

Are tenses recognized as in "Who ships to x?" vs. "Who will ship to x?"

Is the difference between "Who ships to x?", "Who receives from x?" recognized?

Does the database contain basically entities and their attributes, in which case verbs are not needed, or does it have many relationships between entities?

1.2 *Value Recognition Methods*

How are values recognized? by pattern? by dictionary lookup? by database lookup? by context?

How are values input to the dictionary if this is done? manually? automatic capture of database updates?

Are approximate matches supported? phonetic match? upper/lower case differences ignored? don't care (wild card) characters? spelling correction on values?

Are multiple word values supported such as "North Hills"?

Can two attributes share some values such as "New York" for a city and a state field?

Can values also be content words as in "Who ships ships via ship?"

Can values be translated from user view to database view through functions or translate tables? Are the answers translated to the user values?

Can numbers be entered as words in addition to numerals?

Can numbers be used as names as in "IBM 4331"?

1.3 *Subordinate Clauses*

Does the system support clauses which modify an entity such as "What companies that are in North Hills ship to Colonial?"

Are subordinate clauses such as "What company ships to companies that receive from x?" which require a comparison to an independently retrieved set supported?

1.4 *Conjunctions*

Does it support conjunctions between the same entity as in "Who ships to A or B or C?"

Does it support conjunctions between clauses as in "Who ships to A or receives from B?"

Can it convert English "and" to logical "or" and vice versa?

How many conjunctions are allowed? Can it support "Who ships A and B to companies that receive from warehouse X or ship to office Y?"

1.5 *Negation*

Does it support verb negation as in "Who does not ship x?"

What negatives are supported? not? other than? except for? never? but not? neither ... nor? nothing?

Could it handle negation on attributes as in "... a company having no warehouse ..."?
Are the scoping rules for conjunctions and negations defined to the user?
Is there feedback on the scoping of the negation?

1.6 *Ellipsis*
Does it handle ellipsis within a query as in "What company ships to Colonial or to Ajax?"
Does it handle ellipsis across queries as in "What company ships to Colonial? To Ajax?"
How far back can an elliptical reference extend?
Are the scoping rules defined to the user?

1.7 *Anaphoric Reference*
Does it handle references within a query as in "What companies receive from companies that they ship to?"
Does it handle references across queries as in "What companies ship light freight? Where are they located?"
How far back can an anaphoric reference extend?
Are the scoping rules defined to the user?

1.8 *Subset*
Can the user define a subset of the database explicitly?
Through anaphoric reference?
How is it referenced?
How is it refined?
How is it cancelled?

1.9 *Yes/No Questions*
Can the user ask questions to which the correct answer is "yes" or "no"?
Does the system reply "yes" or "no"?
When there is a "yes" answer, does the system elaborate?
When there is a "no" answer, does the system explain why?

1.10 *Function Calls*
Can the system do the standard aggregate functions: sum, min, max, avg, and count?
Can the system produce a query that requires a calculation in the DBMS query language?
Can the system call special functions as in "How many ships are within 500 miles of San Diego?"

1.11 *Updates*
Can the user update through the NLI interface?
What restrictions are placed on update? to a single relation? to an existing tuple?
Are relation updates supported for building new relations? temporary relations from existing relations?

1.12 *View Support*

Can different users have different semantic level views? Can access to specific relations, fields, and tuples be restricted to specific users?

1.13 *Report Generator*

Can the user request formatted reports with headings, totals, sorts and breaks with subtotals?

Can the user call predefined reports with parameters?

Is output automatically paged on the terminal or does it fly across the screen?

Can the user scan or stop long output?

2 User Friendly Features

2.1 *Error Explanation*

To what extent can the system describe why a query will not parse or cannot be understood?

Is there interaction with the user to disambiguate a query?

Can the system describe why a query that did parse cannot be answered by the DBMS?

Can the user correct the error through system interaction or must he reenter the entire query?

Can the user cancel a query while entering it? While running it?

2.2 *Spelling Correction*

Does the system recognize misspelling of keywords? does it automatically correct the misspelling?

Does the system recognize misspelling of values? does it automatically correct the misspelling?

2.3 *Incorrect but Nonambiguous Queries*

Can the user make minor syntactic mistakes such as omitting "the" or making tense and number disagreements as in "How many company ships to warehouse?"

Does the system operate correctly in spite of the mistakes? correct them through user interaction?

2.4 *Metadata Queries*

Is there a built-in help facility?

Can the user ask English questions about the contents and structure of the database that are not answered by the database itself?

Can the user ask about the concepts in the database and how they relate?

Can the user ask about problems with formating a query?

2.5 *Synonym Replacement*

Can the user define synonyms? for a single word? for a phrase?

Are synonyms defined by the system administrator for all users? by users for all users? by individual users for themselves or for a group?

2.6 *Feedback*

Does the system display the interpretation to the user?

Can the user modify an incorrect interpretation?

Does the system estimate the time to answer a query? Give reassurance if there is a long wait?

3 Database Access Issues

3.1 *Degree of DBMS Independence*

Is the database separate from the NLI?

How difficult is it to interface the NLI to a new DBMS?

Can queries be routed to databases on remote computers?

3.2 *Degree of Application Independence*

Is the application definition separated from the basic parsing rules?

How long does it take to define a new application?

What level of expertise is required of the application builder?

How difficult is it to add new values? new concepts? new user views? change database structure?

3.3 *Join Support*

Can a query reference multiple relations? how many?

Must joins be predefined?

What different types of joins are supported: equijoin? outer join? self join? as in "List all employees and manager name if the employee earns more than his manager." where the manager tuple is an instance of an employee.

3.4 *Nested Queries*

Can the user ask queries involving retrieval of a set or aggregate and then use comparison to that retrieval as in: "What companies ship more than the average amount of freight?" "What companies ship to companies in Lakeland?"

3.5 *Group by*

Can the user request aggregates within a group as in: "List companies by neighborhood where there is some company in the neighborhood that ships to Colonial?" "List average shipments by neighborhood."

3.6 *Calculations*

Can the user retrieve calculated fields as in: "List light plus heavy freight shipments."

Can calculations cross relations?

3.7 *Existential and Universal Qualifiers*

Can the system differentiate between "all" and "some"? "Who ships to all companies in Lakeland?" vs. "Who ships to some company in Lakeland?"

3.8 *Repeating Groups*

Can the NLI access data in arrays and repeating groups?

Can the user reference specific instances of an array?

3.9 *Handling of Units and Granularity Differences*

Can conversions be made between user units and database units?

Can the user compare unlike units? as in "Will the Enterprise fit in berth 5?" (where ship length is in meters and berth length is in feet)

3.10 *Time*

Can the user ask for events within a time period as in "What events happened in May?"

Can time comparisons be made as in "What system was running when incident J123 occurred?"

Can consistent earlier database states be referenced?

3.11 *Deductive Inference*

Can facts be inferred that are not explicitly stored?

Can the user ask about hypothetical information as in "If Colonial opens an office in North Hills, will it be in competition with Ajax?"

4 Cost and Performance

4.1 *Development Cost*

What is the cost to develop a new application? to modify it?

What is the cost of the NLI?

What size computer is required to get "real time" response for one user? for 10?

4.2 *Response Time*

Is the response time fast enough to prevent user irritation? on correct queries? on incorrect queries?

6 Summary and Conclusions

For many years, researchers have been attempting to build robust systems for natural-language access to databases. It is not clear that such a system yet exists for general use [OSI79]. There are problems that need to be solved on both the front end, the parsing of the English question, and the back end, the translation of the question into a data management system query. It is important to understand the types of requests, types of functions, and types of databases that can be supported by a specific NLI.

Some general guidelines that can be applied to the selection of applications for current NLI front ends are suggested below:

1. the application should be implemented on a DBMS that has an interactive query language,
2. the DBMS underlying the application should be relational or at least support multiple access paths,
3. the database for the application should not contain arrays either of values or of structures,
4. the input must be controlled to standardize values,
5. there should be few fields that have values that change rapidly, cannot be recognized by a pattern, and that must be used in qualification,
6. the users of the application should have a common use for the data and a common view of the data, and
7. there must be some user who understands the questions that will be asked and is available to work with the developers of the NLI.

We believe that current system development is limited by the need for good semantic modelling techniques and the length of time needed to build the knowledge base required to interface with a new application. When the knowledge base for the NLI is developed, the database as well as sample input must be considered in the design. Parsing of questions to a database cannot be divorced from the database content since semantic interpretation can only be determined in the context of that database. On the other hand, a robust system cannot be developed by considering only database structure and content, because the range of the questions allowed would not accurately reflect the user view of the application and also would not account for all the information that is inferrred at some level.

References

[AHOU72], [BURG75], [BURG80], [CODD74], [CULL80], [DAME81], [DATE77], [EDP82], [GROS83a], [HARR78], [HEND78c], [HONE76], [KELL71], [MART83], [MYLO76], [OLNE78], [OSI79], [SCHA77], [SIMM65], [STON76], [SYST83], [TEMP79], [TEMP80], [THOM69], [THOM83], [WALT77], [WALT78], [WOOD72]

Chapter 4

Studies in the Evaluation of a Domain-Independent Natural Language Query System

Matthias Jarke, Jürgen Krause, and Yannis Vassiliou

Abstract. There is growing consensus that some of the most crucial questions concerning the feasibility and desirability of natural language interfaces to databases can only be resolved by empirical research. This paper reports the results of several empirical studies which investigated the same domain-independent natural language query system, using various applications in two different natural languages - English and German. Taken together, these experiments involved about 100 subjects and over 12000 queries, constituting the bulk of empirical evaluations of natural query language systems reported to date. Some definitive results are derived from the combined experience, and plans are outlined to resolve several of the remaining issues.

1 Introduction

A large number of natural language interfaces (NLI) to information systems have been developed. The continued research interest is evidenced, for example, by no less than 45 papers in [BUND 83]. In industry, early skepticism seems to have given way to last-minute panic: there is hardly a major computer company or software house that is not working on product development.

On the other hand, many practical questions remain unresolved. Fierce battles are still being fought over the best overall architecture for implementing NLI, or - more basically - whether NLI are preferable at all to formal query languages designed with human factors in mind. The problem of how the alternative hypotheses can be verified or at least be made more plausible remains open. Besides this problem of evaluation methodology, three central questions concerning NLI themselves are still awaiting an answer.

1) Can NLI be implemented at all? It seems clear that a full natural language system corresponding to interhuman communication is presently infeasible; any practice-oriented NLI must be application-specific. On the other hand, a NLI would be unacceptable if each user required support by language engineers for an excessive period of time, if the subset of natural language that can be implemented efficiently were not sufficient to support a practical ap-

plication, or if users had insurmountable difficulties recognizing the boundaries of the implemented subset.

2) If NLI can be implemented, do they support human problem solving more successfully than competing end user interfaces, such as formal query languages? A meaningful answer to this question requires measurements beyond the percentage of submitted queries that is accepted by a system.
3) How difficult is it to transport a NLI to a new application? This question is important since it may not be economically feasible to develop a completely new NLI for each new application - and maybe for each user of each application!

These questions must be further refined by user type and application area as well as by type of NLI. This paper focuses on NLI for database querying (NLQS)[1]. Within this group, two essentially different approaches can be distinguished: domain-specific NLQS in which a large portion of the system has to be redeveloped for each new application, and domain-independent systems in which most of the system is portable between applications and the parts to be changed are clearly isolated and relatively small.

Shwartz [SHWA 84] contrasts a *knowledge-based* domain-specific NLI called EXPLORER with domain-independent restricted *subset* systems, which draw on general language knowledge, application-specific vocabularies, and the database itself. He concludes:

> "Natural language systems lacking a knowledge base cannot understand anywhere near as wide a range of information retrieval requests as can knowledge-based systems." (p. 247)

The subset type of NLI, rejected by Shwartz and others [MALK 82, MORI 82], is the focus of this paper. One reason is that only subset systems have reached a degree of maturity where they can be subjected to rigorous empirical testing. There is no indication that this will change in the near future. Indeed, the only commercially successful NLI so far, Intellect [AIC 82], is of the subset type. Unfortunately, no formal performance studies of Intellect have been reported, although some global figures for its predecessor, ROBOT, appear in [HARR 77 c].

The paper examines the three questions raised above in the context of a particular restricted subset NLQS which represents this type of natural language system in a rather pure from. There seems to be no NLQS or other NLI that has been subjected to a comparable number of empirical studies. The first objective of this paper is to present - in a common framework - the experience gained from multiple evaluation methods applied to the same system. A second objec-

[1] For a survey of other natural language applications, see [WALT 83].

tive is to contribute to a better understanding of the overall feasibility and desirability of the domain-independent approach to NLI, based on the empirical assessment of one specific system.

In sect. 2, the NLQS under study is briefly described and a global framework for NLI evaluation methods is given. Sections 3 through 5 describe the design and results of several empirical studies of the NLQS. Section 6 presents a synopsis of the results concerning experimental methodology and NLI performance. Discrepancies and open questions requiring additional research are highlighted. Section 7 briefly summarizes the general conclusions.

2 Research Overview

2.1 Natural Language Query System

The NLQS whose evaluation is reported here [LEHM 78 a, OTT 79 b, OTTZ 80] provides a natural language interface (English, German, Spanish [ZOEP 84 a]) to relational databases. The system does not engage the user in clarification dialog, and to that extent it is similar to any formal database query language. Structurally, the NLQS consists of a generalized parser, a semantic analyzer and executor, and a generalized DBMS (Fig. 2.1). In the sequel, structure and main objectives of the system will be briefly reviewed.

System Structure. The *parser* [BERT 81] accepts general phrase structure grammars written in a modified Backus-Naur form. All parses are produced in parallel, bottom-up, and from right to left. Arbitrary routines can be invoked with any rule. The vocabulary is presented to the parser as part of the grammar. The *semantic analyzer and executor* [LEHM 78 a] consists of a set of interpretation routines which translate the syntactic structures to DBMS executable code. The formal query language SQL serves as the target database query language, supported by the third component - a *relational DBMS* [ASTR 76]. View definitions relate the vocabulary to the database fields. In another version - which was used for the early empirical studies - the experimental relational database system PRTV [TODD 76] was used as the target DBMS and the target language for translation was relational algebra (ISBL).

Transportability. The system emphasizes transportability across application domains, in the same way formal database query languages do. Moreover, it even achieves transportability across natural languages (from German to English, Spanish, and Dutch).

The goal of transportability has three major consequences that influence the design of the NLQS. First, only an application-independent kernel vocabulary is provided. It is the responsibility of the application developer(s) to build a special

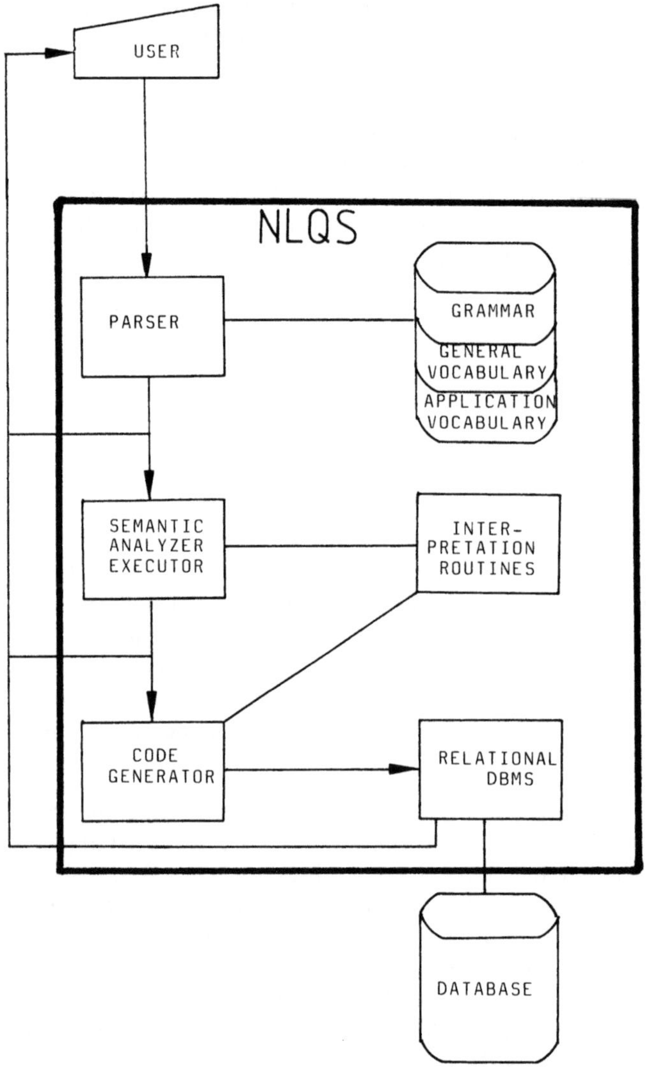

Fig. 2.1. Structure of the natural language query system

application vocabulary. Second, the linguistic component (information about language) is completely separated from the database component (information about domain and data retrieval). Finally, the system has few application-dependent deductive capabilities (the only exceptions being view definitions and the mathematical functions provided by the target language) which draw inferences from stored data and try to understand user intentions. Thus, the system provides limited feedback and seldom assumes control of the interaction.

Application-Specialist Computer-Novice Users. The system requires users to know their application well and to be able to compose questions in their native language. The intended users are neither EDP professionals (having, e.g., database skills) nor linguists. Users are also expected to define their own application-specific vocabulary. Consequently, the system is designed so that the generation of the application vocabulary should neither be a complex process nor require special database and linguistic expertise. This implies certain restrictions in the amount of application-specific linguistic information that can be provided to the system (e.g., no word semantic).

Syntax-Based System. To compensate for the lack of application-specific knowledge bases (which exist only in the form of SQL view definitions), the NLQS goes great lengths in exploiting the systematic connections between syntax and semantics of natural language. Syntactic structures carry meaning which is independent of the application domain. Consequently, the system's grammar is designed with emphasis on this kind of meaning.

2.2 Basic Evaluation Methodologies

The simplest and most widely used approach for the evaluation of NLI is the exchange of intuitive arguments about implementation techniques and language features. For example, the information about natural language systems found in the literature is typically highlighted with a list of supported features (e.g., coordination or ellipsis, see [CODD 78] and chap. 3 in this volume).

Such a list is only useful for the features not included. It can be very misleading since it rarely addresses the important question: "to what degree is the feature supported?" Therefore, it becomes almost impossible to effectively evaluate the usability of any system based on the information given by the system description. Furthermore, it has been shown [LEHM 79, KRAU 80 a, KRAU 82, STOH 82] that opposing arguments of comparable plausibility are confronted without much prospect for a purely argumentative synthesis. There is growing consensus [PETR 76, FINN 79] that only *empirical evaluation* research can lead out of this dilemma.

Answering the three questions, set forth in the introduction with respect to the domain-independent type of NLI, requires a carefully designed methodology for generating and verifying research questions. In this subsection, some of the basic design parameters for empirical investigations of NLQS will be analyzed. The leftmost two columns of Table 2.1 provide an overview of such parameters (compare also [KRAU 82, JARK 83, TURN 84]).

Evaluation Team. The first step in evaluating a natural language system empirically is an on-site test of the parser, often termed as an acceptance test. One or more 'toy' databases are created, and a series of queries are run against these databases by the system designers. Such studies attempt to test supposedly typical, as well as pathological queries. After an iterative process (each iteration corre-

Table 2.1. Design parameters for empirical NLQS evaluation studies and characterization of the studies reported in this paper

Decision variable	Design alternatives	Stage A	Stage B	Stage C
evaluation team	designers	×		
	outside researchers		×	×
evaluation strategy	absolute	×	× field	
	comparative		(×) lab	×
evaluation criteria	quantitative:			
	success	×	×	×
	effort		(×)	×
	qualitative:			
	problems	(×)	×	(×)
	strategies		×	
	level:			
	work task			×
	query	×	×	×
evaluation object	simulated NLI			(×)
	real NLI	×	×	×
type of study	laboratory experiment		(×)	×
	field study	×	×	×
subject selection	students		× lab	
	paid subjects			×
	end users, novices	×	× KFG	
	end users, experts	×	× TA	
database and application	structure:			
	simple	×		
	medium	×	×	×
	complex			
	size:			
	small	×	×	× lab
	large			× field

sponding to an improvement of the grammar and the interpretation routines) the system may reach a steady 'acceptable' state.

There is certainly a need for performing this kind of evaluation but there is also the danger of deriving optimistic conclusions about the usability of the system, after attaining a steady state, or of abandoning useful research efforts if a steady state is not reached. (This happened, for example, to the German natural language systems PLIDIS [KOLV 79] and CONDOR [FISC 82], see [KRAU 83 a].) The system designers cannot be termed 'objective' evaluators. Their vested interest and their detailed knowledge of system capabilities blur their ability to distinguish the needs of future actual users from what the designers want these users to do. In addition, the test applications are commonly several orders of magnitude smaller and conceptually less complex than 'real' applications. Most natural language systems have terminated the evaluation after this acceptance test (unless local test evaluation proved to be a non-ending process.)

Better control is provided by formal evaluation studies conducted by researchers outside the design team. Such an empirical evaluation can be seen as part of a cost-benefit analysis required before introducing a query language into an actual user environment [JARK 85 b]. Several design decisions are of critical importance in this process (cf. Table 2.1).

Evaluation Strategy. The first issue is whether the NLI should be evaluated in the absolute or compared to a competing interface, such as a formal query language. Some useful analyses (e.g., of user problem solving strategies) can be performed in the first case. However, performance evaluations using this strategy are meaningful only if the system under study is either close to perfect, or the results are so disastrous that any alternative would be preferable. Otherwise, a comparative study is necessary.

Evaluation Criteria. This discussion leads to the second design question: how can one measure the costs and benefits of a natural language user interface? Of interest are: the success rate of users working with the system, the effort to achieve such success (or failure), the language and system related problems, the strategies users develop to work around the limitations, and, last but not least, the subjective perceptions and opinions of the users. Additional criteria may be required to control for confounding outside factors.

Orthogonal to these criteria are the amount of skills the user has acquired [SCHN 84], and the level on which performance is evaluated. The former refers to the differentiation between learning and routine task performance [MORA 81], which is closely related to the definition of user types [JARK 85 b, VASS 84]. The latter addresses the distinction between the solution of a problem or work task, for which the database is a tool among others employed by the user, and the generation of an answer to a specific database query.

Evaluation Object. The organizational setting of the study must be decided. Some studies assume a simulated rather than a real NLI (e.g., [CHAP 73, SMAL 77, SHNE 80, MILL 81]). Studies of this type can give valuable hints concerning the desirability of NLI but are usually unsuited for establishing their feasibility.

Type of Study. A more important distinction is between laboratory experiments and field studies of real systems. Laboratory experiments allow for a controlled setting. Methodologies to run them have been extensively studied, and the experiments are economically affordable. Such studies, if performed correctly, are best suited for examining the short-term 'learnability' of a language, identifying language constructs likely to cause user difficulties, and for estimating the number and type of words used for a particular set of tasks, as well as the language features most likely to be employed.

On the other hand, drawing practical conclusions about the overall usability of a natural language system from laboratory experiments may be dangerous [REIS 81]. For example, it is not clear whether field performance will be superior or inferior to laboratory performance, or which factors influence the difference. Surveys of laboratory studies of query languages are given in [REIS 81, JARK 85 b]. The most frequently studied language is SQL which has shown a consistent performance of 55–70% correct queries in paper and pencil tests after a few hours of training. Laboratory studies of NLQS, most not employing real systems, are surveyed in [LEHM 79].

Despite the critical remarks by Petrick [PETR 76] and Tennant [TENN 79], the lack of field studies has hardly changed. Aside from the studies described in this paper, the main exception is a year-long field study of TQA, yielding about 700 queries with an acceptance quota of approximately 65% ([DAME 79], see also chap. 5 in this volume). However, the setting did not allow for the implementation of detailed controls, nor was this intended. Some even more informal studies [WOOD 77 a, HARR 77 c] report only about 20% language-related errors but disregard certain other kinds of failure of the man-machine communication. In general, field studies should be suitable for the evaluation of actual task performance over an extended time period if close observation or carefully designed controls permit the elimination of outside confounding factors. A research design which couples field studies with laboratory experiments, in a way that combines the strengths and reduces the weaknesses of both methods, seems most promising.

Subject Selection. The type and intrinsic motivation of users often has a strong impact on the results of laboratory and field studies. The preferred type of users, actual end users, can be quite demanding and may actually abandon system usage if an alternative way to solve their problems is available. On the other hand, student subjects may be less motivated to achieve good performance. The intermediate solution, using paid subjects, may yield good results if their compensation is related to their success with the system or a good motivation can be achieved in a different way.

Database and Application. Last but not least, the size and complexity of both the application domain and the underlying database may influence the outcome of the experiments, by response time effects [BARB 83] as well as by the impact of complexity on the user's ability to fully understand the application.

2.3 Overview of Evaluation Studies

Experiments with the NLQS have been conducted by different research groups (IBM Scientific Center Heidelberg, University of Regensburg, New York University), using two different natural languages (German and English) and various experimental designs. Three stages of experimentation can be distinguished.

In the first phase (stage A), the development team tested the system informally to uncover errors and gaps in coverage. The second set of experiments (stage B, the KFG study at Heidelberg and at the University of Regensburg since 1978) was still performed in part at the development site and with technical support by the development team but by an external researcher. At the heart of these experiments was a long term (16 months) observation of a single user working on a practical application. Detailed qualitative analyses were performed, and the original field study was complemented by another field study and several minor laboratory experiments.

For the third series of experiments (stage C, the Advanced Language Project (ALP) at New York University from 1981-1983), the system was transfered to a different natural language (English), and to a site where little linguistic or technical support by the development team was available. A quantitatively oriented evaluation strategy was chosen for comparing the NLI to a formal database query language in a partially controlled field study and two controlled laboratory experiments.

The rightmost columns of Table 2.1 characterize each of the three stages by the design parameters presented in the previous section. The following sections provide more detailed information about each stage.

3 Stage A: Smaller Application Studies

Since 1976, the development team tested the system in a series of small evaluation studies on real applications. However, with the exception of one application (SCHOOL), no actual field usage was reached since high error rates required continuous drastic changes of the prototype. An attempted comparison of the NLQS with another natural language interface [KETT 81] failed because the second interface was not ready for use.

An overview of this first stage of system evaluation is given in [LEHM 78] where 451 questions of these tests were analyzed. Krause and Lehmann [KRAU 80 b], and Zoeppritz [ZOEP 83] describe the application areas.

1. *PLANNING* (1976). Data on customers for planning purposes. Two users submitted 59 queries at an error rate of 46%.
2. *SCHOOL* (1977). Data on school attendance and background of pupils. One user submitted 356 queries at an error rate of about 13%.
3. *RECEPTION* (1977). The database contained information about departments. Receptionists used the NLQS to help visitors find appropriate people to answer questions. One user submitted 115 queries at an error rate of 47%.
4. *ROOMS* (1978). Allocation of rooms and office space. Three users submitted 781 queries at an error rate of about 40%.

The tests of stage A can be regarded as debugging tests, attempts to detect functional and grammatical gaps, and trials to obtain hints with respect to the size of the necessary subset and the transportability of the system. All tests of stage A used the German version; no comparison with formal query languages was attempted.

4 Stage B: KFG Study and Related Tests

4.1 Project History and Study Description

The evaluation studies of stage B can be seen as parts of an extended evaluation scheme, outlined in Fig. 4.1. The plan starts with a real application to be analyzed in a field study. Laboratory experiments are based on a typical session of

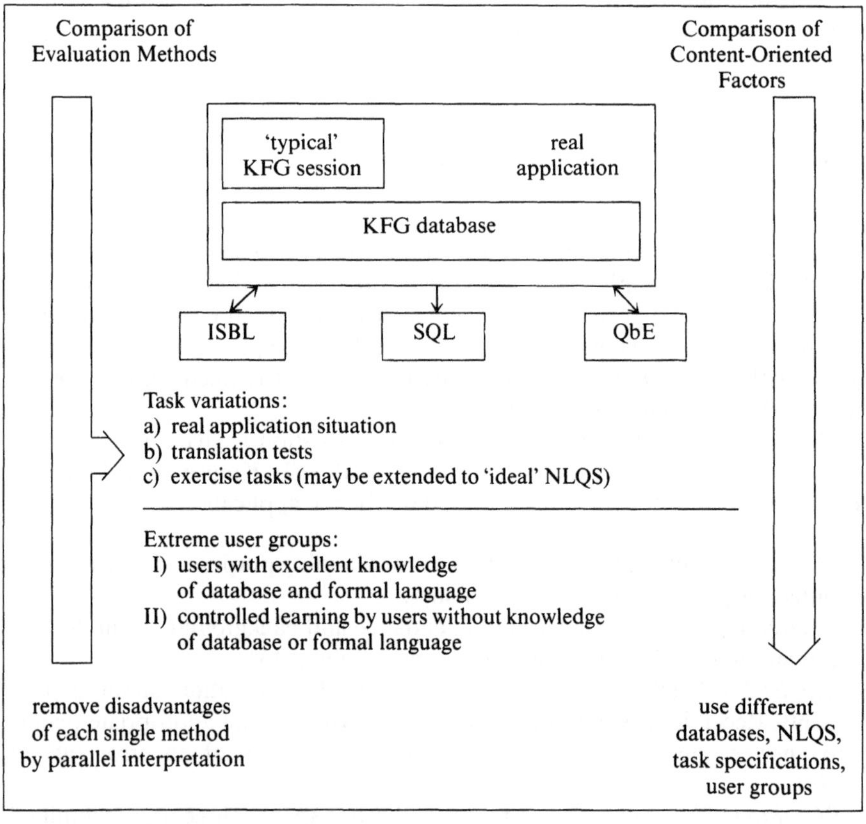

Fig. 4.1. Evaluation plan - KFG studies

this real application. "Typical" means, among other things, that the session contains a representative mixture of dialog types, the linguistic structures of the overall study are represented, and the error rate is near the average. The three formal query languages mentioned in Fig. 4.1 could be changed. It is only important to select types of query languages which have been proposed (or used in practice) for efficient man-machine-interaction.

ISBL, as an example for algebraic query languages, and SQL were advantageous for comparison with the NLQS because the parser translated the natural language queries initially into ISBL, and since 1981 into SQL. The proposed user groups in Fig. 4.1 are extreme points of a broad spectrum of possibilities. One may hypothesize that using different groups is best suited to uncover the common trends.

The field studies and laboratory experiments of stage B consisted of three subgroups:

1. A field study with teachers of the Karl-Friedrich-Gymnasium (KFG) at Mannheim, West Germany (the KFG field study).
2. An effort to transport the same system version to another application (the TA field study).
3. Several laboratory tests to compare error rates in the KFG field study with those achieved by using formal query languages.

4.1.1 KFG Field Study

The KFG field study was carried out by three teachers, supported by the system development team. The teachers wanted to analyze data on student development. For instance, they wanted to know whether low grades in mathematics in earlier years have predictive power for grades at graduation. Typical questions were:

"Wieviele Schüler gehen in Untertertia?"
(How many students attend class 8?)

"Liste die Schüler, die nicht versetzt in Sexta sind."
(List students who are not promoted in class 5.)

The database contained 41 250 grades for 430 students and further information about social background and class repetition. Between August 1978 and September 1979, 7278 questions were asked in 46 sessions. The users worked 157 hours and 26 minutes with the system. Unfortunately, 6603 questions were submitted by a single teacher. Therefore, the KFG field study is in its substance a one-user study, extended by a smaller set of 675 questions by two more users.

4.1.2 TA Study

A preliminary evaluation of the KFG field study [KRAU 80 a] showed that there was a real-world application, which could be queried in a natural language subset with an overall error rate of only 7%. Therefore, a second field study was prepared whose aim was to test whether the successful KFG version could easily be transported to a new application.

The application area of the study was a technical service department of IBM (Technischer Aussendienst = TA). The database included information about EDP systems for which the TA was responsible. The main information groups were: maintenance hours per month and EDP system, details of the systems, the customers, and the organization responsible for the customer. For example, a typical question was:

"Liste die Teams des Wartungsgebietes 424."
(List the teams of maintenance area 424).

The first user was an employee who had worked with the database for five years, using the formal query language IQRP [IBM 76]. Initially, it was planned to bring in other users who had no knowledge of formal query languages. Since it was not possible to build up a version of the TA application with an error rate tolerated by the user (the error rate was about 53% [KRAU 82, chap. 5]), however, the only data for the TA study consisted of queries by the experienced user, submitted in pretests between April 1979 and September 1979.

4.1.3 Laboratory Experiments

The KFG field study was supplemented by laboratory experiments intended to determine whether users could have achieved comparable success with a formal query language, and to measure the time required to learn a formal query language.

4.2 Methodology

4.2.1 KFG Field Study: Research Design and Evaluation Parameters

On the background of the overall evaluation plan, the stage B evaluation reached only some preliminary results. Nevertheless, in particular the KFG field study offers a large amount of experimental data. The analysis used the following primary data:

Computer protocols of the terminal sessions. Each user query, and the responses of the NLQS were stored automatically for later interpretation.

Observations of the users during the terminal sessions. The observer sat next to the user during the sessions. He introduced himself as a researcher with only superficial knowledge of the system, interested in knowing how the user worked with it and what improvements he might desire. The user was not led to expect the observer to help him with any difficulty [KRAU 80 a].

Questionnaires [OTT 79 a] and general statements of the users.

Comments of the users on the results obtained (worked out by the user, when reviewing the results of a session at home). For instance, the user reported which aspects of his problem had been solved.

Results the users achieved (in the case of the KFG field study a research paper written by a user [SCHU 79 b]).

One of the main difficulties in analyzing primary data is the detection, statistical description and detailed study of those phenomena which offer promise for plausible interpretations of general patterns. In the KFG field study, error information proved to be most instructive. Each situation in which the man-machine dialogue failed was defined as an error. Absolute and relative error rates were measured, extensive error classification was performed, and the distribution of the errors over sessions or with respect to different dialogue types was determined. Additionally, the error handling strategies of the user were analyzed, as the basis of an examination of error chains (the starting error and all following errors).

4.2.2 Laboratory Experiments: Research Design and Evaluation Methodology

To compare user performance in the NLQS against a formal query language, five user groups were asked to translate 81 questions from a typical session of the KFG field study into the formal language, ISBL. Group 1 consisted of two users with several years of experience with ISBL who knew the KFG database well and therefore required no training. Groups 2, 3 and 4 consisted of students (altogether 20), who learned ISBL in a controlled procedure before the test. It has been argued that tests with students do not not yield results that are representative for real usage; typical user groups might have more difficulties in learning a formal language. Therefore, six secretaries (group 5) with experience in word processing were trained and tested in the same way as the student groups [KRAU 83 b, KRAU 83 c].

All groups were built up at random. The members of the three student groups attended courses in the department of Linguistic Information Science at the University of Regensburg, and the secretaries were employees of projects in the same department. Thus, the laboratory experiments of the KFG study have the status of pretests, rather than of statistically adequate experiments.

4.3 Experimental Results from stage B

The presentation will be limited to a brief summary of general results, and will omit those data which can be explained by the prototype status of the system (see [KRAU 82]). The experiments provided insights regarding the form of a natural language subset, as well as regarding the correctness of several arguments for and against natural language as a query language for databases.

4.3.1 Results with respect to Some Individual Problems

The literature contains various arguments concerning response time, conciseness of query formulation, change of query patterns over time, and learning time of natural language systems as compared to formal query languages. The stage B studies provided some partial answers to these questions.

Response Time. It has been argued (see, for instance, Ghosh [GHOS 77]) that, in practice, natural language interfaces require an unacceptable amount of computer time for parsing the natural language query. The KFG field study typically showed additional CPU requirements of about 1.5 CPU-seconds for natural language queries over formal language queries (on an IBM 370/145). This means that it is possible to develop natural language translators which work acceptably fast. (This statement does not necessarily cover potential problems resulting from a very large database in combination with a possibly inefficient translation of natural language requests, see sect. 5.)

Conciseness. Woods [WOOD 77 b] suggested as an advantage of formal language queries that formal expressions are more concise than natural language queries. The translation of typical KFG and TA questions into the formal query languages ISBL, IQRP and SQL showed that this conjecture does not hold in reality. Particularly in SQL, one has to expect longer input strings than with NLQS.

Changing Requirements. Malhotra [MALH 75], Woods [WOOD 77 a], and Harris [HARR 77 c] expected based on of observations in shorter evaluation studies that the queries in long term studies could become more and more complicated. The KFG field study did not confirm this fear.

Learning Time. One of the main arguments against the use of formal query languages is that inexperienced users need too much learning time. This hypothesis in favor of natural language could not be verified. Three groups of students could translate the questions of a typical session of the KFG field study into ISBL (in part with fewer errors than the user in the field study) after a maximum learning period of six hours and forty minutes (6-11% errors). These results indicate that the users of the KFG field study might have been perfectly capable of acquiring ISBL skills rather fast. The test with the six secretaries confirmed this results [KRAU 83 b]. After 11 hours of training, they were able to use a formal query language with reasonable success. On the other hand, it seemed that learning a formal language can be a major psychological burden, especially for older users. Because of the nature of the selected tests, the effects of two factors cannot be predicted:

1. The possibility of forgetting the rules of the formal query language after a period of time was not taken into consideration.
2. The concentration of the user might be diverted from the problem to be solved by constructing the formal ISBL expression. This could lead to poorer problem solving than in the application of natural language.

4.3.2 Results with Respect to the Subset Definition

There were mainly three results concerning the problem of how to define the language subset of a practice-oriented NLQS.

The KFG and TA evaluation study confirmed that restricting the application area leads to a considerable *simplification of language analysis*. The vocabulary for all of the system's applications to date falls in the range between 149 and 313 words [ZOEP 84 b]. These observations agree with those made in other practice oriented natural language interfaces (see for instance [HEND 78 a, WALT 78]).

Surface structural variations (for example: "Schueler, die nicht versetzt sind", students who are not promoted, instead of "nicht versetzte Schueler", non-promoted students) are used extensively, even though there is no difference at all, as far as the expected answer is concerned. This result is in contrast with the assumption that users will not change successful input patterns and will generally prefer shorter formulations to reduce input time.

As a corollary, individual *error categories* cause interruptions of varying strength and nature in the man-machine interaction. Errors caused by surface phenomena (for example, word order) lead to serious difficulties [KRAU 82]. The user is often unable to develop effective error strategies, or to learn the restrictions of the language system in order to avoid 'dangerous' constructs. For example, the NLQS recognized only "Schüler, die nicht versetzt in Sexta sind" (Students who are not promoted in class 5), whereas the user wrote: "Schüler, die nicht versetzt sind in Sexta." On the other hand, users can develop successful strategies for errors based on application or user dependent word semantics (where, for example, a synonymous word is not defined).

4.3.3 Conclusions from Stage B

It does not seem promising to work with heavy restrictions in the area of surface structures when defining a subset for natural language interfaces to databases. Possibilities of variation are used extensively and serious interruptions in man-machine interaction occur when the subset barriers concerning surface structure rules are exceeded. However, it appears that application and user dependent semantics remain within narrow confines. This means that the problem of ambiguity is reduced, the quantity of words to be defined is small, necessary relations can be sufficiently well established before the start of a study, and exceeding the subset boundaries causes only minor and easily manageable breaks in man-machine interactions.

From the results of the KFG field study, the realization of functionally capable natural language query components appears to be possible for the user group of application experts. Remaining problems include determining the nature and size of suitable application fields (transferability), and the relative performance in comparison with formal query languages. Natural language queries are not always superior to formal language queries, and vice versa.

5 Stage C: The Advanced Language Project at New York University

5.1 Project History and Study Description

The purpose of the Advanced Language Project (ALP) was to study the English language version of the system in a real application, and in a location remote from that of the development team. The application, a question-answering system about alumni of the Graduate School of Business Administration at New York University, maintains demographic data and donation histories of school alumni, foundations, other organizations, and individuals. There are over 40000 graduates as well as some 5000 non-graduates who have given to the school over the past 20 years. The ALP database contained four base relations with approximately 100000 tuples, substantially more than in previous applications. Data retrieved from this database usually serve as a basis for decision making in fund raising drives.

The research centered on the question of whether - in this setting - the system (as an example for a transportable NLQS) is superior to a formal query language, such as SQL, in terms of learnability, problem-solving success, or effort to use. A comparative study design and mostly quantitative evaluation criteria were chosen for all experiments.

The project design coupled a field study with two controlled laboratory experiments. The experiments began in 1981 with the design and generation of the database and of the application-specific vocabulary, followed by the application and language training and testing of 8 experimental subjects. This skill acquisition phase was organized as a controlled laboratory experiment. After subjects had reached sufficient proficiency in application and language, they performed real work tasks in the actual setting for more than six months (the field study). The field study raised several additional research questions, and the results of the first laboratory test had to be confirmed with a larger number of subjects. Therefore, a second laboratory experiment with 61 subjects was conducted as a paper-and-pencil test in late 1982.

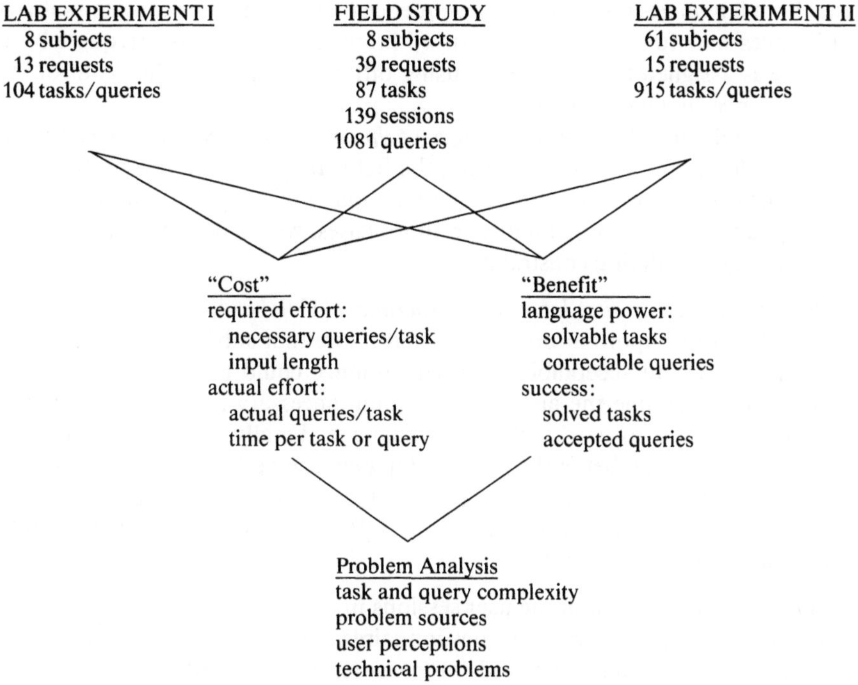

Fig. 5.1. Evaluation plan and descriptive statistics - ALP studies

5.2 *Methodology*

Global design and descriptive statistics of the ALP project are summarized in Fig. 5.1. In the following two subsections, the designs of the field study (together with the first laboratory experiment) and the major laboratory experiment are described.

5.2.1 ALP Field Study: Research Design and Evaluation Parameters

Control of Outside Factors. The decision for a comparative and quantitatively oriented approach inspired a need to control for differences in outside factors, which could blur the results. This problem strongly influenced the research design for the field study.

The first control measure was to use *paid intermediaries* serving the information users or clients. This not only reduced the danger of losing users due to possibly poor performance of the prototype, but it also increased the number of users for statistical purposes.

Furthermore, the use of intermediaries enabled a *counterbalanced and matched* design. The field study was divided into two phases so that each subject used both languages but in different sequence (controlling both for inter-subject differences and for order effects). In addition, each work task (request by a client) was assigned to two subjects using different languages, thus controlling for differences in task complexity.

As a final control measure, *changes of the application-specific system portion* were avoided as far as possible during the field study - only a few problems in the English version were corrected - and a number of *complexity measures* were developed to ensure comparability in those cases, where perfect matching was prevented by scheduling constraints.

Skill Acquisition. The *first laboratory experiment* [TURN 84] served several purposes. The most important one was to make sure that subjects had acquired a level of skill, where acceptable field performance could be expected. Another goal was to determine the amount of training necessary for using a restricted NLI as compared to a formal query language. Finally, the experiment was needed to understand better the relationship between performance in laboratory and field settings; the use of the same subjects, application, and languages seemed to carry some promise in this respect. Previous studies of SQL were used to partially validate the results.

Evaluation Criteria. Data of the user sessions in the *field study* [JARK 85 a] were captured from session logs and questionnaires, and coded using a multi-level coding scheme. The following kinds of measures were applied:

1. Success of subjects in solving decision-support oriented problems, and in phrasing queries acceptable to the system.
2. Effort required for solving the problem (in terms of input length and of time spent).
3. Factors inside and outside the languages that influence success and effort.
4. User reactions to the languages.

These measures apply at four different *levels of measurement* (Fig. 5.2). The main goal is to answer an information *request*, i.e., a problem description given by a client. Each request was given to one or more subjects as *tasks* to be solved in

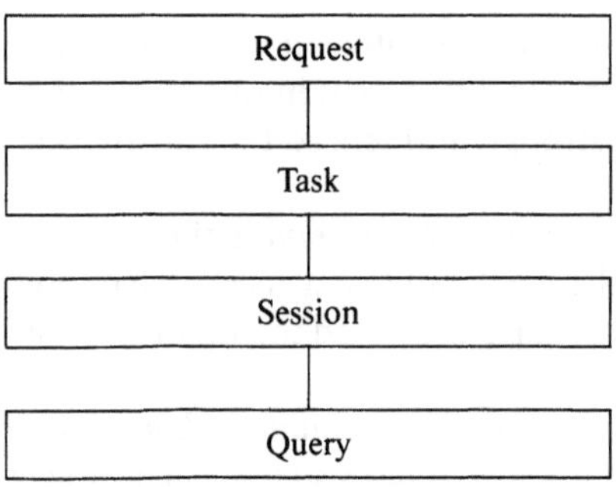

Fig. 5.2. Evaluation hierarchy for the ALP field study

their assigned language. The subject could work on a task during one or more continuous *sessions*. During a session, the subject submitted one or more *queries* to the system. A system evaluation at the query level alone has been common in laboratory experiments with query languages which frequently use translation tasks for testing. However, in the field setting, this approach was deemed insufficient since it does not capture the contribution of each query to overall task performance.

At all levels, coding of session logs and questionnaires was performed independently by at least two persons, namely one of the researchers and one or more graduate research assistants. In addition, redundancy was designed into the criteria definitions that permitted computerized consistency controls to be implemented.

5.2.2 Laboratory Experiment: Research Design and Evaluation Methodology

The paid subjects of the second laboratory experiment [VASS 83 a] were 61 business graduate and undergraduate students. This type of subjects has been termed as 'novice-casual' [JARK 85 b]; they have little knowledge of either programming concepts or of the application domain.

Teaching. All subjects were first given a two hour application description. They were then assigned to three groups. Two groups were taught a language (NLQS or SQL) for three and a half hours and the third group was given no language training. Teaching in SQL followed the pattern established in [REIS 77, WELT 81]; teaching in the natural language subset concentrated on the language system philosophy and on examples of how to get around language restrictions. The application was a scaled-down version of the NYU alumni database, which was used in the field study.

Testing. After training, all subjects were given the same pencil-and paper test consisting of fifteen questions. Exam questions were designed with no bias toward the NLQS or SQL. They described problem situations and subjects were asked to express a query (or a series of queries) to answer them (Fig. 5.3). The group with no language training was asked to employ English queries.

Evaluation Method. Exams were graded by two examiners. A series of measures was used with the goal to facilitate comparisons with other laboratory experiments and with the field study. There were three main objectives in the laboratory experiment: a comparative study between the NLQS and SQL for ease of use (performance), a lexicographic analysis for the number and type of tokens used in the two languages, and an examination of the grammatical constructs employed by natural language users.

For the analysis of word usage, an equal number of natural language and SQL subjects were selected. Among the topics investigated were: tokens used per question and per subject, categories for the individual tokens used (e.g. pro-

AN EXAM QUESTION

Q6.- A list of alumni in the state of California has been requested. The request applies to those alumni whose last name starts with an "S". Obtain such a list containing last names and first names.

NLQS SOLUTION

Q6.- (NLQS). What are the last names and first names of all California Alumni whose last name is like S%?

SQL SOLUTION

Q6.- (SQL).
```
SELECT lastname, firstname
FROM donors
WHERE srccode='al' and state='ca' and lastname like 's%';
```

Fig. 5.3. Example exam question - second ALP laboratory study

nouns, verbs), and commonality of word usage using a similar procedure as the one employed by Miller [MILL 81].

The answers of trained NLQS subjects were further considered for the investigation of the general solution strategies followed, and grammatical correctness and naturalness of the constructs used in answering a question. The latter was graded by a student majoring in English.

5.3 Experimental Results

5.3.1 Results of the ALP Field Study

The results of the field experiment [JARK 85 a], coupled with those of the first laboratory test [TURN 84], concern issues of training, language power, user effort and success, system problems and user perceptions and strategies.

Training. The 8 subjects achieved an acceptable level of skill comparable to that of previous experiments with SQL [REIS 77, GREE 78, WELT 81] after 3 hours of classroom training and several practice terminal sessions followed by a refresher classroom hour. No difference was found between NLQS and SQL performance.

Language Power. Even though no perfect matching was achieved, the assigned tasks in each language were of roughly equal complexity. However, task complexity decreased somewhat over time in the languages. Both languages showed a reasonably good functional coverage of the application but SQL was somewhat more powerful, in the sense that more tasks were solvable and slightly less

Table 5.1. Language power and effort to use - ALP field study

Evaluation criterion	NLQS	SQL
Language power		
% completely solvable tasks	73.8%	84.4%
no. necessary queries per task	4.4	3.2
Effort spent (task level)		
no. queries submitted per task	15.6	10.0
time spent per task (minutes)	120	108
Effort spent (query level)		
no. tokens per query (input)	10.6	34.2
time spent per query (minutes)	7.7	10.6

Table 5.2. Task and query level performance - ALP field study

Experiment	Evaluation criterion	NLQS	SQL
ACTUAL TASK SOLUTION PERFORMANCE			
Field	% essentially correct tasks	17.1%	44.2%
- phase 1	% essentially correct tasks	4.8%	39.1%
- phase 2	% essentially correct tasks	30.0%	50.0%
ACTUAL QUERY ANSWERING PERFORMANCE			
Field	% accepted queries	15.2%	26.5%
Field	% essentially correct queries	22.3%	45.6%

queries were required in principle to resolve a task than in the NLQS. (A task was said to be completely solvable (with x necessary queries) if all the required data were available in the database, and if a specialist could find a way to solve the underlying request with x queries in the given language.)

Effort to Use. There was little difference between the two languages in terms of the total time subjects needed to complete a task. The average number of NLQS queries submitted per task was significantly higher than the number of SQL queries. However, SQL queries were three times longer than natural language queries and required 40% more total time per query, demonstrating the potential savings of using NLQS.

Success in Problem-Solving and Querying. The actual task level performance in both languages was much lower than one would have expected from laboratory results and language power. SQL achieved 44% and the NLQS 17% essentially correct solutions over all tasks. Natural language performance improved considerably (from 4.8% to 30%), after some initial system errors had been removed. In a direct request-by-request comparison, the NLQS was superior in 18% of the paired requests (21% equal, 61% SQL better). Query correctness was equally low, in terms of percentage of accepted queries as well as in terms of percentage of queries judged essentially correct except for trivial errors.

Table 5.3. Reasons for failure - ALP field study

Main problem	TASK LEVEL		SESSION LEVEL	
	NLQS	SQL	NLQS	SQL
lack of data/function	28.5%	14.8%	34.5%	13.0%
user problem	11.5%	55.7%	12.0%	55.6%
interface/system problem	34.3%	11.1%	38.0%	31.4%
combination of problems	25.7%	18.5%	15.5%	0.0%

Problem Analysis. Interface and system unavailability problems - caused by heavy system load, and by the use of hardcopy terminals and noisy dial-up lines - were common to both languages but had a stronger impact on NLQS task performance, since natural language users had more difficulties in recognizing the source of a problem. The large size of the database (as compared to previous studies) also had a negative impact on system performance, not only because of long search times but also because inefficiencies of the NLQS-SQL translation coincided with certain weaknesses in the SQL query optimizer, leading to inefficient query processing. Response times of more than 10-20 minutes were not infrequent.

Otherwise, NLQS failures were mostly attributed to lack of language functionality or omissions in the application design, whereas user errors were the cause of most SQL failures. This can be interpreted in the way that more habitability (tolerance of surface structure variations) must be expected from an NLI than from a formal query language.

Interestingly, the number of typographical errors was quite small. The error rate was almost exactly the same in both language (0.97% respectively 0.94% of all input tokens contained errors), which is at the lower end of the spectrum to be expected from inexperienced typists [EMBL 81]. One might interpret this as an indication that users are very careful in their computer interaction.

User Perceptions and Strategies. Error handling strategies were different for the two languages. Natural language users had the tendency to rephrase a query in a different way, whereas SQL users usually retried the same query with only minor modifications. This gives a hint on the difficulties NLI users had in locating and correcting errors, given the poor error messages of the prototype. Not surprisingly, users rated the suitability of SQL for task solution higher.

5.3.2 Results of the Laboratory Experiment

There were three major objectives in the larger of the two laboratory studies: comparative performance of NLQS and SQL subjects and the impact of training, examination of the effect of subset boundaries for the natural language system, and determination of the grammatical correctness and naturalness of subjects' queries.

Performance. No significant differences in test scores were found between and SQL subjects - see Table 5.4 (t-test, n = 51, p = 0.110). Users of the NLQS required less time and tokens per query - see Table 5.5 (t-test, n = 765, p = .000). It was observed that training in the natural language subset is necessary, as evidenced by the poor performance of the untrained subject group (Table 5.4).

Subset Boundaries. Natural language was less verbose than SQL, but had a larger vocabulary to draw upon (i.e., the number of ***unique*** words used in natural language was higher). Still, it was found that the size of this vocabulary was manageable; approximately 150 words would have to be defined for the application (nouns, adjectives, non-imperative verbs). Furthermore, NLQS subjects shared many such words, while infrequently used words (accounting for forty five percent of all unique words in the vocabulary) could probably have been dropped without serious performance problems (Table 5.6).

Grammatical Correctness and Naturalness. Even after training, NLQS subjects had a strong tendency to write non-grammatical queries. In addition, the sub-

Table 5.4. Performance of subjects - ALP laboratory study

	NO. OF SUBJECTS	CORRECTNESS	
		Mean	S. D.
Trained SQL	17	71.4	22.7
Trained NLQS	34	68.9	23.1
Untrained NLQS	10	28.3	18.9

Table 5.5. Time and tokens per query - ALP laboratory study

	TOKENS PER QUERY	TIME	
		Mean	S. D.
Trained NLQS	21.2	3.06	1.92
Trained SQL	33.8	4.75	3.33

Table 5.6. Summary of word usage - ALP laboratory study

	NUMBER OF WORDS	APPLICATION DEPENDENT	APPLICATION INDEPENDENT	CON-STANT VALUES
UNIQUE WORDS				
NLQS	259	56%	24%	20%
SQL	180	50%	13%	37%
TOTAL WORDS				
NLQS	4478	44%	45%	11%
SQL	6081	28%	61%	11%

Table 5.7. Query level performance overview – ALP experiments (Welty Scale)

Experiment	Essentially NLQS	Correct SQL	At least NLQS	Correctable SQL
Lab I	71.1%	67.3%	78.8%	76.9%
Lab II	44.6%	53.3%	59.2%	68.8%
Field	22.3%	45.6%	75.5%	57.0%

jects used fairly awkward expressions in attempting to meet the artificial restrictions of the NLQS subset.

5.3.3 Conclusion of Stage C

In both languages, performance in the field study appeared to be substantially lower than in the laboratory experiments. Since the evaluation criteria differed, the definitions of essentially correct and correctable queries from [WELT 81] were applied to the queries in all experiments (Table 5.7). There is still a gap between the field and laboratory studies but the results on 'correctable' queries also emphasize the potential of a better adapted system. The SQL results are comparable to those found by Welty and Stemple [WELT 81] who report 67.0% respectively 59.5% 'essentially correct' queries for two groups of subjects. Thus, the ALP laboratory results appear to be consistent with previous research, especially if the extremely short training period in the second experiment (less than three hours) is taken into account.

6 Synopsis of Empirical Studies

In this section, we investigate the relationships between the data gained by the evaluation studies of stage B (KFG) and stage C (ALP). Having a common empirical base, we point out the major results and attempt to explain the differences.

6.1 Assessment of Methods and Research Designs

General Evaluation Plan. In contrast to previous evaluations of NLQS, neither the ALP nor the KFG study were carried out by the development team. Both studies combine field studies and laboratory experiments. Considering the plan underlying the KFG study (see Fig. 4.1), ALP worked in a new application field and a new natural language (English). From this viewpoint, the most important progress is that extensive experiments to compare formal with natural language were conducted in ALP. From the viewpoint of ALP, the most important new element is the orientation on tasks and the analysis of the hierarchical levels request-task-session-query. The KFG laboratory experiments used translation tests and the KFG field study can be seen as one big task. Schütz [SCHU 79 b] describes this task and shows its successful solution with the NLQS. But there is no analysis of subtasks in KFG, nor of the relationships between the hierarchical levels.

Field Studies. The KFG field study extended over a longer period of time (16: 6 months), and the amount of queries was larger (7278:1081). On the other hand, there were eight users in ALP. The ALP users were not real users, in the sense of the KFG and TA field study, but ALP was very close to a real usage. Therefore, there is some common ground for relating results from the KFG and ALP field studies. Results of the KFG field study which can be confirmed by the ALP material will gain more plausibility with respect to their user and application independence. However, there is still a major barrier to bringing the two studies together. Section 4.3 shows that the most important results of KFG came from a *qualitative* analysis of the queries, mainly concerning the internal grammatical structures and error situations, especially error chains and strategies to handle them. In the terminology of ALP, an additional layer is missing between the hierarchical levels session and query, namely 'error chains/query sequences.' Error chains are not determined by the task but by a user's effort to get an answer to one initially erroneous query. This level is only marginally covered by the statistical approach of ALP.

Laboratory Experiments. Laboratory experiments were methodologically stronger in ALP. One question remains open: why are the KFG results so much better? The conjecture that people learn ISBL easier than SQL does not appear to be plausible. Another conjecture is that the result differences can be attributed to differences in the design of the tests (tasks vs. translation test of a typical session).

6.2 Comparison of the Results

6.2.1 Common Results

Based on results of both studies, five statements seem to have a fairly strong empirical backing.

1. Users do not communicate with a NLI in the way they do with a human, as suggested in [CHAP 73] (see also [KRAU 80 a, ZOLT 82, ZOEP 83]). In particular, they are very careful in typing input, as evidenced by a low percentage of typographical errors. It is open, how this would change with widespread availability of automatic spelling correction for NLI.

2. Small vocabulary subsets are sufficient for restricted application areas. This result may not extend to some of the knowledge-based systems which require the definition of all words used (including, in particular, values appearing in the database, see, e.g., [BATE 83]).
3. Natural language is more concise than formal query languages. In particular, SQL requires substantially longer input even for rather simple queries.
4. Formal query languages cannot be rejected on the grounds that a substantial effort is needed to learn them.
5. Neither study confirmed the fear that natural language queries grow more and more complex over time. Rather, there seems to be evidence that users adapt to what they perceive as the system's limitations. In the KFG field study, query complexity remained about stable over time, whereas in ALP it actually decreased.

6.2.2 Open Questions and Discrepancies

On first sight, the main discrepancies between the results of ALP and KFG concern the error rates (Table 6.1). The most plausible explanation regarding the differences in the laboratory experiments seem to be deviations in the test designs. A second startling discrepancy is visible in the number of queries per session, resulting from the differences in time per submitted query. Possible explanations of the poor showing of the NLQS in the ALP field study in contrast to the good results in the KFG field study could be:

Language Dependence. The English syntax of the NLQS has been written on the model of the syntax for German. For example, morphological rules and the user-

Table 6.1. Performance overview NLQS field studies

USER GROUP	NO. USERS	SESSIONS	QUERIES	ERROR RATE
STAGE A				
Planning	2	7	59	46.0%
School	1	6	356	12.9%
Reception	1	4	115	47.0%
Rooms	3	47	781	39.9%
STAGE B				
KFG main 1	1	39	6603	6.9%
KFG user 2	1	5	582	16.9%
KFG user 3	1	1	93	31.1%
TA study	1	1	67	52.7%
STAGE C[a]				
ALP phase 1	4	34	256	77.0%
w/o line noise				69.1%
ALP phase 2	4	31	271	82.3%
w/o line noise				74.9%

[a] ALP figures do not contain incomplete query typing attempts.

independent vocabulary were replaced, and the rules for dependent clause word order were deleted. The interpretation routines are the same as in the German version with some minor modifications [ZOEP 84 a].

ALP was the first application of the English system version. Therefore the simplest explanation of the high error rates would be that there was still a need for debugging tests. The high error rates reported for the stage A experiments (which were achieved in a far better technical environment, using smaller databases and screens instead of hardcopy terminals) give some support to this conjecture. Another more far-reaching conclusion could be that the differences between an efficient English and German subset are more extensive than expected. For instance, so-called ungrammatical queries were used more often in ALP than in KFG.

Database Dependence. While the database schemata of KFG and ALP as well as those of the stage A studies were of comparable complexity (two to six base relations), the size of the ALP database turned out to cause serious response time problems through inefficient translation of natural language into SQL. This does not affect the general concept of the system but stresses the necessity of query optimization in the natural language system.

User Dependence. Since the KFG study was mainly a one-user study, it could be suspected that the main KFG user was a happy coincidence and that the very long usage period and his involvement in the application design provided him with a deeper understanding of the system. On first sight, the fact that KFG was the only application reaching such a low error rate would seem to confirm this assumption. Even the other two KFG users had somewhat higher error rates. However, one has to be cautious: Krause [KRAU 82] shows clearly that the main KFG user had few changes in error rates over time, thus denying a learning effect after the initial phase.

Application Development Dependence. The system had to be adapted to the ALP application by defining the application vocabulary and the relational view definitions. Since the ALP team had difficulties in handling an SQL limitation in the number of views, and the geographical distance between the development team in West Germany and New York worked as an information barrier, it could be that the adaptation of the new application failed to be accurate. On the other hand, one of the system's claims is the ability to have non-linguists define their own application. ALP clearly demonstrated the limitations of this option.

Experimental Design Dependence. The application-specific part of the ALP grammar was hardly changed after initial testing, whereas the KFG application was adapted whenever problems became visible in a user session. On one hand, the KFG experience shows that the NLQS is powerful enough to cover the language subset required for a particular application in an impressive manner (93% success). Moreover, it is perfectly acceptable to expect a certain period of time, during which the system has to be adapted to a user. On the other hand, the question arises: when will this user adaptation terminate? The answer is clearly important for the commercial (rather than technical) feasibility of NLI.

Technical Environment Dependence. A final reason for the high NLQS failure rates in ALP is obvious when looking at the EDP protocols: the poor system performance at New York University (caused by slow and noisy communication lines, and system overload), and difficulties with the operating system.

7 Conclusions

The comparison of several experiments with the same domain-independent natural language query system has yielded methodological results and preliminary conclusions about this type of natural language interface, as well as gaps in the studies and opportunities for future research.

Research Methodology. There seems to be a natural sequence to be followed in the evaluation of a natural language query system in order to yield meaningful results. Starting with exploratory on-site system tests, the strategy proceeds towards a qualitative feature analysis, upon which structured quantitative evaluation models can be based. The ALP experience has demonstrated that such a schema can be exploited to its fullest only if the prototype under study has reached sufficient maturity; otherwise, quantitative analyses must be complemented by qualitative studies in order to separate generalizable results from those influenced by the prototype status of the system. It is also critical to provide an adequate technical environment.

Domain-Independent Natural Language Query Systems. Concerning the three introductory questions set forth about domain-independent natural language query systems, some conclusions can be drawn, whereas other issues require further study. Addressing first the desirability question, we know now that natural language allows for more concise query input and requires less formulation time than a formal query language. However, nobody has been able so far to demonstrate advantages of natural language over formal query languages in terms of learnability, language power, task performance, or query acceptance rates.

Concerning NLQS feasibility, there is no evidence that any of the experiments exceeded the boundaries of what can be easily implemented within the domain-independent subset system approach. Thus, practice-oriented natural language query systems appear to be technically feasible and able to fulfill the purpose they were developed for. However, additional studies will be required to confirm this result.

The third question asked for the cost of adapting a NLQS to a new application. It is not clear how long the adaptation to an application or a new user will take, or to what degree end users will be able to take over this job from specialists in computational linguistics. The experience with ALP indicates that building and stabilizing a new application needs major linguistic information science (computational linguistic) support. That is, different personnel requirements from those for introducing an end user system based on formal query languages may arise (see also [VASS 83 b] and Chap. 3 in this volume).

Future Research. The intensive study of a natural language query system has revealed a number of empirical research questions that have to be answered to bring natural language closer to practical usability. As a first step, it is planned to further explore the reasons for the differences in performance between the ALP and KFG studies in order to make the results more comparable. For KFG, this means that the laboratory experiments will be repeated in a more controlled setting, using queries of the ALP application and SQL as the formal query language. This supplementary test promises interesting results for the comparison of the different design decisions in the laboratory experiments of ALP and KFG.

For ALP, a qualitative re-analysis of the protocols will be performed to make the results compatible with KFG. Another reason for qualitatively reanalyzing the ALP material with respect to error chains comes from the observation that the task orientation in ALP was partly impeded by the high error rates, which in turn led to the existence of almost only error chains in many sessions.

There are first hints that in addition to the performance problems some gaps and inadequacies in the application-dependent part of the NLQS are partially responsible for the high error rates in ALP. There are no hints so far that the general philosophy of domain-independent NLQS is insufficient. But these statements are subject to change pending further evidence.

Acknowledgments

This work is based on several studies in cooperation with the IBM Corporation. The projects would not have been possible without the continued support by members of IBM Heidelberg Scientific Center, in particular, A. Blaser, H. Lehmann, N. Ott, and M. Zoeppritz. Besides the authors, principal investigators of the Advanced Language Project were Ted Stohr, Jon Turner, and Norm White. We would also like to express our gratitude to the subjects who participated the studies presented here, to Robert Tabory for valuable discussions, and to Margi Olson for many helpful suggestions concerning the presentation.

References

[AIC 82], [ASTR 76], [BARB 83], [BATE 83], [BERT 81], [BUND 83], [CHAP 73], [CODD 78], [DAME 81], [EMBL 81], [FINN 79], [FISC 82], [GHOS 77], [GREE 78], [HARR 77 c], [HEND 78 a], [IBM 76], [JARK 83], [JARK 85 a], [JARK 85 b], [KETT 81], [KOLV 79], [KRAU 80 a], [KRAU 80 b], [KRAU 82], [KRAU 83 a], [KRAU 83 b], [KRAU 83 c], [LEHM 78 a], [LEHM 78 b], [LEHM 79], [MALH 75], [MALK 82], [MILL 81], [MORA 81], [MORI 82], [OTT 79 a], [OTT 79 b], [OTTZ 80], [PETR 76], [REIS 77], [REIS 81], [SCHN 84], [SCHÜ 79 b], [SHWA 84], [SHNE 80], [SMAL 77], [STOH 82], [TENN 79], [TODD 76], [TURN 84], [VASS 83 a], [VASS 83 b], [VASS 84], [WALT 78], [WALT 83], [WELT 81], [WOOD 77 a], [WOOD 77 b], [ZOEP 83], [ZOEP 84 a], [ZOEP 84 b], [ZOLT 82]

Chapter 5

An Interactive Customization Program for a Natural Language Database Query System

Fred J. Damerau

Abstract. There has been ample evidence for some time, both from prototype systems and, more recently, commercially available systems that it is possible to build a natural language interface to a data base which allows access to data by naive users. However, these systems have been hand tailored to particular data bases, to a greater or lesser degree, by their developers. (Artificial Intelligence Corporation now trains customers to be their own data base linguists, but the principle of requiring a linguist as a customizer remains the same). It is generally recognized that a fixed, domain independent, natural language query system is not now attainable. Nonetheless, it would clearly be preferable, from a commercial point of view, if a query system product could be delivered to a customer without requiring vendor personnel to adapt it to the domain. This paper describes an interactive system which has the aim of making it possible for a customer who knows his data base but is unfamiliar with linguistic processing to provide an English interface to an SQL/DS data base.

1 Introduction

In the Transformational Question Answering system (TQA) project, we are aiming to build a natural language interface which provides access to data stored in the SQL/DS system [IBM 81], or more generally, data bases which can be accessed by means of the SQL query language.

The customization program described here assumes specifically that the data base architecture is that of SQL/DS. The interface therefore can be built not only from the input of a data base expert, but in part from the contents of the data base, since the data base includes tables which describe the data base itself.

There are three general problems which must be solved in customizing a natural language query system for a particular application, viz., determining:

1) What must be found out
2) How to find it out
3) How to incorporate what is found out into the query system.

The first of these is essentially system independent, whereas the second and third clearly are not. Even 1) is not completely system independent, because not all systems analyze natural languages to the same depth. Since TQA incorporates a transformational grammar which aims at very broad coverage of English sentences, the amount of grammatical information which must be gathered is large. With respect to 2), it is clear that a knowledgeable person will have to be the source for much of the necessary information, but in certain circumstances a considerable amount can come directly from the data base itself, providing the customization system knows how to access diverse data bases.

2 The TQA System

The main component of the TQA system [DAME 80] consists of a transformational parser and a Knuth-style semantic interpreter [KNUT 68]. The parser is separable into a preprocessor, a set of string transformations for local rearrangement, a context free parser giving surface structures, a main transformational component producing underlying forms in the style of generative semantics, and a second transformational component producing structures which reflect the content of the data base. The preprocessor, context free grammar and the main transformational component are constant for all data bases. The interpreter transforms the canonical sentence representation produced by the grammar first into an expression in the domain relational calculus [DATE 81], and then into an SQL expression. An SQL-to-English translation component provides feedback to users as to how the system has understood the original query. The few data dependencies in the interpreter all reside in a small set of tables.

3 The Customization Program

Although the TQA system is meant to interface to SQL/DS, it is presently implemented on a prototype of that system, viz., System R [ASTR 76]. SQL/DS and System R both permit calls to system facilities from a PL/I or COBOL program. The customization program is written in PL/I. It conducts a dialogue with a knowledgeable data base analyst (hereafter referred to as the data base administrator or DBA) interspersed with calls to System R to gather information from the tables in the data base.

To illustrate the process and the kinds of information which must be gathered, consider the data base defined in Fig. 1, in System R commands, with the obvious interpretations. It consists of two tables describing the personnel and organization into projects of a mathematical research department.

A particular manifestation of System R might contain tables from more than one data domain, i. e., might comprise more than one data base. It is necessary to

```
$CREATE TABLE D420S1(
 PHONENO  (CHAR(04) ),
 NAME  (CHAR(24)VAR),
 LOCA  (CHAR(6) ),
 PROJ  (CHAR(29)VAR),
 MANNO  (CHAR(6) )
IN SEGMENT DJOHNS.WPDBS;
$CREATE TABLE D420S2(
 PROJ  (CHAR(29)VAR),
 PROJNO  (CHAR(4) ),
 MANAGER  (CHAR(12)VAR) )
IN SEGMENT DJOHNS.WPDBS;
```

Fig. 1. System R data base definition

```
FOLLOWING WILL BE DISPLAYED THE TABLES IN
THE DATA BASE. PRESS ENTER IF THE TABLE
IS NOT IN THE DOMAIN TO BE QUERIED,
TYPE "Y" IF IT IS PART OF THE DOMAIN

COURSES
D420S1
y
D420S2
y
FACULTY
GEOBASE
LOCATION
LUCF
LUCV
LU1
NEIGHF
PARCFL
PHONE
 .
 .
```

Fig. 2. Identifying the tables in a domain

ask the DBA which tables are in the domain for which an interface is to be generated (Fig. 2). Once the tables have been identified, the program accesses System R catalogues for each of them, extracting the system names for the columns and their system attributes, i. e., character, integer or real. The DBA is then asked to supply synonyms for the column names used by the system, verbal forms, and the desired column heading for retrieved items (Fig. 3). Synonyms and verbal forms are inserted into the lexicon. Column headings are used by the output formatting program when query results are displayed to the user.

The DBA is also asked whether the column is a key in the relation, information needed in semantic interpretation. Next, he is asked if the column contains only numbers and if so, whether or not arithmetic can be performed on them

```
IS THERE AN ORDINARY ENGLISH EXPRESSION
FOR THE COLUMN NAMED "LOCA"
IF SO TYPE THE EXPRESSION, OTHERWISE PRESS ENTER
location
IF THE PLURAL OF THIS EXPRESSIONS IS
"LOCATIONS"
PRESS ENTER. IF THERE IS NO PLURAL TYPE "*"
OTHERWISE ENTER THE CORRECT PLURAL
    .
    .
    .
    .
IS THERE ANOTHER ORDINARY ENGLISH EXPRESSION
FOR THE COLUMN NAMED "LOCA"

IF SO TYPE THE EXPRESSION, OTHERWISE PRESS ENTER
room
IF THE PLURAL OF THIS EXPRESSION IS ROOMS
PRESS ENTER. IF THERE IS NO PLURAL TYPE "*"
OTHERWISE ENTER THE CORRECT PLURAL
```

Fig. 3. Specifying English equivalents for a column name

```
DOES THE MANNO COLUMN CONTAIN ONLY NUMBERS?
yes -
remark: the field contains an employee number
IS ANY ARITHMETIC SENSIBLE ON THESE NUMBERS-
THAT IS, ADD OR MULTIPLY OR
SUBTRACT OR AVERAGE
(BUT NOT NECESSARILY ALL OF THESE)
no
```

Fig. 4. Determine if numeric fields are numbers or identifiers

(Fig. 4). (Notice that a column coded as numeric in the data base might still contain identifiers, and columns which are of type "character" might really contain numbers. Therefore, even though the data type of the column is known, the question must still be asked.)

In the case of columns really containing numbers, one must ask whether the numbers are counts or measurable quantities, what the units and scaling factors are, and the kinds of arithmetic operations which are permitted. For symbolic fields, the program must ask if the values belong to one of the semantic classes, such as human, place, time, etc., that the grammar is sensitive to, and create the proper lexical features. Because file data tend to be stored in some compact form, it is useful to ask if the output form of column values should be different from the internal form. For example, a social security number might be stored as 111223333, but printed as 111-22-3333 (Fig. 5).

```
THIS FIELD HAS 11 CHARACTERS.
IF THE FIELD REQUIRES FORMATTING FOR OUTPUT,
(FOR EXAMPLE, A SOCIAL SECURITY NUMBER MIGHT BE
STORED AS 9 DIGITS, BUT PRINTED AS 11-
  123456789: 123-45-6789)
TYPE X'S FOR THE CHARACTERS FROM THE STORED FIELD
WITH FORMATTING CHARACTERS SEPARATING THE PIECES-
E.G.- XXX-XX-XXXX
OR PRESS ENTER
```

Fig. 5. Identify special print formats

```
THERE ARE ONLY 18 DIFFERENT ENTRIES
IN THIS COLUMN. IF THE ENTRIES ARE CODES WHICH HAVE
ENGLISH EXPRESSIONS, OR WORDS WHICH HAVE SYNONYMS
TYPE "YES", OTHERWISE PRESS ENTER
```

Fig. 6. Determine if a field has coded values

This information also has to be saved for the output formatter. Moreover, our experience with NL query systems in user environments has shown that a user will often input a form [DAME 81] which he has seen in the computer output. Therefore a recognition rule to convert the expanded form to the stored form must be created.

Having found global information about the column from the DBA, the program next scans the entries in the column, or a subset of them if the number of entries is very large. During the scan, the program attempts to break column entries into words, and builds a word frequency dictionary. (The technique of using the data base contents to augment the dictionary is reminiscent of [HARR 77b], with the exception that it is done only once, rather than at each execution, i.e., the customization program is functioning as a compiler.) It also creates a format expression for each entry, keeping track of sequences of digits, alphabetics, and special characters. If the number of unique entries is small compared to the number of rows in the table, all the entries will be entered into the lexicon. Also, the DBA will be asked if the entries are codes, and if so, whether or not he wishes to supply English equivalents, which are also entered into the lexicon (Fig. 6).

Similarly, if some words are very frequent, they will be entered into the lexicon, and the DBA will be asked if they are classifiers for the entries in that column, e.g., "Inc" in a column containing company names.

If the list of formats constructed during the scan over the column contains some which are very frequent, these are saved in a master list and will be used to produce shape recognition rules. By doing this, it is possible to recognize an input sequence such as "31-209" as a room number and assign it the correct column feature, without storing all the possible room numbers [DAME 83].

After all the columns of a table have been processed, the rules pertaining only to that table are written to a system update file, and processing is begun on the next table of the data base, if there is one. When all tables have been processed, dictionary entries and the rules pertaining to multiple tables are written out. It is necessary to defer adding to the lexicon until all tables have been processed, because of the possibility that some words may be relevant to more than one column or more than one table. Naturally, rules dealing with table joins cannot be specified until the join columns for each table pair are known.

Although many details have been omitted, it should now be clear that the amount of information which must be gathered and organized by the program is very large.

4 Examples

The examples in this section illustrate some of the system outputs, and examples of the kind of queries processed, with their SQL translations. Fig. 7 is an example dictionary entry, in LISP notation. Lexical entries are tree structures, with features permissible on the nodes [ROBI 73]. The table name, D420S2, and the column name, MANAGER, are features of the NOUN node, as is the semantic feature, HU, for "human". (Features marked with "+" or "−" are binary features; those beginning with "=" are n-ary features, which have the structure: feature name, list of feature values.)

An example of a program-generated string transformation of a simple kind is given in Fig. 8. This is a shape recognition rule, applying to words not found in the dictionary, which removes the feature "UNKNOWN" and adds the features for a room number if the input word consists of the sequence: two digits, a hyphen, and three digits (indicated by the feature "D02-D03").

Figure 9 is an example of a simple query to the department data base, involving only one table.

Figure 10 is an example of a query involving an essential join over the column "PROJ"; the join is required because both tables in the data base must be accessed.

```
(manager
 (NOM
  (NOUN
   ( (+COLNAME)
   (+SG)
   (-NUMRK)
   (+HU)
   (=COLN (MANAGER D420S2) )
   (V ( (+OGEN) ) MANAGER)
   (INDEX ( (-CONST) (+CODED) ) ) ) ) )
```

Fig. 7. An example dictionary entry

```
(((SHAPE01 STRING OB ALL)
 (X
  (((PROPNOM.1))
   /NOUN
   (((NOUN.3)((+UNKNOWN)(+D02-D03)))
    ((INDEX((+CONST))(W.4))))))
  X)
 NIL
 NIL
 ((DELETE 3 (UNKNOWN))
  (INSERT
   3 ((+COLNAME)(+SG)(=COLN (LOCA D420S1))
    (-NUMRK)(+PL)(-HU)
    (+COLVAL))))
    .
    .
```

Fig. 8. A sample shape recognition rule

```
What is Petrick''s extension?
.
.
SQL QUERY:

WHQ
SELECT UNIQUE A.NAME, A.MANNO, A.PHONENO
FROM D420S1 A
WHERE A.NAME LIKE '%PETRICK%';
```

Fig. 9. Example sentence where retrieval requires only one table

```
Who is Petrick''s manager?

SQL QUERY:

WHQ
SELECT UNIQUE A.NAME, A.MANNO, A.PROJ, B.MANAGER
FROM D420S1 A, D420S2 B
WHERE A.PROJ=B.PROJ
AND A.NAME LIKE '%PETRICK%';
```

Fig. 10. An example sentence involving two tables (a join)

Figure 11 shows the utility of the shape recognition rules. This example was run during an executive demonstration on a data base consisting of the local phone book. The shape rule has identified "31-209" as an entry in the LOC column. Figure 12, from a different telephone book data base, illustrates the utility of finding those columns which contain relatively few entries and including the

```
Who is in 31-209?
.
.
SQL QUERY:
.
.
WHQ
SELECT UNIQUE A.NAME
FROM PHONE A
WHERE A.LOC='31-209';
```

Fig. 11. Use of a shape rule to recognize the column an input word is in

```
How many people are in Montvale?
.
.
SQL QUERY:
.
.
WHQ
SELECT COUNT(UNIQUE A.NAME)
FROM PHONFR A
WHERE A.SITE='MON';
.
.
```

Fig. 12. An example of a dictionary entry coming from the DB

entries plus their elicited synonyms in the dictionary. "Montvale" is recognized as a synonym for "MON" in the SITE column.

5 Discussion

This work is similar in spirit to that of the TEAM project [GROS 83 a], but differs in a number of important respects. From the linguistic point of view, we assume a richer base lexicon than is apparently assumed by TEAM. That is, descriptive adjectives like "cheap" are assumed by us to occur in the base lexicon with appropriate features, for example, "+MONEY" or the like, instead of being elicited from the DBA. In addition, there are numerous differences resulting from the difference of grammatical model. From the data base point of view, major differences result from our assumption of a particular data base architecture, that of SQL/DS. This permits the customization program to access the data base for some of the information it needs, normally resulting in a reduction of the amount of information which must be provided by the individual, i.e., the DBA performing the customization. Because neither approach has been tested to a significant extent, it is not clear whether one approach is superior to the other.

6 Outlook and Conclusion

As a result of experimentation so far, we have decided to make some changes in our parsing system and grammar to facilitate the customization process. One change resulting in markedly simpler rules is a move from binary to n-ary features in the grammar. This allows simpler encoding of the table and column that words are associated with. A number of rules have been generalized so that less specific information is required from the DBA. Our belief is that these simplifications will not seriously affect the ability of the grammar to reject wrong structure.

Once the customization program and grammar changes have been completed, a machine customized query system will be tested against our previous hand-coded system. At that time, we will attempt to create an interface to the White Plains planning department data base [DAME 80] and then run the system on the collection of approximately 1000 sentences which were collected in that experiment. This should provide us with a good indication as to whether the approach outlined above is a viable one for providing transportable natural language query systems.

References

[ASTR 76], [DAME 80], [DAME 81], [DAME 83], [DATE 81], [GROS 83 a], [HARR 77 b], [IBM 81], [KNUT 68], [PLAT 76], [ROBI 73], [WOOD 72]

Part III

Development of Knowledge-Based Natural Language Access Systems

Chapter 6

The Semantics-Based Natural Language Interface to Relational Databases

Jürgen M. Janas

Abstract. An approach for implementing natural language interfaces to relational databases is presented which relies on semantic information about the domain of discourse rather than on the syntax of utterances. Based on a graph-based general procedure for translating natural language questions into formal language queries, the chapter deals with three specific problems of cooperative behavior: ambiguity with respect to the database, conjunction processing, and ellipsis.

1 Introduction

The topic of natural language interfaces to databases has attracted much research interest in recent years (cf. [CODD 78, DELL 77, HABE 79, HEND 78c, KAPL 79, LAND 77, PLAT 76, WALT 76]); in at least one case (cf. [HARR 79]) such a system has become commercially available in the meanwhile. It seems that the restricted domain of discourse that is defined by the contents of some database is appropriate for keeping the problems generally involved with the processing of natural language within acceptable boundaries.

For the sake of user acceptance, however, it is not sufficient that such an interface is able to process correctly a whatever large set of grammatical sentences. Rather, it is indispensable that the system is able to deal adequately with utterances which are imprecise or violate the rules of natural language. The guideline for what constitutes natural language should be the set of utterances that may be understood in a dialog between cooperative people rather than a grammar book.

Most approaches to natural language interfaces are not very well suited to such a claim because they are syntax-oriented. The correct treatment of a natural language utterance in any case requires a complete syntactic analysis of the utterance. Though syntactic analysis may be achieved by the aid of semantic information, there is always a primacy of syntax that seems to derive from the circumstance that the translation of programming languages tacitly has served as a model. Utterances which are only slightly outside the boundaries of the syntax accepted by such a system therefore always require some special treatment if they can be processed at all.

The semantics-based approach to natural language interfaces introduced in this chapter takes an opposite course by primarily relying on semantic information, and by using syntactic information only inasmuch it is necessary to decide among several semantically plausible interpretations of a natural language query. This approach is based on the observation that the relationship between concepts referred to in a natural language utterance is determined largely by the concepts themselves and only to a small degree by the way in which these concepts are combined syntactically. This observation was first made in connection with the extraction of composite index terms from natural language texts (cf. [BRAU 76]) but is well transferable to the area of natural language queries to databases, particularly, because the domain of discourse is confined by the structure and the contents of the database.

As a consequence of such a far-reaching renunciation of syntactic analysis it is scarcely possible to detect and reject nonsensical queries with the semantics-based approach since any utterance presented to the interface will be assumed to be a query to the respective database and the interface will attempt to make sense of it even if there is no sense. Thus, it is a fundamental precondition for the feasibility of a semantics-based natural language interface that the users only ask sensible queries and that they are seriously interested in the answers. Whenever this precondition is fulfilled - and it is reasonable to assume that it is always fulfilled with commercial applications of such interfaces - the absence of syntactic analysis becomes an invaluable strength of the semantics-based approach as it allows any freedom in the wording of the queries.

In Sect. 2, some prerequisites for the subsequent sections are collected; in particular, we clarify the role of a natural language interface within the framework of a database management system and introduce a simple formal database query language into which the natural language queries are to be translated. Section 3 outlines the basic procedure employed for the translation of natural language queries into the formal query language. Each of the remaining sections deals with some particular aspect of natural language query processing that, for the purpose of user acceptance, strongly demands a cooperative system behavior and discuss the treatment of these aspects in the semantics-based approach. Section 4 is concerned with the treatment of natural language queries that contain words or phrases which actually or apparently have ambiguous meanings with regard to the underlying database. Section 5 describes some aspects of the processing of queries which contain conjunctions and thereby pays special attention to sloppy usage of conjunctions in natural language. Finally, in Sect. 6, we discuss the capabilities of the semantics-based approach with regard to the completion of elliptic natural language queries.

2 Prerequisites

In this section prerequisites of various kinds for the subsequent sections are collected. The purpose of Sect. 2.1 is to clarify the actual task of natural language interfaces by describing their interactions with a database management system. In Sect. 2.2, we briefly recall the main constituents of relational databases and then describe that part of the vocabulary used in natural language queries that is dependent on a particular database. Section 2.3 introduces a simple formal database query language into which the natural language queries are to be translated, as well as a graphical representation of this language. Finally, in Sect. 2.4, we introduce the database graph that apart from the information contained in the relation schemata also specifies the admissible joins of relations of a database.

2.1 The Natural Language Interface as a Part of a DBMS

Talking about natural language access to databases, as a matter of fact, is a rather obscuring manner of speaking. It is one of the fundamental characteristics of databases that access to the data is permitted only by taking advantage of the functions of the database management system (DBMS). Therefore it would be more precise to talk about natural language interfaces to an appropriate component of a DBMS than about natural language interfaces to databases.

When trying to identify such an appropriate component of a DBMS one can obviously confine oneself to those parts of the DBMS where the data appear in the form in which they are to be viewed by the end users. Following [ANSI 75], the end-users' view of data is represented by a so-called external schema and there are five classes of users (namely the parametric users, the application programmers, the report specifiers, the update specifiers and the enquiry specifiers) who may access the database via an external schema; for each such class of users, the ANSI/X3/SPARC-architecture provides an individual interface.

The class which is most similar to the class of users who access the database by means of natural language is the class of the enquiry specifiers. They use a formal query language in which certain subsets of the data in the database may be described in order to be retrieved; in particular, the enquiry specifiers are not entitled to update the database. At the enquiry specifiers' interface, the users are forced to work in a strict dialog mode: After a user has input a query (s)he has to wait until the DBMS outputs the answer, only then (s)he may input another query.

In order to avoid duplication of DBMS functions it seems only reasonable to design a natural language interface to a DBMS in such a way that it makes use of the enquiry specifiers' interface. That is, the natural language interface should translate the natural language queries into semantically equivalent queries of the formal query language supported by the DBMS. Still there can be no direct correspondence between the interactions at the enquiry specifiers' interface and at the natural language interface even if semantically equivalent queries are entered.

There are two reasons for this. Firstly, natural language is not as precise as a formal language and therefore the natural language interface component might require additional information from the user in order to process her/his query correctly. Such clarification interactions should preferably be designed as menus that are presented to the user. But even if the translation of a natural language query is possible without additional information, the query should always be presented to the user for confirmation in the way it is comprehended by the interface component, however, rephrased in natural language.

Secondly, the processing of a single natural language query may require several interactions via the enquiry specifiers' interface. On the one hand, this is due to the fact that natural language enables the users to ask queries which cannot be expressed in a single formal query, on the other hand, a cooperative natural language interface may have to do more than merely answering questions directly. This particularly applies to situations when the data required by the user do not exist; for a thorough discussion of this aspect of cooperative behavior, see [JANA 79].

2.2 Vocabulary

Whenever we use the term "database" in the remainder of this chapter, we refer to databases according to the relational model of data the foundations of which were introduced in [CODD 70] and [CODD 71b]. We assume that the reader is familiar with relational databases, e.g. on the level of [DATE 81].

The fundamental concepts of relational databases are relations, attributes and domains. *Domains* are sets of values and *attributes* are symbols. For each attribute A there exists a domain on which the attribute A is defined; we refer to this domain by means of the notation $\mu(A)$. As far as relations are concerned it is useful to distinguish between the relation schema and the actual relation. A *relation schema* is a named set of attributes which is ordered in a arbitrary but fixed way.

A *relation* according to some relation schema is a subset of the Cartesian product of the domains on which the attributes of the relation schema are defined. A relational database consists of a set of relation schemata and a set of relations in such a way that for each relation schema there is a corresponding relation. For simplicity, we assume that the attributes of all the relation schemata of a database have unique names. Moreover, we assume that all relations are at least in first normal form.

Example 2.2.1 (from [CODD 71a])
For representing the relation schemata of a database we use the following notation

{SUPPLIER = (*S#* , SNAME, SLOC),
PART = (*P#* , PNAME, COLOR, WEIGHT, QOH),
PROJECT = (*J#* , JNAME, MGR, JLOC),
SUPPLY = (*SS#* , *SP#* , *SJ#* , *DATE*, QUANITY)}

The primary key attributes of the relations are marked by italics. Concerning the domains on which the individual attributes are defined, the following equations hold:

$$\mu(\mathrm{S\#}) = \mu(\mathrm{SS\#})$$
$$\mu(\mathrm{SLOC}) = \mu(\mathrm{JLOC})$$
$$\mu(\mathrm{P\#}) = \mu(\mathrm{SP\#})$$
$$\mu(\mathrm{QOH}) = \mu(\mathrm{QUANTITY})$$
$$\mu(\mathrm{J\#}) = \mu(\mathrm{SJ\#})$$

Apart from these restrictions, the attributes are assumed to be defined on different domains.

An essential step when designing a natural language interface for some database is to identify those words and phrases of natural language that may be used for referring to the contents of this database; this obviously has to be done anew for each database and special care is required for this task since the semantics-based approach is to a high degree dependent on the quality of this vocabulary.

It can easily be seen that the database-dependent words and phrases that may be employed to express queries addressed to a particular database almost exclusively pertain to the relations, attributes and values of the database. Thus, for each relation, attribute and value that may occur in the database, the set of associated natural language words and phrases has to be established. As a database is always a representation of some part of the real world, such words and phrases that hence will be called *designations* do exist.

Concerning the relation designations it can be observed that there are relations whose tuples preferably are referred to by nouns since they represent entities of the real world and that there are other relations whose tuples mainly are referred to by verbs since they represent relationships and processes in the real world. Still, there is no way of making a definite distinction between these two classes since any relationship or process may be viewed as an entity in its own right at some higher level of abstraction (cf. [CADI 76]). For this reason, all designations of a relation are included in the vocabulary without making further distinctions; the meaning of all these designations is by definition the unique internal name of the respective relation. Note that the sets of relation designations of two relations cannot be identical since otherwise there would be no way of distinguishing these relations from each other by means of natural language.

The attribute designations of an attribute are all the natural language words and phrases that may be used for referring to the feature represented by the attribute; by definition, the meaning of all the attribute designations of an attribute is the unique internal name of that attribute. The sets of attribute designations of different attributes may overlap, however, the sets of attribute designations of two attributes belonging to the same relation cannot be identical since otherwise different features of the same entity could not be distinguished by means of language.

While the sets of relations and attributes of a database can easily be captured, the set of values of a domain may be very large - though always finite. This circumstance prohibits an explicit enumeration of the set of values of a domain in many cases. Still it is of utmost importance that the natural language interface has as much information as possible about the appearance of values in queries in order to be able to decide to which domain(s) a given value may belong. For this reason, [JANA 82] contains a domain description language which aims at describing the set of actually possible values of a domain rather than some superset of this set like STRING or INTEGER. In the following we only sketch some of the more important aspects of this language.

Each domain description relates the actual (internal) values that are used in the database and the corresponding appearances of these values in natural language utterances; different kinds of domains are distinguished and require different kinds of specifications.

For numeric domains (real and integer) the number of digits or, respectively, the admissible interval has to be specified.

The so-called enumeration domains directly correspond to the enumeration types of programming languages like Pascal or Ada; their domain description consists of an exhaustive enumeration of the possible values. For an individual value, several (synonymous) designations may be enumerated. It is advisable to include even designations in the domain description that refer to the respective value only vaguely.

A special case of enumeration domains are binary domains which consist of exactly two values, namely "true" and "false". They require special consideration since a value of such a domain may be expressed in natural language by merely mentioning an attribute designation of an attribute which is defined on that domain (e.g. consider the utterance "Does he speak French?" provided that FRENCH is an attribute defined on a binary domain).

String domains have to be characterized by means of the minimum and maximum length of the strings that may be values of the respective domain, and by an enumeration of the characters these strings may consist of; thus it might be useful to include in the description of the domain of an attribute NAME that the values of this domain may consist of letters and the additional characters "-" and "'".

Pattern domains are sets of strings as well; in contrast to string domains the appearance of their values is described by means of augmented regular expressions on the set of characters available to the users. For instance, local phone numbers should be described as a pattern domain rather than as a numeric domain since the first digit must never be zero.

Some problem areas of natural language query processing, namely the proper treatment of conjunctions and the completion of elliptic queries, require a distinction of "representative" value designations and non-representative value designations. A *representative* value designation is a value designation which in an arbitrary natural language context may take the place of a relation designation, thus referring to an entity or a set of entities represented by the relation. In most cases representative value designations are nouns or proper names. Whether value designations are representative or not is mostly uniform for the whole domain; in any case, a domain description has to lay down which value designations are representative and which are not.

As a result of compiling the designations of relations, attributes and values we obtain a vocabulary of natural language words and phrases which refer to the constituents of the database. It may well happen that several different meanings are attached to a single entry of this vocabulary because the respective designation may be used to address different constituents of the database. The resulting problems of lexical ambiguities will be discussed in Sect. 4.

Example 2.2.2
We close this section by introducing another database schema which will be referred to frequently in Sect. 5 and 6.

{DEPARTMENT (*D#*, DNAME),
EMPLOYEE (*E#*, NAME, PHONE, CITY, JOB, JEXP, ED#,
SALARY, AGE),
CAR (*LIP*, TYPE, PS, COLOR, DRIVER),
HIRE (*HLIP*, HCOMPANY),
INSURANCE (*ILIP*, ICOMPANY)}

Concerning the domains on which the attributes are defined, the following equations hold:

$$\mu(D\#) = \mu(ED\#)$$
$$\mu(E\#) = \mu(DRIVER)$$
$$\mu(LIP) = \mu(HLIP) = \mu(ILIP)$$

The relations HIRE and INSURANCE couple a CAR by means of its license plate (LIP) to the respective company; apart from that the attribute names seem to be self-explanatory.

2.3 A Simple Formal Database Query Language

The database query language into which natural language is to be translated is a simplified version of the retrieval part of the data sublanguage ALPHA (cf. [CODD 71 a]). The language constructs which are omitted here in comparison to ALPHA are universal quantification, negation and predicates other than "=";

the reason for this omission is that these constructs will not be needed in the examples given in the remainder of this paper. Readers who are especially interested in the way these language constructs are treated in the semantics-based approach are referred to [JANA 82].

The basic constituents of our query language are called *terms;* they are defined by means of the following two axioms.

(QL1) If x is a variable, A is an attribute name and v is a value from some domain, then

$$(x.\,A = v)$$

is a term.

(QL2) If x and y are variables and A and B are attribute names, then

$$(x.\,A = y.B)$$

is a term (sometimes called join term).

The variables occurring in terms stand for tuples of the relations; note that it is possible to infer which relation a variable occurring in a term is referring to since all attributes of the database were assumed to be named differently in Sect. 2.2.

Terms may be combined in order to form *expressions* by applying the following axioms

(QL3) If τ is a term, then τ is an expression.

(QL4) If τ_1 and τ_2 are expressions, then both $(\tau_1 \wedge \tau_2)$ and $(\tau_1 \vee \tau_2)$ are expressions.

(QL5) If τ is an expression which contains a free occurence of the variable x, then $\exists x\tau$ is an expression.

With regard to free and bound occurences of variables the conventional rules of predicate calculus apply; hence it is also possible to talk about the free variables of an expression.

In order to be able to construct arbitrary new relations out of the relations of a database, *target lists* are required as additional constituents of our query language.

(QL6) If τ is an expression which contains at least one free variable, then a non-empty list of pairs of variables and attributes is a target list of τ if all free variables of τ occur in the list and if no other than the free variables of τ occur in this list.

(QL7) A query is either an expression which contains no free variables (closed query) or an expression τ which contains at least one free variable together with a target list of τ (open query).

The meaning of the queries according to (QL1) through (QL7) seems to be self-explanatory; we only mention that closed queries essentially are yes/no-questions, whereas the target list of an open query specifies the attributes to be printed as the answer to the query.

Example 2.3.1
The meaning of the open query

$$(x.\text{SNAME}, x.\text{SLOC})\ (\exists y(x.\text{S\#} = y.\text{SS\#}) \wedge \exists z((y.\text{SJ\#} = z.\text{J\#}) \wedge (z.\text{JLOC} = \text{Rome})))$$

might be rephrased as: "Find the names and locations of all suppliers who supply a project in Rome." The closed query

$$\exists x(x.\text{SNAME} = \text{Smith})$$

might be rephrased as: "Is there a supplier named Smith?"

It can clearly be seen that the axioms (QL1) through (QL7) only describe the mere context-free syntax of our query language and that they have to be augmented by additional rules which guarantee that a variable is not used in combinations with attributes from different relations; we will not pursue this problem any further as it is of trivial nature. However, there are other directions of further restricting this query language that seem to be more important with respect to the aim of using it as the target language when translating natural language queries.

Example 2.3.2
The query

$$(x.\text{SNAME})((x.\text{SLOC} = \text{Rome}) \wedge \exists y(y.\text{MGR} = \text{Smith}))$$

is syntactically correct, however, its meaning is obscure at least: "Find the names of all suppliers in Rome and there is a project the manager of which is named Smith." Besides the fact that hardly ever one might ask such a question the answer to it might be not very informative; in particular, if the answer is the empty relation, it is not clear whether this is due to the fact that there are no suppliers in Rome or due to the fact that there is no project manager named Smith.

An inspection of the above example and comparable queries reveals that the reason for the obscurity of their meaning stems from the fact that actually two queries which are not connected by any means are combined in a single expression. This gives rise to the following definition: A query expression is called *strongly connected* if for each pair of variables occurring in the expression there is a join term which connects these variables indirectly via other variables.

It seems to be a matter of taste at first sight that we restrict our further considerations to queries which have strongly connected expressions; yet it will turn out to be of utmost importance for the translation of natural language queries into this query language: As long as a natural language query to be translated yields no strongly connected expression the translation is not yet finished.

In the remainder of this paper, we shall use a graphical version of the query language in order to represent formal queries under construction; this graphical language may also be viewed as an intermediate language from which queries might be translated into other query languages. The relationship between a query according to the axioms (QL1) through (QL7) and its query graph is given by the following procedure:

(QG1) For each variable in the query, introduce a relation-node which is labelled with the name of the relation referred to by the variable.

(QG2) For each attribute name occurring in the target list or in a join term, introduce an attribute-node which is labelled with that attribute name, and connect this node with the relation node corresponding to the variable which is used together with the attribute name.

(QG3) For each join term, connect the two nodes corresponding to the attribute names occurring in the join term.

(QG4) For each term according to (QL1), introduce a value-node labelled with the attribute name and the value occurring in that term and connect it with the relation node corresponding to the variable used in the term.

(QG5) A special marking (*) is attached to all attribute-nodes which correspond to the attribute names in the target list.

Example 2.3.3
The query graph corresponding to the query

$$(x.\mathrm{SNAME})\ \exists y(((y.\mathrm{SS\#}=x.\mathrm{S\#})\wedge(y.\mathrm{SP\#}=113)))\wedge \exists z((z.\mathrm{J\#}=y.\mathrm{SJ\#})\wedge(z.\mathrm{JLOC}=\mathrm{Rome})))$$

depicted in Fig. 2.1.

The graphical representation - in the form given above - is not appropriate for expressing disjunction, but whenever we shall investigate disjunctive queries this will be mentioned explicitly. In any case, query graphs seem to provide more clarity than the calculus-oriented query language. Finally, we note that strongly connected expressions obviously correspond to connected query graphs.

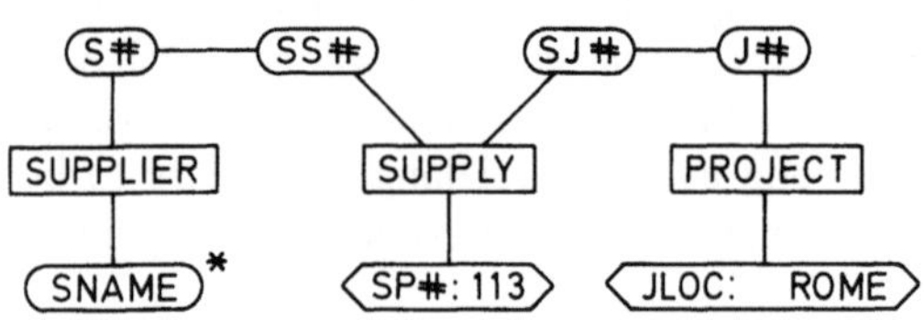

Fig. 2.1

2.4 The Database Graph

Apart from the vocabulary, the translation of natural language queries according to the semantics-based approach requires a second major source of information, namely the database graph. On the one hand, the database graph provides the information contained in the relation schemata, i.e., which attributes belong to which relations. Moreover, it contains information concerning the possible joins of relations.

Obviously, it is not reasonable to compare the values of arbitrary attributes to each other by means of join terms; thus, a comparison of an attribute defined on a domain of city names and an attribute defined on a domain of part numbers would hardly make any sense. The data base designer therefore has to lay down which attributes are comparable to each other and which are not. Starting from a precise definition of the individual domains as outlined in Sect. 2.2, the following guideline can be used: Two attributes are comparable if they are defined on the same domain; this is not true, however, if the domains are as general as STRING or INTEGER.

Though comparability of the attributes in a database is sufficient to rule out a class of meaningless queries on the level of formal queries, it is still rather unsatisfactory when viewed from the level of natural language queries since there are several ways how to express a comparison of two attributes in natural language. Moreover, it is interesting to observe that the way to express a comparison of two attributes mainly depends on the attributes concerned.

One can distinguish three kinds of comparability with respect to the way in which it is expressed in natural language. The first kind which we call *natural correspondence* is not expressed at all in natural language because there is no need to make a distinction between the attributes in natural language. Natural correspondence particularly applies to cases when the attributes in question are a primary key of some relation and a foreign key referring to that relation; since the distinction of such two attributes is only enforced by the relational model of data there is no reason for expressing the distinction in natural language.

The other two kinds of comparability of attributes are called *explicit comparability* and *implicit comparability*. Explicit comparability applies if in natural language a comparison of the two attributes concerned has to be expressed by explicitly mentioning designations of both attributes or a common generic designation of both attributes. Implicit comparability applies if a comparison may also be expressed otherwise, e.g. by using a verb. Implicit comparability always implies that the respective attributes may be compared explicitly in a query as well.

The *database graph* of a database is a labelled graph which for each relation and for each attribute of the database contains a node labelled with the corresponding relation name or attribute name, respectively. Each attribute-node is connected with the relation-node of the relation the attribute belongs to. Moreover, two attribute-nodes are connected if and only if they are comparable; the connecting arc is labelled with p_1 if the comparability is natural correspondence,

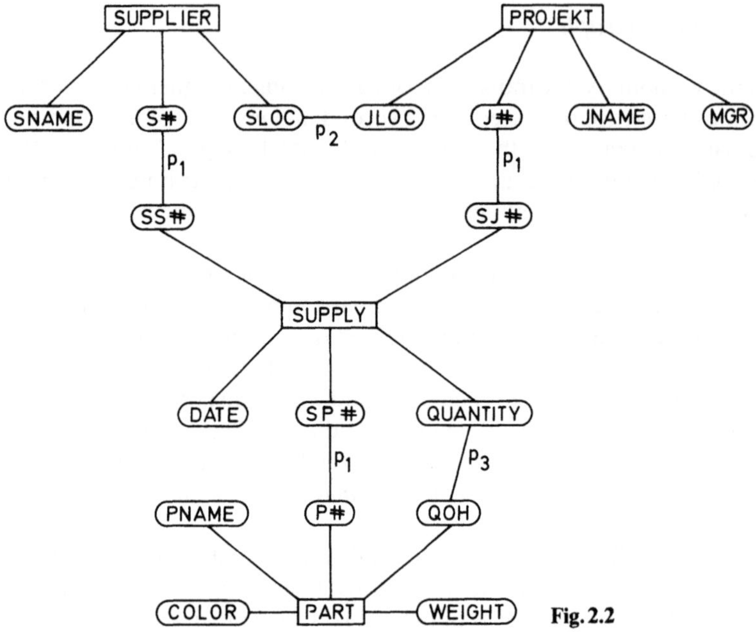

Fig. 2.2

with p_2 if the comparability is implicit comparability, and with p_3 if the comparability is explicit comparability.

Example 2.4.1
Figure 2.2 depicts the database graph of the database given in example 2.2.1.

3 The Basic Translation Procedure

The basic translation procedure translates a natural language query into a corresponding query graph; thereby it mainly makes use of the vocabulary of the respective database, of the order of the designations from that vocabulary in the natural language query and of the database graph of the database to be accessed. It is essential that a natural language utterance to be processed by the basic translation procedure actually is a query referring to this database since otherwise the results would be absolutely unforeseeable. Moreover, we assume that a query to be processed may always be expressed by one or more queries of the formal query language; this particularly implies that neither universal quantification nor negation is required. As far as disjunction is concerned, we have to note that it is not at all taken account of in the basic translation procedure since any occurrence of conjunctions in a query triggers a special treatment of the query (some aspects of which will be discussed in Sect. 5) that operates on the query graph in which disjunctions are neglected. The basic translation procedure consists of five steps which will be described in the following.

(T1) Scan the query for relevant designations.

The natural language query is searched for relation designations, attribute designations and value designations according to the vocabulary. In order to be able to distinguish value designations which belong to string domains, from words which have no meaning with regard to the database it is necessary that the procedure can take advantage of a list of frequently occurring words which have no meaning with regard to the database (e.g., articles, auxiliary verbs etc.). According to the estimates made in [MALH 75] such a list will not exceed 1000 entries.

(T2) Create nodes according to the relevant designations and build the stars of the query.

As the problems of lexical ambiguity will be dealt with separately in Sect. 4, we may assume that each of the designations discovered in step (T1) has a definite meaning. Therefore we are able to create a corresponding relation-node, attribute-node or value-node for each of the designations found in the query; an attribute-node will be created only if no value-node referring to that attribute is generated. Subsequently, additional relation-nodes may have to be included in the resulting set of nodes; this has to be done whenever the set of nodes contains value-nodes or attribute-nodes for which the corresponding relation-node does not belong to this set of nodes. Finally, each value-node and each attribute-node is connected with its corresponding relation-node. Thus we obtain a set of graphs called *stars* because of their graphical appearance; note that a star may consist of a single relation node.

(T3) Establish the sequence of the stars.

For each star there are one or more designations in the wording of the query that correspond to it in a natural way; particularly there is a left-most of those designations in the query for each star. The sequence of these left-most designations within the wording establishes a corresponding ordering of the stars, hence referred to as the sequence of the stars.

Example 3.1
We consider the following query:

> "Find the names of those suppliers who sell part number 113 to a project in London."

During step (T1) the following relevant designations will be discovered:

> names, suppliers, part number, 113, project, London

From these designations, five nodes are generated during step (T2) and an additional relation-node referring to the relation PART is included. Connection

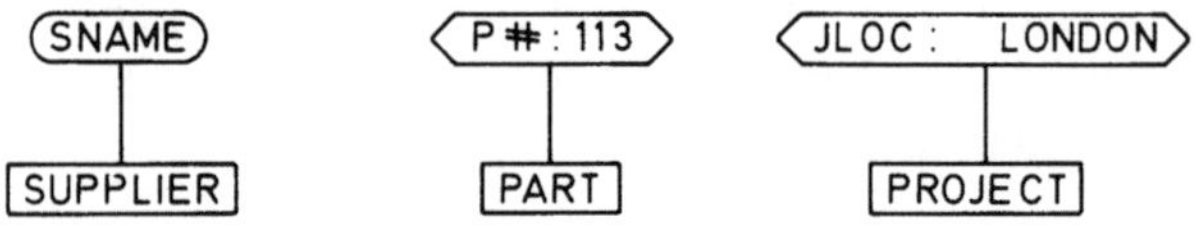

Fig. 3.1

yields the three stars depicted in Fig. 3.1 and their sequence according to step (T3) corresponds to the arrangement in Fig. 3.1 (from left to right).

(T4) Identify the initial star.

By means of the list of words which have no meaning with regard to the database (mentioned in step (T1)) a so-called initial star is chosen; this is done by scanning the wording of the query for words like "print", "find", "display" etc., by determining the following designations, and by attaching markings (*) to the corresponding attribute-nodes and/or relation-nodes. If no such words can be found the first star according to the sequence established in step (T3) becomes the initial star, otherwise an arbitrary star of those which bear markings becomes the initial star.

(T5) Connect the stars in such a way that they form a connected query graph.

The construction of the query graph consists of a series of attempts to connect two stars with each other. Let R1 and R2 be the relations referred to by two stars which are to be connected, let A1 be an attribute of R1 and A2 an attribute of R2; then the following four types of connection are considered:

(C1) The stars are connected by including an arc between their attribute-nodes A1 and A2 if the database graph contains an arc labelled with p_2 or p_3 between A1 and A2.

(C2) The stars are connected by including an attribute-node A2 and by connecting it both with R2 and with the attribute-node A1 if the database graph contains an arc labelled with p_2 between A1 and A2.

(C3) The stars are connected by including two attribute-nodes A1 and A2 and by connecting A1 with R1, A2 with R2 and A1 with A2 if the database graph contains an arc labelled with p_1 between A1 and A2.

(C4) The stars are connected by including two attribute-nodes A1 and A2 and a new star consisting of a relation-node R3 and attribute-nodes A3 and A4 and by connecting A1 to R1 and to A3 and A2 to R2 and to A4 if the database graph contains an arc labelled with p_1 both between A1 and A3 and between A2 and A4.

The actual construction of the query graph proceeds as follows. The initial star is taken as a starting graph and attempts are made to append the stars one to another according to the sequence established in step (T3); however, only connections of the types (C1), (C2) and (C3) are attempted, in this order. Whenever it is not possible to connect a star with the last of the already connected stars by means of a connection of type (C3), the last but one of the already connected stars is considered and so on; still only connections of types (C1) through (C3) are considered. Only if a star cannot be connected at all with the already connected ones, connections of type (C4) are taken into account. As before the last of the already connected stars is the first candidate for trying such a connection; if it fails the preceding stars are considered. If at any time during the construction of the query graph it is not possible to append another star, this may be due to the fact that wrong connections have been made. The procedure therefore requires a backtracking mechanism which may produce alternative connections; the way in which this backtracking mechanism has to operate becomes fairly obvious from the sequence in which the different types of connections are considered.

As described above, the procedure for constructing the query graphs is qualified for generating all varieties of tree-like query graphs. [JANA 82] also considers query graphs that contain cycles; due to the minor practical importance of this class of queries we omit the treatment of such queries here.

Example 3.2
We continue example 3.1; during step (T4) a marking is attached to the attribute-node referring to the attribute SNAME and the star referring to the relation SUPPLIER becomes the initial star. The attempts to connect the second star with the initial one by means of a connection of one of the types (C1) through (C3) fail since there are no corresponding connections in the database graph. As there are no further already connected stars, a connection of type (C4) is tried which results in the graph depicted in Fig. 3.2.

Between the stars referring to the relations PART and PROJECT again no connection of type (C1) through (C3) is possible and therefore a connection be-

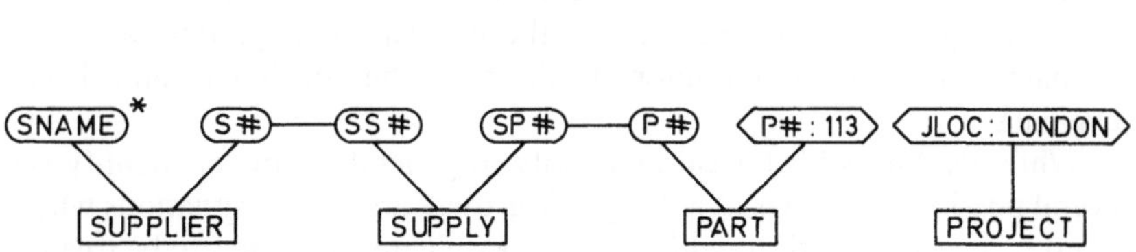

Fig. 3.2

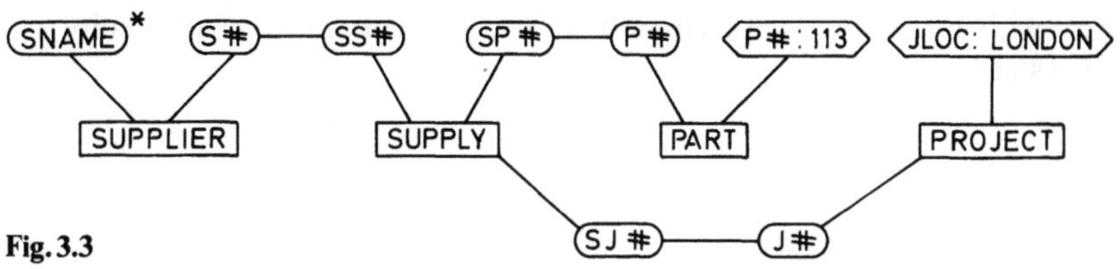

Fig. 3.3

tween the stars referring to SUPPLY and PROJECT is attempted; this time a connection of type (C3) is possible and yields the final query graph (see Fig. 3.3).

4 Lexical Ambiguity

Among other restrictions, the basic translation procedure requires that all relation designations, attribute designations, and value designations have definite meanings. It is unrealistic to assume that unequivocal meanings already exist from the definition of the vocabulary; we have to be prepared for the situation that a large number of the designations of the vocabulary is lexically ambiguous, i.e., they may refer to several different constituents of the database. Given a query which contains one or more of such ambiguous designations, the problem is to find out the actual meaning of these designations as intended by the user.

The easiest way to obtain the intended meaning of some ambiguous designation in a query would certainly be to offer the user a menu containing all possible meanings and let her/him choose. Due to the high rate of ambiguities to be expected, however, this seems to be no feasible solution since it would very quickly discourage even cooperative users. It cannot be excluded that in some cases there is no other possibility than to present such a menu to the user - even human listeners are not able to resolve all kinds of lexical ambiguity - for the sake of user acceptance, however, the problems of lexical ambiguity in general have to be dealt with by the system and not by the user.

In Sect. 4.1, we present a systematic approach to lexical ambiguity of designations referring to constituents of some database. We start by defining different types of ambiguity and then design rule schemata which are appropriate for resolving the individual types of ambiguity by considering a limited context of an ambiguous designation in a query. It is remarkable that these rule schemata are independent of the structure and the contents of any particular database; rather the disambiguation rules required by the natural language interface to some database can be generated automatically from the vocabulary and these rule schemata.

While dealing with lexical ambiguity in general means to identify one of several possible meanings of a designation, there are certain situations where the occurrence of designations with several possible meanings has to be treated differently. In Sect. 4.2, we discuss such cases, which are no ambiguities in the original sense but become manifest in the same way as lexical ambiguities. Section 4.2 ends with a comparative discussion of the treatment of lexical ambiguity in related systems.

4.1 Disambiguation Rules

The ambiguous designations in the vocabulary of a database may be classified according to their possible meanings. With regard to designations that have two possible meanings we distinguish the following nine types of ambiguity:

(A1) The possible meanings are two relations; notation: $<R/S>$.

(A2) The possible meanings are two attributes belonging to the same relation; notation: $<A_R/B_R>$.

(A3) The possible meanings are two attributes belonging to different relations; notation: $<A_R/B_S>$.

(A4) The possible meanings are two values of the same attribute; notation: $<\mu(A_R)/\mu(A_R)>$.

(A5) The possible meanings are two values of different attributes belonging to the same relation; notation: $<\mu(A_R)/\mu(B_R)>$.

(A6) The possible meanings are two values of different attributes which belong to different relations; notation: $<\mu(A_R)/\mu(B_S)>$.

(A7) The possible meanings are a relation and a attribute whereby the attribute may but need not belong to that relation; notation: $<R/A_S>$.

(A8) The possible meanings are a relation and value whereby the value may but need not belong to an attribute of that relation; notation: $<R/\mu(A_S)>$.

(A9) The possible meanings are an attribute and a value whereby the value may but need not belong to that attribute and the attribute of the value may but need not belong to the same relation as that attribute; notation: $<A_R/\mu(B_S)>$.

The most frequently occurring types of ambiguity are (A1) through (A6), whereas (A7) through (A9) will appear very rarely and are included in the above enumeration only for the sake of completeness. It is for this reason that we did not form separate types depending on whether two different relations or only one relation is referred to.

Observation of human understanding of natural language shows that the intended meaning of an ambiguous word is mostly inferred from the meanings of other words appearing in the direct neighbourhood of the word in question. Applied to the processing of natural language queries, we may attempt to infer the intended meaning of an ambiguous designation by identifying another designation in the query in such a way that the meaning of that other designation is semantically connected with one of the possible meanings of the ambiguous designation. Since all the meanings of the vocabulary are constituents (i. e., relations, attributes, values) of the database, a close semantic connection may be assumed whenever the respective meanings are related to each other in one of the kinds to be enumerated below; in detail, a *close semantic connection* holds between

(CSC1) a relation and an attribute of that relation;

(CSC2) a relation and a value of an attribute of that relation;

(CSC3) two attributes of the same relation;

(CSC4) an attribute and a value of that attribute;

(CSC5) an attribute and a value of another attribute of the same relation;

(CSC6) two values of the same attribute;

(CSC7) two values of two different attributes of the same relation.

Example 4.1.1
For each of the seven kinds of close semantic connection, we give a query in which the italicized designations are in the respective close semantic connection with each other.

"Find the *names* of all *suppliers*." (CSC1)

"Print the weight of *part P1091*." (CSC2)

"Display *name* and *weight* of part P1091." (CSC3)

"Print all suppliers whose *name* is *Smith*." (CSC4)

"Find the *location* of *Smith*." (CSC5)

"List all *brown* and *green* parts." (CSC6)

"List all *green bolts*." (CSC7)

If one of the italicized designations in one of the queries above is ambiguous, whereas the other one is not, the intended meaning of the ambiguous designation may be inferred from the definite meaning of the designation in its neighbourhood.

Not each of the seven types of close semantic connection is qualified for resolving an ambiguity of arbitrary type. Thus, when given a query which contains an ambiguity of type (A2), it is obviously of little help to identify an unique relation designation which refers to the relation the two attributes (the possible meanings of the ambiguous designation) belong to. Table 4.1 shows which kinds of close semantic connection are qualified for resolving which types of ambiguity.

It seems peculiar that ambiguities of type (A4) cannot be resolved at all by means of close semantic connections; it will turn out in Sect. 4.2, however, that ambiguities of that type are no proper ambiguities and that they have to be treated in a totally different way.

Table 4.1

	(CSC1)	(CSC2)	(CSC3)	(CSC4)	(CSC5)	(CSC6)	(CSC7)
(A1)	x	x					
(A2)				x			
(A3)	x		x	x	x		
(A4)							
(A5)				x		x	
(A6)		x		x	x	x	x
(A7)	x	x	x	x	x		
(A8)	x	x		x	x	x	x
(A9)	x	x	x	x	x	x	x

Table 4.1 allows for the immediate derivation of a set of context-sensitive *rule schemata* which describe the disambiguation capabilities of the semantics-based approach independently of a particular database. For each entry in the table, we obtain one or two rule schemata of the following shape

$$<X/Y> \rightarrow X/Con(Z)$$

or, respectively

$$<X/Y> \rightarrow Y/Con(Z)$$

The meaning of such a rule schema is that an ambiguous designation of type $<X/Y>$ may be assumed to have the intented meaning X (or Y, respectively) if it appears in the direct neighbourhood of a designation with the meaning Z because a close semantic connection holds between X (or Y, respectively) and Z.

Actual *disambiguation rules* are obtained from these rule schemata by consistently replacing the symbols X, Y, and Z by the internal relation names, attribute names and domain names of some database. We would like to emphasize that it is not the entirety of all possible disambiguation rules that has to be generated. Instead, it is possible to generate automatically the set of exactly those disambiguation rules which are required for resolving the actually occurring ambiguities from the vocabulary of the database.

Example 4.1.2
Imagine the following database schema:

{R1 = (A, B, C),
R2 = (D, E)}

Moreover, assume that according to the definition of the vocabulary, the attributes A and B have one or more designations in common. Since these two attributes belong to the same relation the ambiguity is of type (A2); according to Table 4.1, only a close semantic connection of type (CSC4) is suitable for resolving such an ambiguity. Thus the only applicable rule schemata are

$$<A_R/B_R> \rightarrow A_R/\mathrm{Con}(\mu(A_R))$$
$$<A_R/B_R> \rightarrow B_R/\mathrm{Con}(\mu(B_R))$$

and insertion of attribute names and domain names leads to the following disambiguation rules:

$$<A/B> \rightarrow A/\mathrm{Con}(\mu(A))$$
$$<A/B> \rightarrow B/\mathrm{Con}(\mu(B))$$

Let us further assume that there are common designations of the relations R1 and R2. This ambiguity of type (A1) may be resolved by close semantic connections of type (CSC1) and (CSC2); the corresponding rule schemata are:

a) $<R/S> \rightarrow R/\mathrm{Con}(A_R)$
b) $<R/S> \rightarrow S/\mathrm{Con}(A_S)$
c) $<R/S> \rightarrow R/\mathrm{Con}(\mu(A_R))$
d) $<R/S> \rightarrow S/\mathrm{Con}(\mu(A_S))$

This time consistent insertion of relation names, attribute names and domain names yields several rules for each rule schema:

a) $<R1/R2> \rightarrow R1/(\mathrm{Con}(A)$
   $<R1/R2> \rightarrow R1/\mathrm{Con}(B)$
   $<R1/R2> \rightarrow R1/\mathrm{Con}(C)$
b) $<R1/R2> \rightarrow R2/\mathrm{Con}(D)$
   $<R1/R2> \rightarrow R2/\mathrm{Con}(E)$
c) $<R1/R2> \rightarrow R1/\mathrm{Con}(\mu(A))$
   $<R1/R2> \rightarrow R1/\mathrm{Con}(\mu(B))$
   $<R1/R2> \rightarrow R1/\mathrm{Con}(\mu(C))$
d) $<R1/R2> \rightarrow R2/\mathrm{Con}(\mu(D))$
   $<R1/R2> \rightarrow R2/\mathrm{Con}(\mu(E))$

A disambiguation rule is *applicable* to a designation in a query if that designation features the ambiguity specified by the left-hand-side of the disambiguation rule and if the context of the designation in the query satisfies the restrictions specified by the context-part of the disambiguation rule. With regard to the context-part of the disambiguation rules we only note that there are different levels of detail on which the context of an ambiguous designation may be specified. The weakest kind is to postulate only that one of the possible meanings of the next designation on the left (or right, respectively) in the query is in close semantic connection with one of the possible meanings of the ambiguous designations. For further details with respect to the context-parts of the disambiguation rules the reader has to be referred to [JANA 82].

The *application of a disambiguation rule* to an ambiguous designation in a query requires that the disambiguation rule is applicable to that designation; the result of the application of a disambiguation rule is that the meaning on the right-hand side of the disambiguation rule is assigned to the ambiguous designation in the query.

For a given ambiguous designation in a query, several disambiguation rules may be applicable; as long as all of the applicable disambiguation rules would assign the same meaning to the ambiguous designation, an arbitrary one of them may be applied. If different meanings would be assigned to the ambiguous designation by the applicable disambiguation rules, an application is possible only if there is a majority among the applicable disambiguation rules whose application would yield the same result; in this case an arbitrary rule of this majority may be applied. Otherwise none of the applicable rules is applied - at least temporarily; still one has to consider that a disambiguation of other ambiguous designations in a query may have the effect that no longer all of the disambiguation rules applicable to an ambiguity which temporarily cannot be resolved are applicable and that therefore a majority still may be accomplished. In particular, this implies that a context beyond the next designation in the wording of the query may influence the resolution of an ambiguity.

As a consequence of the above majority heuristics, the result of resolving several ambiguities in one query may differ depending on the sequence in which the ambiguities are resolved; obviously, this is an undesirable effect as the result of disambiguation in such situations would be unreliable at least. To avoid unreliable disambiguations in this sense, it would be safer to try first all possible sequences of disambiguations in a query and then to resolve only those ambiguities for which all possible sequences have yielded the same result. It is obvious that such a procedure will quickly become costly as the number of ambiguous designation in a query rises. It turns out, however, that an inspection of two particular sequences is always sufficient to decide which of the disambiguations are reliable and which not. One of these sequences is the *maximum left-most sequence:* In the maximum left-most sequence always the left-most ambiguous designation for which an application of disambiguation rules is possible is resolved next; this is done until no further disambiguations are possible. The *maximum right-most sequence* is defined analogously. In [JANA 82], a proof of the following theorem is given.

Theorem 4.1.3
If there is a disambiguation sequence for a query that assigns to some ambiguous designation a different meaning than the meaning assigned to this designation by the maximum left-most sequence, also the meanings assigned to this designation by the maximum left-most sequence and by the maximum right-most sequence will differ from each other.

As a consequence of theorem 4.1.3 only the results of the maximum left-most sequence and the maximum right-most sequence have to be compared to each other. If they agree on the meaning of some ambiguous designation this disambiguation may safely be applied since all possible sequences would have yielded this meaning. Otherwise disambiguation would be unreliable and the decision which meaning should be assigned to the ambiguous designation has to be left to the user by offering him a corresponding menu.

Right from the beginning of this section, we have confined ourselves to ambiguous designations with exactly two possible meanings. This is justified since the treatment of ambiguities with more than two possible meanings may easily be reduced to the treatment of ambiguities with exactly two meanings.

The type of an ambiguous designation which has more than two meanings may be specified in an extension of the types (A1) through (A9) in an obvious way. Let $<X_1/\ldots/X_n>$ be such a type; we then consider the set of all rule schemata which are qualified to resolve ambiguities of the types $<X_1/X_2>$, $<X_1/X_3>$, $\ldots <X_n/X_{n-2}>$, $<X_n/X_{n-1}>$ and replace their left-hand sides by the type $<X_1/\ldots X_n>$. Subsequently, we have to remove those rule schemata from the resulting set that are "contradictory"; since all of these rule schemata share the same left-hand side two of them are contradictory if they agree with respect to their context-parts but disagree with respect to their right-hand sides. The remaining rule schemata may be used in the same way as rule schemata for resolving ambiguities with only two possible meanings; this applies to the generation of the actual disambiguation rules as well as to the applicability and application of the disambiguation rules.

4.2 Abnormal Ambiguity

In the previous section, we have seen that ambiguities of type (A4) cannot be resolved at all by means of disambiguation rules. This is not very surprising because an ambiguity of type (A4) applies if the two possible meanings of the designation in question are two different values of the same attribute and there seems to be no way at all to decide which of them is the one intended by the user. As a matter of fact, however, it is not necessary to make such a decision.

Like all ambiguities, an ambiguity of type (A4) derives from a corresponding definition of the vocabulary; particularly with regard to (A4) this means that two (or more) values have intentionally been given the same designation. If we may assume that this did not occur by mistake, the only explanation is that the designation in question is rather a generic term for the different values than an actually ambiguous designation.

The usage of such a generic term in a query obviously requires a different treatment by the natural language interface than the use of ambiguous designations. On the one hand, a generic term may be used intentionally by the user in order to save the time required for explicitly enumerating definite designations of the individual values; on the other hand, the user may not be aware of the definite designations and not even interested in the level of detail they provide. In either case it seems reasonable not to interpret the generic term as one particular value but rather as a reference to the corresponding collection of values.

Example 4.2.1
Suppose that the definition of the vocabulary of some database includes entries for the values of an attribute COLOR, such as "cobalt", "aquamarine", "carmesin" and "purple". Reasonably, the values referred to by the former (latter) two value designations might also be referred to by the additional value designation "blue" ("red"). In this case, a query like

"Find all red cars."

would be interpreted as

"Find all cars which are carmesin or purple."

Such abnormal ambiguities may also occur - though far less frequently - in connection with relations and attributes. Thus, the usage of an ambiguous designation of type (A1) in a query may stem from the fact that the user actually requires information from several relations at the same time; such a possibility has to be taken into account all the more as users who express their queries in natural language need not know the structure of the database to the last detail.

Therefore, if disambiguation of an ambiguity of type (A1) is not possible according to the procedure described in Sect. 4.1, we consider the possibility indicated above. This means that we attempt to construct two (or even more) query graphs, namely one for each of the possible meanings of the ambiguous designation and - if this may be accomplished - connect these query graphs disjunctively. Note that a successful construction of the different query graphs requires the existence of corresponding attributes in the different relations.

Example 4.2.2 (from [KONO 79])
Imagine the following database schema:

{US-SHIP=(NAME, LOCATION),
FOREIGN-SHIP=(F-NAME, F-LOCATION, COUNTRY)}

Stored in separate relations, the database contains the names and current locations of both American and foreign ships as well as the nationality of the foreign ships. In a query like

"Find the names of all ships in the Mediterranean."

the designations "names", "ships" and "Mediterranean" all are ambiguous since they may refer to either of the above relations; a disambiguation by means of the disambiguation rules is not possible. Since the ambiguity of "ships" is of type (A1) an attempt is made to construct separate query graphs for the two possible meanings, namely US-SHIP and FOREIGN-SHIP. In either case, the disambiguation of "names" and "Mediterranean" is possible and a query graph is obtained. Regarding the connection of these two query graphs, we have to note that a connection of such queries is not possible in some query languages since it would require a disjunction on the top level (cf. [PIRO 78] for this problem); in this case, the two queries have to be addressed to the database system one after another; this is one of the rare cases where a natural language query cannot be translated into a single formal query.

We only mention that also ambiguities of the types (A2) and (A3) may turn out to be abnormal ambiguities. As far as type (A2) is concerned, the usage of a corresponding designation in a query may require that several attributes have to be included in the answer relation on account of a single attribute designation; this particularly applies if several attributes of a relation are likely to be frequently accessed together (e.g., "address"). Regarding ambiguities of type (A3), a common designation of two attributes may be used to express a join between these attributes; this may be recognized by inspecting the immediate surroundings of the designation in question (e.g. "the same location as").

The problem of resolving lexical ambiguities is of great importance, especially in the area of natural language interfaces to databases; this particularly applies to non-toy databases where data which are closely related to each other often might be stored in different relations for reasons of efficiency. As a consequence, different relations and attributes have to be referred to rather similarly in natural language. In this respect, it is remarkable that research in the area of natural language interfaces has paid only little attention to the problem of lexical ambiguity. The most common approach (cf. [WALT 76, HARR 77a, CODD 78]) is simply to try to find translations for all possible combinations of meanings hoping this will be possible only for one combination. If disambiguation by means of the context is attempted (cf. [DELL 77, CODD 78]), the employed rules explicitly refer to individual relations, attributes, and domains of a particular database or even to individual designations of these database constituents. In contrast, the treatment of lexical ambiguity described in this chapter is independent of a particular database and allows to generate automatically the actually required disambiguation rules. This latter property is of special importance whenever the part of the real world that is represented by the database will be extended.

5 Conjunctions

In this section, we do not attempt to deal with the entirety of the problems involved in the processing of natural language queries which contain conjunctions. For a more thorough treatment of this problem area within the semantics-based approach the reader has to be referred to [JANA 82]. The purpose of this section is rather to focus on two aspects of cooperative behavior of natural language interfaces to relational databases that are tightly coupled with the usage of conjunctions in natural language.

In Sect. 5.1, we deal with sloppy usage of conjunctions, in particular with situations where the word "and" is used to express logical disjunction. We show

how such situations may be detected and give an algorithm which enumerates the plausible interpretations of a query. It is obvious that such capabilities of a natural language interface may well contribute to the user acceptance of such a system.

In Sect. 5.2, we investigate what information might be relevant to the user in response to her/his query especially in situations where this can be inferred only vaguely from the wording of the query. It turns out that disjunctions within a query considerably influence the set of attributes to be included in the answer relation.

5.1 Connections of Values of the Same Attribute

In all of the examples given so far, the constituents of a query were connected conjunctively (when viewed at the level of a relational calculus representation); this is an immediate consequence of the fact that juxtaposition in language normally corresponds to conjunction in logic. Disjunction always has to be expressed more or less explicitly in order to be understood as disjunction. Therefore, one might suppose that dealing with conjunctions essentially means to identify the positions within a natural language utterance where the implicitly or explicitly conjunctively connected sequence is interrupted explicitly. Unfortunately, this is not true because the use of conjunctions in natural language is rather sloppy from a logician's point of view.

The most frequent sin in this regard is the usage of the word "and" in order to express disjunction; it is so common in all manifestations of natural language that one understands it correctly without even realizing. When dealing with the translation of natural language into some formal representation, however, a literal translation of conjunctions would be disastrous. Instead one has to think of ways to model the human capabilities to understand conjunctions correctly even if they are used in contradiction to logic. As far as conjunctions between value designations referring to the same attribute are concerned, the possibilities of such a modelling and their limitations are investigated in the remainder of this section.

Suppose that the integrity constraints of some database prescribe that a car represented in the database may always have only one color; a query for all cars which are both red and blue then still would be meaningful, however, the answer to it would be of little value because, no matter what the actual contents of the database were, it would always read: "There are no such cars." A user who is familiar with the structure and the contents of the database and is seriously interested in the answer will never ask such a query because (s)he already knows the answer from the start. As we emphasized already in Sect. 1, the above characterized class of users is the only one the semantics-based approach is aiming at. Thus, when given a query which allows for several different interpretations some of which under no circumstances can be fulfilled by the database we may exclude these interpretations from our considerations. With regard to a query like "Find all cars which are red and blue" this implies that the theoretically possible interpretation "cars which are both red and blue" may be neglected and that therefore the only reasonable interpretation is "cars which are red or blue."

Unfortunately, it is not always as easy as in the above example to decide what the meaning of the word "and" is if it is placed between two value designations referring to the same attribute. In general it is quite possible that such an "and" means a logical conjunction.

Example 5.1.1
The query:

> "Find all departments with employees who drive red and blue cars."

according to the above discussion must not be interpreted as:

> "Find all departments with employees who drive cars which are both red and blue."

It may be interpreted as

> "Find all departments with employees who drive cars which are red or blue."

Still there are two more reasonable interpretations which may be rephrased in natural language as follows:

> "Find all departments with employees who drive both at least one red car and at least one blue car."
> "Find all departments which have both employees who drive a red car and employees who drive a blue car."

All of the latter three interpretations are plausible and therefore should be presented to the user in a menu. This requires a formal procedure which discovers all plausible interpretations in such a situation.

The algorithm that discovers the plausible interpretations operates on the query graph of that interpretation in which the "and" is interpreted as a logical disjunction connecting the two (or more) value designations referring to the same attribute. This query graph can always be constructed according to the translation procedure given in Sect. 3. The relation-node to which the value-nodes in question are attached is called the "branching node" of the query graph. The algorithm then proceeds as follows:

(BA1) If the branching node or an attribute-node connected with the branching node bears a marking or if there is more than one direct path from the branching node (via two attribute nodes) to another relation node, then there are no further plausible interpretations.

(BA2) The star of the branching node is replaced by as many instances of itself as there are value-nodes referring to the same attribute; each of these instances contains only one of the value-nodes and is connected with the rest of the query graph in the same way as the original star. The resulting query graph is another plausible interpretation of the query.

(BA3) The (only) relation-node to which there was a direct path from the branching node becomes the new branching node.

(BA4) If the branching node or an attribute-node connected with the branching node bears a marking or if there is more than one direct path from the branching node to another relation-node (paths to an instance of the previous branching node do not count), then there are no further plausible interpretations.

(BA5) The star of the branching node is replaced by as many instances of itself as there are instances of the previous branching node; each of these instances is connected with one instance of the star of the previous branching node and with the rest of the query graph in the same way as the original star of the current branching node. The resulting query graph is another plausible interpretation of the query and the algorithm continues at step (BA3).

Example 5.1.2
We follow the execution of the branching algorithm for the query given in example 5.1.1. Starting point is the query graph depicted in Fig. 5.1 and the first branching node is the relation-node referring to CAR.

Since the corresponding star bears no markings and since there is only one path leading to another relation-node, branching is possible and step (BA2) yields the query graph given in Fig. 5.2; one can easily verify that this graph corresponds to the second plausible interpretation mentioned in example 5.1.1. Now the node referring to the relation EMPLOYEE becomes the new branching node and it turns out in step (BA4) that again branching is possible; as a result of step (BA5) we obtain the query graph displayed in Fig. 5.3 which corresponds to the third plausible interpretation given in example 5.1.1. Finally, the node referring to the relation DEPARTMENT becomes branching node but since it bears a marking the algorithm terminates at step (BA4).

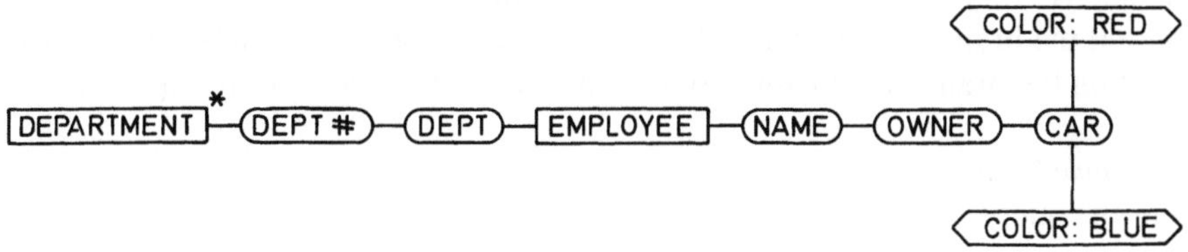

Fig. 5.1

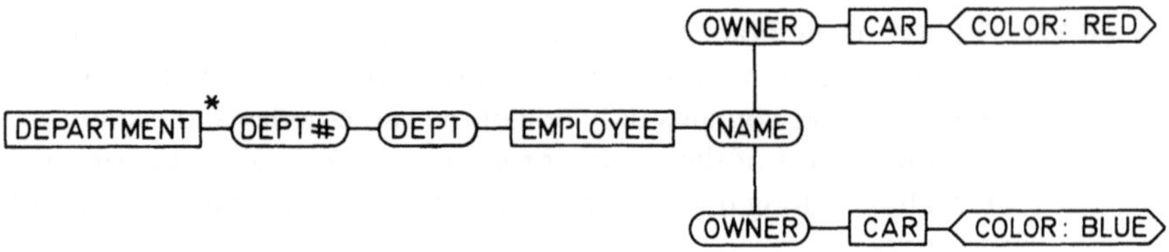

Fig. 5.2

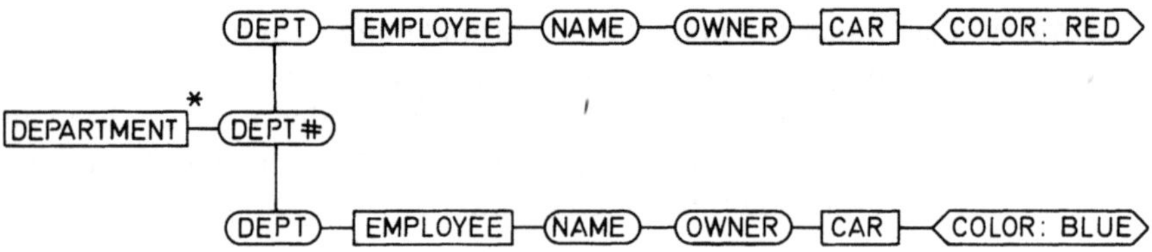

Fig. 5.3

Our branching algorithm still suffers from some deficiencies inasmuch as under certain circumstances it may produce several interpretations that are semantically equivalent, i.e., given arbitrary contents of the database, they will always have the same answers and therefore need not be distinguished at all. Even more annoying, the branching algorithm in its present form sometimes may produce interpretations which cannot be fulfilled no matter what the content of the database is. The reason for both phenomena are functional dependencies holding between certain attributes which are of fundamental importance within the branching process.

In order to be able to suppress the production of undesirable interpretations in the above sense we have to define the "branching attribute" of each generated interpretation. The branching attribute of the interpretation the algorithm starts with is the attribute for which there are two or more value-nodes. The branching attribute of an interpretation generated in step (BA2) or (BA5) is the attribute referred to by the only attribute-node in the query graph that is connected with more than two other nodes.

It can be shown that two interpretations consecutively generated by the branching algorithm are semantically equivalent if the branching attribute of the former interpretation is functionally dependent on the branching attribute of the latter interpretation. Moreover, it can be shown that an interpretation generated in step (BA2) of the branching algorithm cannot be fulfilled at all by the database if the branching attribute of the initial interpretation is functionally dependent on the branching attribute of the interpretation generated in step (BA2).

Example 5.1.3
For the query

"Find the insurance companies of the cars driven by Smith and Jones."

the initial query graph and the two query graphs generated by the branching algorithm are given in Fig. 5.4; their branching attributes are NAME, DRIVER and ILIP. The attribute DRIVER is a foreign key and therefore functionally dependent on E# and vice versa; NAME is functionally dependent on E# since E# is the primary key of EMPLOYEE. Due to the transitivity of functional dependencies NAME is also functionally dependent on DRIVER which means that the second of the interpretations given in Fig. 5.4 needs not be presented to the user because it could never be fulfilled. Moreover, the attribute ILIP is a foreign key and therefore functionally dependent on the attribute LIP and vice versa; additionally DRIVER is functionally dependent on LIP which is the primary key of the relation CAR. Thus we may infer that DRIVER is functionally dependent on ILIP and therefore also the third of the interpretations of the query will be suppressed. A brief look at the two query graphs shows that both decisions are well justified: Since the database contains exactly one driver for each car, neither of the two interpretations in question may ever be fulfilled.

If a query contains more than two value designations that refer to the same attribute, they may be combined in the wording of the query by the use of several conjunctions. As long as all of these conjunctions are "or" it is only natural to connect all of the corresponding value-nodes disjunctively. If all of these conjunctions are "and", we may proceed according to the branching algorithm in the same way as if there were only one "and" which closes an enumeration of value designations. If, however, such an enumeration of value designations is connected both by "and" and by "or" then the user's usage of different conjunctions indicates that the value-nodes are not to be connected in a uniform way. In this case, a connection by means of "and" always requires branching, whereas branching is not considered for connections by means of "or".

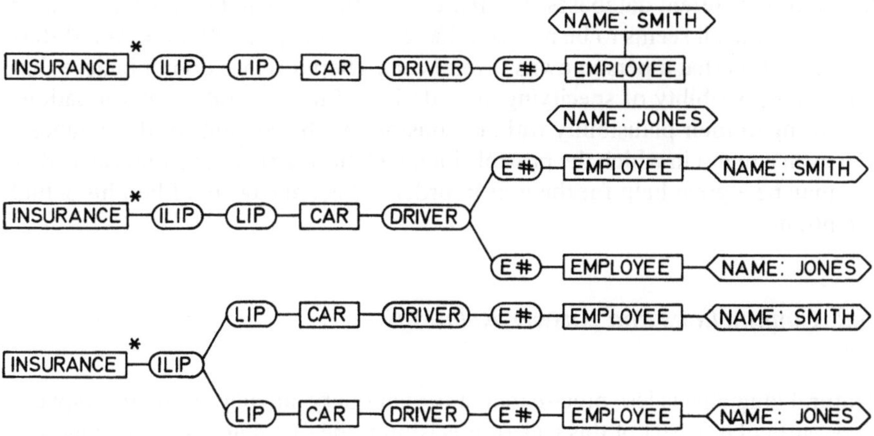

Fig. 5.4

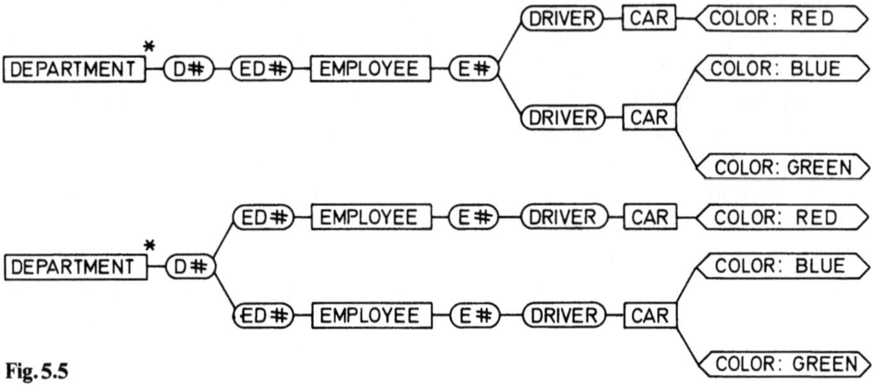

Fig. 5.5

Example 5.1.4
For the query

> "Find all departments with employees who drive red and blue or green cars."

the query graphs depicted in Fig. 5.5 would be generated as the only plausible interpretations of the query. Rephrased in natural language these would read:

> "Find all departments with employees who drive both a car which is red and a car which is blue or green."

> "Find all departments which have both employees who drive a red car and employees who drive a car which is blue or green."

When looking at the different interpretations generated by the branching algorithm, it may be generally noticed that some of them seem to be more plausible to a human reader/listener than others. This particularly applies if examples are taken from different databases. The reasons for this seem to be purely pragmatic in nature; thus it seems to be nearer at hand that a supplier offers several different parts than that a person owns several cars. Therefore, we do not believe that there is a possibility of specifying an ordering of the generated interpretations according to their plausibility without considering the contents of the database. But even a menu in which the possible interpretations appear in a random ordering may be a great help for the user in order to become aware of her/his actual intentions.

5.2 Conjunctions and Answer Relations

Natural language is less precise than a formal query language in many respects. One particular aspect of this lack of precision is the fact that in natural language a user may explicitly or implicitly ask for entire relations rather than for individual attributes of these relations; this is done by asking for relation designations, representative value designations or by the usage of interrogative pronouns. When translating natural language queries into some formal query language, one has to decide which of the attributes of the relation being asked for are to be presented.

The simplest strategy is to present all of the relations's attributes; the large number of attributes that non-toy relations may have normally does not allow such a procedure. Another possible reaction to queries which ask for relations instead of attributes would be to present the attributes of the relation to the user in a menu and to make him tick those attributes (s)he wants to be displayed. This would guarantee that the user always obtains those and only those attributes (s)he is interested in. On the other hand, this strategy would increase the number of interactions necessary for a single query and thus delay the actual dialog.

A compromise between these two strategies is to define a default set of attributes to be displayed for each relation in the database. In reaction to a query which implicitly or explicitly asks for a relation, the corresponding default set of attributes would be displayed. Criteria for the selection of these default sets might be the importance of the individual attributes and considerations with respect to the maximum number of attributes that may be arranged clearly on the screen.

Rigid defaults sets still may lead to some undesirable effects. As an example, imagine a question for red cars where the attribute COLOR is supposed to be an element of the default set of the relation CAR. The column of the attribute COLOR in the answer relation then would contain only the value "red" no matter what the contents of the database are. The display of this attribute would bore the user at best. Therefore, the system should suppress an attribute of the default set whenever it can infer from the query that only a single value is assigned to that attribute in the answer relation. Queries which contain disjunctions, however, require a more thorough treatment with regard to the output attributes.

Example 5.2.1
We consider the following query:

"Find the salary of Smith and Jones."

According to Sect. 5.1, the word "and" is interpreted as a logical disjunction and there is only a single plausible interpretation. A literal execution of this interpretation would result in an answer relation which only consists of two numbers, namely the salary of Smith and the salary of Jones; given such an answer the user could not be sure which salary belongs to which person.

In order to be able to give informative answers to the user's queries, it is necessary to edit attributes which neither have been asked for explicitly nor belong to the respective default set of attributes. In particular, an attribute has to be displayed if two or more value designations pertaining to that attribute are connected disjunctively in a query. In the first place, such a regulation prevents answers like the one demonstrated in example 5.2.1. In general, it is an attempt to provide the user with additional information on aspects (s)he seems to be particularly interested in.

The above regulation can be extended in a natural way to situations where two or more value designations pertaining to different attributes are connected disjunctively in a query; in this case, all these attributes have to be displayed. The output of additional attributes is not possible, however, if the disjunction in question is embedded in another disjunction because the existence of the attributes cannot be guaranteed. A detailed algorithm for the computation of the set of attributes that have to be displayed besides the default set depends on the formal query language into which the natural language queries are to be translated and therefore lies beyond the scope of this paper.

Example 5.2.2
Suppose that the default set of the relation EMPLOYEE only consists of the attribute NAME. The answer relation to the query

"Find all employees in New York and Detroit."

then would comprise the attributes NAME and CITY whereas, the answer relation to the query

"Find all employees who are programmers or live in New York."

would comprise the attributes NAME, JOB and CITY whereas, and the answer relation to the query

"Find all employees who drive a car which is red or blue."

would contain the attribute NAME of the relation EMPLOYEE and the attribute COLOR of the relation CAR. However, the answer relation of the query

"Find all employees who are programmers or drive a car which is red or blue."

only consists of the attribute NAME. The reason for not including the attribute COLOR in the answer relation stems from the fact that the existence of a value for that attribute cannot be guaranteed if an employee is a programmer.

We only mention that, apart from disjunction, there are other determinants which may influence the set of attributes of the answer relation, e.g., negation within a query or intervals of values explicitly or implicitly referred to in a query; for details cf. [JANA 82].

6 Ellipsis

One particularly challenging aspect of the cooperativeness of a natural language interface to databases is the area of elliptic queries. Following traditional linguistic concept formation, a query is called elliptic if one or more of its constituents are omitted; such an omission may apply either to constituents which are of importance with respect to the meaning of the query as intended by the user, or to constituents whose only function is to combine the other constituents of the query in order to form a grammatical utterance.

It is only natural that syntax-oriented approaches to natural language query processing are not very well suited to the processing of elliptic queries because elliptic queries obviously violate the boundaries of normal syntax. Thus, when recognizing a query to be elliptic these systems have to switch to a special mode of processing which either makes use of a special ellipsis-oriented parser or uses the parser in a different way (cf. [HEND 77a] and [WALT 76]). The semantics-based natural language interface, however, can process elliptic queries in the usual way and only uses the previous query as an additional source of information when constructing the query graph of an elliptic query. Moreover, within the semantics-based approach certain kinds of ellipses, namely those where the omitted constituents are not related to the structure or to the contents of the database, do not need any deviation from normal processing whatsoever.

In this section we describe the processing of elliptic queries within the semantics-based approach. We start by giving in Sect. 6.1 a classification of ellipses depending on what part of a query is omitted. In Sect. 6.2, we discuss how ellipsis is detected and investigate the completion of queries which show ellipses of simple kind. In Sect. 6.3, we introduce the concept "query skeleton" which forms the basis for the treatment of ellipses of the more difficult kind that will be studied subsequently.

6.1 A Classification of Ellipses

In the following, elliptic queries are classified according to whether the omitted constituent(s) belong(s) to the target list or to the qualification expression of the formal query language representation of the query. A third class of ellipses reflects natural language queries whose query type (i.e., open query, closed query etc.) cannot be inferred by looking at the query in isolation.

If the wording of a query contains no hint to the query type, this is called an *illocution ellipsis.*

Example 6.1.1
The following query features an illocution ellipsis:

"secretaries in New York"

Depending on which of the following four queries

"Are there secretaries in Chicago?"

"Find all employees in New York."

"How many area managers are there in Orlando?"

"Print the names and age of all dish washers in Miami."

preceeds the elliptic query, it has to be interpreted as

"Are there secretaries in New York?"

"Find all secretaries in New York."

"How many secretaries are there in New York?"

"Print the names and age of all secretaries in New York."

In cases when the above elliptic query is the first query within a user session it is most reasonable to assume that the second of these interpretations was intended by the user.

If the wording of a query implies that the query is an open query but does not contain any hints to the target attribute(s) or target relation(s), respectively, then this is called a *target ellipsis*. From this definition it is clear that a query cannot have both an illocution ellipsis and a target ellipsis.

Example 6.1.2
The following query features a target ellipsis:

"of secretaries in New York."

Depending on which of the following queries

"Print the names and phone numbers of programmers with five years of experience."

"Find the name and department of dish washers with five years of experience."

preceeds the elliptic query, it has to be interpreted as

"Print the names and phone numbers of secretaries in New York."

"Find the name and department of secretaries in New York."

The (inept) case when the above elliptic query is the first query within a user session should be treated like the elliptic query in the previous example.

If the wording of a query contains no or only an incomplete description of the objects to which the query refers, then this is called a *complete* or a *partial qualification ellipsis*.

Example 6.1.3
The following query features a complete qualification ellipsis:

"Age and salary."

If it is preceeded by a query like

"Print the names of all secretaries in New York."

it has to be interpreted as

"Print the age and salary of all secretaries in New York."

An illocution ellipsis may be combined with a qualification ellipsis; in this case the qualification ellipsis may be either partial or complete.

Example 6.1.4
Given the following two consecutive queries

"Print the names of all secretaries in Chicago."

"in New York."

the latter combines an illocution ellipsis and a partial qualification ellipsis; its complete wording would be:

"Print the names of all secretaries in New York."

The second of the following two consecutive queries is an example for the combination of an illocution ellipsis and a complete qualification ellipsis.

"Print the names and address of 10 secretaries in New York."

"20."

Note that this elliptic query might also be a combination of an illocution ellipsis and a partial qualification ellipsis when preceeded by a query which refers to an integer attribute value.

Following from the above definitions, combinations of target ellipses and complete qualification ellipses would not address the database at all and therefore need not be considered. Combinations of target ellipses and partial qualification ellipses are possible. However, even for a human listener it is difficult to tell them from pure target ellipses; therefore it is reasonable to interpret such combinations as pure target ellipses. For similar reasons, partial qualification ellipses that are not combined with an illocution ellipsis may always be interpreted as complete queries.

6.2 Detection of Ellipses

Within a syntax-oriented approach, the detection of elliptic input is rather straightforward. If the parser fails, one has to switch to ellipsis processing; if ellipsis processing fails as well, the input cannot be processed at all. Within the semantics-based approach, we have to make a decision whether a given query is regarded as elliptic or not because dependent on that decision we can make use of the preceding query as an additional source of information or not.

For reasons of brevity we confine ourselves as far as possible to simple open queries (i.e., queries whose natural wording more or less explicitly contains some attributes or relations being asked for or, respectively, whose relational calculus representations contain at least one free variable). However, the semantics-based approach is feasible for a large variety of query types (cf. [JANA 82]): closed queries which are better known as yes/no-questions, queries requiring only restricted retrieval (e.g. "Find five programmers who ..."), queries with interrogative pronouns (e.g. "Who lives in Boston?"), queries containing anaphoric references (e.g. "Find their age.") and several others.

Obviously, each of these query types requires some special treatment at some point during the translation process and thus the type of a query has to be determined at an early point during translation. As a matter of fact, this is done on the occasion of step (T4) of the translation procedure outlined in Sect. 3. For each query type, there are some simple criteria such as the presence of attribute designations, the presence of interrogative pronouns or the presence of possessive pronouns, which - when satisfied - suggest that the respective query is a member of one of the possible query classes. Queries for which no such query class can be found are assumed to be possibly elliptic and are subject to the treatment described in the remainder of this section and in the following section.

In the following, we shall discuss the processing of two kinds of ellipses, whose occurrences are discovered very easily, namely complete qualification ellipses and combinations of illocution ellipsis and complete qualification ellipsis.

Combinations of illocution ellipsis and complete qualification ellipsis always have the shape given in example 6.1.4, i.e., the query only consists of an integer number. Such queries are reasonable only if they follow a question which requires only restricted retrieval (like in example 6.1.4) or if they follow a yes/no-question asking for the existence of some objects in the database. In both cases the query graph of the previous query may be adopted for the elliptic query without any changes. In case the previous query is a closed query which refers to more than one relation it is important to know that the query graphs of closed queries also bear markings. However, these markings do not serve to label the attributes and relations to be presented but they are used for marking the focus of the query which may be referred to by a subsequent query. Thus, when a combination of illocution ellipsis and complete qualification ellipsis follows a closed query referring to several attributes, the restriction relating to the number is placed on the focus node of the closed query.

Example 6.2.1
Given the following two queries

"Are there programmers in the electronics department?"

"10"

the interpretation of the second would be:

"Are there at least 10 programmers in the electronics department?"

rather than:

"Are there at least 10 electronics departments with programmers."

In some cases when a query consists only of an integer number it is not safe to assume a combination of illocution ellipsis and complete qualification ellipsis; this applies if the previous query contains an integer attribute value. The decision then must be left to the user.

Example 6.2.2
Given the following two queries

"Find 3 programmers with 2 years of experience."

"5"

it has to be left to the user which of the following two interpretations (s)he intends.

"Find 5 programmers with 2 years of experience."

"Find 3 programmers with 5 years of experience."

A complete qualification ellipsis has to be considered if the query is an enumeration of attribute designations and relation designations. In this case, the translation procedure from Sect. 3 is pursued until step (T2) only; then, for each of the resulting stars a star in the query graph of the previous query is determined that refers to the same relation. All markings are stripped from the identified stars in the query graph of the previous query and new markings are introduced according to the stars of the elliptic query in the following way: If a star of the elliptic query consists of a single relation-node, then the corresponding relation-node in the query graph is marked. Otherwise, for each attribute-node of a star of the elliptic query a marked attribute-node referring to the same attribute is attached to the corresponding star in the query graph of the previous query. Stars of the elliptic query for which there is no corresponding star in the query graph of the previous query are connected with that query graph by means of a connection of type (C3).

Example 6.2.3
We consider the following two consecutive queries

"Find all secretaries who drive a red car."

"Name, age and phone number."

For the first we obtain the query graph depicted in Fig. 6.1 and for the second a single star with three attributes. According to the procedure described above the star referring to the relation EMPLOYEE is modified, thus yielding the query graph given in Fig. 6.2.

The next pair of queries

"Find the names of all programmers in Detroit."

"Departments."

features a situation where the star of the elliptic query is not contained in the query graph of its preceding query. Therefore, a connection has to be established between the relation-nodes referring to the relations DEPARTMENT and EMPLOYEE. Note that in the resulting query graph (see Fig. 6.3) the marking of the node referring to the attribute NAME deliberately was not deleted. This allows

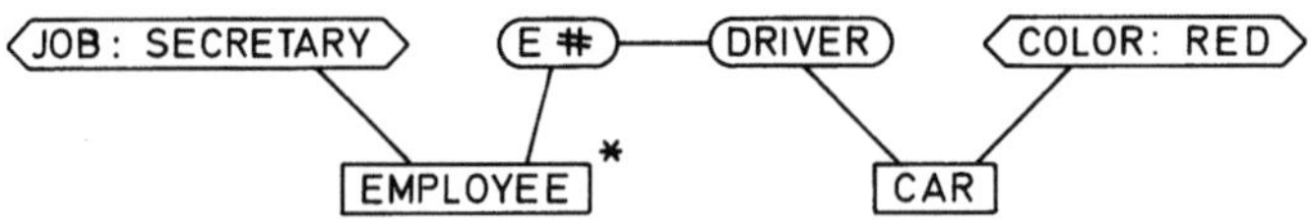

Fig. 6.1

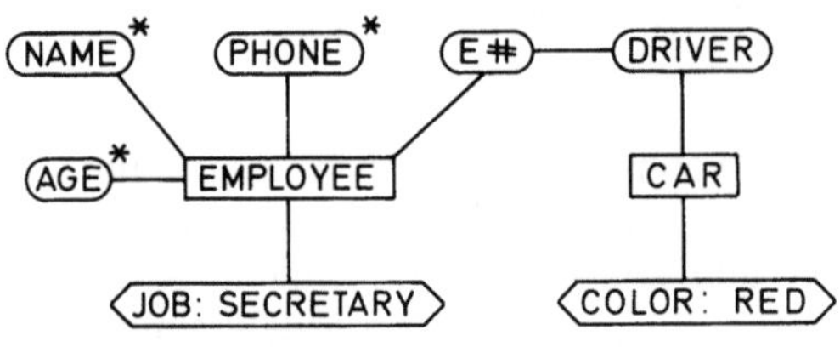

Fig. 6.2

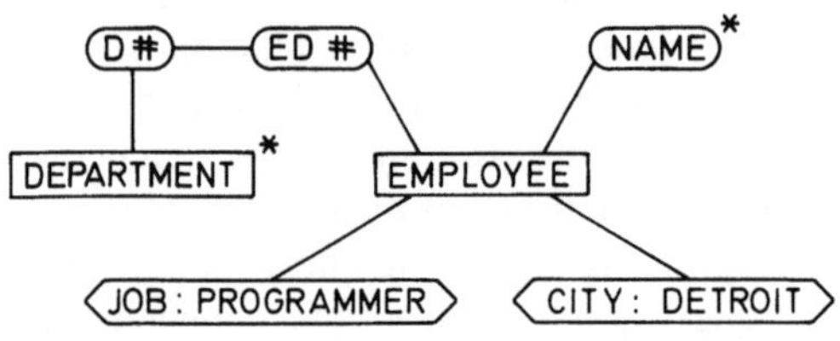

Fig. 6.3

for relating employees and departments in a proper way although the user did not explicitly ask for that.

6.3 *Completing Queries by Comparisons of Query Skeletons*

In this section we shall attempt the completion of target ellipses, pure illocution ellipses and combinations of illocution ellipses and partial qualification ellipses. As far as pure illocution ellipses are concerned, the actual completion is straightforward when taking into consideration the preceding query; the problem is rather to decide that an illocution ellipsis is not combined with a partial qualification ellipsis. This is the reason why we treat these two classes of ellipses together.

Within this section the concept "query skeleton" is of fundamental importance; given a query graph, the *query skeleton* is obtained by applying the following procedure:

(QS1) Delete all value-nodes from the query graph;

(QS2) Delete all attribute-nodes from the query graph which are connected only with a relation-node;

(QS3) Delete all markings (✲) from the nodes of the query graph.

The query skeleton reflects the coarse structure of a query; since elliptic queries frequently show structural similarities to their predecessors, the query skeleton of the preceding query provides a good starting point for completing an elliptic query.

In order to compare an elliptic query to its predecessor on the basis of query skeletons, we need the skeleton of the elliptic query. This is obtained by constructing a preliminary query graph from the elliptic query essentially according to the translation procedure outlined in Sect. 3; deviating from Sect. 3, the first star according to the sequence established in step (T3) is used to start in step (T5). The resulting query graph is reduced to its skeleton by applying (QS1) through (QS3).

The comparison of the query skeletons of an elliptic query and its preceding query yields one of four situations:

(SC1) Both skeletons are identical.

(SC2) The skeleton of the elliptic query is a subgraph of the skeleton of its preceding query.

(SC3) The skeleton of the elliptic query is not a subgraph of the skeleton of its preceding query but the two skeletons have at least one relation-node in common.

(SC4) The two skeletons do not have any relation-nodes in common.

Further processing of the elliptic query depends on which of these situations applies. In situation (SC1) the common skeleton also becomes the skeleton of the final query graph of the elliptic query; it has to be completed by adding value-nodes in an appropriate way. Obviously, the value-nodes in the preliminary query graph of the elliptic query have to be added, whereas possible value-nodes in the query graph of the preceding query referring to the same attributes as the value-nodes in the preliminary query graph must not be added. Value-nodes in the query graph of the preceding query for which there is no corresponding node in the preliminary query graph are added to the final query graph only if the wording of the elliptic query contains no relation designation and no representative value designation of the relation the value-node in question belongs to. This criterion is based on the observation that the use of relation designations often signalizes a shift of focus; since representative value designations may always take the place of relation designations, their occurrences are treated in the same way. The resulting query graph is completed by adding the markings from the query graph of the preceding query; in particular, this may require that some further attribute-nodes are added to the query graph.

Example 6.3.1
For the two consecutive queries

"Find name and age of all programmers in New York."

"in Chicago."

the query skeletons are identical and consist of a single relation-node referring to the relation EMPLOYEE. When constructing the final query graph of the second query, the value-node referring to the attribute CITY in the query graph of the first query is replaced by the corresponding value-node in the preliminary query graph of the second query. Since "Chicago" is a non-representative value designation the value-node referring to the attribute JOB also is adopted from the first query. Finally, the marked attribute-nodes referring to NAME and AGE are added to the final query graph, thus yielding the graph depicted in Fig. 6.4.

The following two queries comprise an example of a value-node that is not adopted from the query preceding the elliptic query although the elliptic query contains no value designation referring to the same attribute.

"Find the salary of programmers in New York."

"employees in Chicago."

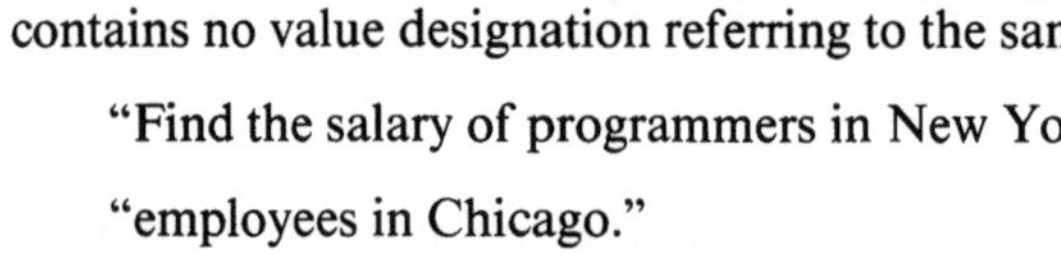

Fig. 6.4

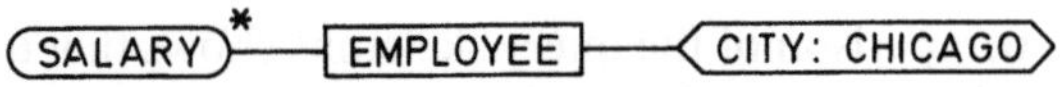

Fig. 6.5

Since the elliptic query contains the relation designation "employee", the value-node referring to the attribute JOB according to the criterion given above must not be attached to the final query graph of the second query. The resulting query graph (see Fig. 6.5) certainly is in agreement with common sense understanding of the second utterance. Note that in this example the same mechanism was used to complete a combination of illocution ellipsis and partial qualification ellipsis (first pair of queries) and to complete a target ellipsis.

In situation (SC2) the set of relation-nodes of the query skeleton of the previous query may be subdivided into three disjoint classes. The first class comprises all relation-nodes which have a marking; such a marking may be attached in the corresponding query graph either to the relation-node itself or to an attribute-node connected with the relation node. The second class comprises all relation nodes without markings for which the skeleton of the elliptic query contains a relation-node referring to the same relation. The third class contains the remaining relation nodes. When building the final query graph of the elliptic query the nodes of the second class obviously have to be considered. The nodes of the first class also are adopted in order to make sure that the completion of the elliptic query and its preceding query agree with respect to their target lists. For the nodes from the third class, we use the following heuristics: A node from the third class is considered for inclusion in the final query graph of the elliptic query if and only if there exists a path in the skeleton of the previous query from this node to a node of the first class that does not contain a node of the second class. As a result of these heuristics, those parts of the previous query that are "cut off" from the target relations by the explicit constituents of the elliptic query will not be considered in the final query graph of the elliptic query.

The nodes of the third class that are not to be considered are deleted from the skeleton of the previous query together with possibly dangling attribute-nodes. The remaining skeleton becomes the skeleton of the final query graph of the elliptic query. For relation-nodes that were contained already in the preliminary skeleton of the elliptic query, the insertion of value-nodes proceeds as described for situation (SC1); for the remaining relation-nodes all value-nodes from the query graph of the previous query are adopted. Finally, the markings of the query graph of the previous query are attached to the final query graph of the elliptic query.

Example 6.3.2
Given the following queries

"Find all employees who drive a car hired from AVIS."

"a black Porsche."

a comparison of the query skeletons shows that the skeleton of the second query (which consists of a single relation-node referring to the relation CAR) is a subgraph of the skeleton of the first query (see Fig. 6.6).

In this skeleton the first class of relation-nodes only contains the node referring to EMPLOYEE, the second class only the node referring to CAR and the third class only the node referring to HIRE. Since the only path from HIRE to EMPLOYEE touches a node the second class, namely the node referring to CAR, the node referring to HIRE together with the otherwise dangling nodes referring to the attributes LIP and HLIP is deleted from the skeleton. Inclusion of value-nodes and markings finally yields the query graph depicted in Fig. 6.7.

We would like to point out that the intended meaning of the elliptic query in the above example might also have been "a black Porsche hired from AVIS." In any case it seems to be more reasonable to end with an interpretation in which certain constituents intended but not explicitly mentioned by the user are missing than to end with an interpretation containing constituents that were neither mentioned nor intended by the user. This provides some justification to our "cut off" heuristics.

Situation (SC3) may be treated rather similarly to (SC2); again, the set of relation-nodes of the query skeleton of the previous query is partitioned into three classes in order to determine the relation-nodes not to be included in the final query graph in the same way as before. This time, however, the resulting query skeleton has to be joined with the preliminary query skeleton of the elliptic query by identifying those nodes with each other that refer to the same relation or attribute, respectively. The attachment of value-nodes and markings proceeds as described before.

Example 6.3.3
For the following two queries

"Find all employees who drive a red car hired from AVIS."

"a car insured by Lloyd's."

we obtain the query skeletons given in Fig. 6.8.

As in example 6.3.2 the relation-node referring to HIRE and the attribute-nodes referring to HLIP and LIP have to be deleted from the skeleton of the first

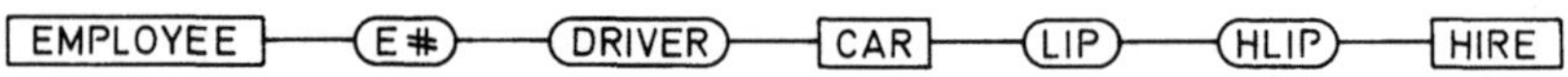

Fig. 6.6

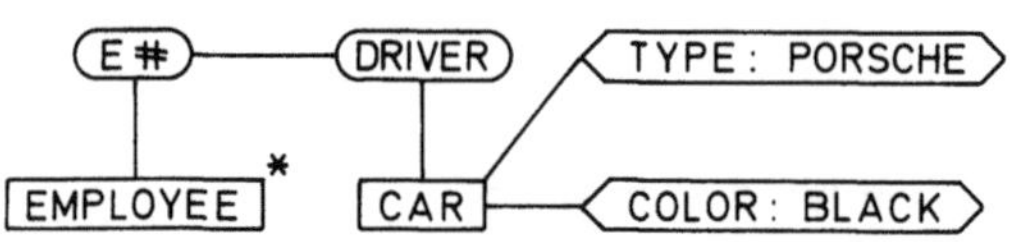

Fig. 6.7

query. Then the two skeletons are joined by identifying the two nodes referring to the relation CAR with each other. When adding value-nodes to the joined skeleton the value-node referring to the attribute COLOR must not be included since the second query contains the relation designation "car" (also cf. example 6.3.1); the resulting query graph for the elliptic query is depicted in Fig. 6.9.

Finally, we have to deal with situation (SC4) where the two skeletons have no common relation-nodes. In this case it is possible that there is no connection with regard to the contents of the two queries, i.e., the second query shows a pure illocution ellipsis. On the other hand, it is possible that the second query is an expansion of the qualification expression of the first one, i.e., the second query shows an illocution ellipsis combined with a partial qualification ellipsis. The decision depends on the first word for the elliptic query: If the first word is a relation designation or a value designation, then a pure illocution ellipsis is assumed and the only thing left to do is to add a marking to that relation-node of the preliminary query graph that corresponds to the first word of the query.

In all other cases - particularly, if the first word of the query is a preposition or a relative pronoun - a combination of illocution ellipsis and partial qualification ellipsis is assumed and a connection between the query skeletons of the elliptic query and the previous query has to be established. For this purpose, first a connection of type (C3) is tried and - if no such connection is possible - then a connection of type (C4) is attempted (cf. Sect. 3 for the different types of connections between query graphs). Value-nodes and markings may be adopted from the preliminary query graph of the elliptic query and the query graph of the preceding query without any modifications.

Example 6.3.4
The query skeletons of the queries

"Find all black Porsches hired from AVIS."

"in department DX042."

have no relation-nodes in common. Because of the preposition at the beginning of the elliptic query, however, a connection with regard to the contents of the two

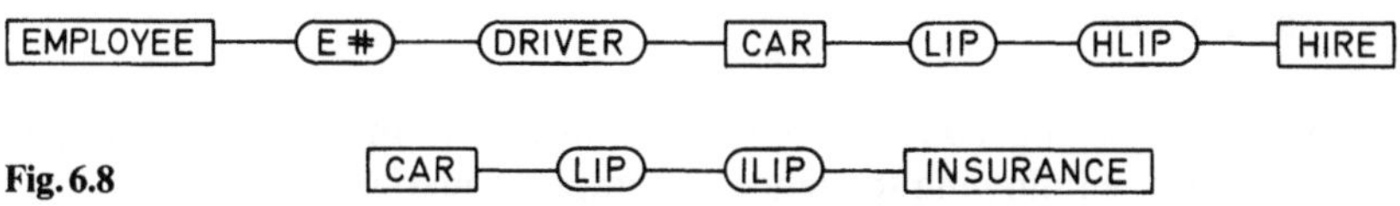

Fig. 6.8

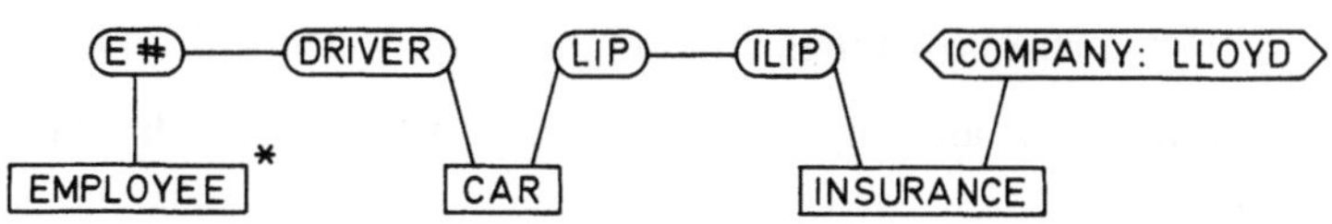

Fig. 6.9

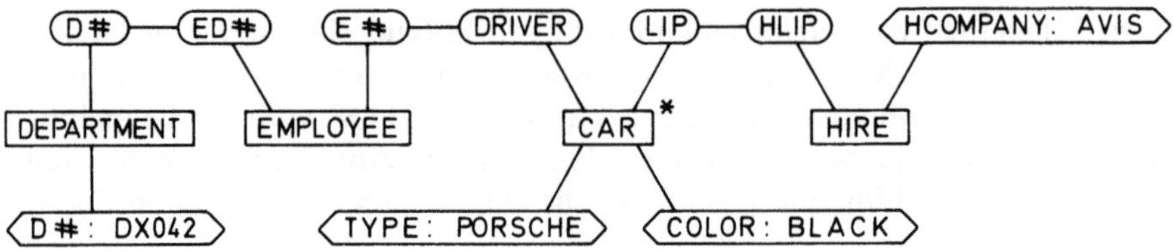

Fig. 6.10

queries is assumed. The attempts to establish a connection of type (C3) between the two query skeletons fail but it is possible to establish a connection of type (C4) between the relation-nodes referring to the relations CAR and DEPARTMENT; this involves the inclusion of an additional relation node, namely one which refers to the relation EMPLOYEE. The finally resulting query graph is given in Fig. 6.10.

All of the examples in this section have examined situations where a single elliptic query is preceded by a complete natural language query. Since completing an elliptic query only requires the query graph of the preceding query, sequences of elliptic queries may be processed as well because at the end of the processing of each elliptic query we obtain a complete query graph for that query which in turn may be used for processing a subsequent elliptic query.

Example 6.3.5
The following sequence of queries:

"How many secretaries drive a Volkswagen?"

"blue with 34 PS."

"name and city."

"programmers who drive a Porsche."

"a car hired from AVIS."

"license plate."

"a Mercedes."

according to the procedures given above would be interpreted exactly in the same way as the following sequence of complete queries.

"How many secretaries drive a Volkswagen?"

"How many secretaries drive a blue Volkswagen with 34 PS?"

"Find name and city of all secretaries who drive a blue Volkswagen with 34 PS."

"Find name and city of all programmers who drive a Porsche."

"Find name and city of all programmers who drive a car hired from AVIS."

"Find name and city of all programmers who drive a car hired from AVIS together with the license plate of the car."

"Find name and city of all programmers who drive a Mercedes together with the license plate of the car."

We would like to close this section on ellipsis by admitting the possibility that some proposed completion of an elliptic query will not meet the user's intents. But since an unequivocal interpretation is not possible even for a human listener/reader (see example 6.3.2) it is fair enough to produce at least plausible interpretations of elliptic queries, thereby imposing the burden on the user that (s)he has to rephrase a query more explicitly every now and then, and not to rule out elliptic queries from the very beginning or to present all interpretations which are plausible to a certain extent to the user in a menu.

7 Conclusion

In this chapter, we have introduced the semantics-based approach to natural language interfaces of relational databases. As we have already pointed out in the introduction the feasibility of such an approach is highly dependent on the cooperation of the user, i.e., whenever a user attempts to fool such an interface (s)he will be able to do so. If, however, the user is seriously interested in taking advantage of the information contained in the database the semantics-based natural language interface will turn out to be a comfortable tool for accessing complex data.

Apart from the high degree of freedom the semantics-based approach offers to the user, it stands out for such properties as portability, adaptability and easy maintainability. Portability is achieved by using a well-defined interface to the database management system, namely the enquiry specifiers' interface. Adaptability derives from the fact that only a minimum of database-dependent information is required for the translation of queries. Maintainability, finally, manifests itself in the easy manner that extensions and structural changes that may occur during the life-cycle of a database may be taken account of in the natural language interface.

Acknowledgment

The author gratefully acknowledges that a due completion of this paper would have been impossible without the stylistic support by Ms. Sabine Janas.

References

[ANSI 75], [BRAU 76], [CADI 76], [CODD 70], [CODD 71a], [CODD 71b], [CODD 78], [DATE 81], [DELL 77], [HABE 79], [HARR 77a], [HARR 79], [HEND 77a], [HEND 78c], [JANA 79], [JANA 82], [KAPL 79], [KONO 79], [LAND 77], [MALH 75a], [PIRO 78], [PLAT 76], [WALT 76]

Chapter 7

Talking it Over: The Natural Language Dialog System HAM-ANS

Wolfgang Hoeppner, Katharina Morik, and Heinz Marburger*

Abstract. This contribution has two objectives. In the first section, the position of language-oriented research in the field of Artificial Intelligence (AI) and its relevance to related disciplines are defined and our theoretical approach in the development of HAM-ANS (*Ham*burg *A*pplication-Oriented *N*atural Language *S*ystem) is outlined. In the following two sections, this system is presented with an emphasis on aspects which are of theoretical interest. Although details of implementation are largely omitted, it is to be emphasized that all of the processes and knowledge bases described have been fully implemented.

After an introduction to the three dialog situations investigated in our project, the organization of the system as a whole is elucidated on the basis of examples taken from one of the domains of discourse: a hotel reservation situation. The final section is devoted to a special problem of pragmatics: representation and application of user modelling in an AI system. Real, unedited dialogs with HAM-ANS covering all three domains are contained with detailed comments on the internal processing in the appendix.

1 Artificial Intelligence and Linguistics

In AI, linguistics is often identified with the Chomskyan paradigm. This is to no small extent due to claims by the Chomskyan group and Chomsky himself, e.g. calling the gTg-theory "the standard theory". Because the Chomskyan work does not satisfy and is not intended to satisfy the demand for a holistic model that explains phenomena of language performance, the restricted view of linguistics as a kind of universal grammar theory leads to the judgment that linguistics is not a matter of high importance for language oriented AI - and language oriented AI is not of relevance for linguistics.

If, however, we view linguistics as a discipline which, as a whole, can only be defined by its interest in language as such, where various linguistic schools of thought differ in their methods and concentration of interest, and their ways of looking at language, then AI language processing - at least with its basic-research oriented branch - can be regarded as a school of linguistics.

* Work on HAM-ANS was supported by the BMFT under contract number 08IT15038.

Stressing, the other way around, the unity of AI fields of research forming a procedural theory of knowledge, AI encompasses a theory of language understanding and production as well as image processing, theorem proving, planning and knowledge representation. Since the classification of newly emerging areas of research under the heading of one discipline or another is more a matter of political than of scientific relevance, we will not attempt to resolve this question.

It is, however, important to touch upon a matter which occasionally creates difficulties in interdisciplinary cooperation. The problem is a misunderstanding on the part of both linguistics and AI research. In AI research, ad-hoc solutions are sometimes defended on the grounds that linguistics failed to has come up with anything more practicable. This reproach seems to be based on the assumption that one of the tasks of linguistics is to establish rules which describe language in a detailed and reliable fashion and which are, moreover, easily translatable into program code. What is overlooked, however, is that

- linguistic descriptions are a product of the paradigms and the evaluatory context in which they are formulated,
- the results of linguistic research - as is always the case with interdisciplinary transfer processes - can only be applied by linguistically trained persons in order to yield answers to questions posed by another discipline,
- these answers cannot have a final, ultimative character.

As the other side of the misunderstanding, representatives of transformational grammar (gTg) have dismissed language-oriented AI as unscientific [DRES 76]. Work with the computer can only be regarded as meaningful if (transformational) rules are programmed. This is the same misunderstanding from another perspective: language oriented AI is viewed as the programming of linguistic hypotheses or theories, and thus misunderstood as a technical extension of existing paradigms. In fact, in the early stages of AI, context-free grammars patterned after linguistic models were programmed and even supplemented by a transformational component [PETR 73]. This approach led, however, to difficulties [BARR 81].

Because we believe that sound language oriented AI needs a basis in linguistics, and claim that language oriented AI should be taken seriously by the linguistic community, we want to state our position as it is related to approaches to linguistics.

Approaches to linguistics (or linguistic schools of thought) can be distinguished on the basis of which conditions and features of observable language use they single out, what they consider language to be, and what context they place language in.

If, for example, language is seen as a concatenation of linguistic objects (structuralism) then the primacy of phonology and syntax is assumed and pragmatics (and often semantics as well) are ignored. AI parser (and grammar) theories fit well in this domain, e.g. GPSG, lexical functional grammar. Interdisciplinary cooperation in this field has grown in the course of the 'syntax revival' that can be observed in the past.

Language as language (learning) capacity narrows linguistic interest not just to the area of competence but to the construction of universally interpretable models of language [DRES 76].

Interest in what humans do when they use language is common to a number of different currents in linguistics; in language oriented AI, which attempts to develop performance models, there are various points of view as well. The three most important linguistic approaches which are also represented in AI research are briefly characterized below in order to elucidate our own approach.

If language use is viewed as the *speech process,* questions of linearization of utterances [LEVE 82], processes of verbalization (HOEN 82] and the temporal perception of spoken language [MARS 80] are emphasized. Delay phenomena and memory limitations, which competence models must set aside [CHOM 65], are a matter of central interest; AI methods (here: simulation) are used as an investigative tool.

The *functional* view of language [SCHM 76] also includes the speaker/hearer in the construction of theories, but concentrates not so much on the cognitive processes of speaking and hearing as on the goals and intentions of speakers/hearers, their knowledge of the world and the processes of interpretation they employ. Language use fulfills a function and is determined by this function. AI methodology is particularly helpful in this area. Knowledge about the world and the goals of the dialog partner can be represented as sources of knowledge in a dialog system, and their effects on language processes can be modeled.

Taking the functionality of language as a point of departure implies also that one and the same model is not appropriate in any random communication situation or instance of language use. For practical purposes it is in any case unrealistic to envision an AI system which would function adequately in any given language-use situation, quite aside from the question of whether such a system is realizable in principle. For this reason, a dialog system is usually designed for a particular area of application, i. e., a situation in which a user wishes to enter or receive information. While the domain of discourse is always represented, i. e., there is a formalism which makes explicit statements to be projected onto a model of a sector of reality, the area of application has up till now been taken into account only through the general framework of the system. That is, systems are designed in such a way that they can carry on a quite sufficient dialog in a particular predetermined area of application [MORI 81]. So, the functionality of language is taken into account only implicitly in AI dialog systems.

The view of language use as a *part of human behavior* is shared by ethnomethodologists, social psychologists, phenomenologists [SCHU 79 a], pragmalinguists and many workers in language oriented AI. Language is investigated in the form of units of behavior, including both those which are directly involved in utterances (speech acts, dialog acts) and those which are determined by non-linguistic plans of action (task oriented dialogs [GROS 78]).

To be sure, language oriented AI is just now taking the first steps towards realizing the inherent possibilities here. Only recently attempts have been made to treat group-specific and individual subjective processes aside from general and goal-oriented cognitive processes in natural language systems.

This view complements what was described earlier. If we take both together, we can characterize the approach taken by one group of language-oriented AI researchers (including ourselves) as follows:

> Taking pragmatics as a point of departure, an attempt is made to construct a *holistic model* of language use. Syntax, semantics and pragmatics cannot be investigated as separate entities.

The Hamburg Application-Oriented Natural Language System (HAM-ANS) has been developed on the basis of these considerations. Our project embraces both the goals of basic research and of application-oriented research; we are, however, not involved in the development of systems for concrete applications. In the following presentation we concentrate mainly on the areas dealing with basic research, see [HOEP 83] and [MORI 83b] for application-oriented work. It should be emphasized that we do not consider the employment of natural language systems in all of the areas of application we are working on to be either practical or desirable. What is involved is rather a selection of communication situations which make it possible to investigate interesting phenomena.

2 The HAM-ANS System

In this section we describe the HAM-ANS system and at the same time concretize the research approach which was sketched in the previous section. We begin by presenting the application classes of man-machine communication that we have chosen (2.1). We then single out one class and describe system behavior using the application: Hotel Room Reservation. First we consider the processing of the dialog structure (2.2) and then illustrate the processing of individual utterances in detail, using a concrete example (2.3).

The described version of HAM-ANS written in UCI-LISP/FUZZY [MEEH 79, LEFA 77] is running under the TOPS10 operating system on a DECsystem 1070 (KI-10). Comprising approximately 900 procedures, the version requires 200 Kwords (à 36 bit).

2.1 Areas of Application

In this section we wish to consider the concept *application orientation* (the second A in HAM-ANS) in more detail and then introduce the three application classes.

The goal of the HAM-ANS project is to design and implement a natural language access system to other software products. By natural language access we mean that the functioning of a program system (e.g., a data base system) can be activated by natural-language utterances and that the output produced by the program system can be communicated in natural language. An access system is not, however, simply reduced to the role of a translator between natural language and the formal language of the program. The manner in which the program system carries out a task is also dependent on the knowledge and the processing of the access system.

An important aspect of language oriented AI research, in addition to basic research, is the application aspect of AI systems: natural language access not only makes program systems installed on computers available to a broader spectrum of users, it can also make communication with the program more efficient [HAHN 83]. With these goals in view, work on HAM-ANS is oriented toward future application, i.e., HAM-ANS is not a directly deployable applied system, but intended to establish a basis for future practical systems.

The problems of the social effects of such systems are directly linked to the application orientation. Making data available to those who are not EDP specialists has its democratizing aspect, but it also contributes to increasing computerization and invasion of privacy by data collection. In our opinion, the appropriateness of the application of natural language systems is mostly dependent on the use which the data made available are put to. Setting the limits on this process is a matter which must be dealt with by an informed public opinion. We ourselves can contribute to the formation of public opinion by providing information.

There have been attempts in language oriented AI research to construct systems which are independent of particular applications. Independence can mean different things. It can, for instance, mean that one and the same system can be used for all areas of application. Such a universal system can only rely on sources of knowledge that are the same for all areas of application as well as those which cover all applications. In this way linguistic abilities are reduced to syntax and morphology as a kind of a natural language empty system. Another possibility is, however, that independence from specific applications is meant to be understood as ease of adaptability or exchangeability of knowledge sources (as for example, the lexicon) for new areas of application. In this case, it is possible to take account of some semantic and inferential capabilities (cf. USL [ZOEP 84], see also Chap. 4 in this volume).

In both approaches the system is, however, limited to particular *application classes*. An application class is characterized by:

- the area of discourse in which natural language communication takes place,
- the program system that the natural language system accesses (i.e., the background system),
- the type of knowledge that the program system makes available, and

- the communication situation for man-machine dialog which can be specified by the intentions of system and user, the function of the system for the actions of the user, and a general characterization of user types (e.g., technical experts, EDP-experts, laymen).

It is our goal to overcome these limitations without sacrificing semantic and pragmatic knowledge [HOEP 83]. The use of different and interchangeable knowledge sources should contribute, rather, to independence from application classes. For this reason we are working with instances of three different application classes for which the HAM-ANS system is parameterized.

Before going into a consideration of these three classes in more detail we must emphasize the fact that our research is confined to written language. This procedure engenders certain limitations, particularly on the prosodic level, which should not, in general, be excluded from consideration. The implementation problems involved here - particularly those of speech analysis - are not yet amenable to solution.

The three application classes treated by the HAM-ANS system are most easily characterized by the types of program system for which natural language access is to be designed. A booking system can be considered as an example of an expert system, an image sequence analysis system processes visually perceivable information, and a data base system organizes mass data and data access.

The booking system area of discourse is a *hotel reservation situation* in which HAM-ANS assumes the role of a hotel employee. The booking system itself is represented here solely by the frame dialog (see Sect. 2.2.). The motivation for selecting this situation was not the need for such a system in a practical application, but rather the relatively obvious intentions of both partners in this type of dialog situation. The caller is interested in booking a hotel room which meets his needs and the system is interested in renting a room. This application class is concerned with consultative dialogs which are supposed to aid the user in making a decision. The system's knowledge about the domain of discourse - hotel rooms - can be viewed as every-day knowledge and is shared by the user, except for the details about specific hotel rooms. The major points of research interest in this application class are the representation and application of an explicit user model (see Sect. 3) and the modeling of dialog strategies, e.g., the generation of interest-based answers.

For the natural language access to an *image sequence analysis* system we envision the following situation. The system has observed a street crossing for a limited period of time and provides the user, who is familiar with the crossing, with information about the observed events. HAM-ANS offers access to an image sequence analysis system [NEUM 82] which provides geometrical scene descriptions (spatial and temporal data) covering a period of 14 seconds with a series of 72 sequential snapshots. As with the hotel reservation situation, everyday knowledge about events at a street crossing is represented in the system. In this situation, the user's plan of action is not a function of system response. The choice of this particular example for the application class was in part motivated by the availability of a vision system in Hamburg. Particularly important for the linguistic and cognitive capabilities of HAM-ANS in this application are the representation and processing of temporal processes and spatial relations, especially the semantics of verbs of locomotion (e.g., *turn off, stop, drive off*) based on referential knowledge. Another point of interest for our research in this area is the cooperative answering and overanswering of yes/no questions (cf. [WAHL 83]).

The choice of the third application class - access to a *data base management system* (DBMS) - was, as with the traffic monitoring situation, determined in part by the availability of such a system in Hamburg [SCHM 80]. Involved here are real data, collected during several international South Atlantic and Indian Ocean expeditions (ship routes, fish catches, oceanographic and ornithological observation data, among other things). In contrast to the two application situations presented above, this data base contains information that, in general, is of interest only for experts. The motivation for practical application is more apparent in this situation. Special research issues are the handling of mass data in natural language communication, the representation and acquisition of knowledge about the structure of the data base and the utilization of dialog coherence for the formulation of optimal data base queries (cf. [MARB 83a, MARB 85]).

2.2 Dialog Structure in the Hotel Reservation Situation

In the following sections we will concentrate our attention primarily on the application class *consultative dialog* in which the HAM-ANS system takes the part of a hotel employee, answering questions posed by a potential customer. A sample dialog from this application class is shown in Fig. 1. The system-internal processing of this same dialog is presented in the appendix, which also contains sample dialogs for the other application classes. In Fig. 1 the system's utterances are printed in capitals.

By taking selected question-answer pairs as examples, we can illustrate the processing strategy for natural language inputs and the fundamental aspects of the system design and the necessary knowledge sources. First let us take a look at the overall structure of a dialog in the hotel reservation situation.

Two dialog phases can be distinguished in this situation: a *frame dialog* and the *consultative dialog* proper. These two phases differ in various respects. In the frame dialog, the initiative lies with the system. The processing with regard to both analysis and generation functions is considerably more superficial in the frame dialog than in the consultative dialog. The structure of the frame dialog (Fig. 2) is implicitly defined by a sequence of speech acts in obligatory order. Variations in linguistic expression are provided for in the form of sentence patterns containing optional elements and variables (e.g., for type of room or the institution the caller represents). The system expects exactly these sentence pat-

[1] *(040 4123 3315)

[2] HOTEL ZUM FETTEN OCHSEN, GUTEN ABEND!
[HOTEL ZUM FETTEN OCHSEN, GOOD EVENING!]

[3] ?Hallo hier ist Karlchen Mueller, Fuchshausen
[Hello, this is Karlchen Mueller from Fuchshausen speaking.]

[4] WAS KANN ICH FUER SIE TUN?
[WHAT CAN I DO FOR YOU?]

[5] ? Sagen Sie, ich moechte ein Doppelzimmer fuer zwei Tage
[I'd like a double room for two days.]

[6] GEWISS ICH WILL MAL SEHEN ...
[YES, OF COURSE, JUST LET ME SEE.]

[7] EIN DOPPELZIMMER BIS ZUM 25.4. HAETTEN SIE GERN?
[YOU WOULD LIKE A DOUBLE ROOM UNTIL APRIL 25TH IS THAT RIGHT?]

[8] ? Nein, das habe ich anders gemeint.
[No, that's not the way I meant it.]

[9] ENTSCHULDIGUNG, DA HABE ICH SIE WOHL MISSVERSTANDEN.
[SORRY, I MUST HAVE MISUNDERSTOOD YOU.]

[10] ? Ich moechte ein Doppelzimmer für drei Naechte mit Bad
[I'd like a double room for three nights with bath.]

[11] EIN DOPPELZIMMER MIT BAD BIS ZUM 26.4. HAETTEN SIE GERN?
[YOUR WOULD LIKE A DOUBLE ROOM WITH BATH UN-
TIL APRIL 26TH IS THAT RIGHT?]

[12] ? Ja genau
[Yes, exactly.]

[13] JA, DA IST NOCH ETWAS FREI. HABEN SIE NOCH IRGENDEINEN BESONDE-
REN WUNSCH?
[YES, WE STILL HAVE SOME VACANCIES. DO YOU HAVE ANY PARTICULAR RE-
QUIREMENTS?]

[14] ? Gibt es im Zimmer einen Sessel oder einen grossen Stuhl?
[Is there an easy-chair or a large chair in the room?]

[15] EIN GROSSER STUHL STEHT NICHT ZUR VERFUEGUNG, ABER EIN SESSEL.
[A LARGE CHAIR IS NOT AVAILABLE, BUT AN EASY-CHAIR.]

[16] ? Wieviele Sitzgelegenheiten sind bequem?
[How many of the chairs are comfortable?]

[17] EINE VON DEN VIER IST RELATIV BEQUEM.
[ONE OF THE FOUR IS RELATIVELY COMFORTABLE.]

Fig. 1.a Sample Dialog

[18] ? Der Sessel?
[The easy-chair?]

[19] JA, RELATIV BEQUEM.
[YES, RELATIVELY COMFORTABLE.]

[20] ? Ausgesprochen bequem?
[Decidedly comfortable?]

[21] NEIN, RELATIV BEQUEM.
[NO, RELATIVELY COMFORTABLE.]

[22] ? Ist dieser Sessel vielleicht weiss?
[Is this easy-chair white, perhaps?]

[23] NEIN, DER SESSEL IST GELB.
[NO, THE EASY-CHAIR IS YELLOW.]

[24] DARF ICH EIN DOPPELZIMMER DANN AUF DEN NAMEN KARLCHEN MUELLER, FUCHSHAUSEN BUCHEN?
[MAY I BOOK A DOUBLE-ROOM THEN UNDER THE NAME KARLCHEN MUELLER, FUCHSHAUSEN?]

[25] ? Augenblick, ich hab noch eine Frage.
[Just a moment, I still have a question.]

[26] JA BITTE?
[YES?]

[27] ? Wo?
[Where?]

[28] BITTE, WIE MEINEN SIE DAS?
[EXCUSE ME, WHAT DO YOU MEAN?]

[29] ? Wo steht denn dieser Sessel?
[Where is this easy-chair?]

[30] DER SESSEL IST VOR DEM FENSTER.
[THE EASY-CHAIR IS IN FRONT OF THE WINDOW.]

[31] ? Und neben was?
[And what is it next to?]

[32] DER SESSEL IST NEBEN EINEM NIEDRIGEN COUCHTISCH.
[THE EASY-CHAIR IST NEXT TO A LOW COFFEE-TABLE.]

[33] DARF ICH EIN DOPPELZIMMER DANN AUF DEN NAMEN KARLCHEN MUELLER, FUCHSHAUSEN BUCHEN?
[MAY I BOOK A DOUBLE-ROOM THEN, UNDER THE NAME KARLCHEN MUELLER, FUCHSHAUSEN?]

Fig. 1.b Sample Dialog (cont.)

[34] ? Nein, so schnell schiessen die Preussen nicht.
[Just a moment, not so fast.]

[35] JA BITTE?
[YES?]

[36] ? Was befindet sich eigentlich auf diesem Couchtisch, der neben dem Sessel steht?
[What is on this coffee-table which is next to the easy-chair?]

[37] KEIN DING IST AUF DEM COUCHTISCH, DER NEBEN DEM SESSEL IST.
[THERE IS NOTHING ON THIS COFFEE-TABLE WHICH IS NEXT TO THE EASY-CHAIR.]

[38] ? Das Zimmer ist doch nicht dunkel?
[The room isn't dark, is it?]

[39] NEIN.
[NO.]

[40] ? Also hell?
[It's bright then?]

[41] JA, VERMUTLICH HELL.
[YES, PROBABLY BRIGHT.]

[42] ? Tatsaechlich?
[Really?]

[43] EIN FENSTER VON IHM IST GROSS.
[ONE OF THE WINDOWS IS LARGE.]

[44] DARF ICH EIN DOPPELZIMMER DANN AUF DEN NAMEN KARLCHEN MUELLER, FUCHSHAUSEN BUCHEN?
[MAY I BOOK A DOUBLE-ROOM THEN, UNDER THE NAME KARLCHEN MUELLER, FUCHSHAUSEN?]

[45] ? Ja, nun habe ich keine weiteren Fragen.
[Yes, I have no further questions.]

[46] ICH HABE ALSO EIN DOPPELZIMMER VOM 23.4. BIS 25.4. AUF DEN NAMEN KARLCHEN MUELLER, FUCHSHAUSEN GEBUCHT.
[FINE, I HAVE BOOKED A DOUBLE-ROOM FOR APRIL 23 TO 25 UNDER THE NAME KARLCHEN MUELLER, FUCHSHAUSEN.]

[47] VIELEN DANK UND AUF WIEDERHOEREN.
[THANK YOU, GOOD-BYE.]

[48] ? Auf wiederhoeren.
[Good-bye.]

ENDE
[END]

Fig. 1.c Sample Dialog (cont.)

terns, and only the information necessary for the system responses in this phase (e.g., name of the caller, length of stay) is extracted.

The present provision for two to three variations for an utterance cannot be considered as broad coverage for the standard situation 'beginning and end of a hotel telephone call', however, the formalism used in the realization of the frame dialog permits an extension of expressive possibilities to any desired degree.

A more important limitation is the lack of connection in content between the frame dialog and the consultative dialog which is embedded in it. The system registers the desires of the caller as is clearly indicated by the booking confirmation (cf. Fig. 1 [46]), but does not, as it would appear (cf. Fig. 1 [13]), compare them with knowledge sources which describe a particular hotel room for the consultative dialog. This kind of comparison would be very easy to arrange, but would only be worthwhile if the system, guided by the desires of the caller, could choose an appropriate hotel room from among several available ones. Such an approach is currently under development. At present the system works with one room at a time. That is, the room may vary from dialog to dialog but at present it is not possible to change rooms in the course of a single dialog. The representation of several rooms, accomplished after this chapter was originally written, required an extensive reorganization of most of the sources of knowledge and the access functions defined for these sources (cf. [MORI 85]).

The transition from the frame dialog to the consultative dialog takes place by running through the initial dialog (cf. Fig. 2). There are two possibilities for making the transition from the consultative dialog to the concluding frame dialog. After answering a fixed number of questions, the system takes the initiative and asks whether the room can be booked (cf. Fig. 1 [24], [33], [44]). If the caller is not amenable to this suggestion, the attempt is repeated at increasingly frequent intervals. A second possibility is to attempt to move into the closing dailog immediately upon a positively interpreted response by the user (e.g., *That's fine*). In the following sections we will illustrate the HAM-ANS system's processing strategy in consultative dialogs using examples from the dialog in Fig. 1.

2.3 Processing of Natural Language Utterances by HAM-ANS

There are various points of departure which can be utilized to give a picture of what actually takes place in an AI system between the points of natural language input and system reaction:

- The architecture of a system, i.e., the interaction between the components of the system, allows conclusions to be drawn about processing strategies, but does not show which sources of knowledge have been consulted.
- The presentation of different knowledge sources and their application for language analysis and generation places emphasis primarily on AI's claims to explicitness but neglects the interaction between the processes.

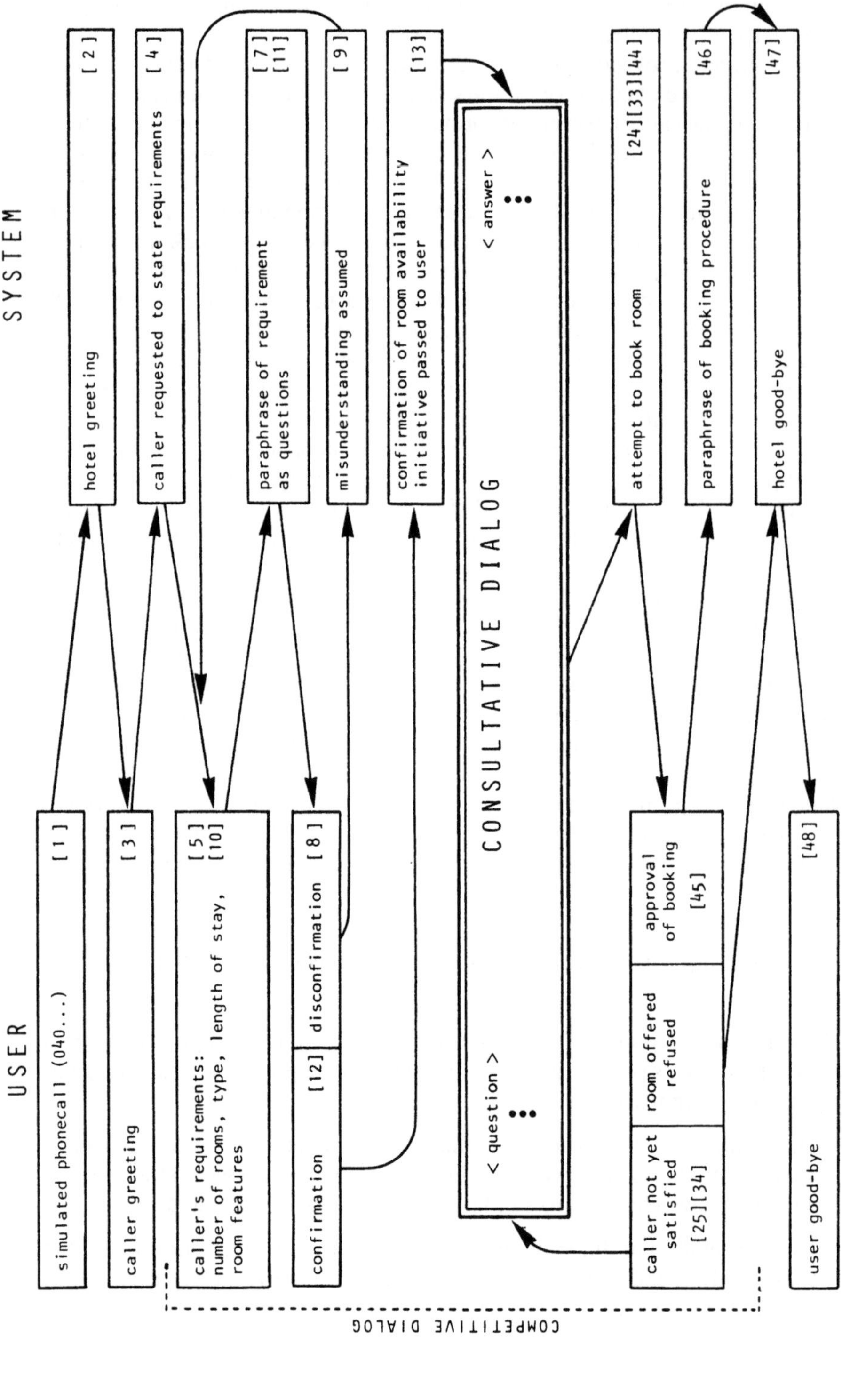

Fig. 2. Dialog structure in the hotel reservation situation

- The description of system abilities in linguistic terms - insofar as this is possible - carries the hidden danger that everything that is understood under these terms may directly be imputed to an AI-system;
- Using the example of the processing of a single utterance makes it possible to describe running processes and necessary knowledge in the most detailed and concrete fashion; coherence is, however, neglected and, as a rule, only those aspects of system capability can be illustrated that are necessary for the particular utterance in question.

Despite the shortcomings noted above, we have decided to use the last mentioned method because it is most clearly oriented toward the actual running processes and aids in reaching a realistic evaluation of the system. The following presentation will be supplemented by an overview of the interrelation of individ-

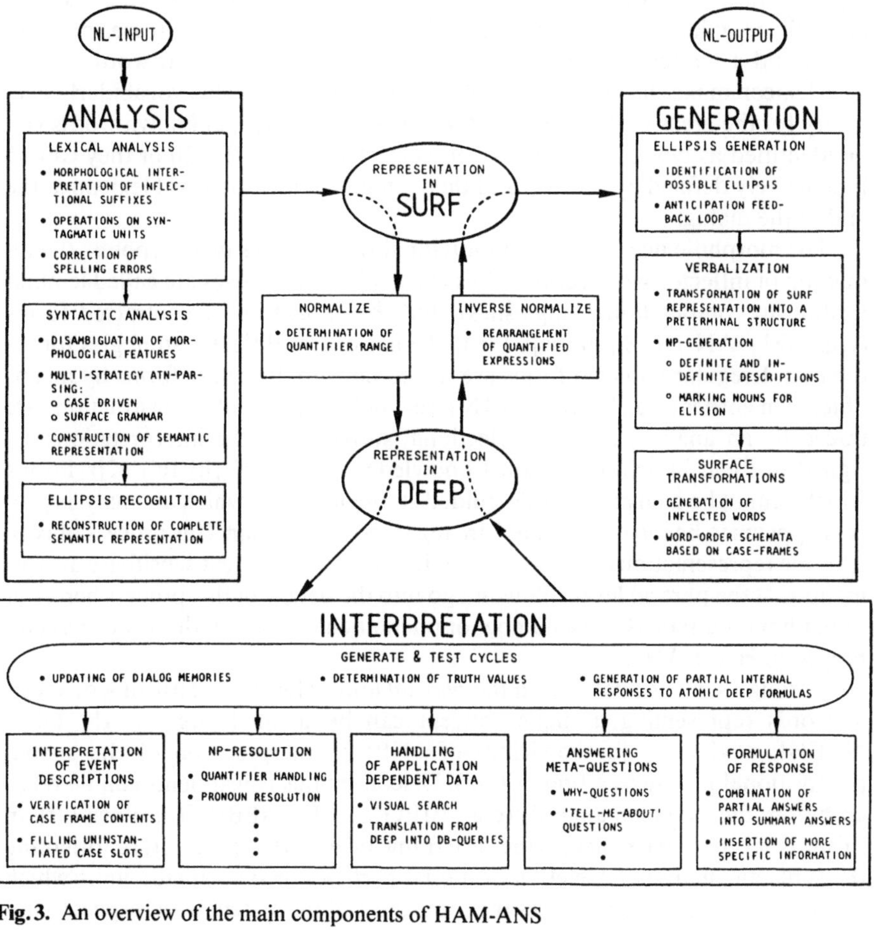

Fig. 3. An overview of the main components of HAM-ANS

ual processing components in Fig. 3 and by a description of the composition and function of the most important knowledge sources.

2.3.1 Analysis

The first question in the consultative dialog in Fig. 1 is:

[14] Gibt es im Zimmer einen Sessel oder einen grossen Stuhl?
[Is there an easy-chair or a large chair in the room?]

After the user has typed in this question, each word is submitted to a process of morphological analysis. The goal of the lexical analysis as a whole is to extract information from the input utterance which will be needed later in the syntactic analysis (e.g., word classes, inflectional features). The most important knowledge source required here is the *word lexicon*. This includes the base forms of all regularly inflected words with their morphosyntactical features (word class, gender), all irregularly inflected words with their surface features (case, number, tense) and a reference to their base forms and all non-inflected word classes. This lexicon makes no claim to completeness. It covers only the vocabularly necessary for the areas of discourse. In the course of a dialog, unknown words can be identified as typographic errors and corrected (cf. [FLIE 83]) or they can be interactively defined by the user and then integrated into the word lexicon at the end of the dialog.

The morphological analysis of individual words serves two purposes: the reduction of inflected word forms to base forms (such processes are called lemmatization in computational linguistics), and the expansion of contracted forms (e.g., AM→AN DEM [on the]). We make use of two different strategies for reduction. Irregular inflected forms are traced back to their base forms by means of lexicon entries (e.g., SIND→SEIN [are→be]), while regular constructions are traced by an analysis of their inflectional suffixes and the interpretations assigned to them in a further lexical knowledge source (cf. [BERG 82]). Forms which cannot be analyzed by rule-guided strategies or for which an analysis process appears to be too complicated are regarded as irregular. This process of context free representation at the word level interacts with context sensitive transformations at the phrasal level. We won't go into the details of this process here, but rather limit our remarks to a number of phenomena for which this process is employed in HAM-ANS.

Through sentence patterns in the *phrasal lexicon* lexemes consisting of several words representing a single concept can be defined (e.g., ... IN DER NAEHE <NP> ... [in-the-vicinity-of<NP>]; interpretation of the spatial prepositional phrase as a preposition). Discontinuous constituents can be related before the syntactic analysis (e.g., BIEG ... AB→ABBIEG ... [turn off], in this way it is possible to access the case frame of ABBIEG [turn off] for orienting the syntactic analysis.). Deletion of modal particles or syntagmatic units which are not yet processable increases the robustness of the system with respect to linguistic variation (e.g., deletion of ... EIGENTLICH ... [actually], ICH WOLLTE MAL FRAGEN, OB ... [I just wanted to ask, if ...]).

This method can be justified on practical if not on linguistic grounds. Finally, with the help of the phrasal lexicon, entire system components which employ a processing strategy other than the usual one can be activated. An example of this is the verbalization of a portion of the semantic network which is triggered by sentence patterns such as WAS VERSTEH ... UNTER D- BEGRIFF X? [WHAT ... MEAN- BY CONCEPT X?]

In example [14] syntagmatic units are treated in such a way that the predicate constituent is represented in an expression interpreted as an existential operator by the syntactic analysis. In the hotel reservation situation, under the assumption of a single special room, this presents no difficulties. The preterminal string [14-a] is generated.

```
[14-a] (SEIN E- SESSEL ODER E- GROSS STUHL VORHANDEN/?)
       [BE A ARMCHAIR OR A LARGE CHAIR AVAILABLE/?]
```

The morphological interpretations obtained from base form reduction from the word lexicon or the features of inflectional suffixes are tied to the elements of this string (see appendix). Base form reduction and replacement of syntagmatic units are applied iteratively because each process can involve transformations that create the inputs for other transformations.

The syntactic analysis in HAM-ANS is based on the ATN-formalism [WOOD 70, BATE 78]. Syntactic analysis in natural language AI systems is not as much concerned with the acceptability of linguistic utterances as with the transformation of utterances into an internal representation which can serve as a point of departure for subsequent processing. For this reason, syntactic analysis does not involve the application of purely syntactic rules and the goal of the analysis is not a syntactic representation, such as a phrase structure or dependency marker. Also typical for the AI approach is that not all utterances are analyzed in the same way (cf. [HAYE 81]). We have already mentioned that different processing strategies are employed for utterances in the frame dialog and the consultative dialog (see Sect. 2.2). Two different strategies are employed in syntactic analysis as well [BOSE 85]. For utterances with verbs whose semantics are limited to a copulative function (BE (locative), STAND, BE AVAILABLE, etc.), we employ a strategy of analysis which is guided by surface structure syntax, i. e., the preterminal string is processed in linear order from left to right. For a linguistically based representation of verb semantics, as, for example, for verbs of locomotion in the traffic scene situation, the *case frame lexicon* provides case frames, which guide the syntactic analysis (cf. [HOEP 82]). This knowledge source is specific for an area of discourse, and it is thus possible to give a verb different semantic interpretations in different domains of discourse. In addition to a listing of obligatory and optional case slots, a case frame contains the semantic restrictions that a syntactic construction - noun phrase, prepositional phrase or adverbial phrase - must fulfill in order to assume a case function. The grammar employed by HAM-ANS at present does not contain provisions for contrafactive sentences or complex subordinations.

As is clear from Fig. 3, the representation languages SURF and DEEP form the connecting links between most of the processing components. Both languages have the same expressive power. The difference - and the reason for employing a two-level internal representation - is that the SURF representation is oriented toward the linguistic surface structure while the DEEP representation is more suitable for the interpretation processes (see below 2.3.2). The most important difference between SURF and DEEP is that the quantifier scope is stipulated in DEEP expressions. The transformation between these two representational levels is carried out by two components: NORMALIZE and INVERSE NORMALIZE (cf. Fig. 3). These components refer to the declarative syntax definitions of both languages.

We will limit our consideration of the transformational components here to the principle used to determine quantifier rank (cf. [HEND 78b]). Each quantifier or question operator (WHICH, HOW MUCH) is assigned an intrinsic rank expressed by a numerical value, which is modified, in a number of cases, by the degree of generality of the quantified noun. An example of this is the treatment of the interrogative pronoun WHAT which the syntactic analysis projects onto the term WHAT THING. Since THING has a very high position in the semantic network, and is therefore a very general concept, the rank of the quantifier is lower in this case than it would be for a NP with a more specific head noun.

The representational power of SURF and DEEP is not easily illustrated since these languages are not describable in terms of their syntax definitions alone. Their semantics are determined by the processes which work with them. An additional difficulty for the description lies in the fact that the representation languages are designed in such a way that their structure and application may be constantly modified and supplemented, and, in fact, are! If, despite these difficulties, we do mention a number of characteristics of SURF and DEEP, it is with the understanding that it is only possible to convey a general impression and in the hope that the further description of the system will broaden this impression.

Characteristic of SURF and DEEP is the capability for representing question operators and logical operators for modal particles of expectation and probability (NATURALLY, PROBABLY), the representation of vague quantifiers (ALMOST ALL), and of predicates modified by linguistic hedges (RATHER COMFORTABLE). In addition, provision is made for constructions with complex coordinated terms, and partitive noun phrases (TWO OF THE FOUR CHAIRS) as well as for metapredicates for deep case roles, verb tense and voice.

The rules of the ATN grammar exploit the definition of the language SURF in order to generate different semantic representations for words with the same lexical categorization, for example. In this manner, quantifiers and question operators are divided into four classes on the SURF level: definite quantifiers (D-, DIES [THE, THIS]), indefinite quantifiers (E-, EINIGE, MEHRERE [ONE, A FEW, SEVERAL]), set operators (ALLE, JEDER, WELCHER [ALL, EACH, WHICH]) and numerical quantifiers (ZWEI, VIER BIS FUENF [TWO, FOUR TO FIVE]). Hence the parser does not only recognize the determiner of a noun phrase (DET) but also begins semantic differentiation. The referential analysis of noun phrases is guided by this classification during the subsequent interpretation of complete DEEP expressions.

In addition to the definition of SURF itself, the *semantic network* which we will examine in the next section plays a role in the SURF structures generated by the syntactic analysis. Based on the position of a concept in a semantic network, it can be determined, for example, whether the noun phrase AN ARMCHAIR is subordinated to the concept FURNITURE and is thus a potential candiate for a case role with the corresponding restriction.

Since the preterminal string [14-a] of the example sentence contains a verb with copula function, the syntactic analysis is controlled by the linear surface structure. Each word with its associated morphosyntactic features is accepted sequentially by a grammar rule and a corresponding SURF expression is generated. After successfully running through the grammar rules, the partial constructs are integrated in a target structure, which in the case of our example is reproduced in [14-b]. The syntactic markings (e.g., *t-o:*) in this structure indicate the type of a partial expression and aid in the efficient processing of these structures.

```
[14-b] (af-d: IS
           (t-o: OR
              (t-s: (q-qt: E-) (lambda: x1 (af-a: ISA x1 SESSEL)))
              (t-s: (q-qt: E-)
                 (d-o: AND
                    (lambda: x3 (af-a: ISA x3 STUHL))
                    (lambda: x2 (af-a: REF x2 GROSS)))))
       T)
```

A more thorough integration of syntactic and semantic analysis processes than is presently utilized in HAM-ANS is possible. In many cases, it appears to be more psychologically adequate to resolve particular noun phrases with regard to their semantic reference either *before* or *during* the syntactic analysis in order to recognize violations of existential presuppositions at the earliest possible point. A similar strategy was employed in the predecessor system HAM-RPM (cf. [HAHN 80, p. 179ff.]). It has proved possible to integrate this strategy into HAM-ANS, since a semantic interpretation of portions of an utterance is easy to realize.

Up to this point we have described syntactic analysis as it is applied to complete utterances. Considerable attention has been paid to fragmentary and ungrammatical utterances in language oriented AI, its goal being a performance model [WEIS 80, HUSS 82]. We will elucidate our approach toward *ellipsis reconstruction* on the basis of example [18] in Fig. 1. For the noun phrase THE EASY CHAIR it is not possible to derive a complete SURF expression corresponding to a complete utterance. However, in the course of the analysis, all the partial structures generated are stored. In addition, the SURF expression for the last complete user entry is stored in the *semantic dialog memory*. If the syntactic analysis fails, an attempt is made to find an expression in the dialog memory

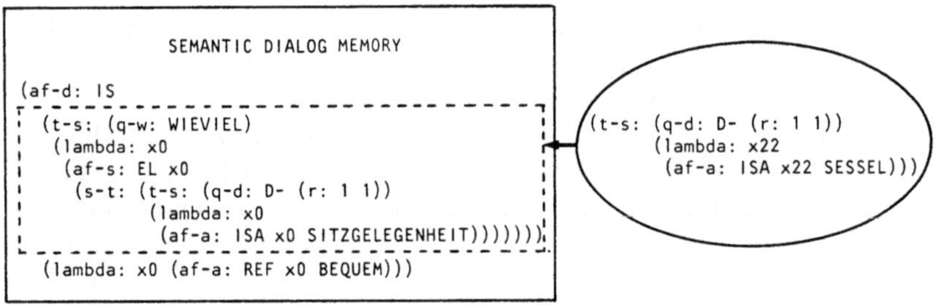

SURF-Structure for Sent.[16]:
How many of the seats are comfortable?

Partial structure for the entry [18]:
The armchair?

Fig. 4. Ellipsis reconstruction

which corresponds syntactically to the most extensive partial structure of the input. This is then replaced by the SURF representation of the input (cf. Fig. 4).

This syntactically oriented procedure can be employed successfully for most *substitution ellipses*. Ellipses which can only be resolved with semantic knowledge, as, for example, when several syntactically identical partial structures are present in the preceding sentence, could be reconstructed with the aid of case frame restrictions. This method would also be applicable for many cases of *expansion ellipses*.

2.3.2 Interpretation

By interpretation we mean the process which transforms the result of the analysis (in HAM-ANS: the DEEP representation of the user utterance) into an internal representation of the system reaction. It is implicitly assumed that the user utterance is a question and that the system response can be viewed as an answer.

Before going into the interpretation process in HAM-ANS in more detail, the knowledge sources required for this process must be presented: the *conceptual* and the *referential semantic network* and the *visual data*.

The *conceptual semantic network* contains seven primitive relations characterizing the semantic relationships between words (the most important ones are contained in Fig. 5). In the referential semantic network, objects in the domain of discourse are represented by a unique name (e.g., CHAIR1, TABLE5) and joined to a node of the conceptual network by an ISA-relation. The characteristics of these reference objects are expressed by the REF-relation. For example (REF CHAIR1 RED), means that the object CHAIR1 is red. In addition, in the representation formalism we use for semantic networks, each relation is assigned a numerical value in the range [0, 1] [LEFA 77]. This value can be utilized by the processing mechanisms. An application of these values might be, for instance, the weakening of the range of application of a relation. The relationship (REF

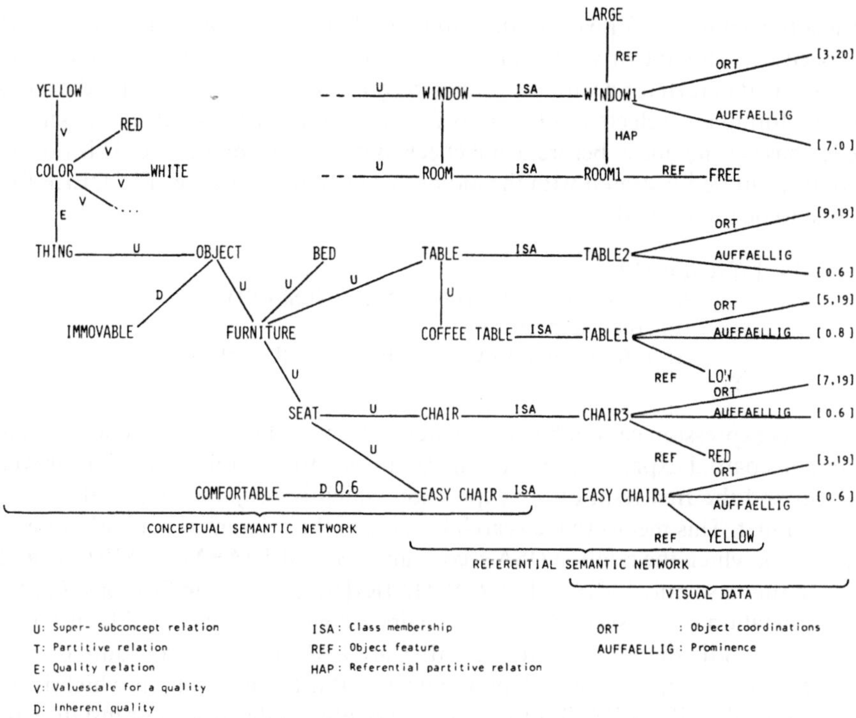

Fig. 5. Conceptual and referential knowledge

CHAIR1 ROT).0.7) can be interpreted by the system as: The object CHAIR1 is rather red.

In the semantics of the network relations, there are numerous dependencies which are assumed as preconditions for the processing mechanisms and others that are explicitly formulated as consistency rules [CHRI 82], aiding in the construction of these knowledge sources.

The *visual data* contain for each object of the domain of discourse an entry for its spatial coordinates, a value for its initial prominence and vertical spatial relations between objects (e.g., ON, UNDER, OVER). The reason for the explicit specification of vertical relations is that in order to enable an efficient search, the hotel room is represented in the system in a two dimensional view, a sort of layout plan. At the end of this section, the utilization of the visual data will be illustrated with an example.

Fig. 5 contains a sample from these three knowledge sources containing the entries relevant to the sample dialog in Fig. 1.

Having presented these three knowledge sources, we can now describe how HAM-ANS interprets DEEP expressions. The interpretation of a DEEP formula is primarily extensional. GENERATE and TEST procedures are recursively activated during the analysis of a DEEP formula. The GENERATE procedures substitute constants for each of the variables of an expression in turn. The TEST procedures attempt to verify fully instantiated formulas. The set of constants substituted in turn for a variable is limited by a heuristic: one of the predications of the formula is selected as the basis for the search for constants in the knowledge base at the outset before being checked by a TEST procedure. This flow of control can be illustrated with the aid of our example sentence. The DEEP formula to be interpreted is:

```
[14-c] (f-d: (t-o: OR
              (t-q: (for: (q-qt: E-) x9) (af-a: ISA x9 SESSEL))
              (t-q: (for: (q-qt: E-) x9)
               (f-o: AND (af-a: ISA x9 STUHL) (af-a: REF x9 GROSS))))
        T)
```

This expression cannot be immediately interpreted in its entirety since it still contains partial expressions including variables (x9). For this reason it is broken down and the first term of the expression which is conjoined with OR is processed first. This means that a search is made in the referential network for constants for which the relation (ISA <constant> SESSEL [ARMCHAIR]) is valid.

In this case only SESSEL1 [ARMCHAIR1] meets the specifications. For the interpretation of the second term, all chairs are generated as possible instances of x9 and individually tested to see if they are LARGE. This procedure is reminiscent of the application of type predicates. But the predication which is exploited by the GENERATE procedures is not always the same. For instance, instead of ISA, NEBEN [NEXT TO] might have occurred. In this case, all objects in the spatial surroundings of the object in question are submitted to the TEST procedures. So, for instance, in [31] of Fig. 1, "Und neben was?" [And next to what?], the set of constants which may be inserted into the corresponding DEEP expression is limited by the predicate NEBEN [NEXT TO]. This flexibility distinguishes the procedure from a pure type approach.

The expressions instantiated by the GENERATE procedures are successively checked by the TEST procedures. In our example STUHL1, STUHL2 and STUHL3 are tested in turn to see whether they are large. Several methods can be employed for the check: either there is a REF-arc with the required characteristic (as, for example, (REF FENSTER1 GROSS) [REF WINDOW1 LARGE]) or else the characteristic in question is assigned to the reference object on the basis of conceptual knowledge (as, for example, for (D GEGENSTAND FEST) [D OBJECT SOLID]). The second method is a simple example of an inference rule, here: inheritance. More complex reasoning is done by inference procedures which are triggered if there is no explicit entry in the network at any level (cf. [HOEP 80]). An example of this is the answering of the question about the brightness of the room [41]. The conclusion that a particular room is bright is drawn from the fact that the room has a window (HAP ZIMMER1 FENSTER1 [HAP ROOM1 WINDOW]) and that this window is large (REF FENSTER1 GROSS [REF WINDOW1 LARGE]). The fact that a particular answer is based on inferences should not be passed over in silence, rather the partner should be given some indication of this, as HAM-ANS does with the modal particle *probably*. In addition, the dialog partner must be able to follow the chain of inference, i.e., inference-based answers require the capability of explanation. In HAM-ANS explanations are generated by verbalizing the relevant steps that are stored in the *inference memory* (cf. [43] in Fig. 1 and [WAHL 81]).

Let us return to example [14-c] and its interpretation. Since a simple existential question is involved, the interpretation of the expression requires only the referential analysis of the two NPs. During the analysis of the expression, DEEP structures are constructed for the individual results. These enter into a DEEP representation which makes the contrast between the two results clear. The two complete expressions, referring to easy chair and chair respectively, are linked with the conjunction BUT yielding the DEEP expression [14-d]:

```
[14-d] (f-o: BUT
        (f-o: NOT
         (f-d: (t-q: (for: (q-qt: E-) x9)
                (f-o: AND (af-a: ISA x9 STUHL) (af-a: REF x9 GROSS)))
         T))
        (f-d: (t-q: (for: (q-qt: (r: 1 1)) x9) (af-a: ISA x9 SESSEL)) T))
```

A number of characteristics of the interpretation processing phase (e.g., interpretation of questions containing locomotion verbs, interpretation of natural language data base queries, pronominal reference and modelling of visual search in a static domain of discourse) could not be illustrated by this example. We will attempt to provide at least a short sketch of these in the next sections.

The interpretation of a DEEP structure containing a case frame, e.g., for utterances with a verb of locomotion, follows a more complicated procedure than the one presented here for a copula structure. The representation for events in the domain of discourse 'traffic scene' does not appear in a fully instantiated form, e.g., as part of a semantic net or a frame hierarchy, but rather includes, in addition to the case frame of each verb, the referential semantics of predicates associated with that verb which make it possible to interpret the visual input data for the movement in question.

This knowledge guides the perceptual process for verifying the movement, e.g., for a turn-off event it specifies that there must be some location on the object's trajectory (a source) and another location - different from the first one - (a goal), and that there must be a significant change of direction between these two locations. If the question lacks some of the optional deep case roles which are necessary for the perceptual verification, the additional information gained during the verification process, i.e., in this example, the source and goal objects, is incorporated in the response. Thus in answering a yes-no question, the system's reaction is not limited to a simple yes or no answer. Rather, an attempt is made to satisfy the implicit desire for information which motivated the question by over-answering in a cooperative fashion (cf. [MARB 83 b]).

Though the principle of the GENERATE and TEST strategy is also applied in the data base application, some differences are worth mentioning. Handling of mass data does not allow for explicitly generating all instances of a certain concept (e.g., ships, when there are several hundreds of them stored in the database) and testing the predicate in question for each instance in turn. Therefore the GENERATE procedures in this application class construct expressions of the DBMS's query language (cf. [O'LEA 83]) which - when interpreted by the DBMS - build virtual relations containing all objects satisfying the restrictions of a certain term (e.g., FRENCH SHIPS). The predicate in questions with copula verbs corresponds to a qualification expression in the query language. Application of the qualification yields the set of tuples of the virtual relation satisfying the whole question, which is then used for building an adequate answer.

This description of the processes which are necessary during the interpretation of a NL data base query is somewhat oversimplified. There are a number of knowledge sources which are very important for the appropriate translation of a DEEP expression into one or more DBMS query language expressions. These contain, among other things, information about the relations in the database (e.g., relation names, attribute names), the connections between concepts and relations, attributes etc., syntactic knowledge about the entries in the relations (e.g., character or number fields) and the syntactic definition of the DBMS query language (cf. [MARB 83 a]).

One coherence feature in natural language dialogs is the use of proforms. At this point, let us briefly investigate the referential analysis of personal pronouns in HAM-ANS. The basis for the determination of a discourse referent is the *referential memory,* which is built up during the process of projecting definite descriptions onto individual objects in the domain of discourse. Each time a definite description is successfully analyzed or generated, an entry is stored in the referential memory (see Fig. 6). This entry includes the name of the object or a set of such names, the DEEP expression of the definite description used, the gender of the NP as well as information about the frequency and the point in time when the reference was made (sum of references and sentence count, respectively). In resolving a pronoun, the last mentioned object with the same gender as the proform is selected. The sum of references is integrated into the evaluation of reference objects during the visual search, which we will briefly describe in the next section.

The visual search process is activated by questions about spatial relations between objects (e.g., [29], [31] in Fig. 1). For this purpose, locations of objects are represented in a modified version of the coordinate form presented above. In the two-dimensional representation of the hotel room, points are selected at regular intervals. All objects that can be perceived when focussing on such points are assigned prominence values. The prominence of an object is calculated from its initial prominence (cf. Fig. 5), the distance from the fixation point in question and a cumulative dialog relevance value - the sum of references from the referential memory. Through this process, different objects are selected as reference points for spatial characterization in different stages of the dialog. The form of representation of visual data as a set of fixation points aids in creating the simu-

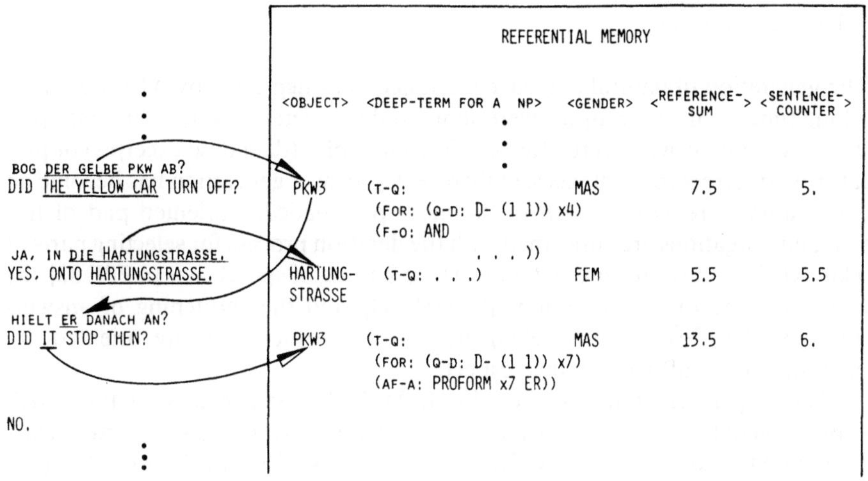

Fig. 6. Pronominal reference

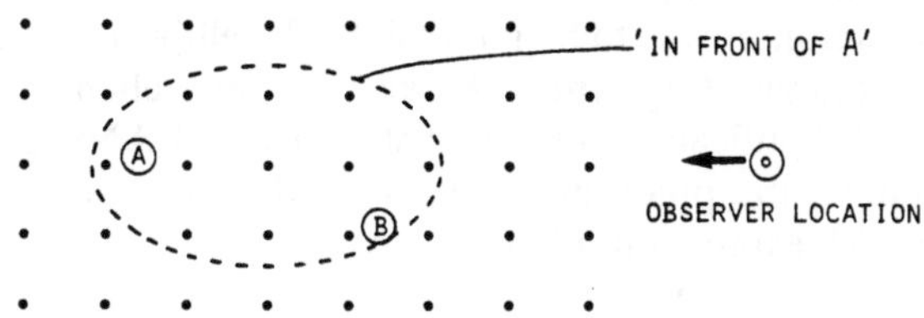

Fig. 7. Semantics of spatial prepositions

lation character of the visual search. A more detailed presentation can be found in [HAHN 80, p. 216 ff.].

The semantics of horizontal spatial relations is procedurally defined from the point of view of an observer. This means, for example, that the relation VOR [IN FRONT OF] holds between an object A and an object B if the object B is visible from a point lying between the point of observation and the fixation point closest to the object A. The result of a visual search process is a set of object names with their assigned values for spatial relations. The object name with the highest value appears in the DEEP representation of the answer. In response to question [29] the following relations are determined:

```
((LINKS-NEBEN TISCH1)0.6) [TO THE LEFT NEXT TO TABLE1 0.6],
((VOR FENSTER1)0.61) [IN FRONT OF WINDOW1 0.61],
((RECHTS-NEBEN BILD1)0.3) [TO THE RIGHT NEXT TO PICTURE1 0.3]
((LINKS-NEBEN STUHL1)0.46) [TO THE LEFT NEXT TO CHAIR1 0.46]).
```

The second relation has the highest value and thus appears in the answer [30]. This selection of the appropriate answer from among the possible correct answers can be seen as the first step in the next processing stage - answer generation.

2.3.3 Generation

The generation of natural language utterances was neglected by AI research for a long time. While user inputs were submitted to a detailed anlysis and interpretation, system answers were often confined to tables (data base excerpts) or prefabricated stereotype sentences. Only recently answer generation has become an active area of research in AI. In the more pragmatically oriented part of this field, investigations are concerned with the decision process for selecting parts of a knowledge source for presentation. The planning of speech acts [APPE 82], the overanswering of user questions [WAHL 83], and the shortening of answers through elliptification also belong here, since surface structure oriented approaches are insufficient in this respect.

The ellipsis generation process in HAM-ANS first decomposes the SURF expression of the complete answer and then compares the resulting partial structures with the corresponding SURF representations of the user's input. The possible ellipses identified by this process are then evaluated on the basis of how understandable the shortened expressions are. This process makes use of ellipsis reconstruction, that is, the partner's understanding is anticipated. If the reconstruction proves to be impossible, the elliptification process is reversed and the next largest fragment is checked for comprehensibility [JAME 82b].

Elliptification is the first step in HAM-ANS' generation process. In our example, the predicate of the second of the two contrasting statements of the SURF expression [14-e]

```
[14-e] (f-o: BUT
        (f-o: NOT
         (af-d: IS
          (t-s: (q-qt: E-)
           (d-o: AND
            (lambda: x9 (af-a: ISA x9 STUHL))
            (lambda: x9 (af-a: REF x9 GROSS))))
          T))
        (af-d: IS (t-s: (q-qt: (r: 1 1)) (lambda: x9 (af-a: ISA x9 SESSEL))) T))
```

is deleted yielding [14-f] (cf. appendix 2 for another example):

```
[14-f] (BUT (FORMULA (f-o: NOT
                      (af-d: IS
                       (t-s: (q-qt: E-)
                        (d-o: AND
                         (lambda: x0 (af-a: ISA x0 STUHL))
                         (lambda: x0 (af-a: REF x0 GROSS))))
                      T)))
       (TERM (t-s: (q-qt: (r: 1 1)) (lambda: x0 (af-a: ISA x0 SESSEL)))))
```

If the presentation of the answer is planned, a linguistic structure must be derived from the internal representation. In this stage – verbalization – HAM-ANS transforms the (partially elided) SURF expression into a preterminal structure, which already contains morphosyntactic features such as number (N), mood (M) and tense (T). The internal object specifiers are transformed into NPs by the NP generation, choosing the proper determiner. In the choice of determiner, the NP generation must rely on knowledge about the dialog partner's state of information. We will go into this in more detail in Sect. 3.2. Whether a noun phrase is to be realized as a pronoun, as in system answer [43], is indicated by a morphosyntactic feature.

In our example [14-f] is transformed into the preterminal structure [14-g]

```
[14-g] (SENTENCE (SENTENCE (SUBJECT (NP (N: SG) E- GROSS STUHL))
                           (PREDICATE (PA: (ZUR/ VERFUEGUNG/
                                            STEH))
                                       (M: IND)
                                       (T: PRES)
                                       NICHT))
                 ABER
                 (SENTENCE (SUBJECT (NP (N: SG) E SESSEL))))
```

The term-predicate classification implied in DEEP and SURF is realized as a subject-predicate classification in copula sentences. The logical structure of SURF and DEEP produces a structure without deep cases for expressions with the operator IS. For other expressions, the corresponding operators are integrated into the preterminal structures as deep case markers. As with analysis, separate processing strategies are also used in generation.

Since HAM-ANS actually *generates* natural language replies in consultative dialogs and does not use prefabricated sentences as in the frame dialog, a third step is necessary in order to generate a natural-language surface structure for a preterminal structure. These surface structure transformations [BUSE 84] first constitute a linear string with the aid of word order rules. During this process, pronouns are inserted if indicated by an appropriate feature, discontinuous verb constituents are generated and punctuation marks added. The second, morphological process inflects word forms in accordance with the syntactic categories they are embedded in.

The output of the surface structure transformations is the system's answer. In our example:

```
[15] EIN GROSSER STUHL STEHT NICHT ZUR VERFUEGUNG, ABER EIN SESSEL.
     [A LARGE CHAIR IS NOT AVAILABLE, BUT AN EASY-CHAIR.]
```

Although the main principle for generation in HAM-ANS is to construct a complete internal representation of the system's response, two exceptions have to be mentioned.

One occurs in the data base application. If the amount of information to be presented is too large or too complicated to be verbalized in a single sentence, the system asks the user what to do with the result of the query. The options are (1) to display it on the terminal in tabular form, or (2) to produce a report file for later examination (cf. appendix 4.1).

The other exception occurs in generating responses to questions about the system's conceptual knowledge. As a first step in this process, the system selects on the basis of the user's question the relevant concepts, properties, values and relations to be verbalized. Then a pattern appropriate to the selected information is instantiated. The syntactic form of these pattern corresponds to types of preterminal structures with slots for accepting certain kinds of substructures. The instantiated forms are then passed through the morphological generation process yielding the surface structure forms (cf. appendix 4.1).

This concludes our survey of HAM-ANS processing procedures as illustrated by our examples. Since it is not possible to illustrate every processing option open to the system with a single example some points had to go unmentioned. In the final section we will turn to a topic of current research interest: What effects do assumptions about the dialog partner have and how can these be modeled in an AI system?

3 User Modeling in HAM-ANS

User modeling is a topic of focal interest for future applied AI systems, which will have to adapt their behavior flexibly to various kinds of users, and for the investigation of the influence that the hearer's image of the speaker and vice versa has on linguistic analysis and generation.

3.1 User Modeling in AI Research

Generally a user model is understood to mean a set of beliefs about a person or group of persons. In this form, the concept has points of relation to: psychology (belief systems, person perception, attribution theory); computer science (user friendliness, user types, personalizing systems); and linguistics (dialog strategies, communicative adequacy, image building in conversations).

The general concept can be made more specific on the basis of several criteria:

1) Is the modeled person the partner in a conversation or the actor in a text?

2) Are beliefs about a specific person or about a group of persons represented?

3) Which aspect of a person is modeled?

We will provide short answers to these questions as they apply to language oriented AI and in particular to our own work, at the same time concretizing concepts that will be used in the following sections.

ad 1) While user models in a text comprehension system refer to persons mentioned in the text, user models in a dialog system refer to the dialog partner. To date there is no system that models both the dialog partner and the persons discussed, although such a project would be a worthwhile undertaking [MORI 81].

ad 2) Beliefs about a particular person are collected during the process of text comprehension in order to connect an actor in a text with the statements that are made about him. In order to understand the actions of a protagonist, it is important to have certain assumptions about his group affiliation at one's disposal at the outset. For example, knowledge about what members of this group usually want may clarify what a particular member is doing. In AI, Carbonell [CARB 81] presented an approach to understanding reports of the activities of groups of persons on the basis of the goals which are attributed to these groups. His system POLITICS explains political events in various ways according to which goals the system imputes to the actors (here: the governments of various countries).

In the course of a dialog, concrete information about the dialog partner can be extracted (e.g., name, bank account number, deposits, interest). If these data are simply entered without influencing the behavior of the system in the dialog, user modeling is not involved. We only speak of user modeling if the system uses such information to modify its behavior toward the user. This is one criterion for the application of this concept. Another criterion, the explicitness of the model, will be explained below.

Individual user modeling is involved if the system stores the results of one dialog session with a particular user under an unambiguous identifier and uses this information in further dialogs with the same user.

In order to utilize beliefs about the user for modifying its behavior, the system must have rules at its disposal that specify which characteristics of the user trigger which behavior of the system. These rules cannot, of course, be based on a particular user since, in that case, they would have to be reformulated for every new user. Rather, they are based either on a profile of the typical user (e.g., in IMP [JAME 83]), or they are based on different user categorizations, each category being assigned a number of user characteristics. In the simplest case, the individual user is assigned to a particular user type and his profile defined accordingly. In the case of more differentiated treatments, a special user profile is assembled from various assignments of several aspects of the partner [RICH 79]. Hence both beliefs about groups of persons and specific beliefs about an individual user derived from these are necessary.

We can now define the profile of a particular user as a user profile. The profile of the typical user is what we call an *apriori user model* [WAHL 82], that of different user types, if a particular psychological approach is employed, a *stereotype* [RICH 79].

We can characterize the user model as that part of the dialog system which contains:

- knowledge about a priori user models,
- rules for the construction of a user profile based on a priori models, and
- rules for different treatment of various dialog partners.

The second condition for user modeling (mentioned above) is that this knowledge must be made explicit, i. e., it must be represented in the system. Implicitly every program system has a user model at its disposal, insofar as the system developers design the man-machine interface for a particular user type and orient the performance of the system around the assumed demands and abilities of the users. It is also possible that a system may have rules at its disposal which direct its behavior in such a way that the system behaves differently toward different users. If, however, there is no knowledge source in the system to which these rules refer, that is, if the user types are simply in the mind of the system designers, it is not proper to speak of user modeling. Differentiated treatment of different users (or user types) is involved here but not their representation. To use the terminology in [SEAR 78], what is involved is a distinction between representational content and representation: the de facto particularized system behavior itself is the representational content, its explicit form in the system is the representation.

ad 3) For the modeling of dialogs, the following factors are of first ranking importance: What a dialog partner believes or knows to be the case, what he believes to be good or bad, and what options for action he has at his disposal. HAM-ANS treats the aspect of knowledge or belief and that of evaluation on a positive-negative scale. In the following section we will discuss the already implemented parts of our system dealing with assumed knowledge in the area of coreference. The design for user modeling with respect to evaluations will be presented in Sect. 3.3.

3.2 *The User's Knowledge*

In the hotel scene it can be assumed that the user is familiar with the typical (minimal) provisions of a hotel room, but not with the details. Similarly in the traffic scene, it is assumed that the user is familiar with the static details of the scene - the streets, buildings, trees, street lights - but not with the pedestrians, automobiles and bicycles.

These presuppositions about the knowledge of the user are represented by a semantic network which has the same types of nodes and arcs as the semantic network that represents the referential knowledge of the system about this sector.

When the user makes a statement that correctly implies or presupposes the existence of an object, the *referential network of the user* is extended with a corresponding entry so that, after the statement has been made, the system knows that the user knows that the object in question exists. In the same way entries are made of the system's statements about the object.

A further knowledge source, the *coreference network,* establishes the connection between the user's knowledge and that of the system. It might be the case, for instance, that in the course of the dialog, an object, e.g., a chair, is mentioned and the system knows that there are several objects of this type present in the scene. In the user's knowledge only one object of this type, only one chair, is present. The definite article is then only available for referring to this one chair which is known to both partners in the dialog. The system must know, however, which chair has already been referred to in the dialog, that is which chair is "the chair". The connection between user knowledge and system knowledge about the domain of discourse which is required here, as in other cases, is established through the coreference network. Fig. 8 illustrates portions of the system's referential network, of the user's network to the extent that this knowledge is shared by both partners (mutual belief), and of the coreference network. A more detailed presentation can be found in [JAME 82].

The networks are used for the generation of determiners. Indefinite determiners are generated when no corresponding entry is present in the user's knowledge. Definite determiners are generated as pragmatic anaphora for objects which can be presumed as known to the user. Since the user's assumptions are presupposed at the beginning of the dialog, an object like THE DOOR or THE BED can be used with the definite article the first time they are referred to.

The choice of attributes for unambiguous identification of an object is also made in accordance with the state of mutual knowledge attained at a given stage of the dialog. If, say, a second chair were to be introduced into the dialog in the above example, the system would have to specify which of the two chairs is

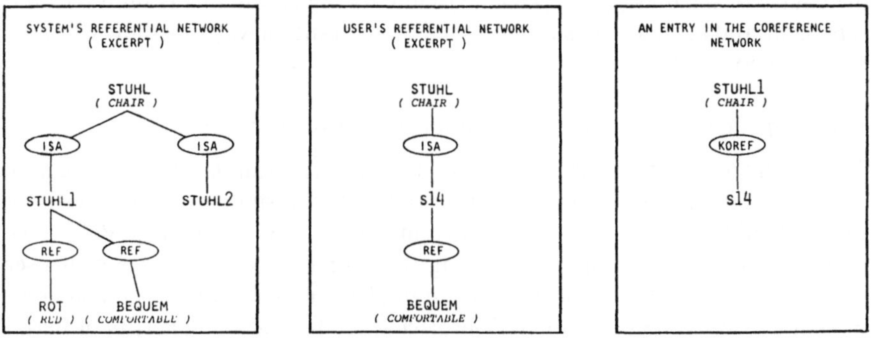

Fig. 8. Referential knowledge of system and user

meant by an additional attribute. In order to accomplish this, it would not be advisable to use a quality which the user cannot associate with a particular chair. For this reason, in our example CHAIR1 is characterized as the COMFORTABLE CHAIR and not as THE RED CHAIR.

In this part of the user modeling there is only one a priori user model which the rules of NP generation refer to but no different user types, for example. A logical extension of the system, already proposed by Jameson (personal communication), would be to provide different sets of presuppositions for different types of users, so that for instance, if the customer is a manager who expects to be speaking to the clerk of a luxury hotel, the system should refer to *the* television set and *the* drinks (in the room) on the first mention.

Up till now a single a priori user model has been sufficient for our investigation of rules for describing and identifying objects. The general model is personalized in the course of the dialog so that it reproduces the knowledge of an individual user in the dialog. When the dialog is completed, the user model of the particular user is erased since it is only applicable within the context of a specific dialog. Thus, no attempt is made to employ individual user modeling.

3.3 User's Evaluation

For a consultative dialog, a system not only has to keep track of the user's beliefs about the domain but also to recognize the user's desires and needs. Consulting consists to no small degree of recognizing the evaluation standards of the client and then finding the best match between these requirements and available objects or services.

In the hotel scene we are working with, we have a consultative situation in which the major goals of the dialog partners are quite fixed: the hotel employee wishes to rent the largest possible number of rooms and the caller desires to book the room which best suits his needs. What the caller considers to be a suitable room is, however, a matter which can only be clarified in the course of the dialog. Only then can a room which meets his requirements be selected. Moreover, in the course of the dialog, it is possible to modify the requirements until they are satisfiable and to choose descriptions of a room in such a way that they will satisfy presumed requirements.

How can such a dialog with the system as advisor be modeled?

The system must recognize and represent the user's standards of evaluation, check the suitability of various rooms according to this standard and, depending on the results of this evaluation, it must initiate various dialog acts. Below, we present a proposal for operationalizing these processes. The concept of user standards and suitability check has been implemented as an independent component in cooperation with the KIT project at the Technical University of Berlin [MORI 83c] and is now being integrated into HAM-ANS.

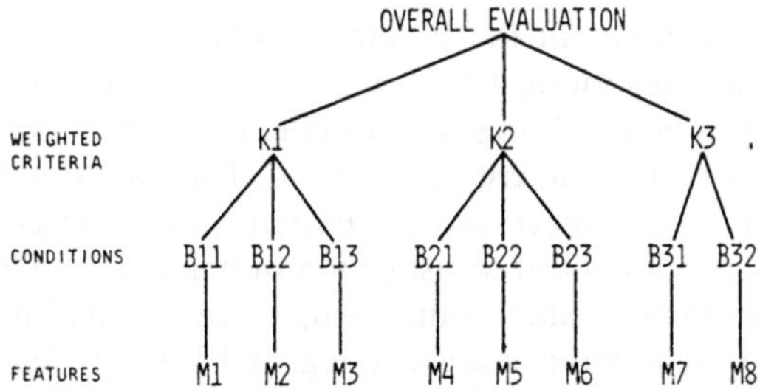

Fig. 9. Evaluation standard

Taking an analysis of value-judgement statements as a point of departure [MORI 83a], a schema involving several stages was developed for the representation of standards of evaluation (cf. Fig. 9).

A good hotel room is, for instance, a *large, bright* room with *comfortable* furnishings, a *hard* bed and a *soft* easy chair; or an *inexpensive* room with a *high* table and a *matching* chair; or a *large* room, with *tasteful* decoration and a *roomy* seating area. Moreover, these criteria are of different degrees of importance for the overall evaluation.

The different criteria applied by various people in evaluating a hotel room are, for the most part, value-judgement expressions which involve a descriptive element. The latter is, however, not sufficient to establish a connection to the features of a hotel room. We need an exact explication of what it means for someone that a hotel room is large, bright, roomy, inexpensive, the furnishings comfortable, the decoration tasteful, etc. The next level is presented then by the conditions necessary for satisfaction of a criterion, e.g., a room is considered to be bright if at least one of its windows is large, or if the color of the walls and the carpet is light, or if the large window faces south or west.

The connection to the features of the room can be established on the basis of the conditions. For this purpose, they are represented to the same degree of detail as the features. If, for instance, no exact measurements for the size of the windows are available, the conditions will not be precisely formulated either. In principle, additional levels can be inserted into the evaluation standard by treating condition as a criterion which is in turn made more explicit by other conditions until a connection to the objective features can be established. For our hotel scenario, this extra effort is not necessary.

In this approach, different standards of evaluation corresponding to different user types vary in:

- the conditions for the fulfillment of a criterion,
- the criteria, and
- the weighting of the criteria.

In contrast to [JAME 83] we do not only model one user type with the corresponding evaluation standard but a number of user types, and we distinguish the stereotypes from the user profiles.

In order for the system to utilize user standards of evaluation for recommending a room, it must attribute specific standards to the particular user. In order to establish this user profile, it could, of course, directly question the user about all of the criteria involved. This would not only be very time consuming but is also unnecessary since criteria are not freely combinable with one another. As psychological investigation in naive personality theory have demonstrated, assumptions about other people are grouped in such a way that they can be judged as being consistent (e.g., [HERK 80]). Similarly, we can also assume that criteria are grouped. These groupings make up the a priori user knowledge. As focal points for the grouping of criteria, we take price class, whether or not children will be in the hotel guest's party, and the reason for the stay in the hotel (i.e., business, vacation). From information on these points, which can be obtained during the introductory dialog, a number of criteria and conditions can be derived at the outset. If the user asks about the fulfillment of a criterion or a condition during the dialog, this could further specify his standard of evaluation.

The system selects a room which is suitable in accordance with the assumed standard of evaluation. In this process, all criteria are first checked on the basis of their conditions. If there is a room in the hotel which meets all of the conditions, the system recommends this room. If there is a room which meets all of the very important criteria but not all of the less important ones, the system makes a qualified recommendation. If there is only a room that meets some criteria, but not others, the system mentions advantages and disadvantages so that the user can ask further questions, which are then interpreted as questions about the fulfillment of conditions.

If advantages and disadvantages are evenly balanced, the system attempts to find a feature of the room which does not figure in the evaluation standard of the user, but which is generally regarded as positive. Such facts might possibly tip the balance in the positive direction.

Finally, if there is no room that meets the user's specificiations, the unfulfillable criteria or conditions are listed. If the user is prepared to drop them, the suitability of the rooms is checked again, if not, the consultative dialog is ended (unsuccessfully).

The schema outlined here is also of theoretical interest for a number of reasons:

- it permits value-judgement statements to be treated;
- it provides a guide for the description of the various room categories - the listing of advantages and disadvantages in accordance with the user's standard of evaluation [RICH 79, MCKE 82];
- it provides the opportunity for alternating speaker initiative since the system poses questions about missing information and draws attention to "inappropriate" demands made by the user;
- it leads to an extension in the kind of speech acts the system can perform, in particular, the recommendation can be modeled in this way.

In order to integrate this schema into HAM-ANS, the system must be expanded. In particular, the frame dialog must be modified and the interpretation component supplemented by an algorithm which determines the suitability of a room.

Further sources of knowledge - the a priori evaluation standards, the user profile and the satisfied and unsatisfied criteria - have to be added. The system's referential network, which at present describes only a single hotel room in great detail, will be supplemented by a referential network that represents several room categories in less detail.

Further processes - the construction of the user profile, the entering of advantages (satisfied criteria) and disadvantages (unsatisfied criteria) - must be added.

The holistic approach, i.e., constantly maintaining a complete running system, involves a considerably greater expense of effort in integrating additional capabilities into the system than is the case with the implementation of isolated components. This effort, however, only demonstrates the interdependence between different cognitive and linguistic abilities and offers a certain amount of safeguards against concepts that do not lend themselves to generalization.

Acknowledgments

We would like to thank T. Christaller, W. v. Hahn, B. Nebel and W. Wahlster for numerous helpful comments, and Russell Block for translation and useful suggestions.

Appendix

1 Overview

The description of the system HAM-ANS is supplemented in this appendix with a documentation of sample sessions (version of spring 1983). It contains a sample dialog from each of HAM-ANS' three application areas: hotel reservation situation, traffic scene, and fishery data. In order to illustrate the real internal functioning of the system, the examples are presented here in a degree of detail which is normally available only during a system demonstration. This detailed description - which approaches 'hands-on experience' - meets Ballard's requirement [BALL 83] for careful descriptions of natural language systems. A more extensive collection of examples of the final system capabilities is contained in [HOEP 84].

All dialogs - except the first one which is given in Fig. 1 in Sect. 2.2 - are presented first without commentary, thus illustrating the system's capability for understanding and generating natural language utterances. Examples from the same dialogs are then repeated with commentary. It is impossible to illustrate all the capabilities of the system on the basis of three short dialogs, but we have attempted to choose sample dialogs which illustrate the largest possible number of characteristics of the system.

The purpose of the commentary is to provide the system constructor with a convenient aid which can, for example, facilitate error analysis or inspection of the flow of control. At the same time the commentary documents for the user what occurs between the input of a natural language utterance and the natural language system reaction.

After the system is activated with the procedure (HAM-ANS <numerical identification of domain of discourse>) parameters are set in an opening dialog, which, i.a., determine the system's input/output behavior. The answer to the question whether the processing steps should be annotated allows selection of one of two options: a general annotation or a selective annotation covering particular processing steps whose functioning calls for closer observation.

If the user selects the back-trace option offered by the system, the complete annotation for the processing of an utterance is stored. After the system has replied, the complete annotation or a selected annotation of individual process steps can be outputted as desired. If spelling correction is desired, a correction component (cf. [FLIE 83]) is activated for unfamiliar words. (This component is

WASCHBECKEN	AUF	ZAHNPUTZBECHER 1
WASH BASIN	*ON*	*WATER GLASS*
		WASCHLAPPEN 1
		WASH CLOTH
		WASCHLAPPEN 2
		WASH CLOTH
		SEIFE 1
		SOAP
BETT 2	AUF	KOPFKISSEN 2
BED	*ON*	*PILLOW*
		BETTUCH 2
		SHEET
		BETTBEZUG 2
		FEATHER BED COVER
		DECKE 2
		FEATHER BED
		TAGESDECKE 2
		BED SPREAD
NACHTTISCH 1	AUF	LAMPE 2
NIGHT TABLE	*ON*	*LAMP*
		WECKER 1
		ALARM CLOCK
		TELEFON 1
		TELEPHONE
BETT 1	AUF	KOPFKISSEN 1
BED	*ON*	*PILLOW*
		BETTUCH 1
		SHEET
		BETTBEZUG 1
		FEATHER BED COVER
		DECKE 1
		FEATHER BED
		TAGESDECKE 1
		BED SPREAD
	IN	MATRATZE 1
	IN	*MATRACE*
TÜR 2	AN	TÜRGRIFF 2
DOOR	*ON*	*DOOR KNOB*
KÜHLSCHRANK 1	AUF	GLAS 1
REFRIGERATOR	*ON*	*GLASS*
		GLAS 2
		GLASS
		GLAS 3
		GLASS
		GLAS 4
		GLASS
SCHREIBTISCH 1	AUF	SCHREIBZEUG 1
DESK	*ON*	*WRITING MATERIALS*
		MATERIALS
		LAMPE 1
		LAMP
		SCHREIB-UNTERLAGE 1
		BLOTTER

not illustrated in the examples.) In this appendix, user inputs are printed in upper and lower case letters, the system responses in upper case. The English translations of the user's questions and the system's responses are enclosed in brackets. In the annotated dialogs the translation reflects the German utterances as closely as possible. The commentary is preceded by '**' or ';;'. The symbol '**' at the beginning of a line indicates the activation of a processing component;

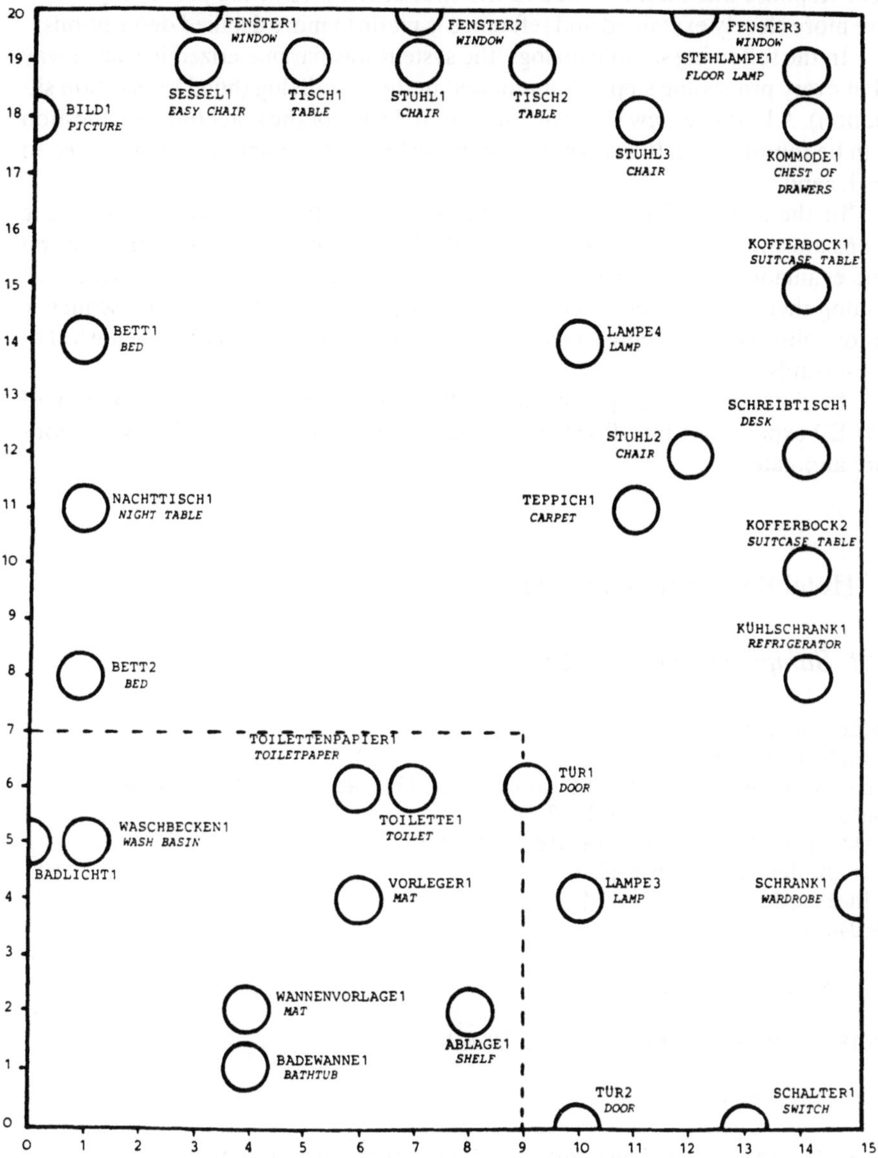

Fig. 10. Spatial arrangement of hotel room

the symbol ';;' introduces annotations to individual processing steps. Indented lines contain values of internal variables in list format and are always part of the previous line of commentary. The values of variables may also be contained in individual lines of commentary. These, like all other values of variables, are printed in capitals. In this manner, identical program operations may have different kinds of annotation. In addition to the system annotation, after each system response attention is called to the special features of the processing; these are more closely examined and reference is made to more detailed descriptions.

In the following sample dialogs, the system was parameterized in such a way that every processing step was annotated in the first dialog (hotel reservation situation). A bird-eye view showing the spatial details of the hotel room in question can be found in Fig. 10 and vertical relationships among objects are presented in its legend.

In the sample dialog covering the traffic situation, only those processing steps are annotated which are concerned with the representational structure and the evaluation of utterances with verbs of locomotion. At the beginning of this dialog there is a bird-eye view of the street crossing (cf. Fig. 11). The sequence under observation is represented by 72 snap shots covering a real-time interval of 14 seconds.

In the sample dialog covering fishery data, only the transformation of DEEP-expressions into PASCAL/R-queries and the results of the evaluations are annotated.

2 Hotel Reservation Situation

2.1 Sample Dialog With Commentaries

```
*(io-options)
Usual IO-Options? >n
Should processing phases be explicated? (Yes/No/Yes: All (=a)) >a
Should backtrace be possible? >n
With correction of typographic errors? >n
Script-driven-dialogue-phase? >j
Linelength ('J' = 72) : >j
*(040 4123 3315)
```

Simulated telephone call

```
HOTEL 'ZUM FETTEN OCHSEN', GOOD EVENING!
```

Hotel greeting.

```
? Hello, this is Karlchen Mueller from Fuchshausen speaking.
WHAT CAN I DO FOR YOU?
```

```
? I'd like a double room for two days.
YES, OF COURSE, JUST LET ME SEE.
YOU WOULD LIKE A DOUBLE ROOM UNTIL APRIL 25TH IS THAT RIGHT?
? Yes, exactly.
YES, WE STILL HAVE SOME VACANCIES. DO YOU HAVE ANY PARTICULAR REQUIREMENTS?
```

End of the stereotyped script-controlled introductory dialog. Initiative passes to the user.

```
? Wieviele von den Sitzgelegenheiten sind bequem?
  [How many seating-accomodations are comfortable?]

** LEXICAL ANALYSIS:

;; Syntagma replacement:

        (WIEVIELE VON DEN SITZGELEGENHEITEN SIND BEQUEM?)

;; Inflectional analysis:

((WIEVIEL ((WORTART IPRN) (FLEXION)))
 (VON ((WORTART PRP) (FLEXION (DAT))))
 (D- ((WORTART DET)
     (FLEXION ((MAS (SG (AKK)) (PL (DAT)))
               (FEM (PL (DAT)))
               (NTR (PL (DAT)))))))
 (SITZGELEGENHEIT
  ((WORTART NOM) (GENUS FEM) (FLEXION ((PL (NOM GEN DAT AKK))))))
 (SEIN ((WORTART AUX) (FLEXION ((PRES (PL (1 3)))))))
 (BEQUEM ((WORTART ADJ) (FLEXION ((POS)))))
 (? ((WORTART SATZZ))))

;; Preterminal string:

((WIEVIEL IPRN FLEXION:)
 (VON PRP FLEXION: (DAT))
 (D- DET
  FLEXION:
  ((MAS (SG (AKK)) (PL (DAT))) (FEM (PL (DAT))) (NTR (PL (DAT))) ))
 (SITZGELEGENHEIT NOM GENUS: FEM FLEXION: ((PL (NOM GEN DAT AKK))))
 (SEIN AUX FLEXION: ((PRES (PL (1 3)))))
 (BEQUEM ADJ FLEXION: ((POS)))
 (? SATZZ))

** SYNTACTIC ANALYSIS:

;; Analysis of a Noun Phrase:

(t-s: (q-w: WIEVIEL)
 (lambda: x14
  (af-s: EL
   x14
   (s-t: (t-s: (q-d: D- (r: 1 1))
          (lambda: x13 (af-a: ISA x13 SITZGELEGENHEIT)))))))
```

```
;; Analysis of predicative adjectives:

(lambda: x17 (af-a: REF x17 BEQUEM))

;; SURF structure:

(af-d: IS
 (t-s: (q-w: WIEVIEL)
  (lambda: x14
   (af-s: EL
    x14
    (s-t: (t-s: (q-d: D- (r: 1 1))
           (lambda: x13 (af-a: ISA x13 SITZGELEGENHEIT)))))))
 (lambda: x17 (af-a: REF x17 BEQUEM)))

** NORMALIZATION:

;; DEEP structure:

(f-d: (t-q: (for: (q-w: WIEVIEL) x18)
       (af-s: EL
        x18
        (s-t: (t-q: (for: (q-d: D- (r: 1 1)) x19)
               (af-a: ISA x19 SITZGELEGENHEIT)))))
 (af-a: REF x18 BEQUEM))

** INTERPRETATION:

;; Evaluation of a formula with the quantifier:

         (q-w: WIEVIEL)

;; Result of the evaluation:

(f-d: (t-q: (for: (q-qt: (r: 1 1)) x18)
       (af-s: EL
        x18
        (s-t: t-q: (for: (q-d: D- (r: 4 4)) x18)
               (af-a: ISA x19 SITZGELEGENHEIT)))))
 (f-o: RELATIV (af-a: REF x18 BEQUEM)))

** INVERSE NORMALIZATION:

;; Answer as Surface structure:

(af-d: IS
 (t-s: (q-qt: (r: 1 1))
  (lambda: x18
   (af-s: EL
    x18
    (s-t: (t-s: (q-d: D- (r: 4 4))
           (lambda: x18 (af-a: ISA x19 SITZGELEGENHEIT)))))))
 (d-o: RELATIV (lambda: x18 (af-a: REF x18 BEQUEM))))

** VERBALIZATION:

;; Verbalized SURF Structure:
```

```
(SENTENCE (SUBJECT (NP (N: SG)
                       E-
                       (ATTRIBUTE (PP VON
                                      (NP D-
                                          (N: PL)
                                          VIER
                                          (ELLIPSIS SITZGELEGENHEIT)))))
          (PREDICATE (PA: SIT) (M: IND) (T: PRES) (AP RELATIV BEQUEM)))

** SURFACE TRANSFORMATIONS:
```

EINE VON DEN VIER IST RELATIV BEQUEM.
[ONE OF THE FOUR IS RELATIVELY COMFORTABLE.]

46.5 Sek.

'How-many' questions with predicate. The use of a global concept requires a search procedure in the semantic network seeking out the global concept and the names of reference objects subsumed under it. Cooperative answer with a precise quantifier, which additionally specifies how many objects of the type "seating accommodation" are available [WAHL 83]; Modification of the quality is characteristic of 'easy-chair' only to a certain degree. Ellipsis of the noun used in the input.

? Der Sessel?
[The easy-chair?]

```
** LEXICAL ANALYSIS:

;; Syntagma replacement:

        (DER SESSEL?)

;; Inflectional analysis:

((D- ((WORTART DET)
      (FLEXION ((MAS (SG (NOM)) (PL (GEN)))
                (FEM (SG (GEN DAT)) (PL (GEN)))
                (NTR PL (GEN))))))
 (SESSEL ((WORTART NOM) (GENUS MAS) (FLEXION ((SG (NOM DAT AKK))))))
 (? ((WORTART SATZZ))))

;; Preterminal string:

((D- DET
 FLEXION:
 ((MAS (SG (NOM)) (PL (GEN)))
  (FEM (SG (GEN DAT)) (PL (GEN)))
  (NTR (PL (GEN)))))
(SESSEL NOM GENUS: MAS FLEXION: ((SG (NOM DAT AKK))))
(? SATZZ))
```

```
** SYNTACTIC ANALYSIS:

** ELLIPSIS RECOGNITION:

;;  This utterance is elliptical and corresponds to the TERM:

(t-s: (q-d: D- (r: 1 1)) (lambda: x22 (af-a: ISA x22 SESSEL)))

;;  It is compared with the previous utterance in the dialog:

(af-d: IS
 (t-s: (q-w: WIEVIEL)
  (lambda: x0
   (af-s: EL
    x0
    (s-t: (t-s: (q-d: D- (r: 1 1))
           (lambda: x0 (af-a: ISA x0 SITZGELEGENHEIT)))))))
  (lambda: x0 (af-a: REF x0 BEQUEM)))

;;  Corresponding part of previous utterance in the dialog:

(t-s: (q-w: WIEVIEL)
 (lambda: x0
  (af-s: EL
   x0
   (s-t: (t-s: (q-d: D- (r: 1 1))
          (lambda: x0 (af-a: ISA x0 SITZGELEGENHEIT)))))))

;;  SURF Structure:

(af-d: IS
 (t-s: (q-d: D- (r: 1 1)) (lambda: x22 (af-a: ISA x22 SESSEL)))
 (lambda: x0 (af-a: REF x0 BEQUEM)))

** NORMALIZATION:

;; DEEP Structure:

(f-d: (t-q: (for: (q-d: D- (r: 1 1)) x23) (af-a: ISA x23 SESSEL))
 (af-a: REF x23 BEQUEM))

** INTERPRETATION:

;;  Evaluation of a formula with the quantifier:

        (q-d: D- (r: 1 1))

;;  Result of the evaluation:

(f-d: (t-q: (for: (q-d: D- (r: 1 1)) x23) (af-a: ISA x23 SESSEL))
 (f-o: RELATIV (af-a: REF x23 BEQUEM)))

;;  The Z-value of the answer is: 1

** INVERSE NORMALIZATION:

;;  Answer as SURF Structure:

(af-d: IS
 (t-s: (q-d: D- (r: 1 1)) (lambda: x23 (af-a: ISA x23 SESSEL)))
 (d-o: RELATIV (lambda: x23 (af-a: REF x23 BEQUEM))))
```

```
**  ELLIPTIFICATION:

;;  SURF structure of the shortened answer:

(d-o: RELATIV (lambda: x0 (af-a: REF x0 BEQUEM)))

**  VERBALIZATION:

;;  Verbalized SURF Structure:

(SENTENCE (PREDICATE (AP RELATIV BEQUEM)))

**  SURFACE TRANSFORMATIONS:
```

JA, RELATIV BEQUEM.
[YES, RELATIVELY COMFORTABLE.]

16.0 Sek.

An incomplete question requires reconstruction of an ellipsis in the predicate [JAME 81]. Elliptification of the subject and the verb in the answer.

? Wo steht denn dieser Sessel?
[Where is this easy-chair?]

```
**  LEXICAL ANALYSIS:

;;  Syntagma replacement:

         (WO STEHT DIESER SESSEL?)

;;  Inflectional analysis:

((WO ((WORTART IPRP)))
 (STEH ((WORTART VRB) (FLEXION ((PRES ((SG (3)) (PL (2)))) (IMP PL)))))
 (DIES ((WORTART DET)
        (FLEXION ((MAS (SG (NOM)) (PL (GEN)))
                  (FEM (SG (GEN DAT)) (PL (GEN)))
                  (NTR (PL (GEN)))))))
 (SESSEL ((WORTART NOM) (GENUS MAS) (FLEXION ((SG (NOM DAT AKK))))))
 (? ((WORTART SATZZ))))

;;  Preterminal string:

((WO IPRP FLEXION:)
 (STEH VRB FLEXION: ((PRES ((SG (3)) (PL (2)))) (IMP PL)) KASUSRAHMEN:)
 (DIES DET
  FLEXION:
  ((MAS (SG (NOM)) (PL (GEN)))
   (FEM (SG (GEN DAT)) (PL (GEN)))
   (NTR (PL (GEN)))))
 (SESSEL NOM GENUS: MAS FLEXION: ((SG (NOM DAT AKK))))
 (? SATZZ))
```

```
** SYNTACTIC ANALYSIS:

;; Analysis of a PP:

(lambda: x45
 (af-a: RAEUMLICH
  IN/ DER/ NAEHE
  x45
  t-s: (q-w: WELCH) (lambda: x46 (af-a: ISA x46 DING)))))

;; Analysis of a Noun Phrase:

(t-s: (q-d: DIES (r: 1 1)) lambda: x49 (af-a: ISA x49 SESSEL)))

;; SURF structure:

(af-d: IS
 (t-s: (q-d: DIES (r: 1 1)) (lambda: x49 (af-a: ISA x49 SESSEL)))
 lambda: x45
  (af-a: RAEUMLICH
   IN/ DER/ NAEHE
   x45
   (t-s: (q-w: WELCH) (lambda: x46 (af-a: ISA x46 DING))))))

** NORMALIZATION:

;; Extraction of a quantifier from an ATOMIC FORMULA:

         (af-a: RAEUMLICH
          IN/ DER/ NAEHE
          x45
          (t-q: (for: (q-w: WELCH) x51) (af-a: ISA x51 DING)))
                                   |
                                   |
                                   v
         (f-d: (t-q: (for: (q-w: WELCH) x51) (af-a: ISA x51 DING))
          (af-a: RAEUMLICH IN/ DER/ NAEHE x45 x51))

;; DEEP structure:

(f-d: (t-q: (for: (q-d: DIES (r: 1 1)) x50) (af-a: ISA x50 SESSEL) )
 (f-d: (t-q: (for: (q-w: WELCH) x51) (af-a: ISA x51 DING))
  (af-a: RAEUMLICH IN/ DER/ NAEHE x50 x51)))

** INTERPRETATION:

;; Evaluation of a formula with the quantifier:

         (q-d: DIES (r: 1 1))

** VISUAL SEARCH:

;; Rating of 0.60 for

         (LINKS/ NEBEN TISCH1)
```

```
;;  Rating of 0.61 for:

        (VOR FENSTER1)

;;  Rating of 0.30 for:

        (RECHTS/ NEBEN BILD1)

;;  Rating of 0.46 for:

        (LINKS/ NEBEN STUHL1)

;;  Result of the evaluation

(f-d: (t-q: (for: (q-d: D- (r: 1 1)) x50) (af-a: ISA x50 SESSEL))
 (af-a: RAEUMLICH VOR x50 FENSTER1))

**  INVERSE NORMALIZATION:

;;  Answer as SURF structure:

(af-d: IS
 (t-s: (q-d: D- (r: 1 1)) (lambda: x50 (af-a: ISA x50 SESSEL)))
 (lambda: x50 (af-a: RAEUMLICH VOR x50 FENSTER 1)))

**  ELLIPSIS GENERATION:

**  VERBALIZATION:

**  NP-GENERATION FOR FENSTER1

;;  The generated NP for FENSTER1 is

        (t-q: (for: (q-d: D-) x52) (af-a: ISA x52 FENSTER))

;;  Verbalized SURF structure:

(SENTENCE (SUBJECT (NP (N: SG) D- SESSEL))
          (PREDICATE (PA: SIT)
                     (M: IND)
                     (T: PRES)
                     (PP VOR (NP (N: SG) D- FENSTER))))

**  SURFACE TRANSFORMATIONS:
```

DER SESSEL IST VOR DEM FENSTER.
[THE EASY-CHAIR IS IN FRONT OF THE WINDOW.]

35.1 Sek.

'Where'-question; visual search for sufficiently prominent objects, which permit a clear description of the location of 'easy-chair'. Generation of a definite description for 'window' guided by the knowledge presupposed for the dialog partner (A priori User Model).

? Und neben was?
[And next to what?]

```
**  LEXICAL ANALYSIS:
```

```
;;  Syntagma replacement:

         (NEBEN WAS /?)

;;  Inflectional analysis:

((NEBEN ((WORTART PRP) (FLEXION (DAT AKK))))
 (WAS ((WORTART IPRN)))
 (/? ((WORTART SATZZ))))

;;  Preterminal string:

((NEBEN PRP FLEXION: (DAT AKK)) (WAS IPRN FLEXION:) (/? SATZZ))

**  SYNTACTIC ANALYSIS:

**  ELLIPSIS RECOGNITION:

;;  This utterance is elliptical and corresponds to a DESCRIPTION:

(lambda: x57
 (af-a: RAEUMLICH
  NEBEN
  x57
  (t-s: q-w: WELCH) lambda: x56 (af-a: ISA x56 DING)))))

;;  It is compared with the previous utterance in the dialog:

(af-d: IS
 (t-s: (q-d: DIES (r: 1 1)) (lambda: x0 (af-a: ISA x0 SESSEL)))
 (lambda: x0
  (af-a: RAEUMLICH
   IN/ DER/ NAEHE
   x0
   (t-s: (q-w: WELCH) (lambda: x0 (af-a: ISA x0 DING))))))

;;  Corresponding part of previous utterance in the dialog:
(lambda: x0

 (af-a: RAEUMLICH
  IN/ DER/ NAEHE
  x0
  (t-s: (q-w: WELCH) (lambda: x0 (af-a: ISA x0 DING)))))

;;  SURF structure:

(af-d: IS
 (t-s: (q-d: DIES (r: 1 1)) (lambda: x0 (af-a: ISA x0 SESSEL)))
 (lambda: x57
  (af-a: RAEUMLICH
   NEBEN
   x57
   (t-s: (q-w: WELCH) (lambda: x56 (af-a: ISA x56 DING))))))

**  NORMALIZATION:
```

```
;;  Extraction of a quantifier from an ATOMIC FORMULA

        (af-a: RAEUMLICH
         NEBEN
         x57
         (t-q: (for: (q-w: WELCH) x59) (af-a: ISA x59 DING)))
                                   |
                                   |
                                   v
        (f-d: (t-q: (for: (q-w: WELCH) x59) (af-a: ISA x59 DING))
         (af-a: RAEUMLICH NEBEN x57 x59))

;; DEEP structure:

(f-d: (t-q: (for: (q-d: DIES (r: 1 1)) x58) (af-a: ISA x58 SESSEL))
 (f-d: (t-q: (for: (q-w: WELCH) x59) (af-a: ISA x59 DING))
  (af-a: RAEUMLICH NEBEN x58 x59)))

**  INTERPRETATION:

;;  Evaluation of a formula with the quantifier:

        (q-d: DIES (r: 1 1))

**  VISUAL SEARCH:

;;  Rating of 0.60 for:

        (TISCH1)

;;  Rating of 0.30 for:

        (BILD1)

;;  Rating of 0.45 for:

        (STUHL1)

;;  Rating of 0.15 for:

        (TISCH2)

;;  Result of the evaluation:

(f-d: (t-q: (for: (q-d: D- (r: 1 1)) x58) (af-a: ISA x58 SESSEL))
 (af-a: RAEUMLICH NEBEN x58 TISCH1))

**  INVERSE NORMALIZATION:

;;  Answer as SURF structure:

(af-d: IS
 (t-s: (q-d: D- (r: 1 1)) (lambda: x58 (af-a: ISA x58 SESSEL)))
 (lambda: x58 (af-a: RAEUMLICH NEBEN x58 TISCH1)))

**  VERBALIZATION:

**  NP-GENERATION FOR TISCH1:

;;  The generated NP for TISCH1 is:

        (t-q: (for: (q-qt: E-) x60) (f-o: AND (af-a: ISA x60
        COUCHTISCH) (af-a: REF x60 NIEDRIG)))
```

```
;;  Verbalized SURF structure:

(SENTENCE (SUBJECT (NP (N: SG) D- SESSEL))
          (PREDICATE (PA: SIT)
                     (M: IND)
                     (T: PRES)
                     (PP NEBEN (NP (N: SG) E- NIEDRIG COUCHTISCH))))

**  Surface transformation:
```

DER SESSEL IST NEBEN EINEM NIEDRIGEN COUCHTISCH.
[THE EASY-CHAIR IS NEXT TO A LOW COFFEE TABLE.]

34.2 Sek.

An incomplete question about spatial relations; visual search for objects in the spatial relation 'next to' to 'easy-chair'. Indefinite coding for 'TISCH 1' [TABLE 1] since it cannot be presumed to be known to the user either a priori or on the basis of the dialog up to this point.

3 HAM-ANS as an Interface to a Scene Analysis System

3.1 Sample Dialog Without Commentaries

*(ham-ans 5)
HALLO!
[HELLO!]

? Wieviele Lastkraftwagen sind vorhanden?
[How many trucks have you seen?]
ZWEI.
[TWO]

? Welche Lastkraftwagen sind denn gefahren?
[Which trucks have gone by?]

EIN HELLER AUF DER HARTUNGSTRASSE.
[A LIGHT-COLORE-ONE ON HARTUNGSTRASSE.]

? Sind ein gelber Personenwagen und ein gruener Kombi vorher abgebogen?
[Did a yellow car and a green stationwagen turn off earlier?]

NEIN, EIN GELBER VON DER HARTUNGSTRASSE IN DIE SCHLUETER-STRASSE, ABER DER GRUENE KOMBI IST VORHER NICHT ABGEBOGEN.
[NO, A YELLOW CAR TURNED OFF HARTUNGSTREET ONTO SCHLUETER-STREET, BUT THE GREEN STATIONWAGON DID NOT TURN OFF FIRST.]

? Sind waehrenddessen ein junger Mann und eine alte Frau auf der Schlueterstrasse gegangen?
[Were a young man and an old woman walking down Schlueterstreet during this time?]

JA, EINE ALTE FRAU UND EIN JUNGER MANN.
[YES, AN OLD WOMAN AND A YOUNG MAN.]

? Hat der gruene Kombi auf der Schlueterstrasse angehalten?
[Did the green station wagon stop on Schlueterstreet?]

JA.
[YES.]

? Wieviele Kombis haben ueberhaupt angehalten?
[How many station wagons altogether have stopped?]

EINER VON DEN DREI AUF DER SCHLUETERSTRASSE.
[ONE OF THE THREE ON SCHLUETERSTREET.]

? Was habe ich sie gerade gefragt?
[What did I just ask you?]

SIE FRAGTEN: WIEVIEL KOMBIS HABEN ANGEHALTEN.
[YOU ASKED: HOW MANY STATION WAGONS HAVE STOPPED.]

? Ist denn ein Kombi losgefahren?
[Did a station wagon drive off?]

JA, EINER AUF DER SCHLUETERSTRASSE.
[YES, ONE ON SCHLUETERSTREET.]

? Uebrigens der helle Lastkraftwagen: Ist er auch auf der Schlueterstrasse gefahren?
[By the way, the light-colored truck: did it drive down Schlueterstreet too?]

JA.
[YES.]

? Wieviele Personenwagen gibt es denn ueberhaupt?
[How many cars are there in all?]

SECHZEHN.
[SIXTEEN.]

? Ist einer von diesen Personenwagen blau?
[Is one of these cars blue?]

JA, ZWEI VON DIESEN SIND ZIEMLICH BLAU.
[YES, TWO OF THEM ARE KIND OF BLUE.]

? Ist denn ein blauer Personenwagen auf beiden Strassen gefahren?
[Did a blue car drive down both streets?]

JA, EIN BLAUER PERSONENWAGEN.
[YES, ONE BLUE CAR.]

? Tschuess
[So long!]

ENDE
[End]

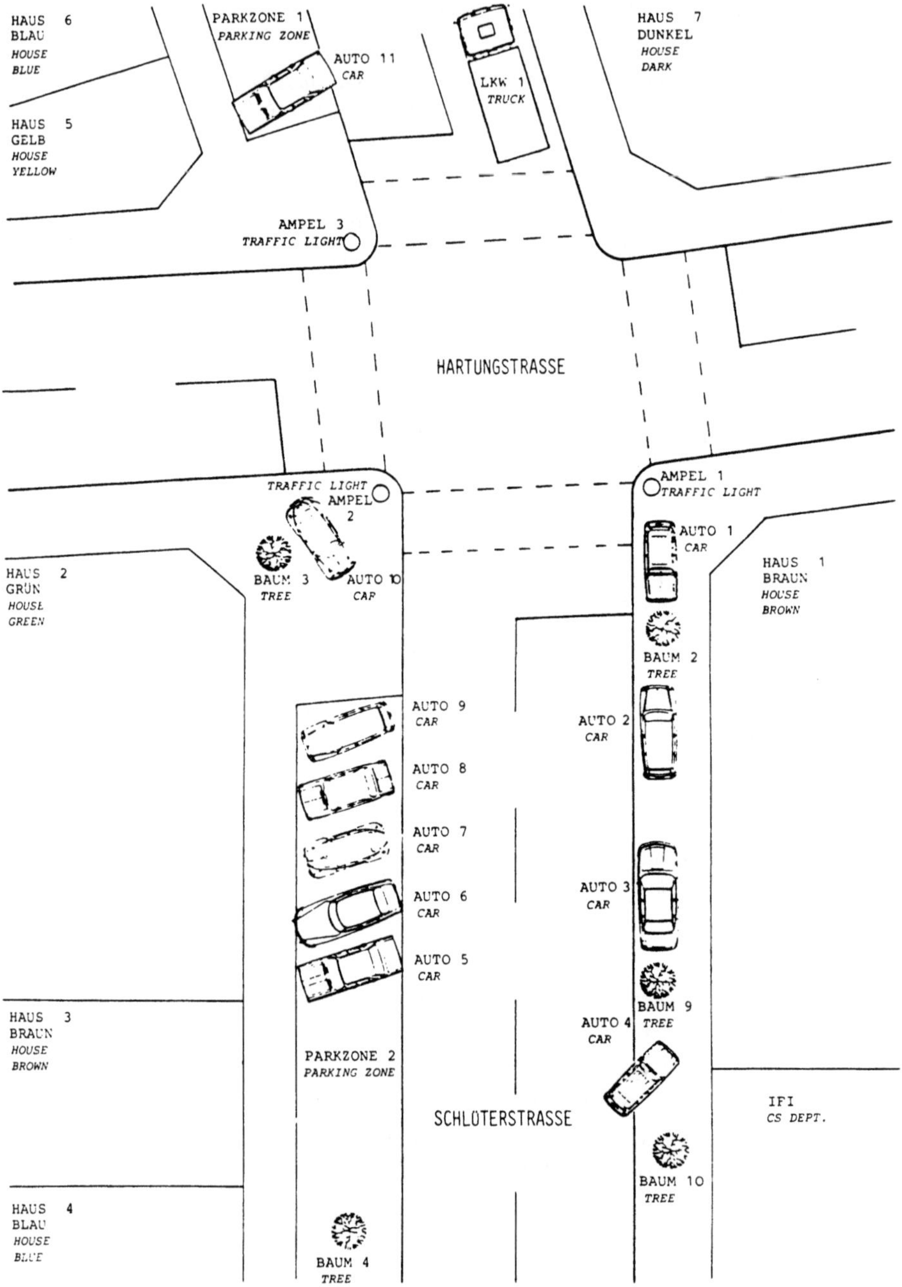

Fig. 11. Bird's-eye view of the street-crossing's static background

3.2 Sample Dialog With Commentaries

```
*(ham-ans 5)
```

HALLO!
[HELLO!]

? Wieviele Lastkraftwagen sind vorhanden?
[How many trucks have you seen?]

ZWEI.
[TWO.]

195.8 Sek.

How-many query. Related to whole scene.

? Welche Lastkraftwagen sind denn gefahren?
[Which trucks have gone by?]

```
** LEXICAL ANALYSIS:

;; Syntagma replacement:

        (WELCHE LASTKRAFTWAGEN SIND GEFAHREN /?)

;; Inflectional analysis:

((WELCH ((WORTART IPRN) (FLEXION)))
 (LASTKRAFTWAGEN
  ((WORTART NOM) (GENUS MAS) (FLEXION ((SG (NOM DAT AKK))))))
 (SEIN ((WORTART AUX) (FLEXION ((PRES (PL (1 3)))))))
 (FAHR ((WORTART VRB) (FLEXION ((PERF (SG (1 2 3)) (PL (1 2 3)))))))
 (/? ((WORTART SATZZ))))

;; Preterminal string:

((WELCH IPRN FLEXION:)
 (LASTKRAFTWAGEN NOM GENUS: MAS FLEXION: ((SG (NOM DAT AKK))))
 (SEIN AUX FLEXION: ((PRES (PL (1 3)))))
 (FAHR VRB
       FLEXION:
       ((PERF (SG (1 2 3)) (PL (1 2 3))))
       KASUSRAHMEN:
       AGENT-LOCATIVE-SOURCE-GOAL-1)
 (/? SATZZ))

** SYNTACTIC ANALYSIS:

;; Case frame:

(r1-s: agent:
 (d-1: role-marker:
  0
  restrictions:
  (lambda: x1 (af-a: ISA x1 FAHRZEUG)))
```

```
 objective:
 source:
 (d-l: role-marker:
  F
  restrictions:
  (lambda: x1 (af-a: ISA x1 VERKEHRSWEG)))
 locative:
 (d-1: role-marker:
  F
  restrictions:
  (lambda: x1 (af-a: ISA x1 VERKEHRSWEG)))
 goal:
 (d-1: role-marker:
  F
  restrictions:
  (lambda: x1 (af-a: ISA x1 VERKEHRSWEG)))
 time:
 path:
 instrument:)

;;  NPs:

        (S-AGENT)

;;  PPs:

        (S-SOURCE S-LOCATIVE S-GOAL)

;;  AGENT parsed:

(lambda: x9
 (af-a: AGENT
  x9
  (t-s: (q-w: WELCH) (lambda: x8 (af-a: ISA x8 LASTKRAFTWAGEN)))))

;;  SURF representation of input sentence:

(af-d: EVENT
 (t-s: (q-qt: E-ACT) (lambda: x10 (af-a: ACT x10 FAHR)))
 (d-e: role-list:
  (r1-s: agent:
   (lambda: x9
    (af-a: AGENT
     x9
     (t-s: (q-w: WELCH) (lambda: x8 (af-a: ISA x8 LASTKRAFTWAGEN)))))
   objective:
   source:
   locative:
   goal:
   time:
   path:
   instrument:)
```

```
  mod:
  (d-m: tense:
   (lambda: x11 (af-a: TENSE x11 PERF))
   voice:
   (lambda: x12 (af-a: VOICE x12 ACTIVE)))))

**  NORMALIZATION:

;;  Extraction of a quantifier from an ATOMIC FORMULA

        (af-a: AGENT
         x9
         (t-q: (for: (q-w: WELCH) x14) (af-a: ISA x14 LASTKRAFTWAGEN)))
                                    |
                                    |
                                    v
        (f-d: (t-q: (for: (q-w: WELCH) x14)
               (af-a: ISA x14 LASTKRAFTWAGEN))
         (af-a: AGENT x9 x14))

;; DEEP structure:

(f-d: (t-q: (for: (q-w: WELCH) x14) (af-a: ISA x14 LASTKRAFTWAGEN))
 (f-d: (t-q: (for: (q-qt: E-ACT) x13) (af-a: ACT x13 FAHR))
  f-e: role-list:
   (rl-d: agent:
    (af-a: AGENT x13 x14)
    objective:
    source:
    locative:
    goal:
    time:
    path:
    instrument:)
   mod:
   (f-m: tense: (af-a: TENSE x13 PERF) voice: (af-a: VOICE x13 ACTIVE)))
  ))

**  INTERPRETATION:

;;  Evaluation of a formula with the quantifier

        (q-w: WELCH)

;;  Evaluation of a formula with the quantifier

        (q-qt: E-ACT)

;;  Object LASTKRAFTWAGEN1 has not moved during the entire scene.

;;  Evaluation of a formula with the quantifier

        (q-qt: E-ACT)
```

```
;; Testing of a partially instantiated case frame:

(f-e: role-list:
 (r1-d: agent:
  (af-a: AGENT FAHR LASTKRAFTWAGEN2)
  objective:
  source:
  locative:
  goal:
  time:
  path:
  instrument:)
 mod:
 (f-m: tense: (af-a: TENSE FAHR PERF) voice: (af-a: VOICE FAHR ACTIVE)))

;; Interval of consideration determined by verb tense and adverb:

          (1. 64)

;; The object becomes visible between time points 56 and 65

;; The interval of consideration modified in accordance with ob-
   ject time is:

          (56 64)

;; Change determined between time points 56 and 57

;; Completed case frame:

(f-e: role-list:
 (r1-d: agent:
  (af-a: AGENT FAHR LASTKRAFTWAGEN2)
  objective:
  source:
  locative:
  (af-a: LOCATIVE FAHR AUF HARTUNGSTRASSE)
  goal:
  time:
  path:
  instrument:)
 mod:
 (f-m: tense: (af-a: TENSE FAHR PERF) voice: (af-a: VOICE FAHR ACTIVE)))

;; Verification of event possible

;; Result of the evaluation:

(f-d: (t-q: (for: (q-s: (LASTKRAFTWAGEN2)) x14) T)
 (f-d: (t-q: (for: (q-qt: E-ACT) x13) (af-a: ACT x13 FAHR))
  (f-e: role-list:
   (r1-d: agent:
    (af-a: AGENT x13 x14)
    objective:
    source:
```

```
    locative:
    (af-a: LOCATIVE x13 AUF HARTUNGSTRASSE)
    goal:
    time:
    path:
    instrument:)
   mod:
   (f-m: tense: (af-a: TENSE x13 PERF) voice: (af-a: VOICE x13 ACTIVE)))
  ))
```

```
** INVERSE NORMALIZATION:

;; Answer as SURF structure:

(af-d: EVENT
 (t-s: (q-qt: E-ACT) (lambda: x13 (af-a: ACT x13 FAHR)))
 (d-e: role-list:
  (r1-s: agent:
   (lambda: x13 (af-a: AGENT x13 (t-s: (q-s: (LASTKRAFTWAGEN2)) T)))
   objective:
   source:
   locative:
   (lambda: x13 (af-a: LOCATIVE x13 AUF HARTUNGSTRASSE))
   goal:
   time:
   path:
   instrument:)
  mod:
  (d-m: tense:
   (lambda: x13 (af-a: TENSE x13 PERF))
   voice:
   (lambda: x13 (af-a: VOICE x13 ACTIVE)))))

** ELLIPSIS GENERATION:

;; SURF structure of the shortened answer:

(r1-s: agent:
 (lambda: x0 (af-a: AGENT x0 (t-s: (q-s: (LASTKRAFTWAGEN2)) T)))
 objective:
 source:
 locative:
 (lambda: x0 (af-a: LOCATIVE x0 AUF HARTUNGSTRASSE))
 goal:
 time:
 path:
 instrument:)

** VERBALIZATION:

** NP-GENERATION FOR LASTKRAFTWAGEN2

;; The generated NP for LASTKRAFTWAGEN2
        (t-q: (for: (q-qt: E-) x15) (f-o: AND (af-a: ISA x15
        LASTKRAFTWAGEN) (af-a: REF x15 HELL)))
```

```
;;  Verbalized structure of answer:

(SENTENCE (AGENT (NP (NP (N: SG) E- HELL (ELLIPSIS LASTKRAFTWAGEN))))
          (LOCATIVE (PP AUG (NP (N: SG) D- HARTUNGSTRASSE))))

**  SURFACE TRANSFORMATIONS:
```

EIN HELLER AUF DER HARTUNGSTRASSE.
[A LIGHT-COLOURED ON HARTUNGSTRASSE]

136.4 Sek.

'Which'-question about objects of the class 'truck', which have executed the movement 'drive'. Processing of sentences with verbs requires, i.a., assignment of constituents to deep-case roles [HOEP 82] and recognition of verb tense. In order to temporally limit the search in the geometrical scene description, an interval of consideration is established in accordance with verb tense and object-existence time. Procedural verb semantics implement the visual search and make possible a cooperative answer with additional specification of the area in which the movement occurred. Ellipsis of the verb and the nouns used in the question produces a short but comprehensible answer. 'Hartungstrasse' is marked definite since stationary objects are presumed 'known' in the A priori Partner Model. Initial characterization 'light' for the reference object LASTKRAFTWAGEN2 (TRUCK2) and indefinite marking since this object cannot be presumed as known to the user. The times at which the events checked took place are entered into a dialog memory.

? Sind ein gelber Personenwagen und ein gruener Kombi vorher abgebogen?
[Did a yellow car and a green station wagon turn off earlier?]

```
;; DEEP structure:

(f-d: (t-o: AND
       (t-q: (for: (q-qt: E-) x31)
        (f-o: AND (af-a: ISA x31 PERSONENWAGEN) (af-a: REF x31 GELB)))
       (t-q: (for: (q-qt: E-) x31)
        (f-o: AND (af-a: ISA x31 KOMBI) (af-a: REF x31 GRUEN))))
 (f-d: (t-q: (for: (q-qt: E-ACT) x26) (af-a: ACT x26 ABBIEG))
  (f-e: role-list:
   (rl-d: agent:
    (af-a: AGENT x26 x31)
    objective:
    source:
    locative:
    goal:
    time:
    (af-a: TIME x26 VORHER T)
    path:
    instrument:)
   mod:
   (f-m: tense: (af-a: TENSE x26 PERF) voice: (af-a: VOICE x26 ACTIVE)))
  ))
```

```
**  INTERPRETATION:
;;  Evaluation of a formula with the quantifier
         (q-qt: E-)
;;  Evaluation of a formula with the quantifier
         (q-qt: E-ACT)
;;  Testing of a partially instantiated case frame
(f-e: role-list:
 (rl-d: agent:
  (af-a: AGENT ABBIEG AUTO20)
  objective:
  source:
  locative:
  goal:
  time:
  (af-a: TIME ABBIEG VORHER T)
  path:
  instrument:)
 mod:
 (f-m: tense:
  (af-a: TENSE ABBIEG PERF)
  voice:
  (af-a: VOICE ABBIEG ACTIVE)))
;;  Interval of consideration determined by verb tense and adverb
         (1. 57)
;;  The object was visible between time 1 and 60
;;  The interval of consideration modified by object time is:
         (1 57)
;;  Change established between time 22 and 23
;;  XY-Change of direction established.
;;  Completed case frame:
(f-e: role-list:
 (rl-d: agent:
  (af-a: AGENT ABBIEG AUTO20)
  objective:
  source:
  (af-a: SOURCE ABBIEG VON HARTUNGSTRASSE)
  locative:
  goal:
  (af-a: GOAL ABBIEG IN SCHLUETERSTRASSE)
  time:
  (af-a: TIME ABBIEG VORHER T)
  path:
  instrument:)
```

```
 mod:
 (f-m: tense:
  (af-a: TENSE ABBIEG PERF)
  voice:
  (af-a: VOICE ABBIEG ACTIVE)))

;;  Verification of event possible

;;  Evaluation of a formula with the quantifier

         (q-qt: E-)

;;  Evaluation of a formula with the quantifier

         (q-qt: E-ACT)

;;  Testing of a partially instantiated case frame

(f-e: role-list:
 (rl-d: agent:
  (af-a: AGENT ABBIEG KOMBI 2)
  objective:
  source:
  locative:
  goal:
  time:
  (af-a: TIME ABBIEG VORHER T)
  path:
  instrument:)
 mod:
 (f-m: tense:
  (af-a: TENSE ABBIEG PERF)
  voice:
  (af-a: VOICE ABBIEG ACTIVE)))

;;  Interval of consideration determined by verb tense and adverb

         (1 . 57)

;;  The object was visible between time 20 and 65

;;  The interval of consideration modified by object time is:

         (20 57)

;;  Change established between time 20 and 21

;;  End of period of observation reached before motion or case agree-
ment could be established.

;;  Verification of event impossible

;;  Result of the evaluation
```

```
(f-o: BUT
 (f-d: (t-q: (for: (q-qt: (r: 1 1)) x31)
       (f-o: AND (af-a: ISA x31 PERSONENWAGEN) (af-a: REF x31 GELB)))
  (f-d: (t-q: (for: (q-qt: E-ACT) x26) (af-a: ACT x26 ABBIEG))
   (f-e: role-list:
    (rl-d: agent:
     (af-a: AGENT x26 x31)
     objective:
     source:
     (af-a: SOURCE x26 VON HARTUNGSTRASSE)
     locative:
     goal:
     (af-a: GOAL x26 IN SCHLUETERSTRASSE)
     time:
     (af-a: TIME x26 VORHER T)
     path:
     instrument:)
    mod:
    (f-m: tense: (af-a: TENSE x26 PERF) voice: (af-a: VOICE x26 ACTIVE))
    )))
  (f-o: NOT
   (f-d: (t-q: (for: (q-d: D- (r: 1 1)) x31)
         (f-o: AND (af-a: ISA x31 KOMBI) (af-a: REF x31 GRUEN)))
    (f-d: (t-q: (for: (q-qt: E-ACT) x26) (af-a: ACT x26 ABBIEG))
     (f-e: role-list:
      (rl-d: agent:
       (af-a: AGENT x26 x31)
       objective:
       source:
       locative:
       goal:
       time:
       (af-a: TIME x26 VORHER T)
       path:
       instrument:)
      mod:
      (f-m: tense:
       (af-a: TENSE x26 PERF)
       voice:
       (af-a: VOICE x26 ACTIVE)))))))

;;  The Z-value of the answer is: 0

**  INVERSE NORMALIZATION:

;;  Answer as SURF Structure:

(f-o: BUT
 (af-d: EVENT
  (t-s: (q-qt: E-ACT) (lambda: x26 (af-a: ACT x26 ABBIEG)))
  (d-e: role-list:
```

```
  (rl-s: agent:
   (lambda: x26
    (af-a: AGENT
     x26
     (t-s: (q-qt: (r: 1 1))
      (d-o: AND
       (lambda: x31 (af-a: ISA x31 PERSONENWAGEN))
       (lambda: x31 (af-a: REF x31 GELB))))))
   objective:
   source:
   (lambda: x26 (af-a: SOURCE x26 VON HARTUNGSTRASSE))
   locative:
   goal:
   (lambda: x26 (af-a: GOAL x26 IN SCHLUETERSTRASSE))
   time:
   (lambda: x26 (af-a: TIME x26 VORHER T))
   path:
   instrument:)
  mod:
  (d-m: tense:
   (lambda: x26 (af-a: TENSE x26 PERF))
   voice:
   (lambda: x26 (af-a: VOICE x26 ACTIVE)))))
(f-o: NOT
 (af-d: EVENT
  (t-s: (q-qt: E-ACT) (lambda: x26 (af-a: ACT x26 ABBIEG)))
  (d-e: role-list:
   (rl-s: agent:
    (lambda: x26
     (af-a: AGENT
      x26
      (t-s: (q-d: D- (r: 1 1))
       (d-o: AND
        (lambda: x31 (af-a: ISA x31 KOMBI))
        (lambda: x31 (af-a: REF x31 GRUEN))))))
    objective:
    source:
    locative:
    goal:
    time:
    (lambda: x26 (af-a: TIME x26 VORHER T))
    path:
    instrument:)
   mod:
   (d-m: tense:
    (lambda: x26 (af-a: TENSE x26 PERF))
    voice:
    (lambda: x26 (af-a: VOICE x26 ACTIVE)))))))
```

```
**  ELLIPSIS GENERATION:

;;  SURF structure of the shortened answer:

(BUT (ROLE-LIST (r1-s: agent:
                 (lambda: x0
                  (af-a: AGENT
                   x0
                   (t-s: (q-qt: (r: 1 1))
                    (d-o: AND
                     (lambda: x0 (af-a: ISA x0 PERSONENWAGEN))
                     (lambda: x0 (af-a: REF x0 GELB))))))
                 objective:
                 source:
                 (lambda: x0 (af-a: SOURCE x0 VON HARTUNGSTRASSE))
                 locative:
                 goal:
                 (lambda: x0 (af-a: GOAL x0 IN SCHLUETERSTRASSE))
                 time:
                 path:
                 instrument:))
(FORMULA
 (f-o: NOT
  (af-d: EVENT
  (t-s: (q-qt: E-ACT) (lambda: x0 (af-a: ACT x0 ABBIEG)))
  (d-e: role-list:
   (r1-s: agent:
    (lambda: x0
     (af-a: AGENT
      x0
      (t-s: (q-d: D- (r: 1 1))
       (d-o: AND
        (lambda: x0 (af-a: ISA x0 KOMBI))
        (lambda: x0 (af-a: REF x0 GRUEN))))))
    objective:
    source:
    locative:
    goal:
    time:
    (lambda: x0 (af-a: TIME x0 VORHER T))
    path:
    instrument:)
   mod:
   (d-m: tense:
    (lambda: x0 (af-a: TENSE x0 PERF))
    voice:
    (lambda: x0 (af-a: VOICE x0 ACTIVE))))))))

**  VERBALIZATION:

;;  Verbalized SURF structure:
```

```
(SENTENCE (SENTENCE (AGENT (NP (N: SG) E- GELB (ELLIPSIS PERSONENWAGEN))
                     )
                    (SOURCE (PP VON (NP (N: SG) D- HARTUNGSTRASSE)))
                    (GOAL (PP (NP (N: SG) D- SCHLUETERSTRASSE))))
          ABER
          (SENTENCE (MAINVERB (T: PERF) (GV: ACTIVE) (M: IND) ABBIEG)
                    (AGENT (NP (N: SG) D- GRUEN KOMBI))
                    (MODIFIER (AP VORHER) NICHT)))
```

** SURFACE TRANSFORMATIONS:

NEIN, EIN GELBER VON DER HARTUNGSTRASSE IN DIE SCHLUETER-
STRASSE, ABER DER GRUENE KOMBI IST VORHER NICHT ABGEBOGEN.
[NO, A YELLOW-ONE FROM HARTUNGSTRASSE INTO SCHLUETER-
STRASSE, BUT THE GREEN STATION WAGON DID NOT TURN OFF EARLIER.]

108.0 Sek.

NPs conjoined with 'and'. The temporal adverb 'earlier' establishes a temporal connection between the events in question here and those in the previous question. The temporal dialog memory is consulted in order to establish a point of reference. The semantics of 'turn off' determines in addition SOURCE and GOAL of the motion. Explicit answers to both parts of the conjoined structure with two sentences. Since the motion cannot be established for one part of the conjoined structure, the two sentences are conjoined with 'but' and the answer is, in the main, negative as indicated by 'no'. Intrasentential ellipsis. Since only one green station wagon appears in the scene, and the user presupposes green station wagons, a definite determiner is chosen.

4 HAM-ANS as a Natural Language Data Base Interface

4.1 Sample Dialog Without Commentaries

* (ham-ans 7)

HALLO!
[HELLO!]

? Was verstehen Sie unter dem Begriff Fahrt?
[What is your definition of the term 'cruise'?]

Eine FAHRT ist ein EREIGNIS. Die FAHRT
ist beschreibbar durch die Eigenschaften SCHIFFSNAME, FAHRTNAME,
ZIEL-SPEZIES, BOX-LATTITUDE-NORD, BOX-LATTITUDE-SUED,
BOX-LONGITUDE-OST, BOX-LONGITUDE-WEST, ANFANGSDATUM, ENDDATUM,
ZIELHAFEN, ZWECK, KOMMENTAR und STARTHAFEN.
[A CRUISSE is an EVENT. The CRUISE is describable by the parameters
VESSEL-NAME, CRUISE-NAME, TARGET-SPECIES, BOX-LATTITUDE-NORTH,
BOX-LATTITUDE-SOUTH, BOX-LONGITUDE-EAST, BOX-LONGITUDE-WEST, DATE-CRUISE-

BEGIN, DATE-CRUISE-END, PORT-OF-DESTINATION, PURPOSE, COMMENT, PORT-OF-EMBARKATION.]

? Definieren Sie uns, was verstehen Sie unter Zweck?
[Define for us what you mean by 'purpose'.]

ZWECK ist eine Eigenschaft von FAHRT. Folgende ZWECKE sind bekannt: KOMMERZIELL und WISSENSCHAFTLICH.
[PURPOSE is an attribute of CRUISE. The following PURPOSES are recognized: COMMERCIAL and RESEARCH.]

? Wieviele Fahrten gibt es?
[How many cruises are there?]

DREI.
[THREE.]

? Wieviele Fahrten sind wissenschaftlich?
[How many are research cruises?]

ZWEI VON DEN DREI.
[TWO OF THE THREE.]

? Welche Fahrten denn?
[Which cruises?]

GROESSE DER ERGEBNISRELATION: 2
[MAGNITUDE OF THE PRODUCT RELATION: 2]

SOLL SIE AUF DEM TERMINAL AUSGEGEBEN WERDEN?> J
[SHOULD IT BE DISPLAYED ON THE TERMINAL? > y]

```
MARION-DUFRESNE                 MD25-FIBEX                    EUPHAUSIA
AND THYSANOESSA
                    -462500 -640436  -515500  -292900 810212 810224 CRO
ZET              CROZET                WISSENSCHA CHIEF SC.HUREAU JC MNH
N-TAAF PARIS
ODISSEY                            FIBEX                      EUPHAUSIA
SUPERBA-KRILL       -520000 -620000   30000    560000 810201 810320 SEV
ASTOPOLIS        SEVASTOPOLIS          WISSENSCHA
```

? Gibt es auch Proben?
[Are there samples too?]

JA, 46.
[YES, 46.]

? Sind zwei bis sechs Proben gezaehlt?
[Have between two and six samples been counted?]

NEIN, SIEBEN.
[NO, SEVEN.]

? Welche Proben denn?
[Which samples?]

GROESSE DER ERGEBNISRELATION: 7
[MAGNITUDE OF THE PRODUCT RELATION: 7]

SOLL SIE AUF DEM TERMINAL AUSGEGEBEN WERDEN? >J
[SHOULD IT BE DISPLAYED ON THE TERMINAL?>y]

AR81 LFE7 GEZAEHLT	*210*
AR81EST6-5 GEZAEHLT	*18*
AR81EST6-6 GEZAEHLT	*22*
AR81ST10-4 GEZAEHLT	*82*
AR81ST12-1 GEZAEHLT	*27*
AR81ST13-3 GEZAEHLT	*248*
AR81ST25-1 GEZAEHLT	*932*

? Welche Proben sind nicht gezaehlt?
[Which samples have not been counted?]

GROESSE DER ERGEBNISRELATION: 39
[MAGNITUDE OF THE PRODUCT RELATION: 39]

SOLL SIE AUF DEM TERMINAL AUSGEGEBEN WERDEN? >n
[SHOULD IT BE DISPLAYED ON THE TERMINAL?]

ANGABE EINES FILENAMENS GEWUENSCHT? >y
[IS SPECIFICATION OF A FILE NAME DESIRED?]

FILENAME <FILE> <EXT> >probe ngz
[FILENAME <FILE> <EXT> >sample ngz]

FILENAME: (PROBE . NGZ)
[FILENAME: (SAMPLE . NGZ)]

? Beschreiben Sie: Was bedeutet die Eigenschaft Messart?
[Describe: What does the parameter 'type of measurement' mean?]

MESSART ist eine Eigenschaft von PROBE. Folgende MESSARTEN sind bekannt: NICHT_BESTIMMT, AUSGELITERT, GEZAEHLT und GEWOGEN.
['TYPE OF MEASUREMENT' is an attribute of 'SAMPLE'. The following TYPES OF MEASUREMENT are recognized: NOT DETERMINED, VOLUME, COUNTED, WEIGHTED.]

? Sind keine Proben ausgelitert?
[Have none of the samples been measured volumetrically?]

JA, KEINE.
[YES, NONE.]

? Sind alle Proben gewogen oder gezaehlt?
[Have all the samples been weighed or counted?]

JA.
[YES.]

? tschuess
[So long!]

Keine neuen Woerter.
TSCHUESS BIS ZUM NAECHSTEN MAL!
[No new words.
SO LONG, TILL NEXT TIME!]

Folgende Files wurden waehrend der Sitzung erzeugt:
The following files were produced during the session:

((PROBE . NGZ))
((SAMPLE . NGZ))

(PROBE . NGZ) Keep, print or delete? >k
(SAMPLE . NGZ)

ENDE
END

4.2 Sample Dialog With Commentaries

*(ham-ans 7)

HALLO!
[HELLO!]

? Was verstehen Sie unter dem Begriff Fahrt?
[What is your definition of the term 'cruise'?]

Eine FAHRT ist ein EREIGNIS. Die FAHRT
ist beschreibbar durch die Eigenschaften SCHIFFSNAME, FAHRTNAME,
ZIEL-SPEZIES, BOX-LATTITUDE-NORD, BOX-LATTITUDE-SUED,
BOX-LONGITUDE-OST, BOX-LONGITUDE-WEST, ANFANGSDATUM, ENDDATUM,
ZIELHAFEN, ZWECK, KOMMENTAR und STARTHAFEN.
[A CRUISE is an EVENT. The CRUISE is describable by the attributes
VESSEL-NAME, CRUISE-NAME, TARGET-SPECIES, BOX-LATTITUDE-NORTH,
BOX-LATTITUDE-SOUTH, BOX-LONGITUDE-EAST, BOX-LONGITUDE-WEST,
DATA-CRUISE-BEGIN, DATA-CRUISE-END, PORT-OF DESTINATION, PURPOSE,
COMMENT, PORT-OF-EMBARKATION.]

52.9 Sek.

A meta-question about the knowledge stored in the system. Answer requires verbalization of nodes and links of the semantic network.

? Definieren Sie uns, was verstehen Sie unter Zweck?
[Define for us what you mean by 'purpose'?]

ZWECK ist eine Eigenschaft von FAHRT. Folgende ZWECKE sind bekannt:
KOMMERZIELL und WISSENSCHAFTLICH.
[Purpose is an attribute of cruise. Following purposes are known:
commercial and research.]

1.8. Sek.

? Wieviele Fahrten gibt es?
[How many cruises are there?]

```
;; DEEP structure:

(f-d: (t-q: (for: (q-w: WIEVIEL) x6) (af-a: ISA x6 FAHRT)) T)

;;  DKRIDB opened.

**  EVALUATION OF DATA BASE QUERIES:

;;  The data base query:

;;  VAR x7 : TYPE OF FAHRT ; BEGIN x7 := FAHRT ; SIZE ( x7 ) END ;

;;  Result of the questions: 3

;;  Result of the evaluation:

(f-d: (t-q: (for: (q-qt: (r: 3 3)) x6) (af-a: ISA x6 FAHRT)) T)
```

DREI.
[THREE.]

25.3 Sek.

Question about the size of a relation, establishment of an area of communication between HAM-ANS and the DBMS PASCAL/R. Opening the data base. Syntax controlled transformation of the internal representation of the question into a data base question [O'LEA 83]. Generation of a complete answer which is then elliptified.

? Wieviele Fahrten sind wissenschaftlich?
[How many cruises are scientific?]

```
;; DEEP structure:

(f-d: (t-q: (for: (q-w: WIEVIEL) x14) (af-a: ISA x14 FAHRT))
 (af-a: REF x14 WISSENSCHAFTLICH))

**  EVALUATION OF DATABASE QUERIES

;;  The data base query:

;;  VAR x15 : TYPE OF FAHRT ; BEGIN x15 := [ EACH x14 IN FAHRT : ( x14 .
 ZWECK = WISSENSCHAFTLICH ) ] ; SIZE ( x15 ) END ;

;;  Result of the question: 2

;;  Result of the evaluation:
(f-d: (t-q: (for: (q-qt: (r: 2 2)) x14)
      (af-s: EL
       x14
       (s-t: (t-q: (for: (q-d: D- (r: 3 3)) x14) (af-a: ISA x14 FAHRT))
        )))
(af-a: REF x14 WISSENSCHAFTLICH))
```

ZWEI VON DEN DREI.
[TWO OF THE THREE.]

23.4 Sek.

Question about the cardinal number of a set of tuples in a relation, which satisfy a particular predicate. The selected tuples are stored in the DBMS on a temporary relational variable. The answer is in the form of a precise quantifier. The total number of cruises is included for reasons of cooperativeness.

```
? Welche Fahrten denn?
  [Which cruises?]

;; DEEP structure:

(f-d: (t-q: (for: (q-w: WELCH) x19) (af-a: ISA x19 FAHRT))
 (af-a: REF x19 WISSENSCHAFTLICH))

**  EVALUATION OF DATABASE QUERIES:

;;  The same question (possibly with different quantifiers)
    has been asked before.

;;  The data base query:

;;  BEGIN SIZE ( x15 ) END ;

;;  Result of the question: 2

GROESSE DER ERGEBNISRELATION: 2
[SIZE OF THE RESULTING RELATION: 2]

SOLL SIE AUF DEM TERMINAL AUSGEGEBEN WERDEN? >j
[SHOULD IT BE DISPLAYED ON THE TERMINAL? >Y]

MARION-DUFRESNE              MD25-FIBEX                     EUPHAUSIA
AND THYSANOESSA     -462500 -640436  -515500  -292900 810212 810224 CRO
ZET              CROZET                 WISSENSCHA CHIEF SC.HUREAU JC MNH
N-TAAF PARIS
ODISSEY                        FIBEX                        EUPHAUSIA
SUPERBA-KRILL       -520000 -620000   300000   560000 810201 810320 SEV
ASTOPOLIS        SEVASTOPOLIS          WISSENSCHA
                                                                18.3 Sek.
```

An incomplete WH-question. The predicate is completed by ellipsis reconstruction since the only difference between this and the previous question is the interrogative. It is sufficient to access the relational auxiliary variable which was formed during processing of the previous sentence (coherence in evaluation). At the time the interrogative 'which' is used a dialog with the user is being conducted about whether the result relation should be out putted and, if so, on which medium.

```
? Gibt es auch Proben?
  [Are there also samples?]

;; DEEP structure:

(f-d: (t-q: (for: (q-qt: EPL) x24) (af-a: ISA x24 PROBE)) T)
```

```
**  EVALUATION OF DATABASE QUERIES:

;;  The data base query:

;;  VAR x25 : TYPE OF PROBE ; BEGIN x25 := PROBE ; SIZE ( x25 ) END ;

;;  Result of the question: 46

;;  Result of the evaluation

(f-d: (t-q: (for: (q-qt: (r: 46 46)) x24) (af-a: ISA x24 PROBE)) T)

;;  The Z-value of the answer is: 1
```

JA, 46 .
[YES, 46.]

15.5 Sek.

Question about whether test samples are in storage. Cooperative answer with specification of the size of the sample.

? Sind zwei bis sechs Proben gezaehlt?
[Have between two and six samples been counted?]

```
;; DEEP structure:

(f-d: (t-q: (for: (q-qt: (r: 2 6)) x31) (af-a: ISA x31 PROBE))
 (af-a: REF x31 GEZAEHLT) )

**  EVALUATION OF DATABASE QUERIES:

;;  The data base query:

;;  VAR x32 : TYPE OF PROBE ; BEGIN x32 := [ EACH x31 IN PROBE :
    ( x31 .
    MESSART = GEZAEHLT ) ] ; SIZE ( x32 ) END ;

;;  Result of the question: 7

;;  Result of the evaluation

(f-d: (t-q: (for: (q-qt: (r: 7 7)) x31) (af-a: ISA x31 PROBE))
 (af-a: REF x31 GEZAEHLT) )

;;  The Z-value of the answer is: 0
```

NEIN, SIEBEN.
[NO, SEVEN.]

19.0 Sek.

Treatment of a complex quantifier. Negative answer since the quantifier in the question does not apply. Specification of the actual number.

? Welche Proben denn?
[Which samples?]

```
;; DEEP structure:

(f-d: (t-q: (for: (q-w: WELCH) x36) (af-a: ISA x36 Probe))
 (af-a: REF x36 GEZAEHLT))

** EVALUATION OF DATABASE QUERIES:

;;  Die Frage wurde bis auf moegliche Quantorunterschiede schon
    einmal gestellt

;;  The data base query:

;;  BEGIN SIZE ( x32 ) END ;

;;  Result of the question: 7
```

GROESSE DER ERGEBNISRELATION: 7
[SIZE OF THE RESULTING RELATION: 7]

SOLL SIE AUF DEM TERMINAL AUSGEGEBEN WERDEN? >j
[SHOULD IT BE DISPLAYED ON THE TERMINAL? >y

```
AR81  LFE7 GEZAEHLT          210
AR81EST6-5 GEZAEHLT           18
AR81EST6-6 GEZAEHLT           22
AR81ST10-4 GEZAEHLT           82
AR81ST12-1 GEZAEHLT           27
AR81ST13-3 GEZAEHLT          248
AR81ST25-1 GEZAEHLT          932
                                                         12.2 Sek.
```

? Welche Proben sind nicht gezaehlt?
[Which samples have not been counted?]

```
;; DEEP structure:

(f-d: (t-q: (for: (q-w: WELCH) x43) (af-a: ISA x43 PROBE))
 (f-o: NOT (af-a: REF x43 GEZAEHLT)))

** EVALUATION OF DATABASE QUERIES:

;;  The data base query:

;;  VAR x45 : TYPE OF PROBE ; BEGIN x45 := [ EACH x43 IN PROBE :
    NOT ( x43 . MESSART = GEZAEHLT ) ] ; SIZE ( x45 ) END ;

;;  Result of the question: 39
```

GROESSE DER ERGEBNISRELATION: 39
[SIZE OF THE RELATION: 39]

SOLL SIE AUF DEM TERMINAL AUSGEGEBEN WERDEN? >n
[SHOULD IT BE DISPLAYED ON THE TERMINAL? >n]

ANGABE EINES FILENAMENS GEWUENSCHT? >j
[SPECIFICATION OF A FILE NAME DESIRED? >y]

FILENAME <FILE> <EXT> >probe ngz
[FILE NAME <FILE> <EXT> >sample ngz]

FILENAME: (PROBE . NGZ)
[FILE NAME: (SAMPLE . NGZ)]

16.4 Sek.

Processing of a WH-question with negated predicate. Possibility of generating a report file for the result relation.

? Beschreiben Sie: Was bedeutet die Eigenschaft Messart?
[Describe: what means the characteristic 'type of measurement'?]

MESSART ist eine Eigenschaft von PROBE. Folgende MESSARTEN sind bekannt: NICHT_BESTIMMT, AUSGELITERT, GEZAEHLT und GEWOGEN.
[TYPE OF MEASUREMENT is an attribute of SAMPLE. The following TYPES OF MEASUREMENT ar known: NOT_DETERMINED, VOLUE, COUNTED and WEIGHED.]

8.0 Sek.

Meta-question about the system's knowledge.

```
? Sind keine Proben ausgelitert?
  [Have none of the samples been measured volumetrically?]

;; DEEP structure:

(f-d: (t-q: (for: (q-qt: KEIN) x50) (af-a: ISA x50 PROBE) )
 (af-a: REF x50 AUSGELITERT) )

**  EVALUATION OF DATABASE QUERIES:

;;  The data base query:

;;  VAR x51 : TYPE OF PROBE ; BEGIN x51 := [ EACH x50 IN PROBE :
    ( x50 . MESSART = AUSGELITERT) ] ; SIZE ( x51 ) END ;

;;  Result of the questions: 0

;;  Result of the evaluation

(f-d: (t-q: (for: (q-qt: (r: 0 0) ) x50) (af-a: ISA x50 PROBE))
 (af-a: REF x50 AUSGELITERT))

;;  The Z-value of the answer is: 1
```

JA, KEINE.
[YES, NONE.]

18.3 Sek.

Processing of the quantifier 'none'. Verbalization of the range (r:0 0) as 'none'.

? Sind alle Proben gewogen oder gezaehlt?
[Have all the samples been weighed or counted?]

```
;; DEEP structure:

(f-d: (t-q: (for: (q-w: ALL) x58) (af-a: ISA x58 PROBE))
 (f-o: OR (af-a: REF x58 GEZAEHLT) (af-a: REF x58 GEWOGEN)))

** EVALUATION OF DATABASE QUERIES:

;; The data base query:

;; VAR x60 : TYPE OF PROBE ; BEGIN x60 := [ EACH x58 IN PROBE :
   ( x58 . MESSART = GEZAEHLT ) OR ( x58 . MESSART = GEWOGEN ) ] ;
   SIZE ( x60 ) END ;

;; Result of the question: 46

;; Result of the evaluation:

(f-d: (t-q: (for: (q-w: ALL) x58) (af-a: ISA x58 PROBE))
 (f-o: OR (af-a: REF x58 GEZAEHLT) (af-a: REF x58 GEWOGEN)))

;; The Z-value of the answer is: 1
```

JA.
[YES.]

17.9 Sek.

Coordinated predicate. Answer shortened to 'Yes' since the result of the evaluation is identical to the SURF-structure of the input.

? tschuess
[So long]

Keine neuen Woerter.
[No new words.]

TSCHUESS BIS ZUM NAECHSTEN MAL!
[SO LONG, TILL NEXT TIME!]

Folgende Files wurden waehrend der Sitzung erzeugt:
[The following files were produced during the session:]

((PROBE . NGZ))
((SAMPLE . NGZ))

(PROBE . NGZ) Keep, print or delete? >k
(SAMPLE . NGZ)

;; DKRIDB geschlossen und PASCAL Dialog beendet

ENDE
[END]

In this dialog no words were used which the system was not already familiar with. The report files generated are listed for the user after the dialog is completed so that he can decide what should be done with them. The data base and the area of communication are closed.

References

[APPE 82], [BALL 80], [BARR 81], [BATE 78], [BERG 82], [BUSE 84], [BUSE 85], [CARB 81], [CHOM 65], [CHRI 82], [DRES 76], [FLIE 83], [GROS 78], [HAHN 80], [HAHN 83], [HAYE 81], [HEND 78], [HERK 80], [HOEN 82], [HOEP 80], [HOEP 82], [HOEP 83], [HOEP 84], [HUSS 82], [JAME 82a], [JAME 82b], [JAME 83], [LEFA 77], [LEVE 82], [MARB 83a], [MARB 83b], [MARB 85], [MARS 80], [MCKE 82], [MEEH 79], [MORI 81], [MORI 83a], [MORI 83b], [MORI 83c], [MORI 85], [NEUM 82], [O'LEA 83], [PETR 73], [RICH 79], [SCHM 76], [SCHM 80], [SCHÜ 79a], [SEAR 78], [WAHL 81], [WAHL 82], [WAHL 83], [WEIS 80], [WOOD 70], [ZOEP 84]

Chapter 8

An Expert Interface for Effective Man-Machine Interaction

Giorgio Brajnik, Giovanni Guida*, and Carlo Tasso**

Abstract. This chapter presents a prototype expert interface (IR-NLI, Information Retrieval Natural Language Interface) to an information retrieval system, developed at the University of Udine in the frame of a broader research effort concerning the topics of cooperative man-machine interaction and expert systems. After a discussion of the novel notion of expert interface, attention is focused on the IR-NLI system for the access to online information services by non-technical users. General specifications, design criteria, and architecture of IR-NLI are presented first. Knowledge representation methods and reasoning mechanisms adopted are then illustrated in detail. In this context, a new mechanism, called task, for representing and using meta-knowledge in rule-based systems is proposed. The internal operation of the system, together with two examples of interaction with the user, are illustrated. The paper concludes with the discussion of some preliminary ideas on how learning capabilities could be introduced in IR-NLI through the task mechanism.

1 Introduction

The study and design of friendly man-machine interfaces has seen remarkable progress in the last decade. Natural language has always been considered a key point in bridging the gap between a casual user and a complex system. In fact, the first difficulty one encounters in approaching an unknown machine and trying to use it, arises from the fact that the machine speaks a language different from that of the user: he cannot talk to it in his native language and he cannot expect to engage in a friendly dialogue. Much effort has been devoted to the study of natural language communication between man and machine, and presently a number of implemented systems exist that can demonstrate enough coverage and robustness in limited subject domains, and can be usefully adopted in real applications. Nevertheless, current interfaces still lack domain competence and their behaviour – although quite natural and friendly – is not cooperative enough to support an effective interaction.

---

* Also with: Artificial Intelligence Project, Politecnico di Milano, Milano, Italy.
** Also with: CISM – International Center for Mechanical Sciences, Udine, Italy.

A brief look at the recent history of the role of natural language processing in the design of man-machine systems can help in analyzing the general trends of this research area. Tracing back to the early seventies, some milestones can be identified in the development of the concept of man-machine interface. We can sum up this evolution in five major steps:

Understanding Imperative Natural Language Sentences
The main goal considered in this first phase is that of enabling a system to understand separate queries or commands expressed in natural language: no shared world knowledge between the system and the user is provided. Several generations of natural language interfaces up to the beginning of the seventies conform to this paradigm [GREE63, LIND63].

Managing Simple Dialogues
The issue of carrying on a (simple) dialogue with the user arises quite naturally from the exigency of overcoming critical situations of misunderstanding. The notion of clarification dialogue to support the system in the comprehension of difficult (imperative) sentences is a good example of this trend [WOOD72, CODD74].

Having a Graceful Behavior
Managing a graceful interaction between man and machine, including most of the features that make a natural conversation easy and pleasant emerges as a necessary capability of a dialogue system. Understanding fragmentary and broken text, dealing with grammatically incorrect sentences, getting confirmation of the correct understanding of an utterance, managing ellipsis and anaphora are only a few of the issues involved in graceful man-machine interaction [HEND78c, HAYE79].

Taking Pragmatics into Account
Several of the above issues point to the need of having complex pragmatic models of communication, beyond syntax and semantics. Knowing how the actors of a dialogue behave, how they manage interpersonal plans, how they use language as a medium to achieve their goals, becomes now a crucial point in the design of effective interfaces [ALLE83, WILE83]. Linguistic knowledge is not enough to master such complex situations: a lot of world knowledge is needed.

Being Cooperative and Supportive
Taking active part into a conversation is not limited, however, to mastering language and world knowledge: an intelligent interface should be able to contribute to the dialogue with its own reasoning capabilities. A natural man-machine interface should be cooperative and supportive for the user and actually help him in the solution of his problems [COHE82, KAPL83, REIC84, REIT83].

This short history denotes a clear trend to move the focus of attention from merely linguistic phenomena towards a more comprehensive understanding of the nature of man-machine interaction, taking into account phenomena that lie behind the linguistic surface and that are expected to play a crucial role in the design of smarter and more effective interfaces. Language is obviously a major problem in man-machine communication, and the use of natural language can surely contribute to bridge the gap between machines and non-technical users. However, language is neither the only impediment nor the main one to an easy and effective use of complex artificial systems. Concepts, models, world knowledge, mental paradigms, intentions, plans, needs, roles which are behind linguistic utterances constitute the real gap between man and machine.

Very often a machine is easily usable only by a person who exactly knows which tasks the machine can perform, how it can be operated, and how it works. But non-technical users are generally not acquainted with all these matters; they only have a rough idea on how to use the machine they are willing to interact with, and some expectations on its capabilities. Moreover, the machine does not care about the user: it does not embody knowledge about possible user profiles, and it does not take into account how its performance can be interpreted by the interacting person and how it can affect his behaviour.

Therefore, the deepest gap between man and machine lays, first of all, at the conceptual level; diversity of language reflects diversity of concepts, and trying to bridge the linguistic gap between man and machine requires, as a prerequisite, a huge amount of shared world knowledge. Only after the conceptual gap is bridged, it is appropriate to address the problem from the linguistic point of view: a neat conceptual context can be an adequate basis to deal with naturalness, robustness, and cooperativeness of discourse.

In this chapter we propose an approach to the design of cooperative man-machine interfaces which explicitly takes into account the conceptual point of view, both to support cooperation and, also, to improve the level of linguistic communication. In order to identify the basic capabilities of such an interface, let us consider a paradigmatic situation where a person (the user), facing a problem in a given subject domain, realizes that some artificial system (the target system) can serve his purpose, and, therefore, decides to use it. But, he does not know enough about how to operate the target system correctly and how to utilize it effectively.

It is straightforward to recognize that the best possible interface - both natural and cooperative - between the user and the target system is, in such a situation, a human intermediary. His expertise covers target system capabilities, use, and operation; he would know about application domains where the target system can be effectively used; he also is knowledgeable about needs, expectations, and mental models of potential users; at last, he fluently speaks the same (natural) language of the user. Such an intermediary can perform, therefore, as an intelligent and active problem solving assistant who can support a wide class of users in the correct and effective use of the target system.

The role of the intermediary between the user and the machine includes three main capabilities:

- assisting the user in the correct and effective use of the target system;
- taking active part in the problem solving process in which the user is engaged;
- possibly training the user in the operation of the target system, gradually making him capable of using it by himself.

In order to perform the job outlined above, the intermediary must have a huge amount of knowledge that can be organized in four classes:

Knowledge About the User:
- problem solving situations where the target system could be used (from the viewpoint of the user);
- user view on the problem domain, including world models and reasoning mechanisms;
- specific exigencies the user wants to satisfy by means of the target system;
- attitude of the user towards the intermediary (cooperative, uncooperative, misleading, suspicious, etc.);
- interest of the user in knowing more about the target system and acquiring the capability of using it directly;
- interpersonal communication model adopted by the user, including language use and terminology.

Knowledge About the Target System:
- functions and limitations;
- operation (how to run it appropriately), including knowledge about the command language;
- general architecture and internal operation;
- problem solving situations where it can be utilized;
- specific use in the solution of classes of problems.

Knowledge About the Problem Domain:
- general knowledge (taxonomic, descriptive, theoretical) on the subject domain;
- general reasoning strategies;
- domain specific (heuristic, experience-based) reasoning mechanisms;
- classes of usual problems in the subject domain.

Knowledge About the Intermediary's Job:
- models of intermediary's professional activity (goals, resources, strategies, tactics, etc.);
- specific models of interpersonal communication (interviewing, convincing, etc.);
- specific (heuristic, experience-based) skills of the intermediary's job.

So far, we have analyzed the main features of a person, a skilled intermediary professional, who is supposed to behave as a living interface to a target system. Our proposal consists in putting the intermediary's competence into an artificial system, which is expert in the specific task of interfacing non-technical users to a complex system. We call this kind of interface an *expert interface.*

The purpose of this paper is to illustrate the research activity performed in the design and experimentation of the *IR-NLI (Information Retrieval Natural Language Interface)* system for the access of non-technical users to online information services. IR-NLI is an expert interface modeled according to the general criteria outlined above, which includes both linguistic coverage and expert competence, and can offer a cooperative and supportive interaction environment. This project has been developed at the University of Udine [GUID82, GUID83 a, GUID83 b] with the aim of experimenting with new techniques for the design of cooperative interfaces and, also with some new ideas concerning the architecture of expert systems [GUID84]. IR-NLI is currently running on VAX-11/780 (it is written in Franz Lisp under the UNIX operating system), and has been tested in the domain of bibliographic information retrieval in a subfield of computer science.

The issue of interfacing online information retrieval systems with user-friendly and cooperative front-ends is not new in the literature. CITE [DOSZ79] is an English language interface for querying an online bibliographic system. Its capabilities include identification of search terms, combinatorial searching, ranked output, relevance feedback, and automatic query modification. CITE does not utilize any of the usual AI techniques for automatic reasoning, and it is therefore unable to include in the search strategy terms which are not supplied by the user in the initial request. Therefore, CITE is mainly addressed to experienced users, who are well acquainted with the most appropriate terminology.

The search statement generator developed by Pollitt [POLL81, POLL82] is an interface to a medical data base, which can be utilized to generate appropriate search commands with a suitable terminology in the domain of cancer therapy. Although sharing with IR-NLI the goal of enabling untrained end users to easily access and search an online database, Pollitt's system is mainly concerned with the problem of constructing and evaluating a non-typing interface, where a touch screen is utilized by the user in order to select the most appropriate concepts, terms, and commands from frames displayed on the screen.

The CONIT system [MARC81 a] is a specialized interface designed to assist a user in directly interacting with several different information retrieval systems. CONIT makes available to the user a generalized query language, and can translate commands of this language into the appropriate commands needed to access whatever specific system is being interrogated. Moreover, CONIT can teach the user the most correct way of utilizing the different commands, and can suggest possible search techniques to be employed. The user is then responsible to decide how to apply these techniques by using the appropriate commands. CONIT does not address the issue of supporting the user in the formulation of the search strategy at a conceptual level, but only provides an instruction aid.

A different, more ambitious point of view is taken in the design of EXPERT [MARC81 b]. Based on the previous experience developed with CONIT, an experimental computerized intermediary system has been developed, which is able to simulate a human expert in the task of assisting inexperienced users of bibliographic retrieval systems. EXPERT interacts with the user through a menu-selection/fill-in-the-blanks dialog which assists the user in data base selection (relying on statistical measures) and supports search formulation and reformulation (this last obtained through relevance feedback techniques). Moreover, EXPERT performs an automatic translation of the search formulation into keyword/stem boolean search commands. EXPERT is implemented as a production system controlled by a forward chaining mechanism. With respect to CONIT, it offers substantially improved capabilities, but it still does not take into account any domain-specific knowledge. Therefore, it can effectively support only users fully acquainted with the subject domain of the search.

All the projects outlined above, although sharing with IR-NLI the same application domain, substantially differ from it in scope. The problems they face are mainly at the linguistic level, and only partially deal with such basic tasks as the analysis of the user's information needs and the design of an appropriate search strategy. Moreover, several crucial issues of conceptual nature, including cooperative behaviour end expert problem solving, are not explicitly addressed.

This chapter is organized as follows. In Sect. 2 a brief introduction to online information retrieval is presented. Section 3 is devoted to the analysis of the specifications of IR-NLI and to the illustration of its general architecture. Section 4 focuses on knowledge representation, and Sect. 5 on the internal operation of the system. In Sect. 6 two examples of interaction with IR-NLI are presented. Section 7 discusses some preliminary ideas on how learning capabilities can be introduced into IR-NLI, and Sect. 8 concludes the chapter.

2 The Information Retrieval Field

2.1 General Issues

In this section we illustrate the basic features of online information retrieval [LANC79, SALT83], the subject domain of the IR-NLI expert interface.

Online services allow interested users to solve information problems by selecting and retrieving relevant documents stored in very large bibliographic or factual data bases, concerning several fields of science, technology, economics, and humanities. *Information retrieval systems* allow access to stored data through a formal query language, which is used for selecting the desired information through a sequence of commands (such as SELECT, FIND, DISPLAY, logical combination of conditions, etc.). Generally, end-users are unwilling (or unable) to interrogate these large files directly, and they rely on the assistance of a specialized information professional, the *intermediary,* who knows how to select appropriate data bases, how to design good search strategies for the retrieval of the desired information, and how to implement them through a suitable formal query language.

In order to clearly point out the peculiarities of this application domain, it is useful to contrast information retrieval systems to data base management systems. We consider two main points.

First, the information stored in a data base has a well defined logical structure, which supports the access to data and helps the user in finding desired information items. In contrast, in an information retrieval system, the stored records (which contain, for example, title, authors, abstract, key words, etc. of a technical paper) identify the content of the documents only in a partial and unstructured way. This implies that retrieval of desired information is much more difficult, since it relies on several loosely defined factors, such as domain-specific knowledge, knowledge about indexing criteria, availability of updated and complete searching referral aids, working experience on the particular database, etc. This first feature is captured by two classical parameters used to measure the effectiveness of a retrieval: recall and precision [SALT83].

Second, while a user of a database generally looks for precise information items to be extracted from the stored files, a user of an online service desires to get information on a given topic, and this does not allow straightforward and exact identification of the relevant records. What documents to extract in order to match the user's request is usually a non-trivial problem that has to be solved by the intermediary.

2.2 *The Actors and Their Role*

Let us continue with the illustration of the scenario of information retrieval by introducing the three actors of a usual search session:

- *the end user:* the person who has some information need that can be satisfied by means of an online service;
- *the intermediary:* the professional who is able to understand and analyze the information needs of the end user and to effectively access the data base in order to retrieve the relevant documents;
- *the data base:* a file of bibliographic (or factual) records which contain references to the literature of a specific subject domain. Generally, a given topic can be dealt with in several data bases, which may differ in the general methodology utilized for indexing and storing documents. Information about the technical peculiarities and the content of a data base (including the criteria employed for collecting relevant information, the attention given to theoretical or practical aspects of the subject, the structure of the records, the list of key-words utilized for indexing the documents, the use of special classifica-

tion schemata, etc.) is supplied by *searching referral aids,* such as reference manuals, thesauri, directories, subject headings, and classification plans.

The interaction between these three actors usually follows a well defined and established procedure, which is structured in the following four phases [MEAD81]:

1. *Presearch Interview*
   It is aimed at precisely clarifying the content and the objectives of the end user's information needs. In this phase the intermediary performs the *conceptualization* of the information problem, i. e. he identifies all concepts present in the end user's request and he analyzes the logical relations existing among them.

2. *Data Base Selection and Strategy Design*
   On the basis of the information gathered during the presearch interview and with the help of searching referral aids, the intermediary chooses the most suitable data base(s) to be interrogated and devises a search strategy which matches end-user goals and needs. By the term *search strategy* we refer to the formal query program (a sequence of statements written in the specific query language of the chosen data base), which can be submitted to the information retrieval system in order to select the relevant documents.

3. *Execution*
   Once a tentative search strategy is available, the intermediary submits it to the information retrieval system, collects the results of its execution, and evaluates them in order to refine, if necessary, the search strategy. Sometimes, phases 2 and 3 are repeated more than once to produce a final version of the search strategy which better fits the end user's needs.

4. *Result Evaluation*
   The output of the search is evaluated by the end user, who may decide to change his requirements (add or substitute some terms, adjust objectives, etc.) or to propose some modification to the search strategy adopted.

From this illustration of the main phases of a search session, it can be noticed that one of the most critical tasks to be performed by the intermediary is the design of a suitable search strategy. In the next section, we illustrate this phase in greater detail, focusing, more specifically, on some of the techniques currently utilized by professional intermediaries.

2.3 Approaches and Tactics for Strategy Design

The term *approach* denotes the abstract way of facing a search problem, reasoning on it, analyzing its facets, and devising a general mode of operation to access the desired information. More precisely, an approach defines the order and the way of combining (through logical operators) the relevant concepts in the design of a search strategy. Five main approaches have been proposed in the literature [MEAD81]:

Most Specific First (MSF)
In this case attention is first focused, in a multifaceted end user's request, on the concept which is the most specific in the query. If, after the search, the number of the retrieved documents is sufficiently low, the search is ended. Otherwise, the remaining concepts are taken into account and the search is repeated. The MSF approach is useful when dealing with a query from which it is possible to extract a concept which is much more specific than the others. In this case, the MSF approach yields the results through very few access operations.

Lowest Posting First (LPF)
This approach is similar to MSF: the concept with the lowest posting count (the number of documents in the data base which are related to a given concept) is searched first; then the results are evaluated and, if necessary, the next lowest posting concept is searched again until a reasonable set of documents is retrieved. Usually, the LPF approach is chosen when the query contains a concept whose posting count is much lower than the others.

Building Block (BBL)
In this approach the query is broken into several concepts or groups of concepts - the facets - and each of them is searched independently. The analysis of each concept (search for related terms, synonyms, possible abbreviations, etc.) is carried out off-line, and only after its completion the information retrieval system is used. The BBL approach involves the lowest interaction degree with the data base system. It is used when a very exhaustive search is desired.

Citation Pearl Growing (CPG)
This is the most empirical and interactive approach: starting from a concept - usually the best known one - a first search is performed; the evaluation of the results so far gathered will then provide further citations and terms which can be used in a subsequent phase of the search. In most cases this try-and-evaluate cycle is repeated a few times until enough information has been collected which eventually leads to the selection of another approach. The CPG approach is mainly used when the user is poorly acquainted with the specific matter, and he does not know the precise terms to be used.

Successive Fractions (SFR)
In this approach, starting from a concept or a limitation specified by the user on the desired documents (e.g., the date, the language, etc.), a search is performed;

another condition (e.g., a concept) is then imposed on the results so far retrieved and a new search is executed. This is repeated until either there are no more conditions to be taken into account or the obtained results are satisfactory.

During the execution of an approach a fundamental activity performed on the facets of a query is *concept analysis*. In this activity, a basic role is played by tactics, which were first defined by Bates [BATE79] as a move made to further a search. From this point of view, a tactic can be understood as a fixed sequence of actions devoted to carry out the analysis.

In our framework the term tactic has been assigned a more specific meaning: a *tactic* is an elementary operation, a single step or action to be performed in order to implement an approach. We can therefore further characterize the concept of search strategy in the following way: a search strategy is the result of the execution of an approach through the application of appropriate tactics. A list of the main tactics usually utilized during concept analysis (BATE79, LANC79] is reported below:

Specify: the search is to be carried out on terms which are more specific than the ones used so far. This tactic can be used when high precision is needed and the current formulation of the query is likely to produce a huge amount of results.

Generalize: the search has to be extended by moving up in the term hierarchy to more general terms and by including several combinations of them in the search formulation. It can be used when the specificity of the current search formulation is too high with respect to the search objectives, and it is likely to produce too few and/or too specific items. It is the opposite of specify.

Exhaust: the search formulation has to include (ANDed together) most of (or all) the terms of the query. This tactic leads to the retrieval of a restricted set of documents, perhaps missing some important ones due to overly stringent conditions.

Reduce: the search formulation has to be relaxed by eliminating one or more of the terms present in it. Reduce is the opposite of exhaust.

Parallel: the search formulation has to be enlarged by including (ORed together) synonyms or related terms. This tactic can be used when the elements in the query are too specific and precise.

Pinpoint: the precision of the search formulation has to be increased by reducing the number of parallel terms. This considerably reduces the degree of recall.

Super: moving upward in the term hierarchy and focusing on a broader term, discarding the original one.

Sub: moving downward in the term hierarchy and focusing on a more specific term, discarding the original one.

Relate: moving at the same hierarchical level towards related terms, and substituting the original term with the new ones (ORed together).

Sibling: including in the search formulation some related terms ORed together with the currently analyzed term. This tactic increases recall, but, at the same time, it is much more reliable than the relate tactic, as it still keeps in consideration the original term.

Superordinate: including in the search formulation some related terms ORed together with the currently analyzed term, and ANDing the result with a broader term. This tactic broadens the search to related terms, still preserving proximity with the original one (because of the broader term ANDed with the related ones). Superordinate can be used when a high recall is desired, without paying the price of a crude broadening.

Subordinate: including in the search formulation some narrower term ORed together, and ANDing the result with the original term. Subordinate is the opposite of superordinate, as it involves a specification over the term rather than a generalization. It can be used when a higher specificity is needed, without the risk of an arbitrary specification.

Rearrange: if a term contains more than one word, reverse or rearrange the words in any reasonable order.

Respell: searching under different spelling variants of the terms.

Respace: searching under different spacing variants of hyphenated words.

Fix: searching under different prefix, subfix, or infix variants.

3 System Architecture and Specifications

3.1 Overview

The general architecture of IR-NLI is shown in Fig. 1. IR-NLI comprises three main modules, devoted to cover the three basic competence areas of the interface, namely: natural language understanding and dialogue, modeling of the intermediary's activity, and generation of the search strategy in the appropriate command language of the target information retrieval system.

The *understanding and dialogue module* is devoted to perform activities of linguistic nature. First, it translates the natural language user's request into a formal *problem internal representation*. Second, it manages (under the control of the reasoning module) a dialogue with the user devoted to expand the problem internal representation with new information. The understanding and dialogue module utilizes for its operation a *vocabulary* and a base of *linguistic knowledge*.

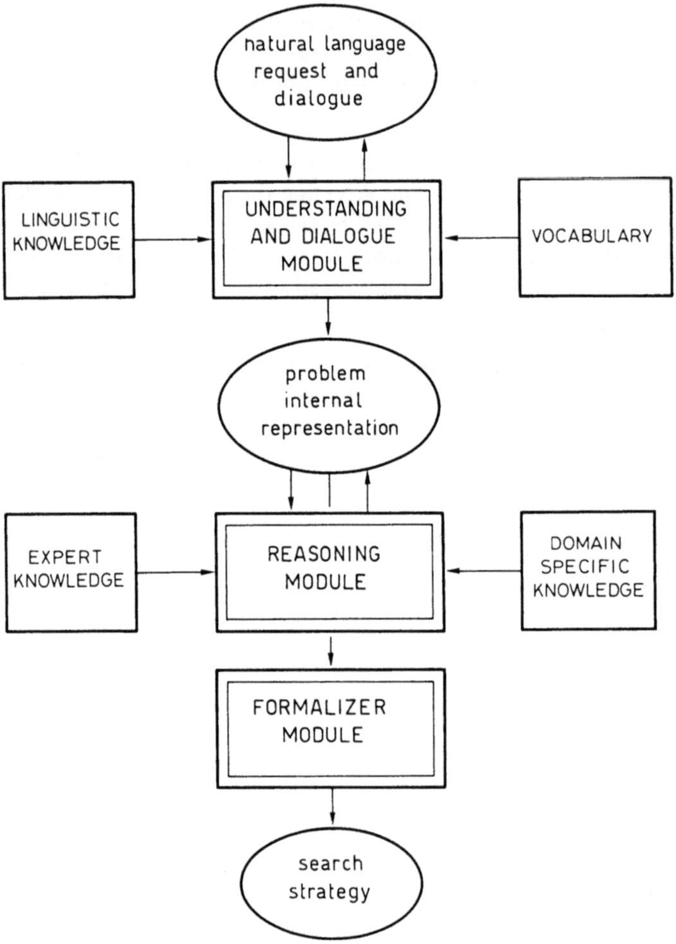

Fig. 1. Overall architecture of IR-NLI

The *reasoning module* is devoted to model the intermediary's activity: it devises the top-level choices concerning the cooperative operation of the interface and controls their execution. To perform this activity it uses a base of *expert knowledge,* which concerns the evaluation of user's request, the management of the presearch interview, the expansion of the problem internal representation, the selection of a suitable approach, the execution of appropriate tactics, the activation of the dialogue with the user, and the generation of a suitable search strategy. The world knowledge (mostly of terminologic nature) necessary to these tasks is contained in a base of *domain specific knowledge.*

The *formalizer module* is activated after the reasoning module has completed its activity, and constructs from the fully expanded problem internal representation the final search strategy to be executed for accessing the target online data base. It is conceived as a parametric translator, capable of producing search strategies in several languages for accessing actual online services, such as SDC ORBIT, Euronet DIANE, and Lockheed DIALOG.

The brief illustration of the overall system architecture shows that the reasoning module constitutes the kernel of IR-NLI, as it is devoted to provide the system with the cooperative behavior typical of an intelligent information retrieval assistant. Therefore, we focus in the following sections only on this part of the system, which embodies the conceptual capabilities that make IR-NLI an example of an expert interface as defined in Sect. 1.

The design of the understanding and dialogue module closely follows the goal-oriented approach developed by the authors and tested in the construction of the NLI system for the enquiry in natural language of a relational data base [GUID82]. The formalizer module can be easily implemented with traditional syntax-directed translation techniques.

3.2 A Rule-Based Architecture for the Reasoning Module

We focus in this section on the basic requirements of IR-NLI and we derive a first set of general technical specification for the reasoning module. The analysis carried out in Sect. 1 on the types of knowledge involved in the intermediary's job, clearly suggests that the rule-based system technology [WATE78, HAYE83] can offer a viable approach to the design of the reasoning module. In fact, several reasons support this choice.

First, a variety of different knowledge types are involved in the subject domain of intelligent information retrieval, including:

- precise classification information about the domain of the search, elicited from thesauri and searching referral aids and stored in the domain-specific knowledge base;
- structured knowledge extracted from technical literature and practical experience about approaches, tactics, and their use in intelligent information retrieval;
- uncertain, judgmental, and often even conflicting knowledge about how to model the intermediary's skill, derived from the analysis of his operation in practical situations;
- incomplete and unreliable data contained in the user's request (often crucial terms or references are missing, while unimportant or misleading concepts are stressed).

Furthermore, the reasoning paradigms of the intermediary are typically data-driven, as they highly depend on the several specific situations which can occur during the search. Therefore, it would not be appropriate to implement them in a fixed algorithm, which should explicitly consider all possible cases.

Moreover, knowledge about the intermediary's job seems to be more easily represented in a declarative way, rather than through fixed procedures. In fact, knowledge necessary to the effective operation of the system is not likely to be available at once before implementation, but it can be acquired, refined, and tested incrementally during system experimentation and tuning.

At last, the search space is estimated to be very large and easily factorable.

3.3 Technical Specifications

The task domain of intelligent information retrieval can hardly be classified in any of the categories of rule-based systems applications defined in [HAYE83]. In fact, it shows several features of different categories, including:

- *Interpretation:* the user's request can, generally, not be assumed to be a faithful description of his real information needs, since it is often incomplete, ambiguous, uncertain, and misleading. More appropriately, the initial user's request can be considered a set of raw data which have to be carefully interpreted in order to capture their deep meaning.
- *Planning:* carrying out a successful dialogue with the user and performing a correct analysis of his request require the basic capability of planning (and dynamic replanning) the choices and actions to be taken.
- *Design:* the construction of a suitable search strategy satisfying given objectives and constraints is a typical design problem, which requires the capability of considering large classes of possible solutions and of taking decisions according to appropriate evaluation criteria.

Sharing features of several application categories constitutes a first impediment to the adoption of traditional rule-based system architectures and suggests that a new paradigm capable of supporting cooperation among interpretation, planning, and design has to be looked for.

Moreover, a first implementation of IR-NLI developed in the past [GUID83b] has shown the inadequacy of a naive approach, based on usual rule-based system techniques, and it has outlined several features that denote the need for new tools capable of fitting the specific peculiarities of an expert interface.

The following technical features can be mentioned:

- The search space is very large, and it shows a tree-like structure comprising loosely connected knowledge islands, i.e. well structured chunks of rules corresponding to the different approaches and tactics of online information retrieval. Therefore, high directionality and specificity of search (guessing) is needed.

- Moreover, in order to ensure a correct recovery in case of a failure during the search, intelligent backtracking capability to the appropriate branching point is necessary. In fact, some kinds of failure may suggest to move to different knowledge islands without trying all alternatives offered by the current one.
- Furthermore, the knowledge island structure of the rule base demands a long-term planning capability which can avoid a fragmentary operation without look-ahead.
- As knowledge about information retrieval naturally comprises a hierarchy of abstraction levels (e.g., rules about approach selection are at a meta-level with respect to rules about tactics to be used for approach implementation), adoption of a mechanism for rule interpretation is suggested which can take advantage of this knowledge structure for improving efficiency of both matching and conflict resolution.
- At last, as the ability of the intermediary is largely based on analogical reasoning, mechanisms of learning from experience should be provided, which enable the reasoning module to refine its skill with operation [CARB83b].

Several of the issues outlined above have major implications for the design of the architecture of the rule-based system for the reasoning module and, more specifically, for the organization and use of meta-knowledge. Therefore, the need arises for a knowledge organization which can fit the many different knowledge types involved in the information retrieval task, and for a mechanism capable of exploiting meta-knowledge in an effective manner.

4 Knowledge Representation

4.1 Domain Specific Knowledge

The *domain specific knowledge base (DKB)* contains knowledge about the subject domain covered by the target online data base to which IR-NLI is connected. The DKB embodies two kinds of knowledge [DEFU84]:

- *linguistic knowledge,* concerning how a concept is currently referred to in the data base through an appropriate linguistic item specific of the subject domain;
- *semantic knowledge,* which expresses classification information and cross-reference relations among terms.

The internal structure of the DKB has been modeled according to the organization of traditional searching referral aids (in particular thesauri and subject classifications). It is constituted by a labelled directed network, in which nodes represent concepts and directed arcs represent relations between concepts. Each node contains:

- a *term*, i.e. the appropriate linguistic item used in the specific domain to denote a concept;
- a boolean flag (Y, N), which indicates whether the term is a *controlled term (CT)*, i.e., whether it belongs to a controlled vocabulary (a collection of standard terms used for document indexing);
- the *posting count (PC)*, i.e., the number of items of the data base in which the term appears;
- an integer value, called *generality level (GL)*, which represents the degree of specificity of the term in a hierarchical subject classification.

Arcs denote the usual cross-reference relationships utilized for structuring thesauri. These include:

- *broader term (BT)*,
- *narrower term (NT)*,
- *related term (RT)*, and
- *used for (UF)*.

The structure of the DKB has been designed in such a way as to be easily constructed from available searching referral aids and online thesauri, possibly in a partially automatic way through appropriate conversion programs.

4.2 Expert Knowledge: Rule Structure and Organization

In addition to the domain specific knowledge, the reasoning module utilizes in its operation an *expert knowledge base (EKB)*, which contains knowledge about the intermediary's skill and expertise. Expert knowledge takes the form of *production rules*.

The *left-hand-side (LHS)* of a rule is constituted by a sequence of logical *conditions* defined over the problem internal representation, that are assumed to be ANDed together. We say that the LHS of a rule is *satisfied* if all conditions in it evaluate to true. The *right-hand-side (RHS)* of a rule can contain:

- *actions* to be executed on the problem internal representation (possibly including interaction with the user or with the DKB), and
- *directives*, i.e. operations which will affect the control flow of the system.

Actions and directives in the RHS of a rule are assumed to be performed, when the rule is executed, in a strictly sequential manner.

Let us now take a closer look at the internal structure of a rule. A rule takes the form of a list of descriptor-value pairs: the *descriptor* is an identifier, and the *value* is either an atomic object (a number, a string, etc.) or a piece of Lisp code. The descriptors currently used for rule representation are:

- ⟨*name*⟩: an identifier (atomic symbol) used for referencing the rule in the EKB;
- ⟨*type*⟩: the type of the rule (domain, matching, or conflict);
- ⟨*weight*⟩: a real value between 0 and 1, which expresses a measure of how reliable the use of the rule is, i. e. an estimation of the quality of the logical implication asserted by the rule;
- ⟨*if-part*⟩: the Lisp-coded LHS (a Lisp predicate);
- ⟨*then-part*⟩: the Lisp-coded RHS (a Lisp function).

An example of the internal structure of a rule is reported below:

```
((name D97-06)
 (type domain)
 (weight 0.8)
 (if-part
  (lambda (p c)
         (and (objective 'high-precision)
              (forall C (concepts)
                       '(forall C1 (concepts)
                                 '(lessp
                                   (abs
                                    (diff
                                      (PC C)
                                      (PC C1)))
                                   100)))
              (setcurrent
                 (exists C (concepts)
                           '(lessp (GL C) 4))))))
then-part
  (lambda
   (p c)
     (activate 'MOST-SPECIFIC-FIRST' on (current)))))
```

In the following, we utilize a simplified description of the rules in order to improve readability. For example, the above rule can be represented in the simplified form as:

D97-06 (0.8)

IF all concepts have similar PC
there exists a concept C. X with low GL

objective is high-precision
THEN activate MOST-SPECIFIC-FIRST on C. X

Both syntax and semantics of the language used for the simplified representation of rules are quite intuitive and will be further clarified without a formal definition.

The EKB has a complex organization. It is first partitioned into three parts called types, each type is then further partitioned into blocks, and blocks are finally grouped together to form classes. Let us analyze each one of these components in turn.

Rules may belong to three different types:

- *domain rules,* which are devoted to represent knowledge about the intermediary's activity, and are used to actually carry out the task assigned to the reasoning module. Their RHS may contain both actions and the directives 'activate' and 'terminate' (see Sect. 5). The rule previously discussed (D97-06) is an example of a domain rule.
- *matching rules,* which contain meta-knowledge devoted to reduce the effort involved in the matching phase during operation of the rule-based system. They allow identification of subsets of domain and conflict rules, which are expected to be relevant in the current context, and will be utilized by the interpreter of the production system in the next steps. These subsets are selected through the directive 'use' contained in the RHS of matching rules. The syntax of 'use' is:

  use ⟨domain block⟩ [⟨conflict block⟩],

  where ⟨domain block⟩ and ⟨conflict block⟩ are the names of subsets of domain and conflict rules in the EKB (note that the second argument of 'use' is optional). The following is an example of a matching rule:

  M65-05 (1.0)
  IF PAR is not empty
  THEN use D12 C18

- *conflict rules,* which contain meta-knowledge devoted to encode criteria for conflict resolution, i. e. for selecting the next rule to be executed from the set of those whose LHS is satisfied in the current context (the conflict set). Conflict rules may contain in the RHS any of the following directives: 'select', 'weigh', 'choose', 'activate', and 'terminate'. The former three directives are used when the conflict set is not empty. Their general form is:

  select ⟨rule name⟩
  weigh
  choose ⟨pattern 1⟩ ⟨pattern 2⟩ . . . ⟨pattern N⟩

  The first directive specifies unconditional selection of the rule referred to by ⟨rule name⟩. The second one causes selection of the rule with highest weight.

The last one chooses the first rule which matches the left-most specified pattern, among ⟨pattern-1⟩, ⟨pattern-2⟩, ..., ⟨pattern-N⟩. Conflict rules devoted to managing the empty conflict set situation may contain the directives 'activate' or 'terminate' since the others are meaningless.
Note that conflict rules may also contain in the RHS any other kind of actions in addition to the above mentioned directives.
Examples of conflict rules are:

```
C41-02  (0.8)
        IF    CONFLICT-SET is not empty
              objective is high-precision
        THEN  weigh

C41-03  (1.0)
        IF    CONFLICT-SET is empty
              objective is high-recall
              number of concepts in the PIR is small
        THEN  activate GENERALIZE
```

Types are further partitioned into *blocks:* domain, matching, and conflict blocks, respectively. Blocks represent small chunks of knowledge that refer to some specific aspect of the subject domain. Therefore, blocks are expected to be relevant to a well identified class of situations during the operation of the reasoning module.

Since both domain knowledge and meta-knowledge are needed to effectively carry out the tasks involved in the operation of the reasoning module, blocks of different types are grouped together to form larger aggregates called *classes*. A class contains one matching block and one or more domain and conflict blocks. Moreover, matching and conflict rules of a class cannot refer (through the directives 'use' and 'select', respectively) to blocks and rules outside the class. Note that a block may belong to several classes.

Names are assigned to classes, blocks, and rules according to the following rules:

- classes are named with a mnemonic string referring to its meaning (e.g., APPROACH-SELECTION, MOST-SPECIFIC-FIRST, PARALLEL, etc.);
- blocks are named with a string made up of a letter belonging to the set {D, M, C} which indicates the type of the block, and a number which identifies the block in the set of blocks of the same type e.g., D27, CO2, M12, etc.);
- rules are named by concatenating the name of the block to which the rule belongs with a number which identifies the rule inside the block (e.g., D27-01, D27-15, M12-02, etc.).

The structure of the EKB outlined above comprises two basic features:

- knowledge is organized into separate chunks, the classes, each referring to a specific facet of the subject domain, such as a subfield of specialist competence, a problem solving approach, an exceptional situation, a phase of the reasoning process, etc.;
- meta-knowledge is contained in two parts of the representation:
  - the directives appearing in the RHS of domain rules, which basically embody knowledge about which class to use next and how to use it, thus allowing implementation of data-driven switching between classes during system operation;
  - the matching and conflict rules, which contain knowledge about which blocks of domain rules to use within a given class and how to use them, thus allowing selective focusing on the specific knowledge actually relevant to the current context.

The proposed representation model appears to be especially suitable for those domains that are highly structured in nature, and contain a lot of meta-knowledge intermixed with domain knowledge. In such cases, it allows easy and natural knowledge acquisition and representation, since appropriate constructs are available to model a large variety of knowledge structures without the need of an unnatural fragmentation. Moreover, the structure of the EKB allows explicit and effective representation of control knowledge that, otherwise, would be lost or dispersed in a flat, hardly usable representation.

4.3 Problem Internal Representation

The *problem internal representation (PIR)* represents the working memory of the rule-based system. Its content is updated at each step of system operation as a consequence of rule execution. Basically, the PIR is splitted into two parts: the *problem information (PI)* and the *control information (CI).*

The PI part of the PIR contains a structured representation of the available knowledge about the search problem.

The sources of such knowledge are:

- the user (through the understanding and dialogue module), who submits to the system his initial request at the beginning of the session (presearch interview), and answers queries formulated by the system whenever he is engaged in a dialogue;
- the DKB (through the reasoning module) which can supply new information whenever needed during system operation.

The users of the PI are the reasoning module and the formalizer module.

The PI part of the PIR is organized as a frame comprising subframes which, in turn, can contain several slots. The general structure of the PI is the following:

- *Concepts:* a sequence of subframes, each containing the representation of a concept supplied by the user or acquired from the DKB. Each subframe comprises the following slots:
  - *name:* a string built up by "C." followed by a sequential number (e.g., C.1, C.2, C.3, etc.), which identifies the concept in the PIR;
  - *term:* the term (or expression) with which the concept is referred to in the DKB;
  - *PC:* the posting count of the term;
  - *GL:* the generality level of the term;
  - *CT:* the flag (Y, N) denoting whether the term is controlled;
  - *DI:* the interest degree the user has assigned to the term;
  - *related:* the list of names of synonyms, spelling variations, and related keywords entered by the user;
  - *derived:* the list of names of concepts acquired from the DKB during the analysis of the concept.
- *Search-logic:* the logic underlying the current search formulation. It is given through a boolean combination (using the operators OR, AND, NOT) of the names of the concepts actually involved in the search formulation.
- *Objective:* the goal of the search stated by the user. The objective may be high-precision, high-recall, or sample, that denote the desire of obtaining only relevant documents, all relevant documents, and just a small set of relevant documents, respectively[1].
- *Limitations:* a subframe representing the constraints supplied by the user to limit the search. Its slots are:
  - *Language:* the language in which a document must be written in order to be relevant to the search (e.g., English, French, etc.);
  - *date:* a time period the publication date of the document must belong to (e.g., >1975, >=1960 and <=1970, etc.);
  - *Treatment:* the nature of documents to be retrieved (e.g., practical, theoretical, general, formal, etc.).
- *Output:* a subframe containing the specifications of the way in which the retrieved documents are to be supplied to the user. It comprises the following slots:

---

[1] The definitions of *precision* and *recall* are:

$$\text{precision} = \frac{\text{No. of relevant documents retrieved}}{\text{No. of documents retrieved}}$$

$$\text{recall} = \frac{\text{No. of relevant documents retrieved}}{\text{No. of relevant documents stored in the data base}}$$

- *Format:* e.g., bibliographic reference, abstract, full format, etc.;
- *Max:* the maximum number of items desired;
- *List:* e.g., sorted by year, sorted by author name, not sorted, etc.;
- *Mode:* e.g., online display, offline print, etc.

• *Search-mode:* a flag to be utilized during search strategy design, indicating whether the search has to be carried out on any field of each record in the data base (free-text), or only on those fields containing controlled terminology (controlled vocabulary).

The CI part of the PIR contains information the system uses for its own work, including partial result and internal state variables. Its entries are called *registers* and are created and deleted dynamically by the system.

A general illustration of the structure of CI is not given here, as it mostly concerns system implementation.

5 Reasoning Mechanism

5.1 The Concept of Task

The mode of operation of the reasoning module basically conforms to the general organization of a rule-based system and comprises a recognize-act cycle including the three activities of matching, conflict resolution, and execution [HAYE83]. However, it embodies a novel concept, the *task,* which allows effective use of meta-knowledge, fully exploiting the structured organization of the EKB and of the PIR illustrated in the previous section.

A *task* can be defined as a triple:

T=(CL, PAR, PRED),

where:

- CL is the name of a class of the EKB;
- PAR is a list of concept names belonging to the PIR, called *parameters;*
- PRED is a predicate defined over the PIR, called *termination predicate.*

Both PAR and PRED may be empty.

Tasks are dynamic entities, created at run time as a consequence of a specific directive, 'activate'. Such a directive takes the following form:

activate CL [on PAR] [until PRED],

where the last two components are optional.

The semantics of the directive 'activate' can be stated as follows: use the rules in CL, focusing on the concepts specified in PAR, until PRED evaluates to true. If parameters are omitted the task will operate on all the concepts appearing in the PIR, and when no termination predicate is specified the task will terminate only if the directive 'terminate' is executed.

We denote by *activation* the process of generating a task, putting together a class with a list of parameters and a termination predicate. Similarly, *termination* denotes the fact that a task ceases to exist when its termination predicate becomes true or the directive 'terminate' is executed, and *execution* refers to the sequence of operations necessary to actually run a task.

Henceforth, we will refer to a task through the name of its CL component. PAR and PRED will be explicitly specified whenever necessary to avoid ambiguity.

5.2 Task Execution

We now illustrate how tasks affect the usual recognize-act cycle of the interpreter of a production system. Task execution is the basic mechanism of operation of the reasoning module, whose kernel is the interpreter of the directive 'activate', called the *task interpreter.*

The basic schema of operation of the task interpreter is illustrated in Fig. 2. Let us analyze this schema in detail. The execution of the directive

activate CL on PAR until PRED

causes both the generation of the task T=(CL, PAR, PRED) and a call to the task interpreter for the execution of T. When T is supplied as input to the interpreter it becomes active and its execution starts.

Let us assume that CL has the following structure:

CL= MB		matching block
DB	={DB1, DB2, ...}	set of domain blocks
CB	={CB1, CB2, ...}	set of conflict blocks

The interpreter will consider in its activity only the concepts contained in PAR, if any; otherwise, the interpreter will operate on the entire PIR. We denote by PIR* the part of the PIR that the interpreter will actually consider during operation.

The interpreter takes first into account the matching block MB of CL and starts the first activity, called *block matching.* This consists of matching the LHS of the rules of MB against PIR*, in order to determine the domain and conflict blocks to be used in the current context. All domain and conflict blocks (belonging to DB and CB, respectively) mentioned in the directive 'use' of the matching

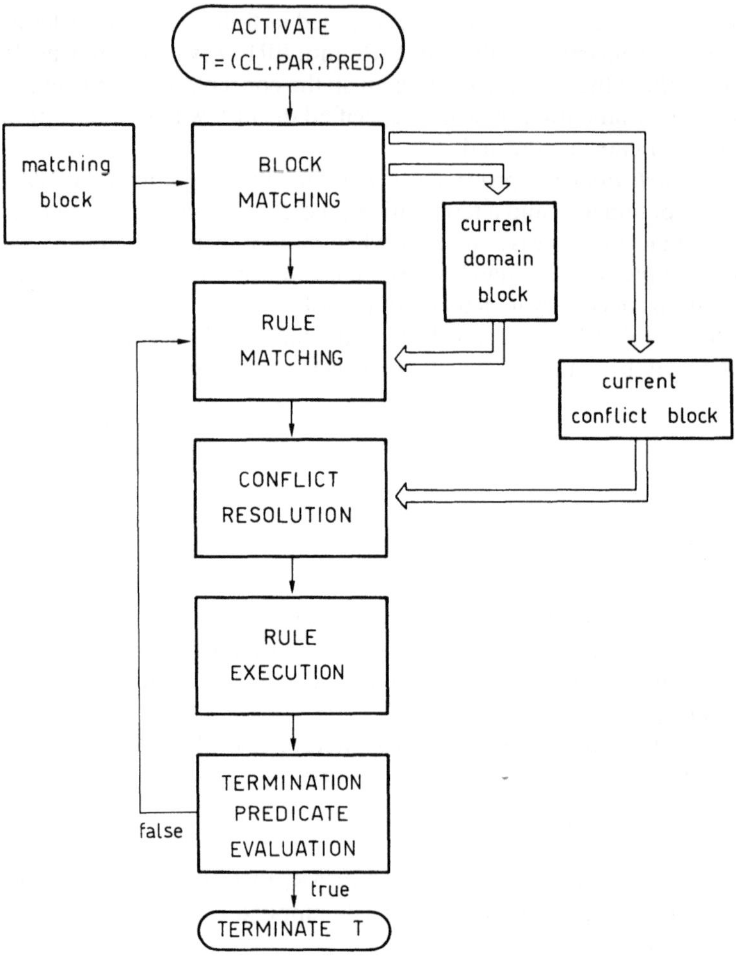

Fig. 2. Schema of operation of the task interpreter

rules whose LHS is satisfied, are merged together to form the current domain and conflict blocks (let us call these DB* and CB*, respectively).

After DB* and CB* have been determined, a usual recognize-act cycle is entered. It comprises three activities:

- *rule matching:* the LHS of the rules in DB* is matched against the current PIR*, and the set of domain rules whose LHS is satisfied is determined (the conflict set).
- *conflict resolution:* the LHS of the rules in CB* is matched against the current PIR*, and the domain rule to be executed next is selected according to the choice determined by execution of the directives appearing in RHS of the con-

flict rules whose LHS is satisfied. If the conflict set is empty, no domain rule can be selected and execution of the directives appearing in the RHS of the conflict rules whose LHS is satisfied will directly determine how task execution will be carried on.

- *rule execution:* the actions and directives appearing in the RHS of the selected domain rule are actually executed and the current PIR* is updated.

If a termination predicate PRED is specified in T, it is now evaluated in relation to the current PIR* *(termination predicate evaluation).* In case it evaluates to true, task execution is terminated; otherwise, control flow is returned to the rule matching activity, and a new recognize-act cycle is started.

Independently of PRED, task execution is also immediately terminated if, during conflict resolution or rule execution, the directive 'terminate' is invoked.

Note that the RHS of both conflict and domain rules can contain the directive 'activate' (possibly in addition to other actions and directives), whose execution causes generation of a new task and a call to the task interpreter. Therefore, if during conflict resolution or rule execution, the directive 'activate' is called upon, the execution of the current task is suspended and a new task becomes active. The suspended task will be resumed, and its execution will continue from the point where it was suspended, after the new task will terminate.

This policy of suspending and resuming task execution is implemented through a stack. The active task is on top of the stack. When a new task is activated, it is pushed on the stack and the point where the current task has been suspended is marked. When a task is terminated it is popped from the stack and the task on top of the stack becomes active again and execution continues from the marked point. If the stack is empty, operation of the task interpreter terminates.

The activity of the task interpreter is initialized by forcing execution of the directive

activate MAIN until (user-is-satisfied)

that pushes the task MAIN on the stack. The class MAIN contains just one matching rule:

```
M01-01 (1.0)
       IF      true
       THEN    use D01
```

and one domain rule:

```
D01-01 (1.0)
       IF      true
       THEN    activate PRESEARCH-INTERVIEW
               activate APPROACH-SELECTION
               activate RESULT-EVALUATION.
```

The operation of the reasoning module is fully determined by the execution of the task MAIN which controls the correct sequencing of phases in a search session and activates appropriate tasks devoted to actually carrying out the activities proper of each phase.

As a closing remark, we note that the intuitive meaning of task activation is that of switching from one domain of competence to another, focusing on a different facet of the problem and using for this a specialized chunk of knowledge. Tasks can therefore be viewed as specialists (or specific separate expert systems with their own domain knowledge and meta-knowledge), that can be invoked in a data-driven way whenever their competence seems to be useful to further the reasoning process. Each specialist can be activated in several different situations, and can adapt, through its own meta-knowledge (matching and conflict rules), to the specific features of the current context.

The task mechanism shares several features with the blackboard architecture of HEARSAY-III [ERMA81] but activation of specialists is, in our approach, only indirectly data-driven. In fact, for a task to be activated it is necessary that a specific situation is recognized by some rule belonging to another task, and, therefore, specialists are not called upon by data on the blackboard, but they are activated by another specialist (although still in a data-driven way as a consequence of rule execution). Therefore, tasks are not fully independent knowledge sources, but each of them must be knowledgeable of other tasks that it can activate during operation, whenever appropriate. This kind of relationships among tasks greatly reduces the non-determinism of the system operation at the meta-level, thus improving efficiency. This also eliminates the need for having structures such as the strategy knowledge sources of the blackboard model for meta-level planning.

The way tasks are activated can also be compared with the use of meta-rules [DAVI80]. In fact, the directive 'activate' can be viewed as a way of selecting a subset of the rule base on which to focus next. However, the activation of a task is not merely a heuristic-guided selection of the rule to be utilized next, but it implies a change of viewpoint and the decision to use a specific chunk of structured knowledge (both at domain and meta-level) to further the reasoning process.

6 Sample Sessions With IR-NLI

6.1 Structure of a Search Session

In this section two sample search sessions with IR-NLI are presented. Focus is centered on the conceptual aspects of IR-NLI operations, disregarding several marginal details. The examples chosen concern two approaches which are very common in practice: namely, Building Block and Citation Pearl Growing.

Before discussing these two examples in detail, we briefly illustrate the general structure of a search session with IR-NLI, which will serve as a background for the following discussion.

Presearch Interview is the initial phase of a search session, where the user formulates the first version of his request. The goal of this activity is to support the user in explicating his information needs, and to enable the intermediary to clearly understand the precise content and objectives of the user's request.

In IR-NLI the user is asked by the system to state a query in English, specifying the topic it relates to, some keywords and synonyms, the facets which are to be considered, the limitations to be imposed on the search, the desired form of the output results, etc. This activity is entirely carried out by the PRESEARCH-INTERVIEW task, whose goal is that of managing the dialogue with the user during the presearch interview, resorting to the understanding and dialogue module for the linguistics aspects of the communication between the user and the system.

After the user's needs have been definitely acquired, the intermediary has to devise the search strategy. The very first step towards this goal consists in completing the initial formulation of the user's request with additional specific information, that can be obtained from available searching referral aids and can be useful for evaluating the content of the request. The intermediary tackles then the most critical phase of his job, namely *approach identification,* the choice of the most appropriate approach to adopt for an effective management of the design of the search strategy. This choice is done without interacting with the information retrieval system, taking into account the following two elements: the objectives of the user, and the nature and richness of the information supplied by the user or obtainable from available searching referral aids.

In IR-NLI this job is performed by the APPROACH-SELECTION task which operates in two steps. First it extracts from the DKB the posting count, generality level, and controlled term flag of the concept involved in the user's request; then, it selects the approach which seems the most suitable one, according to the information currently available.

Concept Analysis, the central activity of a search session, is then started. This phase has the main goal of expanding (through extraction of new concepts from the DKB) the current formulation of the user's request in order to gather all information needed to construct an effective search strategy.

During this phase, the intermediary designs (either interactively with the information retrieval system or off-line) the structure and content of the search strategy, using appropriate tactics according to the chosen approach. This activity is highly data-driven, as the decisions to be taken and the individual steps to be performed strictly depend on the type and content of the pieces of information already gathered in the previous stages of the analysis.

In IR-NLI this phase is carried out by the specific task implementing the chosen approach, which is directly activated by the APPROACH-SELECTION task and can activate, in turn, all other tasks needed for execution of the relevant tactics.

A crucial problem in this phase is deciding when to stop the analysis: either the data gathered so far are enough for strategy construction or the analysis has evolved to an unsatisfactory point. In both cases we are faced with a judgemental step, which can require interaction with the user.

In the case where concept analysis has succeeded in producing the information needed for strategy construction, the formalizer module is activated, and the final search strategy in the appropriate query language is generated. Otherwise, if concept analysis terminates with a failure, backtracking to a previous step of the analysis, or to the approach identification phase takes place and a different solution is tried.

The last phase of a search session is *result evaluation*. This activity begins after the search has been done and results have been made available to the user. Its purpose is to allow the user to evaluate whether his information needs are fully satisfied and the session can be closed, or the search has to be continued, refined, or even repeated from the beginning with a new request. Usually, the responsibility of result evaluation is entirely left to the user, and the intermediary only supports him in expressing his judgements and formulating appropriate requests to further the search.

In IR-NLI this phase is managed by the RESULT-EVALUATION task, which presents to the user the obtained results and, interactively, supports him in evaluating their relevance.

6.2 An Example With the Building Block Approach

In this section we present a first example of a search session carried out by IR-NLI.

As already pointed out in Sect. 5, the task MAIN, which is the first task to be activated at the beginning of a search session, activates the task PRESEARCH-INTERVIEW to support the user in formulating his request. The first operation that the directive 'activate PRESEARCH-INTERVIEW' performs is block matching. The matching block of the class associated to the task PRESEARCH-INTERVIEW contains, among others, the following rule M02-05, which matches the current PIR and is therefore executed.

```
M02-05 (1.0)
       IF     PIR is empty
              PAR is empty
       THEN   use D01
```

The block D01, addressed by the directive 'use', contains rules that perform the presearch interview.

At this point, the user is invited by the system to submit his request. The dialogue between IR-NLI and the user begins as follows:

IR-NLI > `Please, state your request!`

user > `I would like to have references about computer applications in warehousing.`
`I am interested only in English documents not older than three years.`

The first step of the presearch interview is completed; the understanding and dialogue module analyzes the request and extracts the information relevant to the search. The first PIR (PI part) obtained is:

concepts: name = C.1
term = computer applications

name = C.2
term = warehousing

limitations: language = English
date > = 1981

The user has now to supply further information to better specify his needs: in the block D01 there are rules which can manage a bounded scope dialogue for collecting new useful information from the user and expanding the PIR. Some examples of dialogue rules are:

D01-07 (1.0)
IF concepts is empty
THEN get concepts

D01-16 (0.7)
IF PIR has been filled
THEN terminate

where 'get' is a Lisp function which acquires data from the user through a fixed dialogue.

The effect of these rules is the following interaction with the user:

IR-NLI > `Please, specify the scope of the search:`
`- comprehensive: retrieval of all relevant items (high-recall)`
`- limited: retrieval of only relevant items (high-precision)`
`- sample: retrieval of some relevant item`

user > `comprehensive`

IR-NLI > `Now, please, specify the treatment desired (general, practical, theoretical, ...)`

user > practical

IR-NLI > Output desired:
- offline print, online display, . . .
- format: bibliographic reference, abstract, full format, . . .
- sorted, . . .
- maximum number of items desired

user > full format, offline print, not sorted, with at most 50 postings

IR-NLI > Please, specify synonyms, spelling variations, related keywords of each concept contained in your request:

C. 1 computer applications:

user > management information systems

IR-NLI > C. 2 warehousing

user > none

IR-NLI > Please, supply any particular point of view or specific aspect to take into account (design, performance, reliability, security, . . .)

user > cost/benefit evaluation

IR-NLI > For each concept please specify the degree of relevance to the search (score from 1 to 10)

IR-NLI > C. 1 computer applications

user > 10

IR-NLI > C. 2 warehousing

user > 10

IR-NLI > C. 3 cost/benefit evaluation

user > 5

Rule D01-07 allows identification of concepts and related terminology and, moreover, it constructs the search logic. The search-logic reflects the internal logical structure of the initial request.

Once all information that has to be collected in the presearch interview has been supplied by the user (and inserted in the PIR), rule D01-16, above presented, is executed. Therefore, the task PRESEARCH-INTERVIEW terminates, and control is returned to the task MAIN. The updated PIR is now the following:

concepts: name = C. 1
term = computer applications

DI = 10
related = C.3

name = C.2
term = warehousing
DI = 10

name = C.3
term = management information systems

name = C.4
term = cost/benefit evaluation
DI = 5

search-logic: (AND (OR C.1 C.3) C.2 C.4)

objective: high-recall

limitations: language = English
date > = 1981
treatment = practical

output: format = full format
max = 50
list = not sorted
mode = offline print

APPROACH-SELECTION is the next task activated by MAIN. The first step carried out is to get additional information from the DKB. This is accomplished by the task FILL-IN, which is activated if there is at least a concept whose slots 'PC', 'GL', and 'CT' are empty. The actions that FILL-IN takes are straightforward: for each concept considered, it transfers the values of the slots from the DKB to the PIR.

The portion of DKB accessed by FILL-IN in our example is illustrated in Fig. 3 and 4. In these figures, the DKB is represented as a labeled network where two types of nodes appear. The 'closed' ones represent the nodes actually examined by the system in the example, while the 'open' nodes represent concepts that are not taken into account.

After the execution of FILL-IN, the PIR concerning the concept C.1 contains:

concepts: name = C.1
term = computer applications
PC = 12004
GL = 8
CT = Y
DI = 10
related = C.3

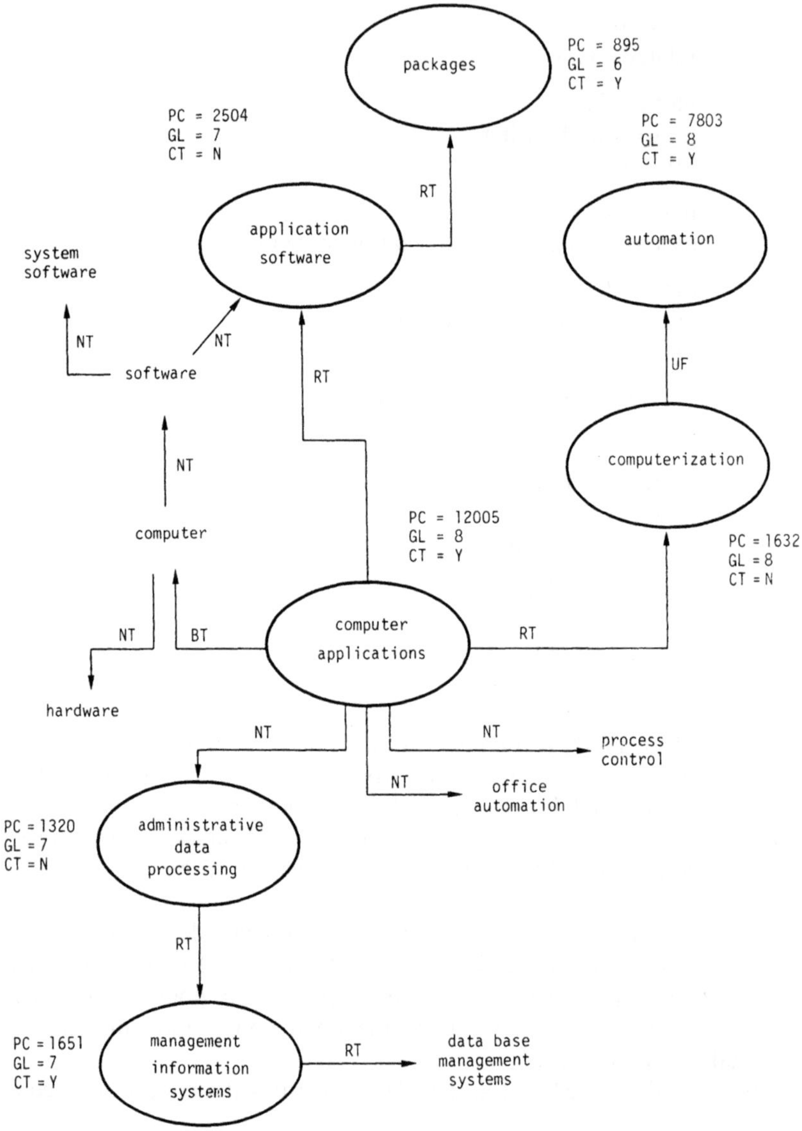

Fig. 3. DKB fragment around the term COMPUTER APPLICATIONS

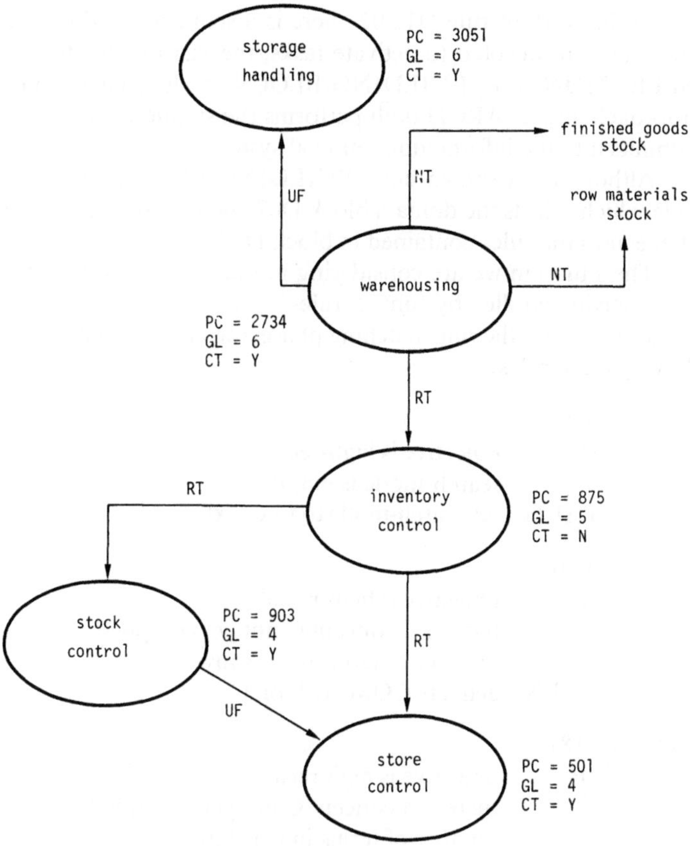

Fig. 4. DKB fragment around the term WAREHOUSING

Similar updates are performed on the other concepts. The second step of APPROACH-SELECTION is the choice of the approach. The domain rule executed is the following one:

D12-02 (0.9)
IF number of concepts is low
all concepts have high PC
all concepts have similar GL
THEN activate BUILDING-BLOCK
activate SEARCH
terminate

The number of concepts is considered to be low when it does not exceed a given constant. Moreover, a concept has high PC when its posting count is greater than a given threshold. Finally, all concepts have similar GL when for any pair of concepts the difference of their generality levels does not exceed a fixed constant.

In the RHS of rule D12-02, there is a sequence of three directives; the first two ones are devoted to activate tasks, the last one to stop the APPROACH-SELECTION task. BUILDING-BLOCK is devoted to implement the BBL approach and SEARCH both performs the synthesis of the search strategy and submits it to the information retrieval system.

Although not shown here, BUILDING-BLOCK first executes a matching rule which selects the domain block D07 and the conflict block C01, and second it executes the rules contained in block D07.

The situation we are considering in our example yields to a conflict resolution activity handled by conflict rules.

In fact, after the rule matching phase, the current conflict set contains the following three rules:

```
D07-01  (0.6)
        IF      objective is high-recall
                search-mode is empty
        THEN    set search-mode to free-text

D07-11  (0.8)
        IF      objective is high-recall
                there is a concept C not yet compiled
                number of terms in C is low
        THEN    activate COMPILE on C

D07-13  (0.8)
        IF      objective is high-recall
                there is a concept C not yet expanded
                number of terms in C is low
        THEN    activate PARALLEL on C
                         until number of terms in C is high
```

where COMPILE refers to the process of specifying spelling variations or truncations of a term, according to the tactics 'rearrange', 'respace', 'respell', and 'fix', while PARALLEL refers to the process by which the terminology related to a term is increased through the tactics 'parallel', 'relate', 'sibling', etc. The conflict rule which matches this conflict situation is:

```
C01-02  (1.0)
        IF      CONFLICT-SET is not empty
                objective is high-recall
        THEN    choose PARALLEL
                       COMPILE
                       GENERALIZE
                       REDUCE
```

whose meaning is trying to solve the conflict by choosing the rule which contains the first-mentioned pattern. In fact, in this situation, due to the high-recall objective, it is better to consider the tactic 'parallel' rather than others, such as 'generalize' or 'reduce'.

In our case rule D07-13 is executed which activates the task PARALLEL, devoted to the expansion of the terminology of the concepts specified in PAR. The expansion is carried out through the application of tactics such as: 'relate', 'sibling', 'generalize', 'parallel', etc.

The following matching rule is first executed:

```
M22-02 (1.0)
       IF      PAR is not empty
       THEN    use D26  C03
```

The rules of the block D26 whose LHS is satisfied in the current PIR are:

```
D26-01 (0.9)
       IF      objective is high-recall
               exists C in PAR with low GL
       THEN    activate RELATE on C

D26-02 (0.7)
       IF      objective is high-recall
               all concepts in PAR have low number of terms
       THEN    activate PARALLEL on terms derived from PAR
```

The conflict is resolved by the rule:

```
C03-04 (1.0)
       IF      CONFLICT-SET is not empty
               objective is high-recall
       THEN    choose RELATE
                      PARALLEL
                      GENERALIZE
                      COMPILE
                      SIBLING
```

which results in the selection of rule D26-01. In this case C is instantiated by C.2 and the task RELATE is activated, which accesses the DKB and expands the terminology of C.2 by including terms linked to C.2 through BT arcs.

After the execution of the task RELATE the portion of PIR concerning C.2 is:

```
concepts:   .
            .
            .
            name = C.2
            term = warehousing
            PC = 2730
            GL = 6
            CT = Y
            DI = 10
            derived = C.5
            .
            .
            .
            name = C.5
            term = inventory control
            PC = 3051
            GL = 7
            CT = Y
            .
            .
            .
```

When RELATE terminates, PARALLEL resumes control. Since its termination predicate (number of terms in PAR is high) has not yet been verified, it continues to match its rules against the PIR and to execute them. In a similar way, other terms are acquired by PARALLEL for the concept C.2.

When the task PARALLEL terminates, control is again transferred to BUILDING-BLOCK which again will match domain rules of block D07 containing the activation of PARALLEL for other concepts. Other tasks are later activated by BUILDING-BLOCK; among these we mention the task COMPILE, charged with the compilation of terms. Some of its domain rules are:

```
D29-02 (1.0)
       IF     HYPHEN is in PAR
       THEN   substitute HYPHEN with SPACE

D29-03 (1.0)
       IF     HYPHEN is in PAR
       THEN   substitute HYPHEN with NULL

D29-07 (0.9)
       IF     '-ing' is in PAR
       THEN   truncate '-ing'
```

D29-08 (0.9)
IF '-ation' is in PAR
THEN truncate '-ation'

D29-12 (0.8)
IF PAR is plural
THEN truncate PAR to singular

Operation continues with execution of all the possible domain rules, and when BUILDING-BLOCK finishes its activity, it terminates and the resulting PIR is the following:

concepts:
name = C.1
term = computer.applic*
PC = 12004
GL = 8
CT = true
DI = 10
related = C.3
derived = C.6 C.7 C.8 C.9 C.10

name = C.2
term = warehous*
PC = 2730
GL = 6
CT = true
DI = 10
derived = C.5 C.11 C.12 C.13

name = C.3
term = management.information.system*

name = C.4
term = cost*.benefit*.evalu*

name = C.5
term = inventory.control

name = C.6
term = applic*.software

name = C.7
term = computeriz*

name = C.8
term = administrative.data.process*

name = C.9
term = autom*

name = C.10
term = package*

name = C.11
term = storage.handl*
name = C.12
term = stock*.control
name = C.13
term = stor*.control

search-logic: (AND (OR C.1 C.3 C.6 C.7 C.8 C.9 C.10)
(OR C.2 C.5 C.11 C.12 C.13)
C.4)

objective: high-recall

limitations: language = English
date > = 1981
treatment = practical

output: format = full format
max = 50
list = not sorted
mode = offline print

search-mode: free-text

After the termination of BUILDING-BLOCK, control is resumed by rule D12-02 of the task APPROACH-SELECTION. Such a rule activates then the task SEARCH which invokes the *formalizer module* to construct the search strategy from the final version of the PIR. In our example, the following program is generated (in a dialect of EUROLANGUAGE):

```
 1. FIND COMPUTER.APPLIC*
 2. FIND MANAGEMENT.INFORMATION.SYSTEM*
 3. FIND APPLIC*.SOFTWARE
 4. FIND COMPUTERIZ*
 5. FIND ADMINISTRATIVE.DATA.PROCESS*
 6. FIND AUTOM*
 7. FIND PACKAGE*
 8. S=1 OR S=2 OR S=3 OR S=4 OR S=5 OR S=6 OR S=7
 9. FIND WAREHOUS*
10. FIND INVENTORY.CONTROL
11. FIND STORAGE.HANDL*
12. FIND STOCK*.CONTROL
13. FIND STOR*.CONTROL
14. FIND S=9 OR S=10 OR S=11 OR S=12 OR S=13
15. FIND COST*.BENEFIT*.EVALU*
16. FIND S=8 AND S=14 AND S=15
17. LIMIT S=16/LANG=ENGLISH
18. LIMIT S=18/YEAR>=1981
19. LIMIT S=17/TREAT=PRACTICAL
20. PRINT F1, 1 ... 50
```

Afterwards, SEARCH submits this program to the information retrieval system which will return the actual results of the search. SEARCH terminates and causes termination of APPROACH-SELECTION. Control is given back to MAIN which activates RESULT-EVALUATION. This task outputs first a ranked list of the retrieved items, and, second, it interacts with the user who supplies the relevance evaluation of the documents. If the results satisfy user's needs, the search session concludes; otherwise, the process continues by repeating the operations specified in the task MAIN.

6.3 An Example With the Citation Pearl Growing Approach

The second example we present deals with the Citation Pearl Growing approach.

The first steps of IR-NLI are just the same as in the previous example: first task MAIN is activated and then task PRESEARCH-INTERVIEW performs the presearch interview.

The initial query is the following one:

IR-NLI > `Please, state your request!`

user > `I would like to have references about cooperative man-machine interfaces for online document retrieval. I am interested in English papers.`

The presearch interview continues then as follows:

IR-NLI > `Please, specify the scope of the search:`
`- comprehensive: retrieval of all relevant items (high-recall)`
`- limited: retrieval of only relevant items (high-precision)`
`- sample: retrieval of some relevant item`

user > `limited`

IR-NLI > `Now, please specify the treatment desired (general, practical, theoretical, ...)`

user > `general`

IR-NLI > `Output desired:`
`- offline print, online display, ...`
`- format: bibliographic reference, abstract, full format, ...`
`- sorted, ...`
`- maximum number of items desired`

user > `full format, online display, sorted by year in ascending order`

IR-NLI > `Please, specify synonyms, spelling variations, related keywords of each concept contained in your request:`

IR-NLI > C. 1 document retrieval

user > none

IR-NLI > C. 2 man-machine systems

user > none

IR-NLI > Please, supply any particular point of view or specific aspect to take into account (design, performance, reliability, security, ...)

user > design criteria

IR-NLI > For each concept please specify the degree of relevance to the search (score from 1 to 10)

IR-NLI > C. 1 document retrieval

user > 10

IR-NLI > C. 2 man-machine systems

user > 10

IR-NLI > C. 3 design criteria

user > 3

PRESEARCH-INTERVIEW terminates as usual when all the possible slots of the PIR are filled with data provided by the user. Control is given back to MAIN which activates task APPROACH-SELECTION.

Task FILL-IN is then activated in order to access the DKB. It produces the following PIR:

concepts:
name = C. 1
term = document retrieval
PC = 3175
GL = 7
CT = N
DI = 10

name = C. 2
term = man-machine systems
PC = 512
GL = 8
CT = N
DI = 10

name = C. 3
term = design criteria
DI = 3

search-logic:	(AND C.1 C.2 C.3)
limitations:	language = English treatment = practical
output:	format = full format list = sorted by year in ascending order mode = online display
objective:	high-precision

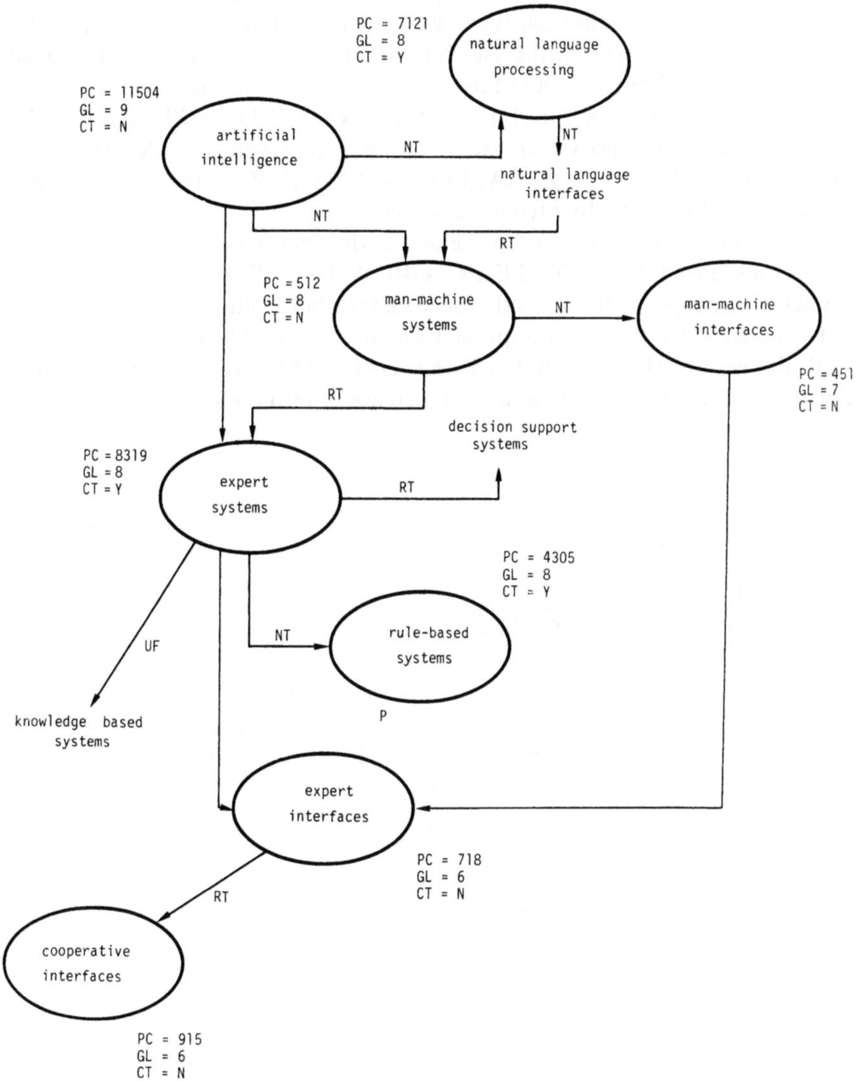

Fig. 5. DKB fragment around the term MAN-MACHINE SYSTEMS

Successively other domain rules, devoted to the choice of the approach, are matched against the current PIR. In particular, the following rule is executed:

D12-06 (0.9)
IF all concepts have loose connection with DKB
THEN activate CITATION-PEARL-GROWING.

By the expression loose connection we mean that the number of arcs in the DKB leaving the node representing a concept is low (bounded by a constant). This corresponds to the situation arising when the intermediary is poorly acquainted with the subject proposed by the user, and decides to follow the CPG approach.

The parts of DKB relevant in this context are shown in Fig. 5 and 6.

With the execution of rule D12-06, the task CITATION-PEARL-GROWING is activated. The goal of this task is to enlarge, when possible, the current PIR by trying tasks such as PARALLEL, GENERALIZE, SPECIFY, etc., and afterwards performing a first tentative search.

The results are collected and presented to the user who will choose interesting citations. Task CITATION-PEARL-GROWING will cease to exist when the number of concepts so discovered exceeds a threshold value.

However, since the CPG approach has been selected because of a 'poor' DKB, the results of CITATION-PEARL-GROWING are not expected to be very effective, leading only to a limited increase of terminology.

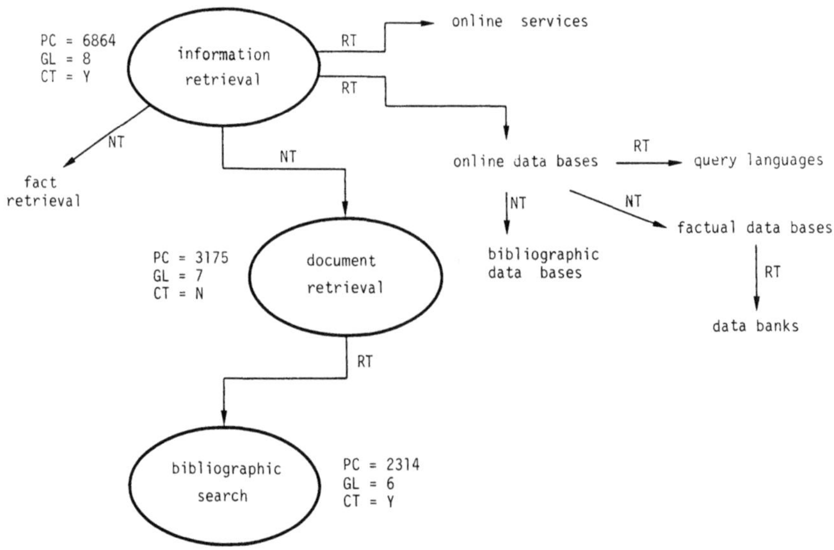

Fig. 6. DKB fragment around the term DOCUMENT RETRIEVAL

In fact, only two terms are found (bibliographic search, expert systems) and are later inserted in the PIR as is shown below:

concepts:	name = C.1 term = document.retrieval PC = 3175 GL = 7 CT = N DI = 10 derived = C.4
	name = C.2 term = man-machine.system* PC = 512 GL = 8 CT = N DI = 10 derived = C.5
	name = C.3 term = design.criteria DI = 3
	name = C.4 term = bibliographic.search PC = 2314 GL = 6 CT = Y
	name = C.5 term = expert.system* PC = 8314 Gl = 7 CT = Y
search-logic:	(AND (OR C.1 C.4) (OR C.2 C.5) C.3)
limitations:	language = English treatment = practical
output:	format = full format list = sorted by year in ascending order mode = online display
objective:	high-precision
search-mode:	free-text

CITATION-PEARL-GROWING now activates the task SEARCH, resulting in the following search strategy:

```
 1. FIND DOCUMENT.RETRIEVAL
 2. FIND BIBLIOGRAPHIC.SEARCH
 3. FIND S=1 OR S=2
 4. FIND MAN-MACHINE.SYSTEM*
 5. FIND EXPERT.SYSTEM*
 6. FIND S=4 OR S=5
 7. FIND DESIGN.CRITERIA
 8. FIND S=3 AND S=6 AND S=7
 9. LIMIT S=8/LANG=ENGLISH
10. LIMIT S=9/TREAT=PRACTICAL
11. PRINT F1
```

Such a search strategy is entered to the information retrieval system and the results are collected. This causes the termination of SEARCH, which in turn leads to the termination of both CITATION-PEARL-GROWING and APPROACH-SELECTION. MAIN activates then task RESULT-EVALUATION that will help the user in the evaluation of the documents extracted from the data base. From these documents the user can identify some new pertinent terms and meaningful citations. The following piece of dialogue supports the user in this job:

IR-NLI > Are you satisfied of the documents I just presented?

user > not completely

IR-NLI > Did you find anything interesting in the above listed document(s)?

user > yes

IR-NLI > Do you think you have to reformulate your request?

user > no

IR-NLI > Then, for each concept, give me please some new key-words and/or synonyms:

IR-NLI > C.1 document retrieval

user > information search
fact retrieval

IR-NLI > C.2 man-machine system

user > natural language processing
expert interfaces
cooperative interfaces

FILL-IN is again activated by RESULT-EVALUATION and extracts new information from the DKB, yielding the following PIR:

```
concepts:    name=C.1
             term=document.retrieval
             PC=3175
             GL=7
             CT=N
             DI=10
             related=C.6 C.7
             derived=C.4

             name=C.2
             term=man-machine.system*
             PC=512
             GL=8
             CT=N
             DI=10
             related=C.8 C.9 C.10
             derived=C.5

             name=C.3
             term=design.criteria
             DI=3

             name=C.4
             term=bibliographic.search
             PC=2314
             GL=6
             CT=Y

             name=C.5
             term=expert.system*
             PC=8319
             GL=7
             CT=N

             name=C.6
             term=information.search
             PC=3128
             GL=8
             CT=N

             name=C.7
             term=fact.retrieval

             name=C.8
             term=natural.language.process*
             PC=3108
             GL=8
             CT=Y
```

	name = C.9 term = expert.interface*
	name = C.10 term = cooperative.interface*
search-logic:	(AND (OR C.1 C.4 C.6 C.7) (OR C.2 C.5 C.8 C.9 C.10) C.3)
limitations:	language = English treatment = practical
output:	format = full format list = sorted by year in ascending order mode = online display
objective:	high-precision
search-mode:	free-text

RESULT-EVALUATION returns control to MAIN. The system now evaluates the termination predicate of MAIN, which results to be false, due to the previous dialogue with the user. The system is therefore again in the initial state, firing thus the domain rule D01-01. This will activate first task PRESEARCH-INTERVIEW, that will not lead to any effect since the PIR is already expanded, and, second, APPROACH-SELECTION. This task will find the PIR suitable for the selection of building block approach, and henceforth, operations will continue in a way analogous to the preceding example.

7 Learning as a Tool for Improving Interface Capabilities

As in all of the fields where intellectual activity is involved, a real expert in the area of expert interfaces and, more specifically, intelligent information retrieval should be able to acquire new knowledge without an enormous effort by refining his skill through experience. Both of these capabilities belong to the sphere of learning [CARB83a, CARB83b], but they are featured by quite different issues and mechanisms:

- the *knowledge acquisition* process allows the expert system to directly and autonomously acquire new knowledge from the outside world, generally expressed in a form which is different from that which it uses internally. This requires that the knowledge acquisition process includes a kind of knowledge compilation from an external form to an internal one. Moreover, knowledge acquisition requires the basic capability of estimating the value of available knowledge and its potential usefulness, in order to choose the pieces of knowledge which are worth to be acquired.

- the *skill refinement* capability allows the expert to improve its performance with experience. Usually, in human experts, experience gathering is a natural consequence of practice, and leads to the indirect acquisition of new meta-knowledge that can be used either to improve efficiency in doing routine jobs or to discover effective strategies for addressing new tasks.

None of the above capabilities is present in IR-NLI. Knowledge acquisition does not take place automatically, as the system cannot acquire new knowledge by itself: knowledge can only be inserted by the designer by directly loading it. Moreover, the lack of any skill refinement capability makes IR-NLI performance quite limited: its behavior is fixed by the designer and its performance can not improve with use.

Of the two limitations mentioned above, the latter is far more important. In fact, while the first deals with the acquisition of domain knowledge, the second basically concerns the acquisition of new meta-knowledge, which is much more difficult to elicit and can hardly be represented in a fixed complete way at the moment of system design.

The extension of the capabilities of IR-NLI (more specifically of the reasoning module) to include some skill refinement capability can focus on three basic issues:

1. improving system efficiency in addressing situations already faced in the past;
2. improving system efficiency in addressing situations similar to other ones already solved in the past;
3. improving system capability of facing new critical situations, i.e., that cannot be solved by means of usual reasoning mechanisms.

All of the issues require that the *history* of the system operation is stored in a long-term memory, which can be structured as a sequence of records, each one representing a situation, the solution adopted, and an evaluation of the resulting performance. This knowledge is already available in the current organization of the reasoning module (namely: the PIR, the sequence of task activations, and the evaluation supplied by the user). It only needs to be appropriately represented and stored.

Once the history of the system is available, the implementation of the above learning capabilities will depend on the different ways in which this knowledge can be used.

The first kind of learning only requires *matching* capabilities between the current situation and those stored in history records. If past cases are found to be identical to the present one (i.e., having the same PIR structure: number of concepts, attributes, relations, objectives, etc. - clearly not the same content) and to have a positive performance value, its solution is simply extracted from the history record and directly utilized.

The system does not improve its performance (i.e., ability to face and solve search problems) but can save search effort and, therefore, it can be more efficient. In other words, it provides the same performance it would have produced anyway, without re-inventing a new one, but simply recalling it from memory.

The second kind of learning requires far more skilled capabilities. First of all, the system must be capable of managing *partial matching,* in order to retrieve from the history situations similar to the current one with a positive performance value. Once such a record is found, the system has to apply some *transformation* in order to adapt the solution of the history case to fit the present one. In doing this, it must carefully take into account the difference that partial matching has shown between the present and the past case. If the transformation fails, the search for other similar cases in the history has to be continued.

Similarly to the previous case, the system does not improve performance, but only tries to be more efficient. This issue clearly depends on the assumption that partial matching plus transformation require less effort than the searching needed to face the current situation anew. We note that this kind of learning, although generally much more costly than the first kind, offers a basic advantage: not only can it contribute to the effective solution of the current situation, but it provides a new meaningful record to be included in the history for possible future use. Therefore, it produces new experience.

The third kind of learning refers to a still more ambitious capability. Similar to the previous case, the system retrieves from the history a set of cases similar to the current one, but for none of them a transformation can be successfully applied. The system has to resort, in this case, to a *synthesis* capability. Taking into account the results of partial matching, the system first decomposes the situations and solutions of the similar cases, extracted from the history, into a collection of situation-solution fragments. It then selects a subset of fragments which are expected to be relevant to the solution of the current situation, and tries to assemble the chosen solution fragments into a new solution. This kind of learning is generally very expressive and can be applied only in critical situations where usual reasoning mechanisms fail. The central issue here is not improving efficiency, but providing a new performance, and, therefore, substantially contributing to the extension of system capabilities and experience.

It is worth noting that the history stored in the long-term memory, usually gathered during system operation, can also be provided directly by human experts as a collection of meaningful cases. This provides a very interesting way of instructing the system, without the need for explicitly eliciting, structuring, and representing meta-knowledge.

The three cases of learning discussed above all rely on the direct use of experience, and do not provide any kind of real acquisition of new meta-knowledge. They enable the system to use knowledge on past cases effectively whenever appropriate to face specific situations, but they do not change its general mode of operation. In other words, they can derive from experience new skill, useful in a particular case, but they do not perform any substantial amount of induction to derive from this specific skill rules of general concern.

Therefore, these three cases of learning may be viewed as a first step towards a more ambitious kind of learning. This would enable the system to elicit the general aspects of the specific situations it encounters during operation, and to code them into new knowledge structures, usable directly in future operation without the need of resorting to the history.

Inductive learning [MICH83] can be quite naturally implemented in IR-NLI through a mechanism that can manipulate tasks. The basic operations it must be able to perform on tasks include:

- *Refinement:* from an existing task new more definite (and, generally, less non-deterministic) tasks are generated, which apply to a smaller number of specific situations;
- *Composition:* two or more tasks are merged to form a single larger task;
- *generalization:* conditions for activation of a task are made less restrictive, so that the task applies to a larger number of situations;
- *Aggregation:* rule that are usually applied in sequences within a task are composed into a single larger rule (or task), thus reducing non-determinism of task execution;
- *Creation:* a new task is constructed by the system.

Note that the above operations generally involve not only the task which they apply to, but also all related tasks that refer to it through the directive 'activate', as, generally, new tasks require new activation conditions.

Presently, little experimentation with the first three kinds of learning has been carried out, while implementation of inductive learning has only been planned as a future activity.

8 Conclusion

In this chapter, we have addressed two main issues; the definition of the new concept of *expert interface,* and the design of a specific rule-based reasoning mechanism, centered on the notion of *task,* suitable to model the behavior of an intelligent intermediary.

These concepts have been practically evaluated in the development of the IR-NLI prototype for intelligent information retrieval, that is presently running on a VAX-11/780 (written in Franz LISP). The experimental work carried out with IR-NLI has revealed several directions for future work. In addition to the major issue of learning already discussed in the previous section, we mention here three basic topics.

A first point concerns the study of a possible enrichment of the DKB with *semantic relationships* embedding world knowledge on the subject domain. Such an extension of the DKB, which presently only contains a few basic terminologic relationships between terms, can be the basis for a more skilled concept analysis and a better elicitation of the information needs of the user. The adoption of a simple kind of semantic net (comprising entities, attributes, and relationships) has already been attempted, and seems promising in several critical situations where the user is not a specialist of the subject domain and can express his needs only in a naive and poorly specific way.

A second topic which is partially connected to the extension of the DKB above discussed, deals with the possibility of computing, for each retrieved document, a *relevance factor*. This should express how close to the information needs of the user a document is expected to be. Relevance factors can serve two purposes:

- supporting the user in evaluating the results of a search;
- offering the user the possibility of constraining the search by specifying a range of acceptable relevance factors for the desired documents.

The design of a mechanism for the computation of relevance factors poses several non-trivial problems and requires precise modeling of such concept as information needs and relevance of a document, that directly refer to the foundations of document indexing and retrieval.

A last issue concerns the extension and generalization of the *task mechanism*, which has been designed to meet the specific requirements of an expert interface, but embodies several concepts about representation and use of metaknowledge that can be the basis for a wider study. A preliminary work in this direction [GUID84] has produced a first outline of a novel expert system architecture supporting a generalization of most of the features of the task mechanism.

References

[ALLE83], [BATE79], [CARB83a], [CARB83b], [CODD74], [COHE82], [DAVI80], [DEFU84], [DOSZ79], [ERMA81], [GREE63], [GUID82], [GUID83a], [GUID83b], [GUID84], [HAYE79], [HAYE83], [HEND78c], [KAPL83], [LANC79], [MARC81a], [MARC81b], [MEAD81], [MICH83], [POLL81], [POLL82], [REIC84], [REIT83], [SALT83], [WATE78], [WILE83], [WOOD72]

References

[AHOU72]
Aho AV and Ullman JD (1972). *The Theory of Parsing, Translation, and Compiling,* Englewood Cliffs, NJ: Prentice-Hall

[AIC82]
Artificial Intelligence Corporation (1982). Intellect Query System Reference Manual, Waltham, Mass.: Artificial Intelligence Corporation

[ALLE83]
Allen J (1983). Recognizing Intentions from Natural Language Utterances, in Brady M and Berwick RC (Eds.), *Computational Models of Discourse,* pp. 107-166, Cambridge, Mass.: MIT Press

[ANSI75]
American National Standards Institute, Study Group on Data Base Management Systems (1977). ANSI/X3/SPARC Interim Report on Data Base Management Systems, FDT (Bulletin of ACM-SIGMOD), 7 (2)

[APPE82]
Appelt DE (1982). Planning Natural Language Utterances to Satisfy Multiple Goals, Report STAN-CS-82, Stanford University

[ASTR76]
Astrahan MM, Blasgen MW, Chamberlin DD, Eswaran KP, Gray JN, Griffiths PP, King WF, Lorie RA, McJones J, Mehl JW, Putzolu GR, Traiger IL, Wade BW and Watson V (1976). System R: Relational Approach to Database Management, *ACM Transactions on Database Systems,* 1 (2), pp. 97-137

[BALL83]
Ballard BW (1983). On the Need for Careful Description of NL Prototypes, *American Journal of Computational Linguistics,* 9 (1), pp. 23-24

[BARB83]
Barber RE and Lucas HC (1983). System Response Time, Operator Productivity, and Job Satisfaction, *Communications of the ACM,* 26 (11), pp. 972-986

[BARR81]
Barr A and Feigenbaum EA (Eds) (1981). *The Handbook of Artificial Intelligence,* London

[BATE78]
Bates MJ. (1978). The Theory and Practice of Augmented Transition Network Grammars, in [BOLC78], pp. 119-159

[BATE79]
Bates MJ (1979). Information Search Tactics, *Journal of the American Society for Information Science,* 30, pp. 205-214

[BATE83]
Bates MJ, Bobrow RJ (1983). A Transportable Natural Language Interface for Information Retrieval, *Proceedings 6th ACM-SIGIR Conference,* Washington, DC

[BECK69]
Becker AL and Arms DG (1969). Prepositions as Predicates, Papers from the Fifth Regional Meeting of the Chicago Linguistic Society, April, Chicago, Illinois University of Chicago
[BERG82]
Bergmann H (1982). Lemmatisierung in HAM-ANS, Memo ANS-10, Universität Hamburg, Forschungsstelle für Informationswissenschaft und Künstliche Intelligenz
[BERT81]
Bertrand O, Daudenarde JJ and du Castel B (1981). User Language Generator. Program Description/Operation Manual, Paris: IBM France
[BOBR84]
Bobrow R (1984). Personal Communication Re: A New Implementation of KL-ONE, May
[BOLC78]
Bolc L (Ed) (1978). *Natural Language Communication with Computers,* Berlin: Springer
[BOLC80]
Bolc L (Ed) (1980). *Natural Language Based Computer Systems,* Munich: Hanser
[BOLC84]
Bolc L (Ed) (1984). *Natural Language Generation Systems,* Berlin: Springer
[BRAC79a]
Brachman RJ (1979). On the Epistemological Status of Semantic Networks, in Findler NV (Ed), *Associative Networks - the Representation and Use of Knowledge in Computers,* pp. 3-50. New York: Academic Press
[BRAC79b]
Brachman RJ, Bobrow RJ, Cohen PR, Klovstad JW, Webber BL and Woods WA (1979). Research in Natural Language Understanding - Annual Report 1 Sept 78-31 Aug 79, Technical Report 4274, Cambridge, Mass.: Bolt Beranek and Newman
[BRAU76]
Braun S and Schwind C (1976). Automatic Semantics-Based Indexing of Natural Language Texts for Information Retrieval Systems, *Information Processing and Management,* 12 (2), pp. 147-153
[BRES78]
Bresnan J (1978). A Realistic Transformational Grammar, in Halle M, Bresnan J and Miller GA (Eds), *Linguistic Theory and Psychological Reality,* Cambridge, Mass.: MIT Press
[BRES82]
Bresnan J (1982). *The Mental Representation of Grammatical Relations,* Cambridge, Mass.: MIT Press
[BUND83]
Bundy A (Ed) (1983). *Proceedings 8th IJCAI Conference,* Karlsruhe, West Germany
[BURG75]
Burger JF, Leal A and Shoshani A (1975). Semantic-Based Parsing and a Natural-Language Interface to Interactive Data Management, *American Journal of Computational Linguistics,* Microfiche 32, pp. 58-71
[BURG80]
Burger JF (1980). Semantic Database Mapping in EUFID, *Proceedings 1980 ACM-SIGMOD Conference,* Santa Monica, Ca
[BURG82]
Burger JF and Templeton M (1982). Recommendations for an Internal Input Language for the Knowledge-Based Systems, System Development Corporation internal paper N-(L-)24890/021/00, January 5
[BUSE84]
Busemann S (1984). Surface Transformations During the Generation of Written German Sentences, in [BOLC84]
[BUSE85]
Busemann S, Hoeppner W, Christaller T, Morik K (1985). Representing and Processing Copula and Full-Verb Sentences in HAM-ANS, in Stoyan H (ed), *GWAI-85,* Berlin: Springer, pp. 187-196

[CADI76]
Cadiou J-M (1976). On Semantic Issues in the Relational Model of Data, *Proceedings 5th Symposium on Mathematical Foundations of Computer Science,* pp. 23-38
[CARB81]
Carbonell JG (1981). *Subjective Understanding: Computer Models of Belief Systems,* Ann Arbor, Mich
[CARB83a]
Carbonell JG (1983). Learning by Analogy: Formulating and Generalizing Plans from Past Experience, in Michalski RS, Carbonell JG and Mitchell TM (Eds), *Machine Learning,* pp. 137-161, Palo Alto, Ca: Tioga
[CARB83b]
Carbonell JG and Michalski RS (1983). Machine Learning: A Historical and Methodological Analysis, *The AI Magazine,* 4 (3), pp. 69-73
[CHAF76]
Chafe WL (1976). Givenness, Contrastiveness, Definiteness, Subjects, Topics, and Point of View, in Li, C N (Ed), *Subject and Topic,* New York: Academic Press
[CHAP73]
Chapanis A (1973). The Communication of Factual Information through Various Channels, *Information Storage and Retrieval,* 9, pp. 215-231
[CHOM65]
Chomsky N (1965). *Aspects of the Theory of Syntax,* Cambridge
[CHRI82]
Christaller T (1982). Konsistenzüberprüfungen bei sich ändernden Wissensbasen, in Wahlster, W. (Ed), *GWAI-82,* pp. 63-71, Heidelberg: Springer
[CODD70]
Codd EF (1970). A Relational Model of Data for Large Shared Data Banks, *Communications of the ACM,* 13 (6), pp. 377-387
[CODD71a]
Codd EF (1971). A Data Base Sublanguage Founded on the Relational Calculus, *Proceedings ACM-SIGFIDET Workshop on Data Description, Access and Control,* pp. 35-68
[CODD71b]
Codd EF (1971). Further Normalization of the Data Base Relational Model, in Rustin R (Ed), *Data Base Systems,* pp. 33-64, Englewood Cliffs, NJ: Prentice-Hall
[CODD74]
Codd EF (1974). Seven Steps to Rendezvous with the Casual User, in Klimbie JW and Koffeman KI (Eds), *Data Base Management,* pp. 179-200, Amsterdam: North-Holland
[CODD78]
Codd EF, Arnold RS, Cadiou J-M, Chang CL, Roussopoulos N (1978). RENDEZVOUS Version 1: An Experimental English-Language Query Formulation System for Casual Users of Relational Data Bases, IBM Research Report RJ2144, San Jose, Ca
[COHE82]
Cohen PR, Perrault CR and Allen JF (1982). Beyond Question Answering, in Lehnert WG and Ringle MH (Eds), *Strategies for Natural Language Processing,* pp. 245-274, Hillsdale, NJ: Lawrence Erlbaum
[CULL80]
Cullinane Corporation (1980). IQS Summary Description, May
[DAME80]
Damerau FJ (1980). The Transformational Question Answering (TQA) System: Description, Operating Experience, and Implications, IBM Research Report RC 8287, Yorktown Heights, NY
[DAME81]
Damerau FJ (1981). Operating Statistics for the Transformational Question Answering System, *American Journal of Computational Linguistics,* 7 (1), pp. 30-42
[DAME83]
Damerau FJ (1983). Shape Descriptor for Unidentified Words in a Natural Language Processing System, *IBM Technical Disclosure Bulletin,* 26, pp. 2648-2649

[DATE77]
Date CJ (1977). *An Introduction to Database Systems,* 2nd ed., Menlo Park, Ca: Addison-Wesley
[DATE81]
Date CJ (1981). *An Introduction to Database Systems,* 3rd ed, Reading, Mass.: Addison-Wesley
[DAVI80]
Davis R (1980). Meta-Rules: Reasoning about Control, *Artificial Intelligence,* 5, pp. 179-222
[DEFU84]
Defude B (1984). Knowledge Based Systems Versus Thesaurus: An Architecture Problem about Expert Systems Design, in van Rijsbergen CJ (Ed), *Research and Developments in Information Retrieval,* pp. 267-280, Cambridge, UK: Cambridge University Press
[DELL77]
Dell'Orco P, Spadavecchia VN and King M (1977). Using Knowledge of a Data Base World in Interpreting Natural Language Queries, *IFIP 77 Congress Proceedings,* pp. 139-144
[DONE78]
Donelson W (1978). Spatial Management of Data, *Proceedings ACM-SIGGRAPH Conference,* Atlanta, Ga
[DOSZ79]
Doszkocs TE and Rapp BA (1979). Searching MEDLINE in English: A Prototype User Interface with Natural Language Query, Ranked Output, and Relevance Feedback, *Proceedings 42nd ASIS Annual Meeting,* 16, pp. 131-137
[DRES76]
Dresher BE and Hornstein N (1976). On some Supposed Contributions of Artificial Intelligence to the Scientific Study of Language, *Cognition,* 4, pp. 321-398
[EDP82]
Query Systems for End Users, *EDP Analyzer,* 20 (9), September 1982
[EMBL81]
Embley DW and Nagy G (1981). Behavioral Aspects of Text Editors, *ACM Computing Surveys,* 13 (1), pp. 33-70
[ERMA81]
Erman LD, London PE and Fickas SF (1981). The Design and an Example of Use of HEARSAY-III, *Proceedings 7th IJCAI Conference,* Vancouver, BC, pp. 409-515
[FINN79]
Finnin T, Goodman B and Tennant H (1979). JETS: Achieving Completeness through Coverage and Closure, Working Paper, University of Illinois, Champaign/Urbana
[FISC82]
Fischer HG (Ed) (1982). *Information Retrieval und natürliche Sprache. Integrierte Verarbeitung von Daten und Texten im Modell CONDOR,* Munich, West Germany
[FLIE83]
Fliegner M (1983). Überlegungen zur automatischen Schreibfehlerkorrektur für ein KI-System, Memo GEN-18, Universität Hamburg, Forschungsstelle für Informationswissenschaft und Künstliche Intelligenz
[GAZD81]
Gazdar G, Pullum GK and Sag I (1981). Auxiliaries and Related Phenomena in a Restrictive Theory of Grammar, *Language,* 58, pp. 591-638
[GHOS77]
Ghosh SP (1977). *Data Base Organization for Data Management,* New York, NY: Academic Press
[GNAN80]
Gnanamgari S, (1980). Providing Automatic Graphic Displays through Defaults, *Proceedings Third National Conference of the Canadian Society for Computational Studies of Intelligence*
[GOLD83]
Goldberg A and Robson D (1983). *Smalltalk-80: The Language and Its Implementation,* Reading, Mass.: Addison-Wesley

[GREE63]
Green BF, Wolf AK, Chomsky C and Laughery K (1963). Baseball: An Automatic Question Answerer, in Feigenbaum E and Feldman J (Eds), *Computers and Thought,* pp. 207-233, New York, NY: McGraw-Hill

[GREE78]
Greenblatt D and Waxman J (1978). A Study of Three Database Query Languages, in Shneiderman B (Ed), *Databases: Improving Usability and Responsiveness,* pp. 77-97, New York: Springer

[GREE81]
Greenfeld NR (1981). Jericho: A Professional's Personal Computer System, *Proceedings 8th Intl. Symp. Computer Architecture,* Rochester, Maine

[GROS78]
Grosz BJ (1978). Focusing in Dialog, in Waltz DL (Ed), *TINLAP-2: Theoretical Issues in Natural Language Processing-2,* pp. 96-103, Urbana-Champaign

[GROS80a]
Grosz BJ and Hendrix G (1980). Focusing and Description in Natural Language Dialogues, in Joshi AK et al. (Eds), *Elements of Discourse Understanding,* Cambridge, UK: Cambridge University Press

[GROS80b]
Grosz BJ and Hendrix G (1980). A Computational Perspective on Indefinite Reference, Artificial Intelligence Center Technical Note No 181, Menlo Park, Ca.: SRI International

[GROS83a]
Grosz BJ (1983). TEAM: A Transportable Natural-language Interface System, *Proceedings Applied Natural Language Conference,* Santa Monica, Ca

[GROS83b]
Grosz B and Stickel M (1983). Research on Interactive Acquisition and Use of Knowledge, SRI Project 1894, Final Report, Menlo Park, Ca.: SRI International

[GUID82]
Guida G and Tasso C (1982). NLI: A Robust Interface for Natural Language Person-Machine Communication, *International Journal of Man-Machine Studies,* 17, pp. 417-433

[GUID83a]
Guida G and Tasso C (1983). IR-NLI: An Expert Natural Language Interface to Online Data Bases, *Proceedings ACL Conference on Applied Natural Language Processing,* pp. 31-38, Santa Monica, Ca

[GUID83b]
Guida G and Tasso C (1983). An Expert Intermediary System for Interactive Document Retrieval, *Automatica,* 19 (6), pp. 759-766

[GUID84]
Guida G and Tasso C (1984). A New Approach to the Design of Expert System Architectures, in Plander I (Ed), *Proceedings 3rd Intl Conf on Artificial Intelligence and Information - Control Systems of Robots,* pp. 405-423, Amsterdam: North-Holland

[HABE79]
Habel C, Rollinger CR, Schmidt A and Schneider H-J (1979). Ein logik-orientierter Ansatz zum automatischen Text-verstehen, Report No 1/79, Technische Universität Berlin, Semantic Network Project

[HAHN80]
von Hahn W, Hoeppner W, Jameson A and Wahlster W (1980). The Anatomy of the Natural Language Dialogue System HAM-RPM, in [BOLC80], pp. 119-253

[HAHN83]
von Hahn W (1983). The Contribution of Artificial Intelligence to the Human Factors of Application Software, in Blaser A, Zoeppritz M (Eds), *Enduser Systems and their Human Factors,* pp. 128-138, Heidelberg: Springer

[HARR77a]
Harris LR (1977). Natural Language Data Base Query: Using the Data Base Itself as the Definition of World Knowledge and as an Extension of the Dictionary, Technical Report TR 77-2, Dartmouth College, Department of Mathematics, Hannover

[HARR77b]
Harris LR (1977). ROBOT: A High Performance Natural Language Data Base Query System, *Proceedings 5th IJCAI Conference,* pp. 903-904

[HARR77c]
Harris LR (1977). User Oriented Data Base Query with the ROBOT Natural Language System, *Proceedings 3rd VLDB Conference,* Tokyo, pp. 303-311

[HARR78]
Harris LR (1978). The ROBOT System: Natural Language Processing Applied to Data Base Query, *Proceedings ACM 78 Annual Conference*

[HARR79]
Harris LR (1979). Experience with ROBOT in 12 Commercial Natural Language Data Base Query Applications, *Proceedings 6th IJCAI Conference,* pp. 365-368

[HAYE79]
Hayes PJ and Reddy R (1979). An Anatomy of Graceful Interaction in Spoken and Written Man-Machine Communication, CMU-CS-79-144, Carnegie-Mellon University, Department of Computer Science, Pittsburgh, PA

[HAYE81]
Hayes PJ and Carbonell JG (1981). Multi-Strategy Parsing and its Role in Robust Man-Machine Communication, Report CMU-CS-81-118, Carnegie-Mellon University, Pittsburgh

[HAYE83]
Hayes-Roth F, Waterman DA and Lenat DB (Eds) (1983). *Building Expert Systems,* Reading, Mass: Addison-Wesley

[HEND77]
Hendrix GG (1977). Human Engineering for Applied Natural Language Processing, *Proceedings 5th IJCAI,* pp. 183-191

[HEND78a]
Hendrix GG (1978). A Natural Language Interface Facility and its Application to a IIASA Data Base, in Rahmstorf G and Ferguson M (Eds), *Proceedings Workshop on Natural Language for Interaction with Data Bases,* Laxenburg, Austria, pp. 87-94

[HEND78b]
Hendrix GG (1978). Semantic Aspects of Translation, in Walker DE (Ed), *Understanding Spoken Language,* pp. 193-228, New York

[HEND78c]
Hendrix GG, Sacerdoti ED, Sagalowicz D and Slocum J (1978). Developing a Natural Language Interface to Complex Data, *ACM Transactions on Database Systems,* 3 (2), pp. 105-147

[HERK80]
Herkner W (Ed) (1980). *Attribution - Psychologie der Kausalität,* Bonn, Stuttgart, Wien

[HERO80]
Herot CF and Wilson GA (1980). Semantics Versus Graphics - To Show or Not to Show, Technical Report CCA-80-09, Cambridge, Mass.: Computer Corporation of America

[HOBB79]
Hobbs J and Robinson J (1979). "Why ask", *Discourse Processes,* 2 (4)

[HOEN82]
Hoenkamp E, Kempen G (1982). Incremental Sentence Generation: Implications for the Structure of a Syntactic Processor, in Horecky J (Ed), *Proceedings COLING 82,* pp. 151-156, Amsterdam, New York, Oxford

[HOEP80]
Hoeppner W (1980). Repräsentationsstrukturen und Inferenzen für zusammengesetzte Objekte, in Rollinger C-R, Schneider H-J (Eds), *Inferenzen in natürlichsprachlichen Systemen der KI,* pp. 151-172, Berlin

[HOEP82]
Hoeppner W (1982). ATN-Steuerung durch Kasusrahmen, in Wahlster W (Ed), *GWAI-82*, pp. 213-226, Heidelberg: Springer
[HOEP83]
Hoeppner W, Christaller T, Marburger H, Morik K, Nebel B, O'Leary M and Wahlster W (1983). Beyond Domain-Independence: Experience with the Development of a German Language Access System to Highly Diverse Background Systems, in [BUND83], pp. 588-594
[HOEP84]
Hoeppner W, Busemann S, Christaller T, Marburger H, Morik K, Nebel B (1984). Commented Terminal Sessions with a Natural Language System, Research Unit for Information Science and Artificial Intelligence, Memo ANS-23, University of Hamburg
[HONE76]
Honeywell (1976). WWMCCS: World Wide Data Management System User's Guide, Honeywell DB97 Rev 3, April
[HUSS82]
Hussmann M and Genzmann H (1982). Performanz-orientiertes Parsing - Ansätze zur robusten Analyse natürlicher Sprache, Memo GEN-5, Universität Hamburg, Forschungsstelle für Informationswissenschaft und Künstliche Intelligenz
[IBM76]
IBM (1976). MIS/370 Anwendung. IV Informations-Systeme
[IBM81]
IBM Corporation (1981). SQL/Data System Concepts and Facilities, Endicott, New York: IBM Corporation
[JACK77]
Jackendoff R (1977). *X-Bar Syntax: A Study of Phrase Structure*, Cambridge, Mass: MIT Press
[JAME82a]
Jameson A (1982). Documentation for Three HAM-ANS Components: Ellipsis, NORMALIZE and NORMALIZE-1, Memo ANS-4, Universität Hamburg, Forschungsstelle für Informationswissenschaft und Künstliche Intelligenz
[JAME82b]
Jameson A and Wahlster W (1982). User Modeling in Anaphora Generation: Ellipsis and Definite Description, *Proceedings ECAI-82*, Orsay, France, pp. 222-227
[JAME83]
Jameson A (1983). Impression Monitoring in Evaluation-Oriented Dialog. The Role of the Listener's Assumed Expectations and Values in the Generation of Informative Statements, in [BUND83], pp. 616-620
[JANA79]
Janas JM (1979). Towards more Informative User Interfaces, *Proceedings 5th VLDB Conference*, Rio de Janeiro, pp. 17-23
[JANA82]
Janas JM (1982). Natürlichsprachliche Schnittstellen zu relationalen Datenbanken: Ein semantisch orientierter Ansatz, PhD Dissertation, Hochschule der Bundeswehr München, Neubiberg
[JARK83]
Jarke M (1983). Zur Beurteilung natürlichsprachlicher Endbenutzerschnittstellen von Datenbanken, in Schmidt JW (Ed), *Sprachen für Datenbanken*, pp. 42-60, Heidelberg: Springer
[JARK85a]
Jarke M, Turner JA, Stohr EA, Vassiliou Y, White NH and Michielsen K (1985). A Field Evaluation of Natural Language for Data Retireval, *IEEE Transactions on Software Engineering*, SE-11 (1), pp. 97-114

[JARK85b]
Jarke M and Vassiliou Y (1985). A Framework for Choosing a Database Query Language, *ACM Computing Surveys,* 17 (3), pp. 213-240
[JARK86]
Jarke M (Ed) (1986). *Managers, Micros, and Mainframes: Integrating Systems for End Users,* London: John Wiley
[JOSH80]
Joshi AK and Levy LS (1980). Phrase Structure Trees Bear more Fruit than You would Have Thought, University of Pennsylvania, Philadelphia, Pa
[KAPL79]
Kaplan SJ (1979). Cooperative Responses from a Portable Natural Language Data Base Query System, Ph D dissertation, University of Pennsylvania, Philadelphia, Pa
[KAPL83]
Kaplan SJ (1983). Cooperative Responses from a Portable Natural Language Database Query System, in Brady M and Berwick KC (Eds), *Computational Models of Discourse,* pp. 167-208, Cambridge, Mass: MIT Press
[KAY83]
Kay M (1983). Unification Grammar (Ms)
[KAYG76]
Kay A and Goldberg A (1976). Personal Dynamic Media, Technical Report SSL 76-1, Xerox Palo Alto Research Center, Palo Alto, Ca
[KELL71]
Kellogg CH, Burger JF, Diller T and Fogt K (1971). The CONVERSE Natural Language Data Management System: Current Status and Plans, *Proceedings ACM Symposium on Information Storage and Retrieval,* pp. 33-46, College Park, MD: University of Maryland
[KETT81]
Kettler W, Schmidt A and Zoeppritz M (1981). Erfahrungen mit zwei natürlichsprachlichen Abfragesystemen, TR 81.01. 001, IBM Heidelberg Scientific Center
[KNUT68]
Knuth DE (1968). Semantics of Context-Free Languages, *Mathematical Systems Theory,* II, pp. 127-145
[KOLV79]
Kolvenbach M, Loetscher A, Dutz HD (Eds) (1979). *Künstliche Intelligenz und natürliche Sprache. Sprachverstehen und Problemlösungen mit dem Computer,* Tübingen
[KONO79]
Konolige K (1979). A Framework for a Portable Natural-Language Interface to Large Data Bases, Technical Note 197, Stanford Research Institute, Artificial Intelligence Center
[KRAU80a]
Krause J (1980). Natural Language Access to Information Systems: An Evaluation Study of its Acceptance by End Users, *Information Systems,* 4, pp. 297-318
[KRAU80b]
Krause J and Lehmann H (1980). The User Specialty Language. A Natural Language Based Information System and its Evaluation, in Krallmann D (Ed), *Dialogsysteme und Textverarbeitung,* pp. 127-146, Essen
[KRAU82]
Krause J (1982). *Mensch-Maschine-Kommunikation in natürlicher Sprache,* Tübingen: Niemeyer
[KRAU83a]
Krause J (1983). Praxisorientierte natürlichsprachliche Frage-Antwort-Systeme: Zur Entwicklung vor allem in der Bundesrepublik Deutschland, *Nachrichten für Dokumentation,* 34 (4/5), pp. 188-194
[KRAU83b]
Krause J (1983). Linguistic Components in (Office) Information Systems and a General Evaluation Strategy for Automatic Indexing, *Journal of Information and Optimization Sciences,* 87

[KRAU83c]
Krause J, Schneider C, Spettel G and Wormser-Hacker C (1983). *EVAL: Zur Evaluierung informationslinguistischer Komponenten von Informationssystemen,* Regensburg
[LANC79]
Lancaster FW (1979). *Information Retrieval Systems,* New York: John Wiley
[LAND77]
Landsbergen SP and Scha RJH (1977). An Outline of the Question-Answering System PHLIQA1, Reprints from the Workshop on Logic and Data Bases, pp. XI.1-XI.16, Toulouse
[LANG78]
Langacker RW (1978). The Form and Meaning of the English Auxiliary, *Language,* 54, pp. 853-882
[LEFA77]
Lefaivre RA (1977). FUZZY Reference Manual, New Brunswick, NJ: Rutgers University
[LEHM78a]
Lehmann H (1978). Interpretation of Natural Language in an Information System, *IBM Journal of Research and Development,* 22 (5), pp. 560-572
[LEHM78b]
Lehmann H, Ott N and Zoeppritz M (1978). User Experiments with Natural Language for Database Access, *Proceedings 7th International Conference on Computational Linguistics,* Bergen
[LEHM79]
Lehmann H and Blaser A (1979). Query Languages in Database Systems, TR 79.07.004, IBM Heidelberg Scientific Center
[LEVE82]
Levelt W (1982). Linearization in Describing Spatial Networks, in Peters S and Saarinen E (Eds), *Processes, Beliefs, and Questions. Essays on Formal Semantics of Natural Language and Natural Language Processing,* pp. 199-220, Dordrecht
[LIND63]
Lindsay RK (1963). Inferential Memory as the Basis of Machines which Understand Natural Language, in Feigenbaum EA and Feldman J (Eds), *Computers and Thought,* New York: McGraw-Hill
[MALH75]
Malhotra A (1975). Design Criteria for a Knowledge-Based English Language System for Management: An Experimental Analysis, PhD dissertation, Massachusetts Institute of Technology, Cambridge, Mass
[MALK82]
Malkovsky M (1982). TULIPS-2 Natural Language Learning System, *Proceedings Coling 82,* Prague
[MARB83a]
Marburger H and Nebel B (1983). Natürlichsprachlicher Datenbankzugang mit HAM-ANS: Syntaktische Korrespondenz, natürlichsprachliche Quantifizierung und semantisches Modell des Diskursbereichs, in Schmidt JW (Ed), *Sprachen für Datenbanken,* pp. 26-41, Berlin: Springer
[MARB83b]
Marburger H and Wahlster W (1983). Case Role Filling as a Side Effect of Visual Search, *Proceedings First EACL Meeting,* Pisa, pp. 188-195
[MARB85]
Marburger H (1985). Kooperativität in natürlichsprachlichen Zugangssystemen, in Brauer W, Radig B (eds), *Wissensbasierte Systeme. GI-Kongreß 1985,* Berlin: Springer, pp. 135-144
[MARC81a]
Marcus RS (1981). A Translating Computer Interface for End-User Operation of Heterogeneous Retrieval Systems: I. Design, II. Evaluations, *Journal of the American Society for Information Science,* 32, pp. 287-317

[MARC81b]
Marcus RS (1981). An Automated Expert Assistant for Information Retrieval in the Information Community: An Alliance for Progress, *Proceedings 44th ASIS Annual Meeting*, pp. 270-273
[MARS80]
Marslen-Wilson WD and Tyler LK (1980). The Temporal Structure of Spoken Language Understanding, *Cognition*, 8, pp. 1-71
[MART83]
Martin PA, Appelt DA and Pereira FC (1983). Transportability and Generality in a Natural-Language Interface System, in [BUND83], pp. 573-581
[MCKE82]
McKeown K (1982). Generating Natural Language Text in Response to Questions about Database Structure, Ph D dissertation, University of Pennsylavania, Philadelphia, Pa
[MEAD81]
Meadow CT and Cochrane PA (1981). *Basics of Online Searching*, New York: John Wiley
[MEEH79]
Meehan JR (1979). The New UCI-LISP Manual, Hillsdale
[MICH83]
Michalski RS (1983). A Theory and Methodology of Inductive Learning, in Michalski RS, Carbonell JG and Mitchell TM (Eds), *Machine Learning*, pp. 83-134, Palo Alto, Ca: Tioga
[MILL81]
Miller LA (1981). Natural Language Programming: Styles, Strategies, and Contrasts, *IBM Systems Journal*, 20 (2), pp. 184-215
[MORA81]
Moran T (1981). An Applied Psychology of the User, *ACM Computing Surveys*, 13 (1), pp. 1-12
[MORI81]
Morik K (1981). Verarbeitung von externer und interner Situation in Überzeugungssystemen, in Siekmann J (Ed), *GWAI-81*, pp. 287-296, Berlin: Springer
[MORI82]
Morik K (1982). Differenzstudie zu früheren sprachverarbeitenden Systemen in der Bundesrepublik Deutschland, HAM-ANS Report 6, Forschungsstelle für Informationswissenschaft und Künstliche Intelligenz, Universität Hamburg
[MORI83a]
Morik K (1983). Wertäußerungen und Repräsentation von Bewertungen, Memo ANS-14, Universität Hamburg, Forschungsstelle für Informationswissenschaft und Künstliche Intelligenz
[MORI83b]
Morik K (1983). Demands and Requirements for Natural Language Systems - Results of an Inquiry, in [BUND83], pp. 647-649
[MORI83c]
Morik K and Rollinger C-R (1983). Partnermodellierung im Evidenzraum, in Neumann B (Ed), *GWAI-83*, pp. 158-168, Berlin: Springer
[MORI85]
Morik K (1985). User Modeling, Dialog Structure and Dialog Strategy in HAM-ANS, *Proceedings 2nd EACL Conference*, Geneva, pp. 268-273
[MYLO76]
Mylopoulos J, Borgida A, Cohen P, Roussopoulos N, Tsotsos J and Wong H (1976). TORUS: A Step Towards Bridging the Gap between Data Bases and the Casual User, *Information Systems*, 2 (1), pp. 49-64
[NEUM82]
Neumann B (1982). Towards Natural Language Description of Real-World Image Sequences, in Nehmer J (Ed), *GI - 12. Jahrestagung*, pp. 349-358, Berlin: Springer

[NIEVE83]
Nievergelt J (1983). Die Gestaltung der Mensch-Maschine-Schnittstelle, in Schmidt JW (Ed), *Sprachen für Datenbanken,* pp. 1-10, Berlin: Springer

[O'LE83]
O'Leary M (1983). PEVAL: Towards an Interface Between the HAM-ANS Core System and PASCAL/R Databases, Memo ANS-15, Universität Hamburg, Forschungsstelle für Informationswissenschaft und Künstliche Intelligenz

[OLNE78]
Olney J (1978). Enabling EUFID to Handle Negative Expressions, SDC SP-3996 Systems Development Corporation

[OSI79]
Operating Systems, Inc. (1979). An Assessment of Natural Language Interfaces for Command and Control Database Query, Logicon/OSI Division report for WWMCCS System Engineering, OSI Report R79-026

[OTT79a]
Ott N (1979). Bericht über die KFG-Studie, IBM Heidelberg Scientific Center TN 79.03

[OTT79b]
Ott N (1979). Das experimentelle, auf natürlicher Sprache basierende Informationssystem USL, *Nachrichten für Dokumentation,* 30 (3), pp. 129-140

[OTTZ80]
Ott N and Zoeppritz M (1979). USL - An Experimental Information System Based on Natural Language, in [BOLC80], pp. 256-282

[PAXT77]
Paxton WH (1977). A Framework for Speech Understanding, Ph D thesis, Stanford University, Stanford, Ca

[PETR73]
Petrick SR (1973). Transformational Analysis, in Rustin R (Ed), *Natural Language Processing,* pp. 27-41, New York: Algorithmics Press

[PETR76]
Petrick SR (1976). On Natural Language Based Computer Systems, *IBM Journal of Research and Development,* 20 (4), pp. 314-325

[PIRO78]
Pirotte A (1978). Linguistic Aspects of High-Level Relational Languages, in *Data Base Technology, 2 (Infotech State of the Art Report),* pp. 271-300, Maidenhead, UK

[PLAT76]
Plath WJ (1976). REQUEST: A Natural Language Question-Answering System, *IBM Journal of Research and Development,* 20 (4), pp. 326-365

[POLL81]
Pollitt AS (1981). An Expert System as an Online Search Intermediary, *Proceedings 5th Intl. Online Information Meeting,* London, pp. 25-32

[POLL82]
Pollitt AS (1982). A Search Statement Generator for Cancer Therapy Related Information Retrieval, *Proceedings 6th Intl. Online Information Meeting,* London, pp. 405-413

[REIC84]
Reichman-Adar R (1984). Extended Person-Machine Interface, *Artificial Intelligence,* 22, pp. 157-218

[REIS77]
Reisner P (1977). Use of Psychological Experiments as an Aid to the Development of a Query Language, *IEEE Transactions on Software Engineering,* SE-3 (3), pp. 218-229

[REIS81]
Reisner P (1981). Human Factors Studies of Database Query Languages: A Survey and Assessment, *ACM Computing Surveys,* 13 (1), pp. 13-31

[REIT83]
Reiter R (Chairperson), Gallaire H, King JJ, Mylopoulos J and Webber BL (1983). A Panel on AI and Databases, in [BUND83], pp. 1199-1206

[RICH79]
Rich E (1979). Building and Exploiting User Models, Report CMU-CS-79-119, Carnegie-Mellon University, Pittsburgh, Pa

[ROBI70]
Robinson JR (1970). Dependency Structures and Transformational Rules, *Language*, 46, pp. 259-285

[ROBI73]
Robinson JR (1973). An Inverse Transformational Lexicon, in Rustin R (Ed), *Natural Language Processing*, pp. 43-60, New York: Algorithmics Press

[ROSS69]
Ross JR (1969). Adjectives as Noun Phrases, in Reibel DA and Schane SA (Eds), *Modern Studies in English*, Englewood Cliffs, NJ: Prentice Hall

[SALT83]
Salton G and McGill MJ (1983). *Introduction to Modern Information Retrieval*, New York: McGraw-Hill

[SCHA77]
Scha RJH (1977). Phillips Question-Answering System PHLIQA1, in [WALT77]

[SCHM76]
Schmidt SJ (1976). *Texttheorie*, Munich, West Germany

[SCHM80]
Schmidt JW and Mall M (1980). PASCAL/R Report, Report IFI-HH-B-66/80, Universität Hamburg

[SCHN84]
Schneider M (1984). Ergonomic Considerations in the Design of Control Languages, in Vassiliou Y (Ed), *Human Factors and Interactive Computer Systems*, pp. 141-161, Norwood, NJ: Ablex

[SCHU79a]
Schuetz A and Luckmann T (1979). *Strukturen der Lebenswelt*, Frankfurt

[SCHU79b]
Schuetz F (1979). Noten am KFG. Zufall oder Notwendigkeit, in Elternvereinigung des KFG Mannheim (Eds), *Karl-Friedrich-Gymnasium Mannheim. Jahresbericht*, pp. 39-87

[SEAR77]
Searle JR (1977). A Classification of Illocutionary Acts, *Proceedings Texas Conference on Performatives, Presuppositions and Implicatures*, Arlington, Va

[SEAR78]
Searle JR (1978). Intentionality and the Use of Language, *Studies in the Linguistics Sciences*, 8 (2), pp. 149-162, Urbana: University of Illinois

[SHNE80]
Shneiderman B (1980). *Software Psychology*, Winthrop

[SHWA84]
Shwartz SP (1984). Natural Language Processing in the Commercial World, in Reitman W (Ed), *Artificial Intelligence Applications for Business*, pp. 235-248, Norwood, NJ: Ablex

[SIMM65]
Simmons RF (1965). Answering English Questions by Computer - a Survey, *Communications of the ACM*, 8 (1), pp. 53-70

[SMAL77]
Small D and Weldon LJ (1977). The Efficiency of Retrieving Information from Computers using Natural and Structured Query Languages, Report SAI-78-655-WA, Science Applications, September

[STOH82]
Stohr EA, Turner JA, Vassiliou Y and White NH (1982). Research in Natural Language Systems, *Proceedings 15th Annual Hawaii Conference on System Sciences*, Honolulu, Hw

[STON76]
Stonebraker M, Wong E, Kreps P and Held G (1976). The Design and Implementation of INGRES, *ACM Transactions on Database Systems*, 1 (3), pp. 189-222

[SUTH63]
Sutherland IC (1963). Sketchpad: A Man-Machine Graphical Communications System, Technical Report LL-TR-296, Lincoln Labs, MIT, Cambridge, Mass.
[SYST83]
Systems-Software, August 1983
[TEMP79]
Templeton MP (1979). EUFID: A Friendly and Flexible Frontend for Data Management Systems, *Proceedings National Conference of the Association for Computational Linguistics*
[TEMP80]
Templeton MP (1980). A Natural Language User Interface, *Proceedings "Pathways to System Integrity"*, Washington, D.C., Chapter of the ACM
[TENN79]
Tennant HR (1979). Evaluation of Natural Language Processors, Ph D dissertation, University of Illinois, Urbana
[TESN76]
Tesniere L (1976). *Elements de Syntaxe Structurale*, 2nd Ed, Paris: Editions Klincksieck
[THOM69]
Thompson FB, Lockemann PC, Dostert BH and Deverill R (1969). REL: A Rapidly Extensible Language System, *Proceedings 24th ACM National Conference*, pp. 399-417
[THOM83]
Thompson B and Thompson F (1983). Introducing Ask, A Simple Knowledgeable System, *Proceedings Conference on Applied Natural Language Processing*, pp. 17-24
[TODD76]
Todd SJP (1976). The Peterlee Relational Test Vehicle, *IBM Systems Journal*, 15 (4), pp. 285-308
[TURN84]
Turner JA, Jarke M, Stohr EA, Vassiliou Y and White NH (1984). Using Restricted Natural Language for Data Retrieval - A Plan for Field Evaluation, in Vassiliou Y (Ed), *Human Factors and Interactive Computer Systems*, pp. 163-190. Norwood, NJ: Ablex
[VASS83a]
Vassiliou Y, Jarke M, Stohr EA, Turner JA and White NH (1983). Natural Language for Database Queries: A Laboratory Study, *MIS Quarterly*, 7 (4), pp. 47-61
[VASS83b]
Vassiliou Y, Jarke M, Stohr EA, Turner JA and White NH (1983). Application Development for Natural Language Query Systems, *Proceedings IEEE Workshop on Languages for Automation*, Chicago, pp. 288-293
[VASS84]
Vassiliou Y and Jarke M (1984). Query Languages - A Taxonomy, in Vassiliou Y (Ed), *Human Factors and Interactive Computer Systems*, pp. 47-82. Norwood, NJ: Ablex
[WAHL81]
Wahlster W (1981). *Natürlichsprachliche Argumentation in Dialogsystemen. KI-Verfahren zur Rekonstruktion und Erklärung approximativer Inferenzprozesse*, Berlin: Springer
[WAHL82]
Wahlster W (1982). Natürlichsprachliche Systeme. Eine Einführung in die sprachorientierte KI-Forschung, in Bibel W and Siekmann JH (Eds), *Künstliche Intelligenz. Frühjahrsschule Teisendorf*, pp. 203-284, Berlin: Springer
[WAHL83]
Wahlster W, Marburger H, Jameson A and Busemann S (1983). Over-Answering Yes-No Questions: Extended Responses in a NL Interface to a Vision System, in [BUND83], pp. 643-646
[WALT76]
Waltz DL, Conrad F, Finin T, Goodman B, Green F, Hadden G (1976). The PLANES System: Natural Language Access to a Large Data Base, Report T-34, University of Illinois, Coordinated Science Laboratory, Urbana
[WALT77]
Waltz DL (Ed) (1977). Natural Language Interfaces, *ACM SIGART Newsletter*, 61

[WALT78]
Waltz DL (1978). An English Language Question Answering System for a Large Relational Database, *Communications of the ACM*, 21 (7), pp. 526-539
[WALT83]
Waltz DL (1983). Artificial Intelligence: An Assessment of the State-of-the-Art and Recommendations for Future Directions, *The AI Magazine*, 4 (3), pp. 55-67
[WASO78]
Wasow T (1978). Remarks on Processing, Constraints, and the Lexicon, in Waltz DL (Ed), *TINLAP-2: Theoretical Issues in Natural Language Processing-2*, Urbana: University of Illinois
[WATE78]
Waterman DA and Hayes-Roth F (Eds) (1978). *Pattern-Directed Inference Systems*, New York, NY: Academic Press
[WEIN81]
Weinreb D and Moon D (1981). Lisp Machine Manual, Cambridge, MA: Massachusetts Institute of Technology, Artificial Intelligence Laboratory
[WEIS80]
Weischedel RM and Black JE (1980). Responding Intelligently to Unparsable Inputs, *American Journal of Computational Linguistics*, 6 (2), pp. 97-109
[WELT81]
Welty C and Stemple DW (1981). Human Factors Comparison of a Procedural and a Non-Procedural Query Language, *ACM Transactions on Database Systems*, 6 (4), pp. 629-649
[WILE83]
Wilensky R (1983). *Planning and Understanding*, Reading, MA: Addison-Wesley
[WOOD70]
Woods WA (1970). Transition Network Grammars for Natural Language Analysis, *Communications of the ACM*, 13 (10), pp. 591-606
[WOOD72]
Woods WA, Kaplan RM and Nash-Webber B (1972). The Lunar Sciences Natural Language Information System: Final Report, BBN Report 2378, Bolt Beranek and Newman Inc., Cambridge, MA
[WOOD77a]
Woods WA (1977). Lunar Rocks in Natural English: Explorations in Natural Language Question Answering, in Zampolli (Ed), *Linguistic Structures Processing*, Amsterdam: North Holland
[WOOD77b]
Woods WA (1977). A Personal View of Natural Language Understanding, in [WALT77], pp. 17-20
[YONK78]
Yonke MD (1978). A Lisp Machine Should Only be Thought of as an Expensive Terminal, *Proceedings 11th Annual Microprogramming Workshop*, Pacific Grove, Ca
[ZOEP83]
Zoeppritz M (1983). Human Factors of a 'Natural Language' Enduser System, in Blaser A and Zoeppritz M (Eds), *Enduser Systems and their Human Factors*, pp. 62-93, Heidelberg: Springer
[ZOEP84a]
Zoeppritz M (1984). *Syntax for German in the User Specialty Languages System*, Tübingen
[ZOEP84b]
Zoeppritz M (1984). Datenabfrage in natürlicher Sprache: Diskussion von Eigenschaften der natürlichen Sprache aufgrund von Beobachtungsdaten, in Ochl, H (Ed), *Online '84 Proceedings*, Berlin.
[ZOLT82]
Zoltan, E., Weeks, G. and Ford, WR (1982). Natural Language Communication with Computers: A Comparison of Voice and Keyboard Input, in Johannsen, G and Rijsdorp, JE (Eds), *Analysis, Design, and Evaluation of Man-Machine Systems*, pp. 27-28, Baden-Baden

List of Authors

Giorgio Brajnik
Istituto di Matematica,
Informatica e Sistemistica,
Universita di Udine
Udine
Italy

John Burger
System Development Corporation
Santa Monica, CA
USA

Fred J. Damerau
IBM Corporation
Thomas J. Watson Research Center
Yorktown Heights, NY
USA

Giovanni Guida
Istituto di Matematica,
Informatica e Sistemistica
Universita di Udine
Udine
Italy

Wolfgang Hoeppner
Fachbereich Informatik
Projekt WISBER
Universität Hamburg
Jungiusstraße 6
D-2000 Hamburg 36
Federal Republic of Germany

Jürgen M. Janas
Universität der Bundeswehr München
Fachbereich Informatik
D-8014 Neubiberg
Federal Republic of Germany

Matthias Jarke
Universität Frankfurt
Fachbereich Informatik
Dantestraße 9
D-6000 Frankfurt am Main 11
Federal Republic of Germany

Jürgen Krause
Linguistische
Informationswissenschaft
Universität Regensburg
Universitätsstraße 31
D-8400 Regensburg
Federal Republic of Germany

Heinz Marburger
Fachbereich Informatik
Projekt WISBER
Universität Hamburg
Jungiusstraße 6
D-2000 Hamburg 36
Federal Republic of Germany

Katharina Morik
Fachbereich Informatik
Projekt KIT
TU Berlin
Franklinstraße 28/29
D-1000 Berlin 10

Jane J. Robinson
Artificial Intelligence Center
SRI International
Menlo Park, CA 94025
USA

Carlo Tasso
Istituto di Matematica,
Informatica e Sistemistica
University di Udine
Udine
Italy

Marjorie Templeton
System Development Corporation
Santa Monica, CA
USA

Yannis Vassiliou
Computer Applications and
Information Systems
Graduate School of Business
Administration
New York University
90 Trinity Place
New York, NY 10006
USA

Frank Zdybel
Xerox Palo Alto Research Center
Palo Alto, CA 94304
USA

Subject Index

On Conceptual Modelling:

Perspectives from Artificial Intelligence, Databases, and Programming Languages

Editors: **M. L. Brodie, J. Mylopoulos, J. W. Schmidt**

1984. 25 figures. XI, 510 pages. (Topics in Information Systems). ISBN 3-540-90842-0

Conceptual modelling relates to all areas of computer science, but especially to artificial intelligence, databases, and programming languages. Here is the first published collection of state-of-the-art research papers in these domains. Its purpose is to consider conceptual modelling as a topic in its own right rather than as an aspect of data modelling, and to present and compare research on knowledge representation, semantic data models, and data abstraction in this context.

The contributions consist of overviews and reports, each chapter having been written and edited for readers in all three areas. Also included are transcripts of symposium discussions which took place among the contributors during a workshop on conceptual modelling at Intervale; these interdisciplinary discussions of each paper clarify many aspects which might otherwise remain obscure to non-specialists. Key features of the book include introductions to pertinent concepts, and the integration of recent results; focus on twelve research projects, involving specific applications such as database design; and challenging suggestions for further research, especially in the concluding comments by leading experts in the three main fields of inquiry.

Springer-Verlag
Berlin Heidelberg
New York Tokyo

Springer

MIX
Papier aus verantwortungsvollen Quellen
Paper from responsible sources
FSC® C105338

If you have any concerns about our products,
you can contact us on
ProductSafety@springernature.com

In case Publisher is established outside the EU,
the EU authorized representative is:
Springer Nature Customer Service Center GmbH
Europaplatz 3, 69115 Heidelberg, Germany

Printed by Libri Plureos GmbH
in Hamburg, Germany